Implementing AWS: Design, Build, and Manage your Infrastructure

Leverage AWS features to build highly secure, fault-tolerant, and scalable cloud environments

Yohan Wadia
Rowan Udell
Lucas Chan
Udita Gupta

BIRMINGHAM - MUMBAI

Implementing AWS: Design, Build, and Manage your Infrastructure

First published: January 2019

Production reference: 1290119

Published by Packt Publishing Ltd.
Livery Place
35 Livery Street
Birmingham
B3 2PB, UK.

ISBN 978-1-78883-577-0

www.packtpub.com

`mapt.io`

Mapt is an online digital library that gives you full access to over 5,000 books and videos, as well as industry leading tools to help you plan your personal development and advance your career. For more information, please visit our website.

Why subscribe?

- Spend less time learning and more time coding with practical eBooks and Videos from over 4,000 industry professionals

- Improve your learning with Skill Plans built especially for you

- Get a free eBook or video every month

- Mapt is fully searchable

- Copy and paste, print, and bookmark content

Packt.com

Did you know that Packt offers eBook versions of every book published, with PDF and ePub files available? You can upgrade to the eBook version at `www.packt.com` and as a print book customer, you are entitled to a discount on the eBook copy. Get in touch with us at `customercare@packtpub.com` for more details.

At `www.packt.com`, you can also read a collection of free technical articles, sign up for a range of free newsletters, and receive exclusive discounts and offers on Packt books and eBooks.

Contributors

About the authors

Yohan Wadia is a client-focused evangelist and technologist with an experience of more than 8 years in the cloud industry. He focuses on helping customers succeed with cloud adoption. As a technical consultant, he guides customers with pragmatic solutions that leverage cloud computing through either Amazon Web Services, Windows Azure, or Google Cloud Platform and make practical and business sense.

Rowan Udell has been working in development and operations for 15 years. He has held a variety of positions, such as SRE, front-end developer, back-end developer, consultant, technical lead, and team leader. His travels have seen him work in start-ups and enterprises in the finance, education, and web industries in Australia and Canada. He currently works as a senior consultant with Versent, an AWS advanced partner in Sydney. He specializes in serverless applications and architectures on AWS and contributes actively in the Serverless Framework community.

Lucas Chan has been working in the field of technology since 1995 as a developer, systems admin, DevOps engineer, and a variety of other roles. He is currently a senior consultant and engineer at Versent and a technical director at Stax. He's been running production workloads on AWS for over 10 years. He's also a member of the APAC AWS Warriors program and holds all five of the available AWS certifications.

Udita Gupta is an AWS Certified Solutions Architect and an experienced cloud engineer with a passion for developing customized solutions, especially on the Amazon Web Services Cloud platform. She loves developing and exploring new technologies and designing reusable components and solutions around them. She particularly likes using the serverless paradigm, along with other upcoming technologies such as IoT and AI. A highly animated creature and an avid reader, Udita likes to spend her time reading all kinds of books, with a particular interest in Sheryl Sandberg and Khaled Hosseini.

Packt is searching for authors like you

If you're interested in becoming an author for Packt, please visit authors.packtpub.com and apply today. We have worked with thousands of developers and tech professionals, just like you, to help them share their insight with the global tech community. You can make a general application, apply for a specific hot topic that we are recruiting an author for, or submit your own idea.

Table of Contents

Preface

AWS is one of the biggest market leaders for cloud computing. With this Learning Path, you'll explore techniques to easily manage applications on the AWS cloud.

You'll begin with an introduction to serverless computing, its advantages, and the fundamentals of AWS. The following chapters will guide you on how to manage multiple accounts by setting up consolidated billing. You'll learn to set up reliable and fast hosting for static websites, share data between running instances, and back up your data for compliance. The Learning Path holds much promise when it comes to enhancing your application delivery skills, with the latest AWS services such as CodeCommit, CodeDeploy, and CodePipeline to provide continuous delivery and deployment, while also securing and monitoring your environment's workflow. It'll also add to your understanding of the services AWS Lambda provides to developers. To refine your skills further, it demonstrates how to design, write, test, monitor, and troubleshoot Lambda functions.

By the end of this Learning Path, you'll be able to create a highly secure, fault-tolerant, and scalable environment for your applications.

This Learning Path includes content from the following Packt products:

- AWS Administration: The Definitive Guide, Second Edition by Yohan Wadia
- AWS Administration Cookbook by Rowan Udell, Lucas Chan
- Mastering AWS Lambda by Yohan Wadia, Udita Gupta

Who this book is for

If you are an IT professional or a system architect who wants to improve infrastructure using AWS, then this course is for you. It is also for programmers who are new to AWS and want to build highly efficient, scalable applications.

What this book covers

Chapter 1, *What's New in AWS?*, contains a brief introduction to some of the key enhancements and announcements made to the existing line of AWS services and products.

`Chapter` 2, *Managing EC2 with Systems Manager*, provides a brief introduction to using EC2 Systems Manager to manage your fleet of EC2 instances. It also covers an in-depth look at how to work with SSM agents, Run Command, as well as other systems manager features, such as automation, patching, and inventory management.

`Chapter` 3, *Introducing Elastic Beanstalk and Elastic File System*, explains how to leverage both Elastic Beanstalk and the Elastic File Systems services to build and scale out web applications and deploy them with absolute ease.

`Chapter` 4, *Securing Workloads Using AWS WAF*, discusses some of the key aspects that you can leverage to provide added security for your web applications using AWS WAF and AWS Shield. The chapter also provides some keen insights into how you can protect your web applications against commonly occurring attacks such as cross-site scripting and SQL injections.

`Chapter` 5, *Governing Your Environments Using AWS CloudTrail and AWS Config*, introduces you to the concept and benefits provided by leveraging AWS CloudTrail and AWS Config. The chapter covers in-depth scenarios using which you can standardize governance and security for your AWS environments.

`Chapter` 6, *Access Control Using AWS IAM and AWS Organizations*, takes a look at some of the latest enhancements made to the AWS IAM service. It also walks you through how you can manage your AWS accounts with better efficiency and control using AWS organizations as a Service.

`Chapter` 7, *Transforming Application Development Using the AWS Code Suite*, covers an indepth look at how you can leverage CodeCommit, CodeDeploy, and CodePipeline to design and build complete CICD pipelines for your applications.

`Chapter` 8, *Powering Analytics Using Amazon EMR and Amazon Redshift*, provides practical knowledge and hands-on approach to process and a run large-scale analytics and data warehousing in the AWS Cloud.

`Chapter` 9, *Orchestrating Data Using AWS Data Pipeline*, covers how you can effectively orchestrate the movement of data from one AWS service to another using simple, reusable pipeline definitions.

`Chapter` 10, *Managing AWS Accounts*, covers everything you need to know to manage your accounts and get started with AWS organizations.

`Chapter` 11, *Using AWS Compute*, dives deep into how to run VMs (EC2 instances) on AWS, how to auto scale them, and how to create and manage load balancers.

Chapter 12, *Management Tools*, provides an overview of how to audit your account and monitor your infrastructure.

Chapter 13, *Database Services*, shows you how to create, manage, and scale databases on the AWS platform.

Chapter 14, *Introducing AWS Lambda*, covers the introductory concepts and general benefits of serverless computing, along with an in-depth look at AWS Lambda. The chapter also walks you through your first steps with AWS Lambda, including deploying your first functions using the AWS Management Console and the AWS CLI.

Chapter 15, *Writing Lambda Functions*, covers the fundamentals of writing and composing your Lambda functions. The chapter introduces you to concepts such as versioning, aliases, and variables, along with an easy-to-follow code sample.

Chapter 16, *Testing Lambda Functions*, discusses the overall importance of testing your function for code defects and bugs. It also introduces you to some out-of-the-box testing frameworks in the form of Mocha and Chai, and summarizes it all by demonstrating how you can test your functions locally before actual deployments to Lambda.

Chapter 17, *Event-Driven Model*, introduces the concept of the event-based system and how it actually works. The chapter also provides a deep dive into how Lambda's event-based model works with the help of event mappings and a few easy-to-replicate, real-world use cases.

Chapter 18, *Extending AWS Lambda with External Services*, discusses the concept and importance of Webhooks and how they can be leveraged to connect your serverless functions with any third-party services. The chapter also provides a few real-world use cases, where Lambda functions are integrated with other services such as Teamwork, GitHub, and Slack.

Chapter 19, *Build and Deploy Serverless Applications with AWS Lambda*, provides you with a hands-on approach to building scalable serverless applications using AWS services such as SAM and Step Functions with a few handy deployment examples.

Chapter 20, *Monitoring and Troubleshooting AWS Lambda*, covers how you can leverage AWS CloudWatch and X-ray to monitor your serverless applications. The chapter also introduces other third-party tools, such as Datadog and Loggly, for effectively logging and monitoring your functions.

Chapter 21, *AWS Lambda - Use Cases*, provides a comprehensive set of real-world serverless use cases with some easy-to-follow code examples and snippets.

Chapter 22, *Next Steps with AWS Lambda*, summarizes the next phase in the evolution of serverless applications and discusses how new and improved enhancements in Lambda are expected to come about in the near future.

To get the most out of this book

To start using this book, you will need the following software installed on your local desktop:

- An SSH client such as PuTTY, a key generator such as PuTTYgen, and a file transferring tool such as WinSCP
- Any modern web browser, preferably Mozilla Firefox.
- You'll need at least one AWS account with full administrative access.
- You'll also need a text editor to edit YAML/JSON CloudFormation templates, and the AWS CLI tools, which are supported on common operating systems (macOS/Linux/Windows).

Download the example code files

You can download the example code files for this book from your account at www.packt.com. If you purchased this book elsewhere, you can visit www.packt.com/support and register to have the files emailed directly to you.

You can download the code files by following these steps:

1. Log in or register at www.packt.com.
2. Select the **SUPPORT** tab.
3. Click on **Code Downloads & Errata**.
4. Enter the name of the book in the **Search** box and follow the onscreen instructions.

Once the file is downloaded, please make sure that you unzip or extract the folder using the latest version of:

- WinRAR/7-Zip for Windows
- Zipeg/iZip/UnRarX for Mac
- 7-Zip/PeaZip for Linux

The code bundle for the book is also hosted on GitHub at `https://github.com/PacktPublishing/Implementing-AWS-Design-Build-and-Manage-your-Infrastructure`. In case there's an update to the code, it will be updated on the existing GitHub repository.

We also have other code bundles from our rich catalog of books and videos available at `https://github.com/PacktPublishing/`. Check them out!

Conventions used

There are a number of text conventions used throughout this book.

`CodeInText`: Indicates code words in text, database table names, folder names, filenames, file extensions, pathnames, dummy URLs, user input, and Twitter handles. Here is an example: "The `input()` method is used to get an input from the user."

A block of code is set as follows:

```
exports.myHandler = function(event, context, callback) {
console.log("value = " + event.key);
console.log("functionName = ", context.functionName);
callback(null, "Yippee! Something worked!");
};
```

Any command-line input or output is written as follows:

```
# aws lambda list-functions
```

Bold: Indicates a new term, an important word, or words that you see onscreen. For example, words in menus or dialog boxes appear in the text like this. Here is an example: "If you need something different, click on the **DOWNLOADS** link in the header for all possible downloads: "

Warnings or important notes appear like this.

Tips and tricks appear like this.

Get in touch

Feedback from our readers is always welcome.

General feedback: If you have questions about any aspect of this book, mention the book title in the subject of your message and email us at customercare@packtpub.com.

Errata: Although we have taken every care to ensure the accuracy of our content, mistakes do happen. If you have found a mistake in this book, we would be grateful if you would report this to us. Please visit www.packt.com/submit-errata, selecting your book, clicking on the Errata Submission Form link, and entering the details.

Piracy: If you come across any illegal copies of our works in any form on the Internet, we would be grateful if you would provide us with the location address or website name. Please contact us at copyright@packt.com with a link to the material.

If you are interested in becoming an author: If there is a topic that you have expertise in and you are interested in either writing or contributing to a book, please visit authors.packtpub.com.

Reviews

Please leave a review. Once you have read and used this book, why not leave a review on the site that you purchased it from? Potential readers can then see and use your unbiased opinion to make purchase decisions, we at Packt can understand what you think about our products, and our authors can see your feedback on their book. Thank you!

For more information about Packt, please visit packt.com.

What is New in AWS? 1

Having spent many years in the IT industry, you get to see a lot of new technologies, products, and platforms that start to evolve, gradually mature, and eventually be replaced by something that's faster and better! I guess in some ways, this concept applies to this book as well.

I still remember the time when I first started exploring AWS way back in 2009, when it was the early days for the likes of EC2 and CloudFront, still adding new features to them, SimpleDB and VPC just starting to take shape, and so on; the thing that really amazes me is how far the platform has come today! With more than 50 different solutions and service offerings ranging from big data analytics, to serverless computing, to data warehousing and ETL solutions, digital workspaces and code development services, AWS has got it all! Which is one of the reasons why I have always been a huge fan of it! It's not only about revenue and the number of customers, but how well do you adapt and evolve to changing times and demands.

So here we are, back at it again! A new book with a lot of new things to learn and explore! But before we begin with the deep dives into some really interesting and powerful services, let's take this time to traverse a little way back in time and understand what has been happening in AWS over this past year, and how the services that we explored in the first edition are shaping up today!

In this chapter, we will be covering the following topics:

- Improvements in existing AWS services.
- A brief introduction to newer AWS services and what they are used for.

Improvements in existing services

There have been quite a few improvements in the services that were covered back in the first edition of *AWS Administration - The Definitive Guide*. In this section, we will highlight a few of these essential improvements and understand their uses. To start off, let's look at some of the key enhancements made in EC2 over the past year or two.

Elastic Compute Cloud

Elastic Compute Cloud (**EC2**) is by far one of the oldest running services in AWS, and yet it still continues to evolve and add new features as the years progress. Some of the notable feature improvements and additions are mentioned here:

- **Introduction of the t2.xlarge and t2.2xlarge instances**: The **t2** workloads are a special type of workload, as they offer a low-cost burstable compute that is ideal for running general purpose applications that don't require the use of CPU all the time, such as web servers, application servers, LOB applications, development, to name a few. The *t2.xlarge* and *t2.2xlarge* instance types provide 16 GB of memory and 4 vCPU, and 32 GB of memory and 8 vCPU respectively.
- **Introduction of the I3 instance family**: Although EC2 provides a comprehensive set of instance families, there was a growing demand for a specialized storage-optimized instance family that was ideal for running workloads such as relational or NoSQL databases, analytical workloads, data warehousing, Elasticsearch applications, and so on. Enter I3 instances! I3 instances are run using non-volatile memory express (NVMe) based SSDs that are suited to provide extremely optimized high I/O operations. The maximum resource capacity provided is up to 64 vCPUs with 488 GB of memory, and 15.2 TB of locally attached SSD storage.

 This is not an exhaustive list in any way. If you would like to know more about the changes brought about in AWS, check this out, at `https://aws.amazon.com/about-aws/whats-new/2016/`.

Availability of FPGAs and GPUs

One of the key use cases for customers adopting the public cloud has been the availability of high-end processing units that are required to run HPC applications. One such new instance type added last year was the F1 instance, which comes equipped with field programmable gate arrays (FPGAs) that you can program to create custom hardware accelerations for your applications. Another awesome feature to be added to the EC2 instance family was the introduction of the Elastic GPUs concept. This allows you to easily provide graphics acceleration support to your applications at significantly lower costs but with greater performance levels. Elastic GPUs are ideal if you need a small amount of GPU for graphics acceleration, or have applications that could benefit from some GPU, but also require high amounts of compute, memory, or storage.

Simple Storage Service

Similar to EC2, **Simple Storage Service (S3)** has had its own share of new features and support added to it. Some of these are explained here:

- **S3 Object Tagging**: S3 Object Tagging is like any other tagging mechanism provided by AWS, used commonly for managing and controlling access to your S3 resources. The tags are simple key-value pairs that you can use for creating and associating IAM policies for your S3 resources, to set up S3 life cycle policies, and to manage transitions of objects between various storage classes.

- **S3 Inventory**: S3 Inventory was a special feature provided with the sole purpose of cataloging the various objects and providing that as a useable CSV file for further analysis and inventorying. Using S3 Inventory, you can now extract a list of all objects present in your bucket, along with its metadata, on a daily or weekly basis.

- **S3 Analytics**: A lot of work and effort has been put into S3 so that it is not only used just as another infinitely scalable storage. S3 Analytics provides end users with a medium for analyzing storage access patterns and defines the right set of storage class based on these analytical results. You can enable this feature by simply setting a storage class analysis policy, either on an object, prefix, or the entire bucket as well. Once enabled, the policy monitors the storage access patterns and provides daily visualizations of your storage usage in the AWS Management Console. You can even export these results to an S3 bucket for analyzing them using other business intelligence tools of your choice, such as Amazon QuickSight.

- **S3 CloudWatch metrics**: It has been a long time coming, but it is finally here! You can now leverage 13 new CloudWatch metrics specifically designed to work with your S3 buckets objects. You can receive one minute CloudWatch metrics, set CloudWatch alarms, and access CloudWatch dashboards to view real-time operations and the performance of your S3 resources, such as total bytes downloaded, number of 4xx HTTP response counts, and so on.

- **Brand new dashboard**: Although the dashboards and structures of the AWS Management Console change from time to time, it is the new S3 dashboard that I'm really fond of. The object tagging and the storage analysis policy features are all now provided using the new S3 dashboard, along with other impressive and long-awaited features, such as searching for buckets using keywords and the ability to copy bucket properties from an existing bucket while creating new buckets, as depicted in the following screenshot:

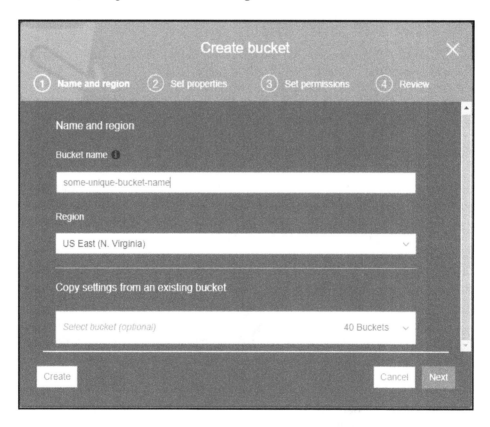

- **Amazon S3 transfer acceleration**: This feature allows you to move large workloads across geographies into S3 at really fast speeds. It leverages Amazon CloudFront endpoints in conjunction with S3 to enable up to 300 times faster data uploads without having to worry about any firewall rules or upfront fees to pay.

Virtual Private Cloud

Similar to other services, **Virtual Private Cloud** (**VPC**) has seen quite a few functionalities added to it over the past years; a few important ones are highlighted here:

- **Support for IPv6**: With the exponential growth of the IT industry as well as the internet, it was only a matter of time before VPC too started support for IPv6. Today, IPv6 is extended and available across all AWS regions. It even works with services such as EC2 and S3. Enabling IPv6 for your applications and instances is an extremely easy process. All you need to do is enable the **IPv6 CIDR block** option, as depicted in the VPC creation wizard:

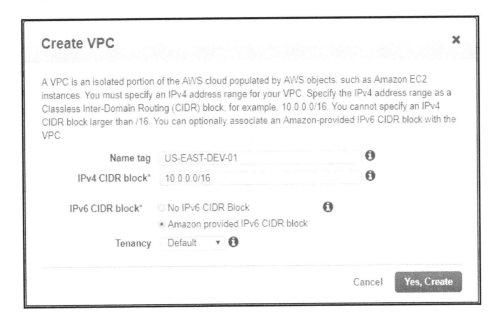

Each IPv6 enabled VPC comes with its own /56 address prefix, whereas the individual subnets created in this VPC support a /64 CIDR block.

- **DNS resolution for VPC Peering**: With DNS resolution enabled for your VPC peering, you can now resolve public DNS hostnames to private IP addresses when queried from any of your peered VPCs. This actually simplifies the DNS setup for your VPCs and enables the seamless extension of your network environments to the cloud.
- **VPC endpoints for DynamoDB**: Yet another amazing feature to be provided for VPCs later this year is the support for endpoints for your DynamoDB tables. Why is this so important all of a sudden? Well, for starters, you don't require internet gateways or NAT instances attached to your VPCs if you are leveraging the endpoints for DynamoDB. This essentially saves costs and makes the traffic between your application to the DB stay local to the AWS internal network, unlike previously where the traffic from your app would have to bypass the internet in order to reach your DynamoDB instance. Secondly, endpoints for DynamoDB virtually eliminate the need for maintaining complex firewall rules to secure your VPC. And thirdly, and most importantly, it's free!

CloudWatch

CloudWatch has undergone a lot of new and exciting changes and feature additions compared to what it originally provided as a service a few years back. Here's a quick look at some of its latest announcements:

- **CloudWatch events**: One of the most anticipated and useful features added to CloudWatch is CloudWatch events! Events are a way for you to respond to changes in your AWS environment in near real time. This is made possible with the use of event rules that you need to configure, along with a corresponding set of actionable steps that must be performed when that particular event is triggered. For example, designing a simple back-up or clean-up script to be invoked when an instance is powered off at the end of the day, and so on. You can, alternatively, schedule your event rules to be triggered at a particular interval of time during the day, week, month, or even year! Now that's really awesome!

- **High-resolution custom metrics**: We have all felt the need to monitor our applications and resources running on AWS at near real time, however, with the least amount of configurable monitoring interval set at 10 seconds, this was always going to be a challenge. But not now! With the introduction of the high-resolution custom metrics, you can now monitor your applications down to a 1-second resolution! The best part of all this is that there is no special difference between the configuration or use of a standard alarm and that of a high resolution one. Both alarms can perform the exact same functions, however, the latter is much faster than the other.

- **CloudWatch dashboard widgets**: A lot of users have had trouble adopting CloudWatch as their centralized monitoring solution due to its inability to create custom dashboards. But all that has now changed as CloudWatch today supports the creation of highly-customizable dashboards based on your application's needs. It also supports out-of-the box widgets in the form of the *number* widget, which provides a view of the latest data point of the monitored metric, such as the number of EC2 instances being monitored, or the *stacked graph*, which provides a handy visualization of individual metrics and their impact in totality.

Elastic Load Balancer

One of the most significant and useful additions to ELB over the past year has been the introduction of the Application Load Balancer. Unlike its predecessor, the ELB, the Application Load Balancer is a strict Layer 7 (application) load balancer designed to support content-based routing and applications that run on containers as well. The ALB is also designed to provide additional visibility of the health of the target EC2 instances as well as the containers. Ideally, such ALBs would be used to dynamically balance loads across a fleet of containers running scalable web and mobile applications.

This is just the tip of the iceberg compared to the vast plethora of services and functionality that AWS has added to its services in just a span of one year! Let's quickly glance through the various services that we will be covering in this book.

Introduction of newer services

We will be exploring and learning things a bit differently by exploring a lot of the services and functionalities that work in conjunction with the core services:

- **EC2 Systems Manager**: EC2 Systems Manager is a service that basically provides a lot of add-on features for managing your compute infrastructure. Each compute entity that's managed by EC2 Systems Manager is called a *managed instance* and this can be either an EC2 instance or an on-premise machine! EC2 Systems Manager provides out-of-the-box capabilities to create and baseline patches for operating systems, automate the creation of AMIs, run configuration scripts, and much more!

- **Elastic Beanstalk**: Beanstalk is a powerful yet simple service designed for developers to easily deploy and scale their web applications. At the moment, Beanstalk supports web applications developed using Java, .NET, PHP, Node.js, Python, Ruby, and Go. Developers simply design and upload their code to Beanstalk ,which automatically takes care of the application's load balancing, auto-scaling, monitoring, and so on. At the time of writing, Elastic Beanstalk supports the deployment of your apps using either Docker containers or even directly over EC2 instances, and the best part of using this service is that it's completely free! You only need to pay for the underlying AWS resources that you consume.

- **Elastic File System**: The simplest way to define **Elastic File System**, or **EFS**, is an NFS share on steroids! EFS provides simple and highly scalable file storage as a service designed to be used with your EC2 instances. You can have multiple EC2 instances attach themselves to a single EFS mount point which can provide a common data store for your applications and workloads.

- **WAF and Shield**: In this book, we will be exploring quite a few security and compliance providing services that provide an additional layer of security besides your standard VPC. Two such services we will learn about are WAF and Shield. **WAF**, or **Web Application Firewall**, is designed to safeguard your applications against web exploits that could potentially impact their availability and security maliciously. Using WAF you can create custom rules that safeguard your web applications against common attack patterns, such as SQL injection, cross-site scripting, and so on.

Similar to WAF, Shield is also a managed service that provides security against DDoS attacks that target your website or web application:

- **CloudTrail and Config**: CloudTrail is yet another service that we will learn about in the coming chapters. It is designed to log and monitor your AWS account and infrastructure activities. This service comes in really handy when you need to govern your AWS accounts against compliances, audits, and standards, and take necessary action to mitigate against them. Config, on the other hand, provides a very similar set of features, however, it specializes in assessing and auditing the configurations of your AWS resources. Both services are used synonymously to provide compliance and governance, which help in operational analysis, troubleshooting issues, and meeting security demands.
- **Cognito**: Cognito is an awesome service which simplifies the build and creation of sign-up pages for your web and even mobile applications. You also get options to integrate social identity providers, such as Facebook, Twitter, and Amazon, using SAML identity solutions.
- **CodeCommit, CodeBuild, and CodeDeploy**: AWS provides a really rich set of tools and services for developers, which are designed to deliver software rapidly and securely. At the core of this are three services that we will be learning and exploring in this book, namely CodeCommit, CodeBuild, and CodeDeploy. As the names suggest, the services provide you with the ability to securely store and version control your application's source code, as well as to automatically build, test, and deploy your application to AWS or your on-premises environment.
- **SQS and SNS**: SQS, or **Simple Queue Service**, is a fully-managed queuing service provided by AWS, designed to decouple your microservices-based or distributed applications. You can even use SQS to send, store, and receive messages between different applications at high volumes without any infrastructure management as well. **SNS** is a **Simple Notification Service** used primarily as a pub/ sub messaging service or as a notification service. You can additionally use SNS to trigger custom events for other AWS services, such as EC2, S3, and CloudWatch.

- **EMR: Elastic MapReduce** is a managed *Hadoop as a Service* that provides a clustered platform on EC2 instances for running Apache Hadoop and Apache Spark frameworks. EMR is highly useful for crunching massive amounts of data as well as to transform and move large quantities of data from one AWS data source to another. EMR also provides a lot of flexibility and scalability to your workloads with the ability to resize your cluster depending on the amount of data being processed at a given point in time. It is also designed to integrate effortlessly with other AWS services, such as S3 for storing the data, CloudWatch for monitoring your cluster, CloudTrail to audit the requests made to your cluster, and so on.

- **Redshift:** Redshift is a petabyte scale, managed data warehousing service in the cloud. Similar to its counterpart, EMR, Redshift also works on the concept of clustered EC2 instances on which you upload large datasets and run your analytical queries.

- **Data Pipeline**: Data Pipeline is a managed service that provides end users with an ability to process and move datasets from one AWS service to another as well as from on-premise datastores into AWS storage services, such as RDS, S3, DynamoDB, and even EMR! You can schedule data migration jobs, track dependencies and errors, and even write and create preconditions and activities that define what actions Data Pipeline has to take against the data, such as run it through an EMR cluster, perform a SQL query over it, and so on.

- **IoT and Greengrass:** AWS IoT and Greengrass are two really amazing services that are designed to collect and aggregate various device sensor data and stream that data into the AWS cloud for processing and analysis. AWS IoT provides a scalable and secure platform, using which you can connect billions of sensor devices to the cloud or other AWS services and leverage the same for gathering, processing, and analyzing the data without having to worry about the underlying infrastructure or scalability needs. Greengrass is an extension of the AWS IoT platform and essentially provides a mechanism that allows you to run and manage executions of data pre-processing jobs directly on the sensor devices.

Managing EC2 with Systems Manager

2

EC2 instances have long been a core service provided by AWS and EC2 still continues to evolve with newer sets of features and instance types added every year. One such really awesome service added during AWS re:Invent 2016 was the EC2 Systems Manager!

In this chapter, we will be learning a lot about the EC2 Systems Manager and its associated sub-services; namely:

- **Run Command**: Service that allows you to execute commands directly on an EC2 Systems Manager enabled EC2 instance
- **State Manager**: Allows you to specify a desired state for an EC2 Systems Manager enabled EC2 instance
- **Patch management**: Provides administrators with the ability to manage the deployment of patches over EC2 instances
- **Automations**: Allows administrators to automate the deployment of certain tasks
- **Inventory**: Service that collects and manages a list of software inventory from your managed EC2 instances

Sound exciting? Then what are we waiting for? Let's get started!

Introducing EC2 Systems Manager

As the name suggests, EC2 Systems Manager is a management service that provides administrators and end users with the ability to perform a rich set of tasks on their EC2 instance fleet such as periodically patching the instances with a predefined set of baseline patches, tracking the instances' configurational state, and ensuring that the instance stays compliant with a state template, runs scripts and commands over your instance fleet with a single utility, and much, much more! The EC2 Systems Manager is also specifically designed to help administrators manage hybrid computing environments, all from the comfort and ease of the EC2 Systems Manager dashboard. This makes it super efficient and cost effective as it doesn't require a specialized set of software or third-party services, which cost a fortune, to manage your hybrid environments!

But how does AWS achieve all of this in the first place? Well, it all begins with the concept of managed instances. A managed instance is a special EC2 instance that is governed and managed by the EC2 Systems Manager service. Each managed instance contains a **Systems Manager** (**SSM**) agent that is responsible for communicating and configuring the instance state back to the Systems Manager utility. Windows Server 2003–2012 R2 AMIs, Windows Server 2003–2012 R2 AMIs will automatically have the SSM agent installed. For Linux instances, however, the SSM agent is not installed by default. Let's quickly look at how to install this agent and set up our first Dev instance in AWS as a managed instance.

Getting started with the SSM agent

In this section, we are going to install and configure an SSM agent on a new Linux instance, which we shall call as a Dev instance, and then verify it's working by streaming the agent's log files to Amazon CloudWatch Logs. So let's get busy!

Configuring IAM Roles and policies for SSM

First, we need to create and configure IAM Roles for our EC2 Systems Manager to process and execute commands over our EC2 instances. You can either use the Systems Manager's managed policies or alternatively create your own custom roles with specific permissions. For this part, we will be creating a custom role and policy.

To get started, we first create a custom IAM policy for Systems Manager managed instances:

1. Log in to your AWS account and select the **IAM** option from the main dashboard, or alternatively, open the IAM console at `https://console.aws.amazon.com/iam/`.

2. Next, from the navigation pane, select **Policies**. This will bring up a list of existing policies currently provided and supported by AWS out of the box.

3. Type `SSM` in the **Policy Filter** to view the list of policies currently provided for SSM.

4. Select the **AmazonEC2RoleforSSM** policy and copy its contents to form a new policy document. Here is a snippet of the policy document for your reference:

```
{
    "Version": "2012-10-17",
    "Statement": [
        {
            "Effect": "Allow",
            "Action": [
                "ssm:DescribeAssociation",
                ..... SSM actions list
            ],
            "Resource": "*"
        },
        {
            "Effect": "Allow",
            "Action": [
                "ec2messages:AcknowledgeMessage",
                "ec2messages:DeleteMessage",
                "ec2messages:FailMessage",
                "ec2messages:GetEndpoint",
                "ec2messages:GetMessages",
                "ec2messages:SendReply"
            ],
            "Resource": "*"
        },
        {
            "Effect": "Allow",
            "Action": [
                "cloudwatch:PutMetricData"
            ],
            "Resource": "*"
        },
        {
            "Effect": "Allow",
            "Action": [
```

```
            "ec2:DescribeInstanceStatus"
        ],
        "Resource": "*"
    },
    {
        "Effect": "Allow",
        "Action": [
            "ds:CreateComputer",
            "ds:DescribeDirectories"
        ],
        "Resource": "*"
    },
    {
        "Effect": "Allow",
        "Action": [
            "logs:CreateLogGroup",
            "logs:CreateLogStream",
            ..... CloudWatch Log actions
        ],
        "Resource": "*"
    },
    {
        "Effect": "Allow",
        "Action": [
            "s3:PutObject",
            "s3:GetObject",
            "s3:AbortMultipartUpload",
            "s3:ListMultipartUploadParts",
            "s3:ListBucketMultipartUploads"
        ],
        "Resource": "*"
    },
    {
        "Effect": "Allow",
        "Action": [
            "s3:ListBucket"
        ],
        "Resource": "arn:aws:s3:::amazon-ssm-packages-*"
    }
  ]
}
```

5. Once the policy is copied, go back to the **Policies** dashboard and click on the **Create policy** option. In the **Create policy** wizard, select the **Create Your Own Policy** option.

6. Provide a suitable **Policy Name** and paste the copied contents of the **AmazonEC2RoleforSSM** policy into the **Policy Document** section. You can now tweak the policy as per your requirements, but once completed, remember to select the **Validate Policy** option to ensure the policy is semantically correct.

7. Once completed, select **Create Policy** to complete the process.

With this step completed, you now have a custom IAM policy for System Manager managed instances.

The next important policy that we need to create is the custom IAM user policy for our Systems Manager. This policy will essentially scope out which particular user can view the System Manager documents as well as perform actions on the selected managed instances using the System Manager's APIs:

1. Once again, log in to your AWS IAM dashboard and select the **Policies** option as performed in the earlier steps.

2. Type SSM again in the **Policy Filter** and select the **AmazonSSMFullAccess** policy. Copy its contents and create a custom SSM access policy by pasting the following snippet in the new policy's **Policy Document** section:

```
{
    "Version": "2012-10-17",
    "Statement": [
        {
            "Effect": "Allow",
            "Action": [
                "cloudwatch:PutMetricData",
                "ds:CreateComputer",
                "ds:DescribeDirectories",
                "ec2:DescribeInstanceStatus",
                "logs:*",
                "ssm:*",
                "ec2messages:*"
            ],
            "Resource": "*"
        }
    ]
}
```

3. Remember to *validate* the policy before completing the creation process. You should now have two custom policies, as shown in the following screenshot:

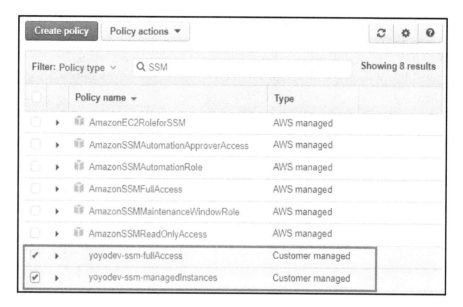

With the policies created, we now simply create a new instance profile role, attach the full access policy to the new role, and finally verify the trust relationship between Systems Manager and the newly created role:

1. To create a new role, from the IAM management dashboard, select the **Roles** option from the navigation pane.
2. In the **Create Role** wizard, select the **EC2** option from the **AWS service** role type, as shown in the following screenshot. Next, select the **EC2** option as the *use case* for this activity and click on the **Next: Permissions** button to continue:

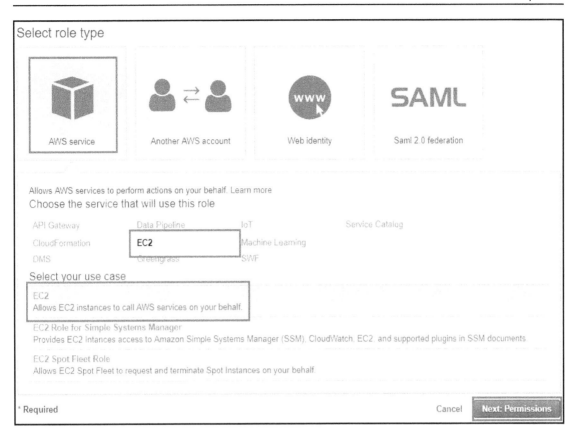

3. In the **Attach permissions policy** page, filter and select the **ssm-managedInstances** policy that we created at the beginning of this exercise. Click on **Review** once done.

4. Finally, provide a suitable **Role name** in the **Review** page and click on **Create role** to complete the procedure!

With the role in place, we now need to verify that the IAM policy for your instance profile role includes `ssm.amazonaws.com` as a trusted entity:

1. To verify this, select the newly created role from the **IAM Roles** page and click on the **Trust relationships** tab.
2. Here, choose the **Edit Trust Relationship** option and paste the following snippet in the policy editor, as shown. Remember to add both *EC2 and SSM* as the trusted services and not just one of them:

```
{
  "Version": "2012-10-17",
  "Statement": [
    {
      "Sid": "",
      "Effect": "Allow",
      "Principal": {
        "Service": [
          "ec2.amazonaws.com",
          "ssm.amazonaws.com"
        ]
      },
      "Action": "sts:AssumeRole"
    }
  ]
}
```

3. With the new trust policy in place, click on **Update Trust Policy** to complete the process. Congratulations!
4. You are almost done with configuring the Systems Manager! A final step remains, where we need to attach the second policy that we created (SSM full access) to one of our IAM users. In this case, I've attached the policy to one of my existing users in my AWS environment, however, you can always create a completely new user dedicated to the Systems Manager and assign it the SSM access policy as well.

With the policies out of the way, we can now proceed with the installation and configuration of the SSM agent on our simple Dev instance.

Installing the SSM agent

As discussed at the beginning of the chapter, the Systems Manager or the SSM agent is a vital piece of software that needs to be installed and configured on your EC2 instances in order for Systems Manager to manage it. At the time of writing, SSM agent is supported on the following sets of operating systems:

- **Windows**:
    - Windows Server 2003 (including R2)
    - Windows Server 2008 (including R2)
    - Windows Server 2012 (including R2)
    - Windows Server 2016

- **Linux** (64-bit and 32-bit):
    - Amazon Linux 2014.09, 2014.03 or later
    - Ubuntu Server 16.04 LTS, 14.04 LTS, or 12.04 LTS
    - Red Hat Enterprise Linux (RHEL) 6.5 or later
    - CentOS 6.3 or later

- **Linux** (64-bit only):
    - Amazon Linux 2015.09, 2015.03 or later
    - Red Hat Enterprise Linux 7.x or later
    - CentOS 7.1 or later
    - SUSE Linux Enterprise Server 12 or higher

To install the agent on a brand new instance, such as the one we will create shortly, you simply need to ensure that the instance is provided with the necessary SSM IAM role that we created in the previous section, as well as to provide the following code snippet in the **User data** section of your instance's configuration:

```
#!/bin/bash
cd /tmp
wget
https://s3.amazonaws.com/ec2-downloads-windows/SSMAgent/latest/debian_amd64
/amazon-ssm-agent.deb
sudo dpkg -i amazon-ssm-agent.deb
sudo start amazon-ssm-agent
```

The user data script varies from OS to OS. In my case, the script is intended to run on an Ubuntu Server 14.04 LTS (HVM) instance. You can check your SSM agent install script at `http://docs.aws.amazon.com/systems-manager/latest/userguide/sysman-install-ssm-agent.html#sysman-install-startup-linux`.

Once the instance is up and running, SSH into the instance and verify whether your SSM agent is up and running or not using the following command. Remember, the following command will also vary based on the operating system that you select at launch time:

```
# sudo status amazon-ssm-agent
```

You should see the agent running, as shown in the following screenshot:

```
ubuntu@ip-192-168-32-188:~$
ubuntu@ip-192-168-32-188:~$ sudo status amazon-ssm-agent
amazon-ssm-agent start/running, process 1494
ubuntu@ip-192-168-32-188:~$
ubuntu@ip-192-168-32-188:~$
```

You can, optionally, even install the agent on an existing running EC2 instance by completing the following set of commands.

For an instance running on the Ubuntu 16.04 LTS operating system, we first create a temporary directory to house the SSM agent installer:

```
# mkdir /tmp/ssm
```

Next, download the operating-specific SSM agent installer using the `wget` utility:

```
# wget
https://s3.amazonaws.com/ec2-downloads-windows/SSMAgent/latest/debian_amd64
/amazon-ssm-agent.deb
```

Finally, execute the installer using the following command:

```
# sudo dpkg -i amazon-ssm-agent.deb
```

You can additionally verify the agent's execution by tailing either of these log files as well:

```
# sudo tail -f /var/log/amazon/ssm/amazon-ssm-agent.log
# sudo tail -f /var/log/amazon/ssm/errors.log
```

Configuring the SSM agent to stream logs to CloudWatch

This is a particularly useful option provided by the SSM agent, especially when you don't want to log in to each and every instance and troubleshoot issues. Integrating the SSM agent's logs with CloudWatch enables you to have all your logs captured and analyzed at one central location, which undoubtedly ends up saving a lot of time, but it also brings additional benefits such as the ability to configure alarms, view the various metrics using CloudWatch dashboard, and retain the logs for a much longer duration.

But before we get to configuring the agent, we first need to create a separate log group within CloudWatch that will stream the agent logs from individual instances here:

1. To do so, from the **AWS Management Console**, select the **CloudWatch** option, or alternatively, click on the following link to open your CloudWatch dashboard from `https://console.aws.amazon.com/cloudwatch/`.

2. Next, select the **Logs** option from the navigation pane. Here, click on **Create log group** and provide a suitable name for your log group, as shown in the following screenshot:

3. Once completed, SSH back into your Dev instance and run the following command:

```
# sudo cp /etc/amazon/ssm/seelog.xml.template
/etc/amazon/ssm/seelog.xml
```

4. Next, using your favorite editor, open the newly copied file and paste the following content in it. Remember to swap out the `<CLOUDWATCH_LOG_GROUP_NAME>` field with the name of your own log group:

```
# sudo vi /etc/amazon/ssm/seelog.xml
<seelog minlevel="info" critmsgcount="500" maxinterval="100000000"
 mininterval="2000000" type="adaptive">
 <exceptions>
```

```
<exception minlevel="error" filepattern="test*"/>
</exceptions>
<outputs formatid="fmtinfo">
<console formatid="fmtinfo"/>
<rollingfile type="size" maxrolls="5" maxsize="30000000"
filename="{{LOCALAPPDATA}}\Amazon\SSM\Logs\amazon-ssm-agent.log"/>
<filter formatid="fmterror" levels="error,critical">
<rollingfile type="size" maxrolls="5" maxsize="10000000"
filename="{{LOCALAPPDATA}}\Amazon\SSM\Logs\errors.log"/>
</filter>
<custom name="cloudwatch_receiver" formatid="fmtdebug" data-log-
group="<CLOUDWATCH_LOG_GROUP_NAME>"/>
</outputs>
CODE:
```

5. With the changes made, save and exit the editor. Now have a look at your newly created log group using the CloudWatch dashboard; you should see your SSM agent's error logs, if any, displayed there for easy troubleshooting.

With this step completed, we have now successfully installed and configured our EC2 instance as a **Managed Instance** in Systems Manager. To verify whether your instance has indeed been added, select the **Managed Instance** option provided under the **Systems Manager Shared Resources** section from the navigation pane of your EC2 dashboard; you should see your instance listed, as shown here:

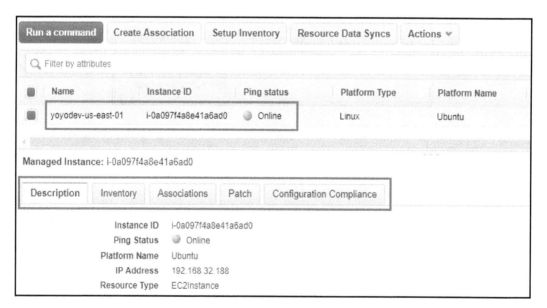

In the next section, we will deep dive into the various features provided as a part of the Systems Manager, starting off with one of the most widely used: Run Command!

Introducing Run Command

Run Command is an awesome feature of Systems Manager, which basically allows you to execute remote commands over your managed fleet of EC2 instances. You can perform a vast variety of automated administrative tasks, such as installing software or patching your operating systems, executing shell commands, managing local groups and users, and much more! But that's not all! The best part of using this feature is that it allows you to have a seamless experience when executing scripts, even over your on-premises Windows and Linux operating systems, whether they be running on VMware ESXi, Microsoft Hyper-V, or any other platforms. And the cost of all this? Well, it's absolutely free! You only pay for the EC2 instances and other AWS resources that you create and nothing more!

Here's a brief list of a few commonly predefined commands provided by Run Command along with a short description:

- `AWS-RunShellScript`: Executes shell scripts on remote Linux instances
- `AWS-UpdateSSMAgent`: Used to update the Amazon SSM agent
- `AWS-JoinDirectoryServiceDomain`: Used to join an instance to an AWS Directory
- `AWS-RunPowerShellScript`: Executes PowerShell commands or scripts on Windows instances
- `AWS-UpdateEC2Config`: Runs an update to the EC2Config service
- `AWS-ConfigureWindowsUpdate`: Used to configure Windows Update settings
- `AWS-InstallApplication`: Used to install, repair, or uninstall software on a Windows instance using an MSI package
- `AWS-ConfigureCloudWatch`: Configures Amazon CloudWatch Logs to monitor applications and systems

Before we proceed with the actual execution of the Run Commands, it is important to remember that the Run Command requires both the SSM agent as well as the right set of permissions and roles to work with. So if you haven't performed the SSM agent's installation or the setup of the IAM polices and roles, then now would be a good time to revisit this!

In this section, let's look at a simple way of executing a simple set of commands for our newly added managed instance:

1. To begin with, first log in to the **AWS Management Console** and select the **EC2** service from the main dashboard. Alternatively, you can even launch the EC2 dashboard via `https://console.aws.amazon.com/ec2/`.

2. Next, from the navigation pane, select the **Run Command** option from the **Systems Manager Services** section. You will be taken to the **Run Command** dashboard where you will need to select the **Run a command** option to get started.

3. In the **Run a command** page, the first thing we need to do is select a **Command document** that we can work with. A command document is basically a statement or set of information about the command you want to run on your managed instances. For this scenario, we will select the `AWS-RunShellScript` command document to start with.

4. In the next **Select Targets by** section, you can optionally choose whether you wish to execute your command document manually by selecting individual instances or specify a particular group of instances identified by their *tag* name.

5. The **Execute on** criteria provides you with the option to select either the **Targets** or **Percent** of instances you wish to execute the command document on. Selecting **Targets** allows you to specify the exact number of instances that should be allowed to execute the command document. The execution occurs on each instance one at a time. Alternatively, if you select the **Percent** option, then you can provide a percentage value of the instances that should be allowed to run the command at a single time.

6. You can optionally set the **Stop after x errors** to halt the execution of your command document in case an instance encounters an error.

7. Finally, you can paste your execution code or shell script in the **Commands** section as shown in the following screenshot. In this case, we are running a simple script that will install and configure a Zabbix monitoring agent on our Dev instance for easy monitoring of our EC2 resources:

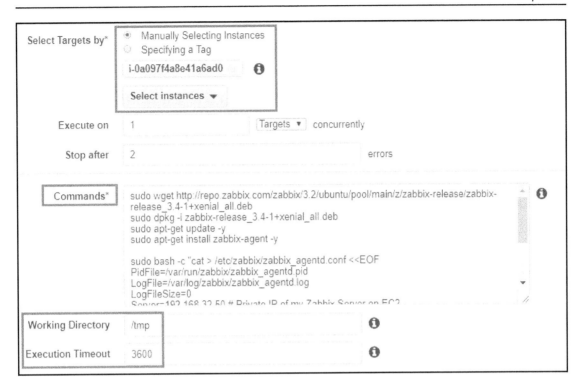

 You can learn more about Zabbix and its features at `https://www.zabbix.com/product`.

8. Copy and paste the following code snippet or, alternatively, tweak it according to the EC2 instance operating system that you may have selected for this exercise:

```
sudo wget
http://repo.zabbix.com/zabbix/3.2/ubuntu/pool/main/z/zabbix-release
/zabbix-release_3.4-1+xenial_all.deb
sudo dpkg -i zabbix-release_3.4-1+xenial_all.deb
sudo apt-get update -y
sudo apt-get install zabbix-agent -y

sudo bash -c "cat > /etc/zabbix/zabbix_agentd.conf <<EOF
PidFile=/var/run/zabbix/zabbix_agentd.pid
LogFile=/var/log/zabbix/zabbix_agentd.log
LogFileSize=0
Server=192.168.32.50 # Private IP of my Zabbix Server on EC2
ServerActive=192.168.32.50 # Private IP of my Zabbix Server on EC2
Include=/etc/zabbix/zabbix_agentd.d/*.conf
```

```
EOF"

sudo service zabbix-agent status
sudo service zabbix-agent restart
```

9. The rest of the options provide other configurational items such as setting up an optional *working directory* where the commands get executed on the remote managed instances.

   Additionally, you can even choose to **Enable SNS notifications** as well as write your command output logs to S3 using the **Advanced Options** sections, as shown here:

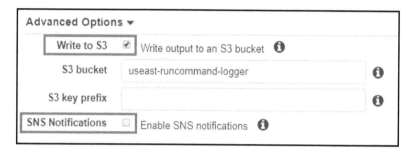

10. Once the configuration items are filled in, simply select the **Run** option to start the execution of your command document. During this time, Systems Manager will invoke the execution of your supplied commands over the list of managed instances that you provided. If there is an error during the execution, Systems Manager will halt the execution and display the **Status** of your output as either **Success** or **Failed**.

Simple isn't it? You can use this same mechanism to manage and execute commands remotely over your fleet of EC2 instances with ease and consistency and even leverage the AWS CLI to perform the same set of actions we have explored in this section.

In the next section, we will be learning a bit about yet another really useful feature provided by Systems Manager: State Manager.

Working with State Manager

State Manager is a powerful tool that helps to govern and manage the configuration of a managed system. For example, by using State Manager you can enforce a particular firewall rule for your fleet of managed instances and set that as the required **State** that needs to be enforced at all times. If the rules change outside of State Manager, it will automatically revert to match the required state's configuration, thus maintaining compliance and enforcing standardization over your environment.

Working with State Manager is quite simple and straightforward. You start off by selecting a state document (JSON based) that specifies the settings you need to configure or maintain your EC2 instances. These documents come predefined and you can create customized versions of them. With the document created, you can then select the individual managed instances, which can be either EC2 instances or even on-premises virtual machines, as well as specify a schedule for when and how often you wish to apply these states. It's that simple!

But before we go ahead with the invocation of our State Manager, let's first understand the concept of state documents a bit better as these documents are the foundation on which your Systems Manager works.

State documents are nothing more than simple JSON-based steps and parameters that define certain actions to be performed by Systems Manager. AWS provides dozens of such documents out of the box, which can be used to perform a variety of tasks such as patching your instances, configuring certain packages, configuring the CloudWatch Log agents, and much more! Additionally, you can even create your own custom document as well! There are three types of documents that are supported by Systems Manager:

- **Command**: Command documents are leveraged by the Run Command to execute commands over your managed instances. Alternatively, State Manager uses the command documents to apply certain policies as well. These actions can be run on one or more targets at any point during the life cycle of an instance.
- **Policy**: Used by the State Manager, policy documents are used to enforce a policy on your managed instances.
- **Automation**: These documents are more often used by the automation service within Systems Manager to perform common maintenance and deployment tasks. We will be learning more about automation documents a bit later in this chapter.

To view System Manager's predefined documents, from the EC2 dashboard navigation pane, select the **Documents** option under the **Systems Manager Shared Resources** section. Here you can use any of the predefined documents as per your requirements for State Manager, however let's quickly create a very simple custom document based on the **aws:configurePackage** definition:

1. To create your own document, select the **Create Document** option from the **Documents** dashboard as shown here:

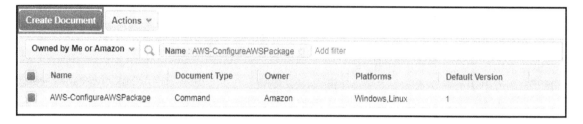

2. In the **Create Document** wizard, start off by providing a suitable **Name** for your document. In this case, I've provided the name `yoyodev-ssm-configure-packages`. Do note that the name cannot contain any spaces.

3. Next, from the **Document Type** dropdown, select **Command** as the option type and paste the following JSON code in the **Content** section as shown here:

```
{
        "schemaVersion": "2.0",
        "description": "Install or uninstall the latest version or
specified version of LAMP stack.",
        "parameters": {
                "action": {
                        "description": "(Required) Specify whether or not to
install or uninstall the package.",
                        "type": "String",
                        "allowedValues": [
                                "Install",
                                "Uninstall"
                        ]
                },
                "name": {
                        "description": "(Required) The LAMP package to
install/uninstall.",
                        "type": "String",
                        "allowedValues": [
                                "apache2",
                                "mysql-server",
                                "php"
```

```
                              ]
                      },
                      "version": {
                              "description": "(Optional) A specific version of the
          package to install or uninstall.",
                              "type": "String",
                              "default": "",
                              "allowedPattern":
          "(^(?:(\\d+)\\.)(?:(\\d+)\\.)(\\d+)$|^$)"
                      }
              },
              "mainSteps": [{
                      "action": "aws:configurePackage",
                      "name": "configurePackage",
                      "inputs": {
                              "name": "{{ name }}",
                              "action": "{{ action }}",
                              "version": "{{ version }}"
                      }
              }]
      }
```

4. With the document pasted, you can now click on **Create Document** to complete the document creation process.

The document comprises two primary sections: a `parameters` section, which contains a list of actions to be performed by the document, followed by a `mainSteps` section that specifies the action, which in this case is the `aws:configurePackage` to be performed by the document. In this case, the document when invoked will ask the user to select either `apache2`, `mysql-server`, or `php` from the dropdown list followed by an optional version number of the software you select. You can then select whether you wish to install or uninstall this particular package from your fleet of managed EC2 instances and simply execute the document when done!

Now that your custom document is created, let's quickly configure the State Manager to invoke it:

1. From the **Systems Manager Services** section in the EC2 navigation pane, select the **State Manager**. In the State Manager dashboard, select the **Create Association** option to get started with configuring State Manager.
2. Provide a suitable **Association Name** for your association. Note that this is an optional field and you can skip it if you want.

3. Next, from the **Select Document** section, filter and select the custom document that we created in our earlier step. On selection, you will notice the subfields change according to what we provided as parameters in the document. Let's quickly configure this and create our association.

4. In the **Targets** section, select your Dev instance or any of your managed instances which you wish to associate with this State Manager. Finally, go ahead and configure the **Schedule** that will trigger the association based on either a CRON or a rate schedule.

5. Last but not the least, configure the **Action** and select the appropriate package **Name** from the **Parameters** section as shown in the following screenshot:

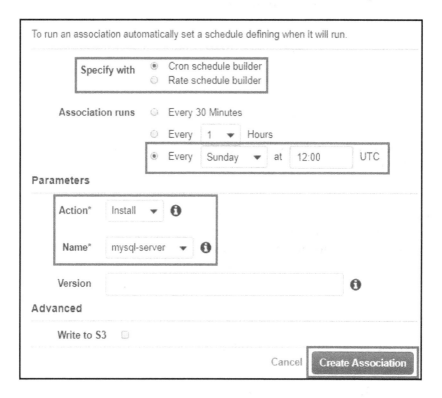

6. You can optionally enable the **Write to S3** checkbox to log the State Manager's execution in your own custom S3 bucket. For this scenario, I have not selected this option.

7. Finally, complete the State Manager's association process by selecting the **Create Association** option.

You can now view and modify your associations using the State Manager dashboard. Alternatively, you can even choose to enable your association immediately by selecting the **Apply Association Now** option as well.

In the next section, we will be looking at yet another simple and easy-to-use feature provided by Systems Manager that helps automate simple instance and deployment tasks, called System Manager Automation!

Simplifying instance maintenance using System Manager Automation

System Manager Automation is a managed service that provides a single, centralized interface for executing and monitoring commonly occurring instance management tasks such as patching, performing backups, executing scripts, and much more. Let's first get started by understanding a few necessary prerequisites that are required to be configured in order for automation to work in your environments.

Working with automation documents

As discussed briefly during the introduction to the State Manager service, automation documents are simple JSON-based documents that are designed to help you get started with the automation service quickly and efficiently. You can leverage the predefined automation documents or, alternatively, create your own set. In this section, we will look at how to leverage an existing automation document to patch your Dev EC2 instance and create a new AMI from it:

1. From the **EC2 Management Console**, select the **Documents** option from the **Systems Manager Shared Resources** section.
2. Using the **Documents** dashboard, you can filter and view only the documents that have **Automation** set as the **Document Type**.

3. Select **AWS-UpdateLinuxAmi** and click on the **Content** tab to view the automation document as shown here:

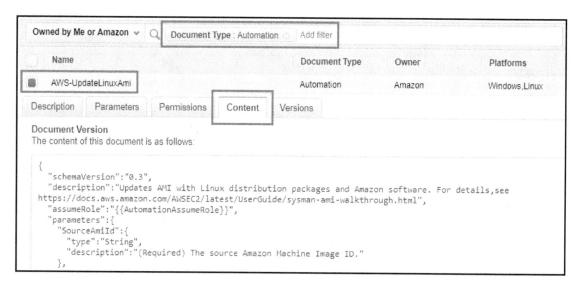

The **AWS-UpdateLinuxAmi** document comprises five distinctive steps, each explained briefly here:

- **launchInstance:** This step basically launches a new EC2 instance using your Systems Manager IAM instance profile as well as with a user data script that will install the latest copy of the SSM agent on this instance. The SSM agent is vital as it will enable the next steps to be executed using the Run Command as well as State Manger.

- **updateOSSoftware:** With the instance launched and the SSM agent installed, the next step is responsible for updating the packages in your Linux instance. This is done by executing an update script that methodologically updates the packages and any other software that may be marked for upgrades. You also get the capability to include or exclude a particular set of packages from this step using the `IncludePackages` and `ExcludePackages` parameters respectively. If no packages are included, the program updates all available packages on the instance.

- **stopInstance:** Once the instance is updated with the latest set of packages, the next action simply powers off the instance so that it can be prepped for the image creation process.

- **createImage:** This step creates a new AMI from your updated Linux instance. The image contains a descriptive name that links it to the source ID and creation time of the image.
- **terminateInstance**: The final step in the automation document, this step essentially cleans up the execution by terminating the running Linux instance.

Let's look at few simple steps using which we can invoke this particular automation document manually using the automation dashboard.

Patching instances using automation

In this section, we will be manually invoking the **AWS-UpdateLinuxAmi** automation document for patching our Linux instance and later creating a new AMI out of it:

1. To do this, first select the **Automations** option present under the **Systems Manager Services** section.
2. From the **Automations** dashboard, select the **Run automation document** option.
3. From the **Document name** field, select the **AWS-UpdateLinuxAmi** document and populate the required fields in the **Input parameters** section as described here:
    - `SourceAmiId`: Provide the source Amazon Machine Image ID from which the new instance will be deployed.
    - `InstanceIamRole`: Provide the IAM role name that enables Systems Manager to manage the instance. We created this role earlier during the start of this chapter as a part of SSM's prerequisites.
    - `AutomationAssumeRole`: Provide the ARN of the IAM role that allows automation to perform the actions on your behalf.
    - `TargetAmiName`: This will be the name of the new AMI created as a part of this automation document. The default is a system-generated string including the source AMI ID and the creation time and date.
    - `InstanceType`: Specify the instance type of instance to launch for the AMI creation process. By default, the *t2.micro* instance type is selected.
    - `PreUpdateScript`: You can additionally provide the URL of a script to run before any updates are applied. This is an optional field.
    - `PostUpdateScript`: Provide an optional post update script URL of a script to run after package updates are applied.

- `IncludePackages`: Include specific packages to be updated. By default, all available updates are applied.
- `ExcludePackages`: Provide names of specific packages that you wish to exclude from the updates list.

4. With the fields populated, simply select the **Run automation** option as shown in the following screenshot:

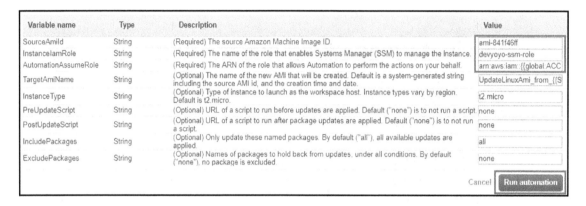

5. The automation document takes a couple of minutes to completely execute. You can verify the output of the execution using the **Automations** dashboard as well.
6. Simply select your automation job **Execution ID** to view the progress of each individual step as shown in the following screenshot. Optionally, you can verify the output of each step by selecting the adjoining **View Outputs** link as well:

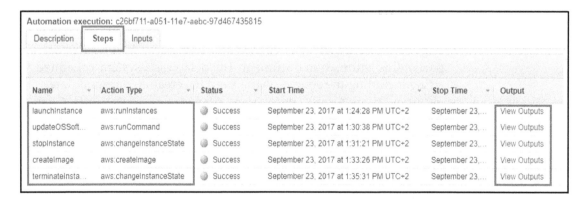

With this completed, you can now run similar automation tasks by creating your own automation documents and executing them using the steps mentioned herein. But what if you wanted to trigger these steps based on some events or schedules? Well, that's exactly what we will look into in the next section, *Triggering automation using CloudWatch schedules and events*.

Triggering automation using CloudWatch schedules and events

Although you can trigger automation documents manually, it's far better to either schedule or automate the execution of automation jobs using CloudWatch schedules and events.

Let's first understand how you can leverage CloudWatch events to trigger simple notifications of Systems Manager Automation events. These events can be used to notify you of whether your automation task succeeded, failed, or simply timed out:

1. First, log in to the CloudWatch dashboard. Alternatively, you can open CloudWatch via `https://console.aws.amazon.com/cloudwatch/`.
2. Next, from the navigation pane, select the **Events** option to bring up the **Create rule** page. Here, select **Event Pattern** from the **Event Source** section.
3. With this done, we now need to build our event source. To do so, from the **Service Name** drop-down list, search and select the option **EC2 Simple Systems Manager (SSM)**, as shown here:

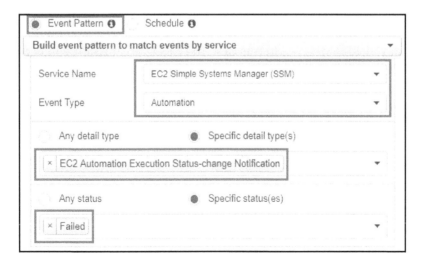

4. With the service selected, you can now opt to select a corresponding SSM **Event Type** as well, for example in this case I wish to be notified when a particular **Automation** task fails. So in the **Event Type** drop-down list, I've selected the **Automation** option. You can alternatively select other SSM services as well.

5. Next, in the detail type section, I've opted to go for the **EC2 Automation Execution Status-change Notification** option. Correspondingly, I've also selected **Failed** as the **Specific status(es)** for my event. This means that if and when a failed status event is generated as a result of an automation job, it will trigger a corresponding action which can be as simple as sending a notification using an SNS service or even triggering a corresponding Lambda function to perform some form of remediation action.

6. Your **Event Pattern Preview** should resemble something similar to the snippet here:

```
{
  "source": [
    "aws.ssm"
  ],
  "detail-type": [
    "EC2 Automation Step Status-change Notification",
    "EC2 Automation Execution Status-change Notification"
  ]
}
```

Similarly, you can even configure a CRON expression or fixed rate of execution of your automation jobs by selecting the **Schedule** option in the **Event Source** section:

1. Provide a suitable **Cron expression** depending on your requirements, for example, I wish to run the **AWS-UpdateLinuxAmi** automation document every Sunday at 10 P.M. UTC. In this case, the CRON expression will become `0,18,?,*,SUN,*`.

2. With the schedule configured, move on to the **Targets** section and select the **SSM Automation** option from the **Targets** drop-down list as shown in the following screenshot:

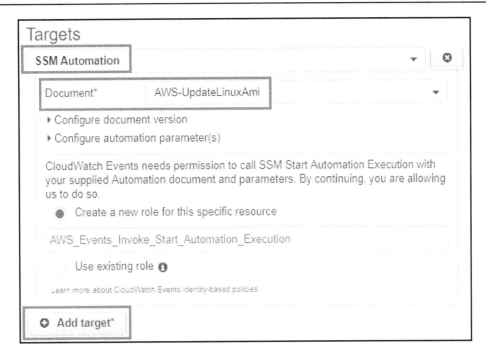

3. Next, configure the **AWS-UpdateLinuxAmi** parameters as we discussed earlier, and once the desired fields are populated, click on **Add target*** to complete the configuration.

With this step completed, you can now instantaneously trigger your automation jobs based on events as well as schedules, all powered by CloudWatch! Amazing isn't it?

In the next and final section, we will be learning a bit about yet another simple and easy to use SSM service that enables you to manage and patch your instances with ease.

Managing instance patches using patch baseline and compliance

Regularly patching your instances with the right set of security patches is an important activity that can take up a lot of time and effort if performed manually on each individual instance. Luckily, AWS provides a really efficient and easy way of automating the patching of your managed instances using the concept of Patch Manager services, provided as an out-of-the-box capability with SSM.

As an administrator, all you need to do is scan your instances for missing patches and leverage Patch Manager to automatically remediate the issues by installing the required set of patches. You can, alternatively, even schedule the patching of your managed instance or group of instances with the help of SSM's maintenance window tasks.

In this section, we will explore a quick and easy way of creating a unique patch baseline for our Dev instances and later create and associate a maintenance window for this, all using the EC2 Management dashboard. So let's get started with this right away!

First up, you will need to ensure that your instance has the required set of IAM Roles as well as the SSM agent installed and functioning as described at the beginning of this chapter. With these basics out of the way, we first need to configure the patch baseline with our set of required patches:

1. To do so, launch your EC2 dashboard and select the **Patch Baselines** option from the **Systems Manager Services** section. Patch Manager includes a default patch baseline for each operating system supported by Patch Manager. This includes Windows Server 2003 to 2016, Ubuntu, RHEL, CentOS, SUSE, and even Amazon Linux as well. You can use these default patch baselines or alternatively you can create one based on your requirements. Here, let's quickly create a custom baseline for our Dev instances.
2. Select the **Create Patch Baseline** option to bring up the **Create Patch Baseline** dashboard. Here, provide a suitable **Name** for your custom baseline.
3. From the **Operating System**, select **Ubuntu** as the OS choice. You will notice the patching rules change accordingly based on the OS type you select.

4. Next, in the **Approval Rules** section, create suitable patch baseline rules depending on your requirements. For example, I wish to set the Python packages to an **Important** priority and with a **High** compliance level as well. Similarly, you can add up to 10 such rules for one baseline, as shown in the following screenshot:

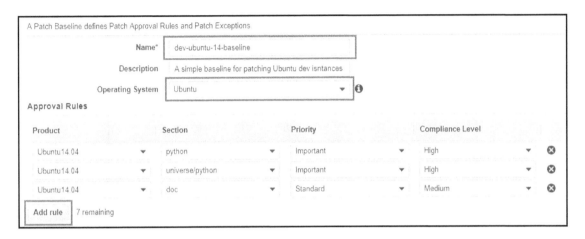

5. In the final section, **Patch Exceptions**, you can optionally mention the **Approved Packages**, **Rejected Packages**, and the **Compliance Level** for these patches collectively. In this case, I've left these values as their defaults and selected the **Create Patch Baseline** option to complete the process.

With your new patch baseline created, you now have the option to promote the same as the **Default Baseline** by selecting the new baseline from the **Patch Baselines** dashboard and clicking on the **Set Default Patch Baseline** option from the **Actions** tab.

Moving on to the next part of this walkthrough, we will now go ahead and set up the maintenance window for our newly created patch baseline:

1. To do so, select the **Maintenance Windows** option from the **Systems Manager Shared Resources** section. Click on **Create maintenance window** to get started with the process.
2. In the **Create maintenance window** page, provide a suitable **Name** for your window as well as an optional **Description**.

3. Next, in the **Specify schedule** section, you can opt to either use a *CRON scheduler* or a *rate expression* to define the schedule for your maintenance window. For this scenario, I've opted for the **Cron schedule builder** option and provided a window that starts every Sunday at 12:00 UTC:

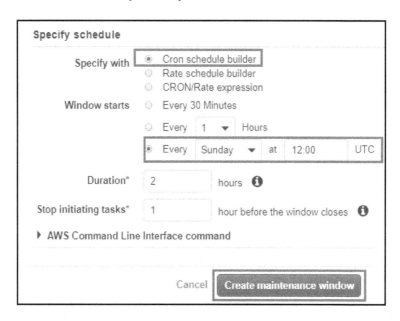

4. In the **Duration** as well as the **Stop initiating tasks** field, specify the timeline in hours that the maintenance window has to last for, as well as the number of hours before you want the system to stop initiating new tasks. Once all the required fields are populated, click on **Create maintenance window** to complete the creation process.

With the maintenance window created, we next need to add some targets for execution. Targets are individual EC2 instances or a group of EC2 instances that are identified by tags. To configure targets, select your newly created maintenance window then from the **Actions** tab and select the option **Register targets**:

1. In the **Register targets** page, provide a **Target Name** for your maintenance window's target with an optional **Description**.
2. Next, select the target EC2 instances you wish to associate with this target by either opting to **Specify Tags** or even by **Manually Selecting Instances** as shown in the following screenshot. For this scenario, I've already provided the tag *OS:Linux* to my Dev instances; alternatively, you can manually select your instances as well:

Maintenance window   mw-05bc51ca25c0d704a (dev-ubuntu-14-base-maintenance)

| Target Name | dev-ubuntu-14-Target |
| Description | Ubuntu 14.04 dev instances |

Owner information

Targets

Targets are the instances you would like to register with maintenance window. You can choose to target by both managed instance and tag.

Select Targets by   ⦿ Specifying Tags
                     ○ Manually Selecting Instances
                     Select tag key pairs to add targets that are tagged with these key pairs:

Tags

Tag Name	Tag Value
OS ▼	Linux ▼ ⊗
Add Tag 4 remaining	

Cancel   **Register targets**

3. Once completed, select the **Register targets** option to complete the process.

With the target instances registered with our maintenance window, the final step left to take is associate the maintenance window with our patch baseline:

1. In order to do this, we need to select the newly created *maintenance window*; from the **Actions** tab, select the option **Register run command task**.

2. Here, in the **Register run command task** page, fill in the required details such as a *name* for your new Run Command followed by an optional **Description**.

3. Next, from the **Command document** section, select the **AWS-RunPatchBaseline** document. You will also see the targeted instance associated with this Run Command already, as we configured it in our earlier steps.

4. Finally, in the **Parameters** section, select the appropriate IAM Role, provide a suitable count for the *Run Command to stop after* receiving a certain amount of errors, and last but not least, don't forget to select whether you wish to **Install** or simply **Scan** the target instances for the required set of patches.

5. With all the fields completed, click on **Register task** to complete this configuration.

Awesome isn't it? With just a few simple clicks you have now set up an effective patch management solution for your Dev instances, and without the need for any specialized software or expertise! But before we wind up this chapter, let's look at one last simple and really useful service provided by Systems Manager, which helps collect and inventorize metadata about your AWS as well as on-premises instances.

Getting started with Inventory Management

Inventory Management or just Inventory is yet another managed service provided by Systems Manager that is responsible for collecting operating system, application, and instance metadata from your AWS instances as well as those present and managed by Systems Manager in your on-premises environments. You can use this service to query the inventory metadata for mapping, understanding, and remediating EC2 instances based on certain software or regulatory compliances.

Let's look at a very simple example of enabling the inventory service for our Dev instance using the AWS Management dashboard:

1. To begin with, you will require both the SSM agent as well as the required IAM Roles configured on your managed instance. Once this is completed, select the **Managed Instances** option from the **Systems Manager Shared Resources** section.
2. Here, select your Dev instance and click on the **Setup Inventory** option as shown in the following screenshot:

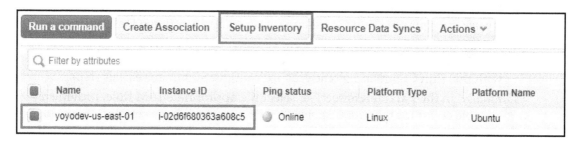

3. On the **Setup Inventory** page, most of the options will be quite familiar to you by now, such as the **Targets** and **Schedule** sections, so I'm not going to dwell on them here again. The more important section here is the **Parameters** section, using which you can choose to either **Enable** or **Disable** different types of inventory collections. For example, since we are working with Linux instances, I've chosen to disable the *Windows updates* parameters while keeping the rest enabled.

4. The final field **Write execution history to S3** basically allows you to write and store the inventory data centrally in an S3 bucket. This comes in really handy when you wish to collate your inventory data from multiple instances at a central location and then query this data either using services such as Amazon Athena or QuickInsights. Once completed, click on **Setup Inventory** to complete the inventory setup process.

You can now view the collected metadata of your EC2 instance by selecting it from the **Managed Instances** page and clicking on the **Inventory** tab. Here, choose between the various **Inventory Types** drop-down lists to view your instance specific metadata. You can toggle between **AWS:Application**, **AWS:AWSComponent**, **AWS:Network**, and **AWS:InstanceDetailedInformation**, just to name a few.

3
Introducing Elastic Beanstalk and Elastic File System

In the previous chapter, we started off by learning a lot about an awesome managed service called Systems Manager, which can perform virtually any and all tasks related to your EC2 instances, such as automating script executions, patching your instances, maintaining state and compliance, and much more. In this chapter, we will take things up a notch by introducing two really awesome services: Elastic Beanstalk, a service that can help you develop and deploy rich web applications in just a few clicks, and Elastic File System, a service that provides a massively scalable shared filesystem for your EC2 instances! So, keeping this in mind, let's have a quick look at the various topics that we will be covering in this chapter:

- Introducing Elastic Beanstalk and how it works
- How to manage applications, environments, and configurations with ease using Elastic Beanstalk
- Pushing your applications to AWS using the Elastic Beanstalk CLI
- Getting started with Elastic File System and its various use cases
- Hosting a highly scalable and available WordPress site using Elastic Beanstalk and Elastic File System

So much to do, so let's get started right away!

Introducing Amazon Elastic Beanstalk

One of the key features of a cloud is to provide its users and developers with a seamless and easy to use platform for developing and deploying their applications. That's exactly where Elastic Beanstalk comes in. Elastic Beanstalk was first launched in the year 2011, and has continuously evolved to become a full-fledged PaaS offering from AWS.

Elastic Beanstalk is your one-stop shop for quickly deploying and managing your web applications in AWS. All you need to do is upload your code to Beanstalk, and voila! Elastic Beanstalk takes care of the entire application's deployment process, from EC2 capacity provisioning to auto-scaling the instances and even load balancing using an ELB! Elastic Beanstalk does it all so that you can concentrate on more important tasks, such as developing your applications and not getting bogged down with complex operational nuances.

But for me, Beanstalk is much more than just the deployment and management of your applications. Let's look at some of the key benefits of leveraging Elastic Beanstalk for your web applications:

- **Deployment support**: Today, Beanstalk supports standard EC2 instances and Docker containers as the basis for your application's deployment. This enables you to host your web applications and your microservices-based apps on AWS with relative ease.
- **Platform support**: Beanstalk provides a rich set of platforms for developers to deploy their apps on. Today, the list includes Java, PHP, Python, .NET, Node.js, and Ruby, with more languages and platforms to be added in the future.
- **Developer friendly**: It is extremely easy to build and deploy your applications over to AWS using Beanstalk. You can leverage a wide variety of options, including the AWS Management Console or its CLI, a code repository such as Git, or even an IDE such as Eclipse or Visual Studio to upload your application, and the rest is all taken care of by Beanstalk itself.
- **Control**: With Beanstalk, you get complete control over your underlying AWS resources as well as the environments on which your application runs. You can change the instance types, scale the resources, add more application environments, configure ELBs, and much more!
- **Costs**: One of the best things about Beanstalk is that it's absolutely free! Yes, you heard it right! Free! You only pay for the AWS resources that are spun up based on the configurations that you provide and nothing more. Amazing isn't it?

With these pointers in mind, let's look at some of the essential concepts and terminologies that you ought to know before getting started with Elastic Beanstalk.

Concepts and terminologies

Here's a look at some of the common concepts and terminologies that you will often come across while working with Elastic Beanstalk:

- **Applications**: An application in Elastic Beanstalk is basically a collection of Beanstalk's internal components, and includes environments, versions, events, and various other things. Think of an Elastic Beanstalk application as a high-level container which contains different aspects of your application.
- **Application versions**: Application versions are nothing more than different versions of an application's code. Each version of your application's code is stored in an S3 Bucket that is auto-created and managed by Beanstalk itself. You can create multiple versions of your application code and use this for deployment to one or more environments for testing and comparison.
- **Environments**: An Elastic Beanstalk environment is yet another logical container that hosts one application version at a time on a specified set of instances, load balancers, auto scaling groups, and so on. Typically, you would have an environment for development, one for acceptance testing, and another one for production hosting, however, there are no hard and fast rules on this.

An environment comes in two flavors, and you can choose between the two during your initial environment setup phase. The first is called a **web server environment**, and is basically created for applications that support HTTP requests, such as web applications and so on. The second is called a **worker environment**, where the application pulls tasks from an Amazon SQS Queue. Here's a look at each of these flavors in a bit more detail:

- **Web server environment**: As mentioned earlier, this particular environment is well suited to hosting and managing web frontend applications, such as websites, mobile applications, and so on. As part of this environment, Beanstalk provisions an internet-facing Elastic Load Balancer, an autoscaling group with some minimalistic configuration settings, and a small number of EC2 instances that contain your application code along with a pre-installed agent called **Host Manager**. The Host Manager agent is a key component in the entire setup process, as it is responsible for deploying and monitoring the application as well as periodically patching the instance and rotating the logs.

Here's a representational diagram depicting a simple application being scaled using a web server environment. Note the RDS instance in the diagram as well. You can also choose to set up an RDS instance for your application using Elastic Beanstalk, or add it to the application stack manually later:

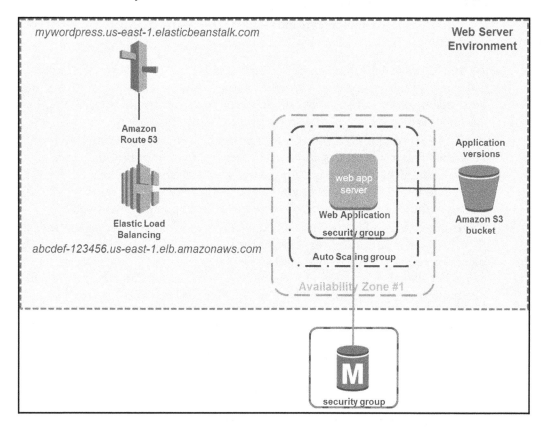

An additional point worth mentioning here is that every environment has a unique CNAME, for example `mywordpress`. The CNAME maps to a URL which is in the form of `mywordpress.us-east-1.elasticbeanstalk.com`. This URL is aliased in Amazon's DNS service Route53 to an Elastic Load Balancing URL, something like `abcdef-123456.us-east-1.elb.amazonaws.com`, by using a CNAME record.

- **Worker environment**: The worker environment works in a very different way to the web server environment. In this case, Elastic Beanstalk starts up an SQS Queue in your environment and installs a small daemon into each of the worker instances. The daemon is responsible for regularly polling the queue for newer messages, and if a message is present, the daemon pulls it into the worker instance for consumption, as depicted in the following diagram:

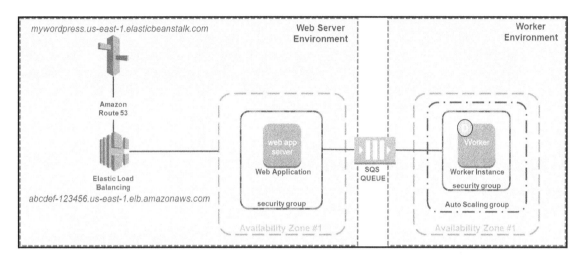

Ideally, you can use a combination of web and worker environments to host your applications, so that there is a clear decoupling of your web frontend resources and your backend processing worker instances. Keep in mind that there are a lot more design considerations that you also ought to think about while setting up your environments, such as how the scalability is going to be handled and storage options for data depending on the type of data, for example S3 for logs and RDS for application-centric data, security, fault tolerance, and much more.

With this section completed, let's move on to the fun part and see how to get started with using Elastic Beanstalk!

Getting started with Elastic Beanstalk

In this section, we will be performing a deep dive into how to set up a fully-functional Dev and Prod environment for our simple WordPress application using Elastic Beanstalk. Before we get started, here is a list of some prerequisite items that you need to have in place before we can proceed:

- A valid AWS account and user credentials with the required set of privileges to run the AWS CLI and the Elastic Beanstalk CLI.
- A sandbox/Dev instance to download the WordPress installation and later use it to push the application code over to the respective Beanstalk environment. Note that you can also use other resources, such as a Git URL or an IDE, but for now we will be focusing on this approach.

Creating the Dev environment

Let's first start off by creating a simple and straightforward development environment for our WordPress site. To do so, execute the following steps:

1. Sign in to the AWS Console and select the Elastic Beanstalk option from the **Services** filter, or alternatively, launch the Elastic Beanstalk console by launching the URL `https://console.aws.amazon.com/elasticbeanstalk` in a browser of your choice.
2. Next, select the **Create New Application** option to get started. Remember, an application is the highest level of container for our application code, which can contain one or more environments as required.
3. In the **Create New Application** dialog box, provide a suitable **Application Name** and an optional **Description** to get started with. Click on **Create** once completed.
4. With the basic application container created, you can now go ahead and create the development environment. To do so, from the **Actions** drop-down list, select the **Create New Application** option.
5. Here, you will be provided with an option to either opt for the **Web server environment** or the **Worker environment** configuration. Remember, an environment type can be selected only once here, so make sure that you select the correct tier based on your application's requirements. In this case, I've opted to select the **Web server environment**, as shown in the following screenshot:

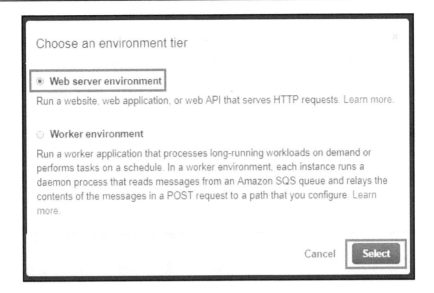

6. On the **Create a new environment** wizard page, provide a suitable **Environment name** for your WordPress site. Since this is a development environment, I've gone ahead and named it `YoyoWordpress-dev`. Next, in the **Domain** field, provide a unique name for your website's domain URL. The URL will be suffixed by the region-specific Elastic Beanstalk URL, as shown in the following screenshot:

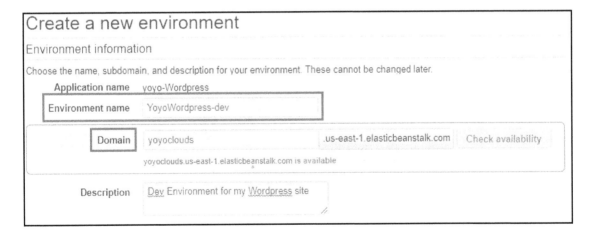

7. Next, type in a suitable **Description** for your new environment, and move on toward the **Base configuration** section. Here, from the **Platform** dropdown, select the **Preconfigured platform** option and opt for the **PHP** platform, as depicted in the following screenshot. PHP is our default option as WordPress is built on PHP 5.6. Today, Beanstalk supports packer builder, Docker containers, Go, Java SE, Java with Tomcat, .NET on Windows Server with IIS, Node.js, PHP, Python, and Ruby, with more platform support coming shortly:

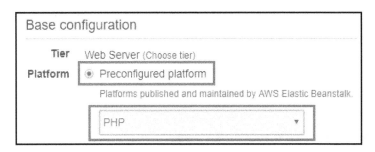

8. Now, here's the part where you need to keep your calm! Leave the rest of the options as their default values and select **Configure more options**, not the **Create environment** option! Yes, we will be configuring a few additional items first and will create our development environment later!

9. On the **Configure Environment** page, you can opt to select one of the three preconfigured **Configuration presets** options, based on your application's requirements. The presets are briefly explained here:
   - **Low cost (Free tier eligible)**: This particular configuration will launch a single (**t2.micro**) instance with no load balancing or autoscaling group configured. This is ideal if you just want to get started with an application using the basics or wish to set up a minimalistic Dev environment, as in this case.
   - **High availability**: Unlike the low-cost preset, the high-availability configuration comes pre-equipped with an autoscaling group that can scale up to a default of four instances or more, and an Elastic Load Balancer that has cross-zone load balancing and connection draining enabled by default. Besides this, you also get a host of CloudWatch alarms created for monitoring, as well as security groups for your instance and Load Balancer.
   - **Custom configuration**: You can additionally opt to configure your environment based on other parameters. You can select this preset, and modify each and every component present within your environment as you see fit.

10. With the **Configuration preset** set to **Low cost (Free tier)**, the next item that we can modify is the **Platform configuration**. Elastic Beanstalk supports the following PHP platform configurations:

PHP Language	Amazon Linux AMI	PHP version
PHP 7.1	2017.03.1	PHP 7.1.7
PHP 7.0	2017.03.1	PHP 7.0.21
PHP 5.6	2017.03.1	PHP 5.6.31
PHP 5.5	2017.03.1	PHP 5.5.38
PHP 5.4	2017.03.1	PHP 5.4.45

11. Since we are using a WordPress application, we need to modify the platform as well, to accommodate for the correct PHP version.

    To do so, select the **Change platform configuration** option. This will bring up the **Choose a platform version** dialog, as shown here:

12. Here, from the drop-down list, search and select the **64bit Amazon Linux 2017.03 v2.5.0 running PHP 5.6** option, as WordPress execution is stable with PHP 5.6. Once done, click on **Save** to complete the process.

13. With the **Platform configuration** changed as per our requirements, we can now move on to configuring the add-on services such as **security**, **notifications**, **network**, **database**, and much more! For example, let's quickly configure the networking for our WordPress Dev environment by selecting the **Modify** option in the **Network** pane.

14. In the **Network** pane, you can opt to launch your environment in a custom **VPC**, as well as other instance-specific settings such as enabling **Public IP address**, selecting the **Instance subnets** based on your VPC design, and finally assigning **Instance security groups** for your Dev instances. In this case, I already have a custom VPC created specifically for the development environment that contains one public subnet and one private subnet, with a default security group as well. Here is an overview of the network configuration setup for my environment. You can tweak this to match your requirements:

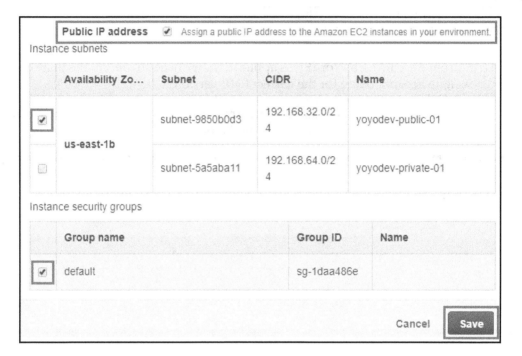

15. Once the settings are made, click on **Save** to complete the networking changes. You can perform other configurational changes as you see fit, however, since this is only a development environment, I've opted to leave the rest of the options as default for now. Once completed, select the **Create environment** option to finish the environment creation process.

Once the environment creation process is initiated, it will take a couple of minutes to complete its execution, as depicted in the following screenshot. Here, you will see Elastic Beanstalk create a new security group as well as an Elastic IP address for your EC2 dev instance. During this stage, the environment also transitions from a **Pending** to an **Ok** state, and you can view the environment, your application's logs, and the status:

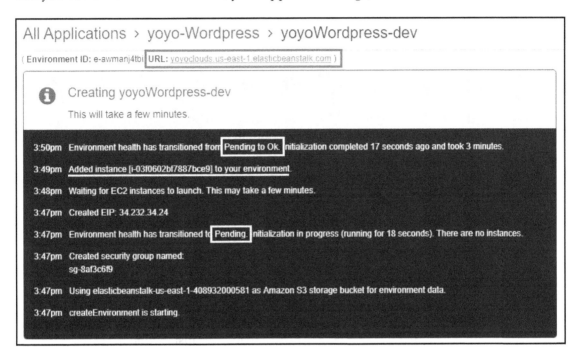

With your environment up and running, you can also verify it using the URL provided as an output of your environment's creation by using the environment dashboard. Upon selecting the URL, you will be redirected to a new application landing page in your web browser which basically verifies that your environment is configured to work with PHP 5.6.

But where is our WordPress application? That's exactly what we will be deploying next using a really simple and easy-to-use Elastic Beanstalk CLI.

Working with the Elastic Beanstalk CLI

With your environment deployed using the AWS Management Console, we now shift our focus to leveraging the Elastic Beanstalk CLI, or EB CLI, to push the application code over to the newly created environment.

The EB CLI is a powerful utility that can be used to operate and manage your entire Elastic Beanstalk environment using a few simple CLI commands. It is also designed to work with AWS development services such as CodeBuild and CodeCommit, as well as other third-party code repository services such as Git.

In this section, we will first be looking at a few simple steps for installing the EB CLI on a simple Linux instance, later followed by configuring and pushing our WordPress application to its respective development environment:

1. To do so, we first need to ensure that the instance is updated with the latest set of packages. In my case, I'm performing the steps on a simple Ubuntu 14.04 LTS instance, however, you can alternatively use your own on-premises virtual machines.

2. Run the following command to update your OS. The command will vary based on your operating system variant:

   ```
   # sudo apt-get update
   ```

3. Next, we need to ensure that the instance has the required Python packages installed in it. Note that if you are using the Amazon Linux AMI, then by default it will already have the necessary Python packages installed in it:

   ```
   # sudo apt-get install python python-pip
   ```

    AWS CLI and the EB CLI require Python 2 version 2.6.5+ or Python 3 version 3.3+.

4. With the Python packages installed, we now move forward and set up the AWS CLI using the following commands:

   ```
   # pip install awscli
   # aws configure
   ```

The first command installs the CLI, while the other runs you through a simple wizard to set up the AWS CLI for your instance. To learn more about how to configure the AWS CLI, you can check out this URL: `http://docs.aws.amazon.com/cli/latest/userguide/installing.html`.

5. Finally, we go ahead and install the EB CLI. The installation is pretty straightforward and simple:

```
# pip install awsebcli
```

6. That's all there is to it! You now have a functioning Elastic Beanstalk CLI installed and ready for use. So let's now go ahead and download the required WordPress code ZIP file locally and use the EB CLI to push it into the development environment:

```
# sudo git clone https://github.com/WordPress/WordPress.git
```

7. Extract the contents of your WordPress ZIP file into a new folder, and run the following command from within the WordPress directory:

```
# eb init
```

The `eb init` command is used to initialize and sync the EB CLI with your newly created development environment. Follow the on-screen instructions to configure the EB CLI's settings, such as **Selecting a default region** to operate from, **Selecting an application to use**, and so on. Remember, the default region has to match your current development environment's region as well, which in my case is **us-east-1**:

1. With the EB CLI set up, the only step left now is to deploy the WordPress application to the development environment using yet another EB CLI command called simply `eb deploy`:

```
# eb deploy
```

During the deployment process, the CLI creates an application version archive in a new S3 bucket within your environment. Each application deployment will result in subsequent version creations within S3 itself. After this, you will see your application code get uploaded to your development environment, as depicted in the following screenshot:

```
root@YoYoNux:~/WordPress#
root@YoYoNux:~/WordPress# eb deploy
Creating application version archive "app-a83e4-171007_132524".
Uploading: [###############################################] 100% Done...
INFO: Environment update is starting.
INFO: Deploying new version to instance(s).
INFO: New application version was deployed to running EC2 instances.
INFO: Environment update completed successfully.

root@YoYoNux:~/WordPress# █
```

2. The environment simultaneously changes its state from **Ok** to **Pending** as the application is uploaded and set up in your development instance. Once the application becomes available, the health state of the environment will yet again transition from **Pending** to **OK** to **Info**.

3. You can verify whether your application has uploaded or not by refreshing the application URL (`yoyoclouds.us-east-1.elasticbeanstalk.com`) on your environment's dashboard. You should see the WordPress welcome screen, as shown in the following screenshot:

Note, however, that this setup still requires a MySQL database, so don't forget to go to the RDS Management Console and create a minimalistic MySQL database, or even better, an Aurora DB instance, for your development environment. Remember to note down the database username, password, and the DB host and database name itself; you will need these during your WordPress configuration!

With this step completed, let's take a few minutes to understand the various options for configuring and monitoring your newly deployed application using the environment dashboard!

Understanding the environment dashboard

The environment dashboard is your one-stop shop for managing and monitoring your newly deployed applications, as well as the inherited instances. In this section, we will quickly look at each of the sections present in the environment dashboard and how you can leverage them for your applications.

To start off with, the **Dashboard** view itself provides you with some high-level information and event logs depicting the current status of your environment. To learn more about the recent batch of events, you can opt to select the **Show All** option in the **Recent Events** section, or alternatively select the **Events** option from the navigation pane.

The **Dashboard** also allows you to upload a newer version of your application by selecting the **Upload and Deploy** option, as shown in following screenshot. Here, you can see a **Running Version** of your WordPress application as well. This is the same application that we just deployed using the EB CLI.

You can also control various aspects of your environment, such as **Save Configuration**, **Clone Environment**, and **Terminate Environment**, as well using the **Actions** tab provided in the right-hand corner of the environment dashboard:

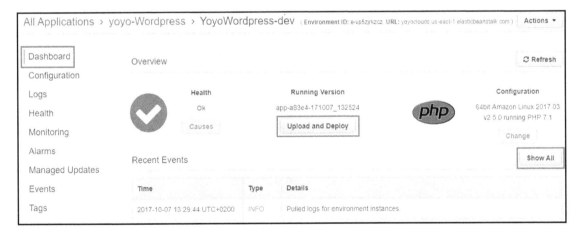

Moving on from the **Dashboard**, the next tab in the navigation pane that is worth checking out is the **Configuration** section. Let's look at each of the configuration options in a bit more detail, starting off with the **Scaling** tile:

- **Scaling**: Here, you can opt to change your **Environment Type** from a **Single instance** deployment to a **Load balancing, auto scaling** enabled environment simply by selecting the correct option from the **Environment Type** drop-down list. You can even enable **Time-based scaling** for your instances by opting for the **Add scheduled action** option.

- **Instances**: In the next tile, you can configure your instance-specific details for your environment, such as the **Instance type**, the **EC2 key pair** to be used for enabling SSH to your instances, the **Instance profile**, and other options as well, such as the root volume type and its desired size.

- **Notifications**: Here, you can specify a particular **Email** address, using which, notifications pertaining to your environment—such as its events—are sent using the Amazon SNS.

- **Software configuration**: This section allows you to configure some key parameters for your application, such as the application's **Document root**, the **Memory limit** for running your PHP environment, and the logging options. But the thing that I really love about the software configuration is the **Environment properties** section. With this, you can pass secrets, endpoints, debug settings, and other information to your application without even having to SSH into your instances, which is simply amazing! We will be learning a bit about environment properties and how you can create simple environment variables and pass them to your WordPress application a bit later in this chapter.

- **Health**: One of the most important configuration items in your environment, the **Health** section allows you to configure the **Health Check URL** for your application, as well as to enable detailed health reporting for your environment using a special agent installed on your systems. This agent monitors the vitals of your EC2 instance, captures application-level health metrics, and sends them directly to Beanstalk for further analysis. This, in conjunction with the **Application Logs**, helps you to drill down into issues and mitigate them all using the Elastic Beanstalk Console itself.

- **NOTE**: You can find the agent's logs in your instance's `/var/log/healthd/daemon.log` file.

Apart from the **Configuration** tab, Elastic Beanstalk also provides you with a **Logs** option, where you can request either the complete set of logs or the last 100 lines. You can download each instance's log files using this particular section as well:

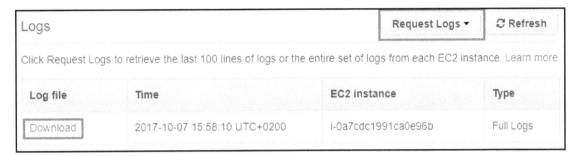

And last but not least, you can also leverage the **Monitoring** and **Alarms** sections to view the overall **Environment Health**, as well as other important metrics, such as **CPU Utilization**, **Max Network In**, and **Max Network Out**. To configure the alarms for individual graphs, all you need to do is select the alarm icon adjoining each of the graphs present in the **Monitoring** dashboard, as shown in the following screenshot:

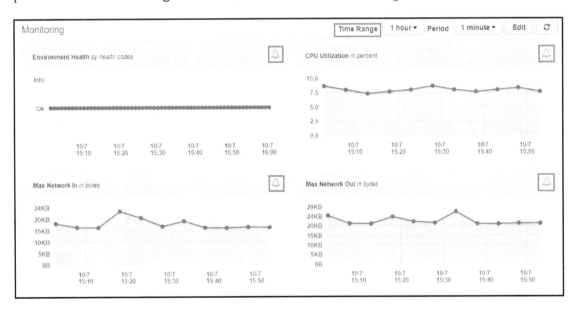

A corresponding **Add Alarm** widget will pop up, using which you can configure the alarm's essentials, such as its **Name**, the **Period**, and **Threshold** settings, as well as the required **Notification** settings.

In this way, you can use the environment dashboard and the EB CLI together to perform daily application administration and monitoring tasks. In the next section, we will be leveraging this environment dashboard to clone and create a new production environment from the existing development environment.

Cloning environments

With the development environment all set and working, it is now time to go ahead and create a production environment. Now, technically, you could repeat all the processes that we followed earlier for the development environment creation, and that would work out well indeed, but Elastic Beanstalk offers a really simple and minimalistic approach to creating new environments while using an existing one as a template. The process is call cloning, and it can be performed in a few simple clicks, using the environment dashboard itself:

1. To get started, simply select the **Actions** tab from the environment dashboard page and select the option **Clone Environment**. This will bring up the **New Environment** page, as shown here:

2. Here, start off by providing an **Environment name** for the new environment, followed by a unique prefix for the **Environment URL**. Remember, this is a clone from the earlier development environment that we created, so, by default, it will contain the same Amazon Linux instance with the WordPress application that we pushed in during the Dev stages. This is not a concern as we can always use the EB CLI to push the production version of the application as well. But for now, fill in the rest of the details and select the **Clone** option.

The new environment undergoes the same initialization and creation process as it did earlier, creating separate security groups, assigning a new Elastic IP, and launching a new EC2 instance with the same application version that was pushed in the development environment.

Once completed, you should now have two very similar environments up and running side by side, but isn't a production environment supposed to be more than just one instance? Well, that's precisely what we will be configuring in the next section.

Configuring the production environment

Now that we have had a good tour of the environment dashboard, it should be relatively easy to configure the production environment as per our requirements. Let's start off by increasing the instance count for our production environment:

1. Select the **Scaling** configuration tile from the newly created production environment's configuration dashboard and change the **Environment type** from **Single instance** to **Load balancing, auto scaling**. The instance count settings as well as the auto scaling features, will only be available once the new changes are reflected in the environment. Click **Apply** once done.

 To verify that the changes have indeed been propagated, you can copy the newly created Elastic Load Balancer DNS name into a web browser and verify that you can access the WordPress getting started wizard.

2. Next, you can also change the default instance type from **t1.micro** to something a bit more powerful, such as **t2.medium** or **t2.large**, using the **Instances** configuration section.

3. Once your major settings are done, you will also require a new RDS backed MySQL database for your production instances. So go ahead and create a new MySQL DB instance using the RDS Management Console at `https://console.aws.amazon.com/rds/`.

For handling production-grade workloads, I would strongly recommend enabling multi-AZ deployment for your MySQL database.

4. Remember to make a note of the database name, the database endpoint, as well as the username and password, before moving on to the next steps!
5. Next, using the production environment URL, launch your WordPress site and fill in the required database configuration details, as depicted in the following screenshot:

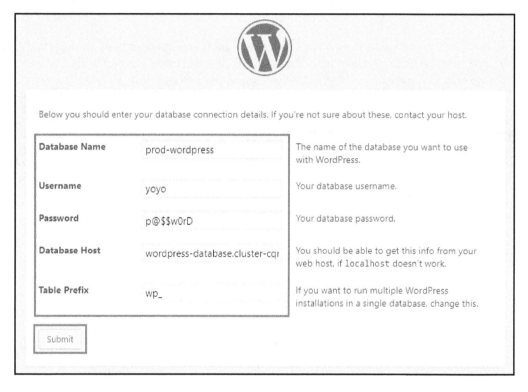

This method of configuring database settings is not ideal, especially when it comes to a production environment. Alternatively, Elastic Beanstalk provides you with the concept of environment properties that enable you to pass key-value pairs of configurations directly to your application.

6. To do so, you need to select the **Configuration** section from your **Production** dashboard, and within that, opt to modify the **Software** configuration.

7. Here, under the **Environment Properties** section, fill out the required production database variables, as depicted in the following screenshot:

But where do these variables actually end up getting configured? That's where we leverage the WordPress configuration file called wp-config.php and configure all these variables into it. Upon loading, PHP will read the values of each of these properties from the environment property that we just set in Elastic Beanstalk.

8. Open your wp-config.php file using your favorite text editor, and change the database section, as shown in the following snippet:

```
/** The name of the database for WordPress */
define('DB_NAME', getenv('DB_NAME'));

/** MySQL database username */
define('DB_USER', getenv('DB_USER'));

/** MySQL database password */
define('DB_PASSWORD', getenv('DB_PASSWORD'));

/** MySQL hostname */
define('DB_HOST', getenv('DB_HOST'));
```

9. Save the file and push the newly modified code into the production environment using the eb deploy command. Simple isn't it?

Here's what the new environment should look like after the deployments:

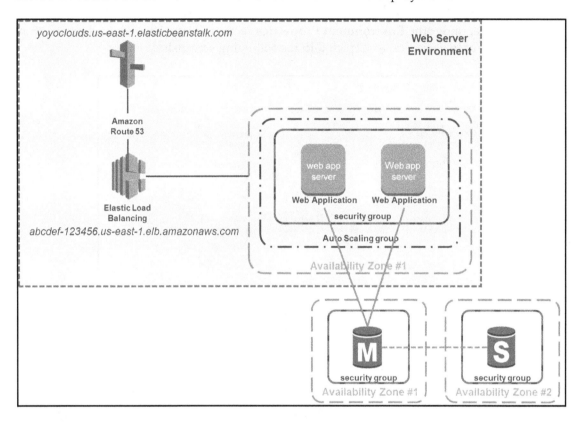

Looking good so far, right? With this done, your WordPress setup should be able to scale in and out efficiently without you having to worry about the load balancing needs or even about the MySQL instances. Additionally, now that we have configured the instances to fetch the database information from Elastic Beanstalk itself, we no longer have to worry about what will happen to our site if the underlying WordPress instances restart or terminate. This is exactly what we set out to do in the first place, but there's still a small catch. What about the content files that you will eventually upload on your WordPress website, such as images and videos? These uploads will end up getting stored on your instance's local disks, and that's a potential issue as you may end up losing all of your data if that instance gets terminated by the auto-scaling policies. Luckily for us, AWS has a solution to this problem, and that's exactly what we are going to learn about next.

Introducing Amazon Elastic File System

AWS, for one, has really put in a lot of innovation and effort to come up with some really awesome services, and one such service that I personally feel has tremendous potential is the Elastic File System. Why is it so important? Well, to answer this question, we need to take a small step back and understand what type of storage services AWS offers at the moment.

First up, we have the object stores in the form of Amazon S3 and Amazon Glacier. Although virtually infinite in scaling capacity, both these services are known to be a tad slower performance-wise compared to the EC2 instance storage and the EBS. This is bound to happen, as the likes of EBS is specially designed to provide fast and durable block storage, but, as a trade-off, you cannot extend an EBS volume across multiple Availability Zones. Elastic File System or EFS, on the other hand, provides a mix of both worlds by giving you the performance of an EBS volume combined with the availability of the same volume across multiple AZs, and that is really awesome! To summarize, EFS is a massively scalable file storage system that allows you to mount multiple EC2 instances to it simultaneously across AZs, without having to worry about the durability, availability, or performance of the system.

How does EFS actually work, you ask? Well, that's exactly what we will learn about in the next section.

How does it work?

EFS works in a very simple and minimalistic way, so as to reduce the amount of configurations that you need to perform and manage as an end user. To start off, EFS provides you with the ability to create one or more filesystems. Each filesystem can be mounted to an instance or instances, and data can be read as well as written to them. Mounting the filesystem requires your instances to have support for the Network File System version 4.0 and 4.1 (NFSv4) protocol. Most Linux operating systems come with the necessary support, however, you may have to install the NFS client on these machines if it is not there to connect to an EFS. So, how is this useful for our WordPress application? Well, for starters, once you have an Amazon Elastic File System in place, you can have multiple EC2 instances connect to it simultaneously and use it as a scalable shared drive that can extend even to petabytes if the need arises. Also, the Amazon Elastic File System does not have any downtime or repercussions if your EC2 instances reboot or even terminate; the data will persist on the filesystem until you manually delete it or terminate the filesystem itself. There are some rules and limitations, however, when it comes to using the Elastic File System, which you ought to keep in mind.

You can mount an Amazon EFS on instances in only one VPC at a time, and both the filesystem and the VPC must be in the same AWS region.

Once the filesystem is created, you will be provided with a DNS name for identifying it within your region. Additionally, you will also be required to create one or more supporting mount targets within your VPC, which basically acts as a connectivity medium between your instances present within a subnet and the filesystem. Here is a representational diagram of how an Elastic File System interacts with EC2 instances using mount targets:

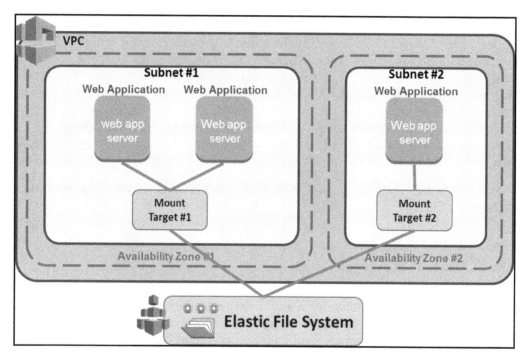

As an administrator, you can create one mount target in each Availability Zone present in a given region. You can also create a mount target in each of the subnets presents within a particular VPC, so that all EC2 instances in that VPC share that mount target. In the next section, we will be exploring a few simple steps required for setting up your own Elastic File System.

Creating an Elastic File System

Setting up your own Elastic File System is as easy as it gets! You can start off by launching the Elastic File System dashboard from the AWS Management Console, or alternatively, by visiting the URL `https://console.aws.amazon.com/efs/`:

1. On the EFS landing page, select the option **Create file system** to get started.
2. In the **Configure file system access** page, you can start off by first selecting the **VPC** you want to associate the filesystem with. Remember, you can have multiple filesystems per VPC, however, they cannot be extended across regions:

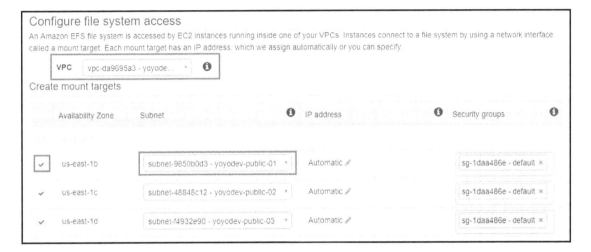

3. With the VPC selected, the associated subnets will automatically populate themselves based on the Availability Zones that they are a part of in the **Create mount targets** section. Here, you can select the appropriate subset that you wish to associate with the Elastic File System, along with its corresponding security group. In my case, I've selected the individual public subnets from my VPC, as the WordPress application instances will be deployed here, and these instances will require access to the filesystem for storing the images and other content.
4. With the fields populated, select the **Next Step** option to proceed.

5. The next step is all about **Configuring optional settings** for your Elastic File System. Here, you can **Add tags** to describe your filesystem and select the appropriate **Performance mode** for the filesystem, based on your requirements. Today, EFS provides two modes: the **General Purpose**, which is ideal for running the majority of workloads, and a **Max I/O** mode, which is specifically designed for when your environment needs to scale to tens of thousands of EC2 instances, all connecting to this single filesystem itself. **Max I/O** mode provides much better performances compared to **General Purpose**, however, there is the chance of a slightly higher latency when handling file operations here.

6. The final option left is **Enable encryption**, which, if checked, will leverage a KMS key from your existing AWS account and encrypt all the data stored in the filesystem at rest:

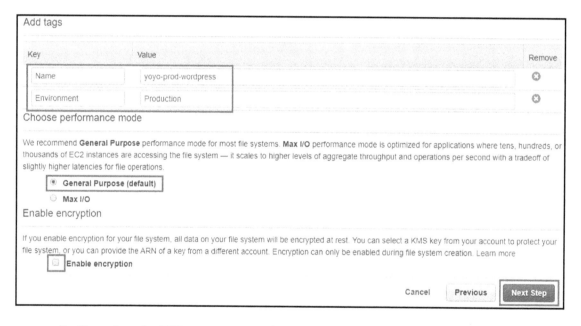

7. Complete the EFS setup process by reviewing the configuration changes on the **Review and create** page, and finally, click on **Create** to enable the filesystem. This process takes a couple of minutes, but once completed, you will be shown the **DNS name** of your newly created filesystem. Make a note of this name as you will be required to reference it in our Elastic Beanstalk environment as well.

So far, so good! We have our production environment up and running on Elastic Beanstalk, and now we have created a simple yet powerful Elastic File System. In the next section, we will look at how you can integrate the two services for use by WordPress using Elastic Beanstalk's configuration files concept.

Extending EFS to Elastic Beanstalk

Although Elastic Beanstalk takes complete care of your environment's provisioning and configuration, there are still methods which you can used to control the advanced configuration of your environment, such as integrating your application with the likes of other AWS services, such as ElastiCache, or even EFS for that matter. This can be performed using a variety of services provided by Beanstalk itself; for example, by leveraging Beanstalk's **Saved configurations**, or even using **Environment Manifest** (YML) files. But in this particular section, we will be concentrating on integrating the EFS service with our WordPress application using specialized **Configuration Files** called .ebextensions.

These .ebextensions are simple YAML formatted documents ending with a .config file extension. Once the .ebextensions file is created, you need to place this in the root folder of your application's source code, within a special directory named .ebextensions, and finally, deploy your application over to Beanstalk.

These configuration files are so powerful that you don't even have to connect to your instances through SSH to issue configuration commands. You can configure your environment entirely from your project source by using .ebextensions:

1. To start using .ebextensions for your WordPress setup, first we need to create a folder named .ebextensions within the root of your WordPress application. Type the following command from your Dev instance:

   ```
   # cd wordpress && sudo mkdir .ebextensions
   ```

2. Create a new file with an extension of .config, and paste the following contents into it:

   ```
   # sudo vi efs.config

   ### PASTE THE FOLLOWING CONTENTS ###
   packages:
     yum:
       nfs-utils: []
       jq: []
   files:
     "/tmp/mount-efs.sh" :
   ```

```
      mode: "000755"
      content: |
        #!/usr/bin/env bash
        mkdir -p /mnt/efs
        EFS_NAME=$(/opt/elasticbeanstalk/bin/get-config environment |
jq -r '.EFS_NAME')
        mount -t nfs4 -o
nfsvers=4.1,rsize=1048576,wsize=1048576,hard,timeo=600,retrans=2
$EFS_NAME:/ /mnt/efs || true
        mkdir -p /mnt/efs/uploads
        chown webapp:webapp /mnt/efs/uploads
commands:
  01-mount:
    command: "/tmp/mount-efs.sh"
container_commands:
  01-rm-wp-content-uploads:
    command: rm -rf /var/app/ondeck/wp-content/uploads
  02-symlink-uploads:
    command: ln -snf /mnt/efs/uploads /var/app/ondeck/wp-
content/uploads
```

You can find the complete copy of the previous code at https://github.
com/yoyoclouds/Administering-AWS-Volume2.

This file causes Elastic Beanstalk to mount the newly created EFS volume on the instance's /mnt/efs directory, and also removes the wp-content/uploads, directory if it exists, and symlinks it to /mnt/efs/uploads so that it persists and is shared between instances:

1. Once the file is created, use the eb deploy command once again to push the application directory and the newly added .ebextensions directory to your production environment.
2. Last but not least, sign in to your production environment and select the **Configuration** option from the *environment* dashboard. Here, select the **Software** configuration tile and add the following key-value pair into the **Environment Properties** section, as shown:

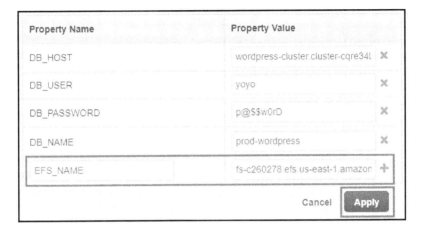

3. Here, the **EFS_NAME** has to have the newly created EFS filesystem's DNS name as its value. This is the same DNS name that we copied a while back once the EFS was created.

Once the deployment changes states and is made available, select the environment URL and verify whether the WordPress configurations are all working as intended or not. If you have made it this far, then you should have a really awesome, highly available, scalable, WordPress site up and running! Awesome, isn't it?

Securing Workloads Using AWS WAF

4

In the previous chapter, we learned a lot about how to leverage Amazon Elastic Beanstalk as well as Amazon Elastic File System to build and deploy highly scalable and available applications with the utmost of ease! However, there is one critical aspect that we didn't talk too much about in the previous chapter, and that is, of course, security! *"How do I safeguard my applications and workloads against malicious software and threats?"* This is exactly the question we will try and answer through a combination of two simple, yet very powerful, AWS services, namely AWS Shield and AWS **Web Application Firewall**, or **WAF**.

Keeping this in mind, let's have a quick look at the various topics that we will be covering in this chapter:

- Introducing AWS WAF and how it works
- Securing our WordPress site by leveraging WAF and using web ACLs
- Learning about additional WAF conditions for protection against cross-site scripting and SQL injections
- Automated deployment and configuration of AWS WAF using CloudFormation templates
- Monitoring AWS WAF using Amazon CloudWatch
- A brief introduction to AWS Shield and how it works
- Understanding AWS Shield Advanced and how to leverage it

There is so much to do, so let's get started right away!

Introducing AWS Web Application Firewall

Security has always been, and always will be, a key concern for a lot of organizations that run their workloads and applications on the cloud. That is precisely why AWS offers a wide assortment of managed services that you, as a cloud administrator, should leverage in order to protect and safeguard your workloads from any compromises or threats. In this section, we are going to explore one such simple, yet really powerful, service, called AWS WAF, or Web Application Firewall.

AWS WAF is basically a firewall that helps you to protect your internet-facing applications from common web-based threats and exploits. It is basically a service that enables you to specify a set of web security rules or ACLs that can allow or restrict a certain type of web traffic across Amazon CloudFront as well as the **Application Load Balancer** (**ALB**). As of now, WAF can be used to create customized rules that can safeguard your applications against attacks, such as SQL injections, cross-site scripting, **Distributed Denial of Services** (**DDoS**), bad bots, scrapers, and much more! You can easily create new rules and attach them to your existing ACL list as per your requirements, enabling you to respond to and mitigate changing traffic patterns more rapidly.

WAF also comes equipped with a powerful API, by using which you can automate the deployments of ACL rules as well as manage them programmatically. Alternatively, for the UI people out there, WAF provides customization CloudFormation templates which will allow you to get started with a complete WAF-based security solution in less than a few minutes! We will be looking at how to deploy this template for securing our own WordPress application as well a bit later in this chapter.

 WAF is priced based on the number of ACL rules which you deploy, as well as on the number of web requests that your application receives.

Here is a quick summary of benefits that you can obtain by levering AWS WAF:

- **Enhanced protection**: Apart from your standard VPC and security groups, you can additionally safeguard your applications against commonly occurring web attacks by leveraging WAF's ACL rules.
- **Advanced traffic filtering**: Unlike your simple NACLs or security groups, WAFs provide you with an ability to define custom rules and conditions based on the characteristics of your incoming web request, such as values present in the headers, origin IP address of the request, whether the request has any SQL code present in it, and so on. Using these conditions, you now have the ability to basically allow, block, or filter traffic based on such preset conditions.

- **Easy management**: With WAF rules defined and managed in one central location, you can easily reuse and propagate your custom ACLs across multiple CloudFront CDNs as well as Application Load Balancers, and monitor the traffic as well as mitigate any issues, all using the same WAF API or web user interface.
- **Cost effective security solution**: One of the best parts of leveraging WAF is that there are absolutely no upfront fees or costs associated with it. You simply pay based on the number of rules you create using WAF as well as the amount of traffic your web application receives, and not a penny more!

With this basic set of information, let's have a look at how WAF actually works!

Concepts and terminologies

As discussed briefly, WAF can be enabled over your standard ALBs and over your CloudFront distributions. But before we get started with configuring WAF and its various rules and ACLs, we first need to understand some of its commonly used terms and terminologies:

- **Conditions**: Conditions form the core of your WAF rulesets. These are basically configurable characteristics that you want WAF to monitor in each of your incoming web requests. At the time of writing this book, WAF supports the following list of conditions:
    - **IP match**: You can use this condition to check whether the incoming web request originated from a specified black/whitelisted IP addresses or not. You can then plot corresponding actions to be performed against the same based on your requirements, such as not allowing any incoming traffic other that the whitelisted IP range, and so on. AWS WAF supports /8, /16, /24, /32 CIDR blocks for an IPv4 address.
    - **String and regex match**: A string match or a regex match condition can be used to specify a part of an incoming web request and its corresponding text that you wish to control access to. For example, you can create a match or regex condition that checks the user agent headers and its value against a preset *string* or *expression*. If the condition matches, you can opt to either allow or block that particular traffic using WAF rules.

- **SQL injection match**: You can use this condition to inspect certain parts of your incoming web requests, such as the URI or query string, for any malicious SQL code. If a pattern matches, you can then opt to block all traffic originating from that particular request's IP range.
- **Cross-site scripting match**: Hackers and exploiters can often embed malicious scripts within web requests that can potentially harm your application. You can leverage the cross-site scripting match condition to inspect your incoming request URI or headers for any such scripts or code, and then opt to block the same using WAF rules.
- **Geographic match**: You can use this condition to list countries that your web request originated from and accordingly block or allow the same based on your requirements.
- **Size constraint match**: You can use the size constraint match condition to check the lengths of specified parts of your incoming web requests, such as the query string or the URI. For example, you can create a simple WAF rule to block all requests which have a query string greater than 100 bytes, and so on.

- **Rules**: With your conditions defined, the next important aspect of configuring WAF are the rules. Rules basically allow you to combine one or more conditions into a logical statement, which can then be used to either allow, block, or count a particular incoming request. Rules are further classified into two categories:
  - **Regular rules**: Regular or standard rules, apply one or more conditions to your most recent batch of incoming web requests. For example, a rule to block all incoming traffic from the IP range `40.40.5.0/24` or if there is any SQL-like code in the query string of your request, and so on.
  - **Rate-based rules**: Rate-based rules are very much like your regular rules apart from one addition: the rate limit. You can now configure conditions and pass a rate limit along them as well. The rule will only trigger if the conditions match or exceed that particular rate limit which was set.

 Rate limits are checked by WAF within a 5-minute window period.

For example, you may configure a simple condition that blocks all incoming traffic from the IP range `40.40.5.0/24` with a rate limit of 10,000. In this case, the rule will only trigger a corresponding action (allow, block, count) if the condition is met and the number of incoming requests in a 5-minute period exceed 10,000 requests. Requests that do not meet both the conditions are simply not compared towards the rate limit and hence will not be blocked by this rule.

- **Web ACLs**: Once the rules are defined, you combine them into one or more web ACLs. Here, you have the ability to define an action for your rule if it gets triggered; for example, allow, block, count, or even perform a default action that gets triggered in case a request doesn't match any of the conditions or rules specified. Web ACLs work on a priority basis, so the rule listed first is the one that gets compared to the incoming request first. This makes it extremely important to know the order in which you create and assign your rules in a web ACL.

Here is a simple representation of how conditions, rules, and web ACLs work together in WAF:

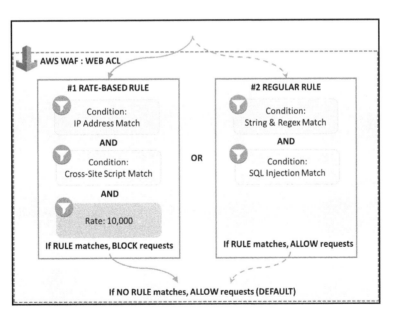

With the concepts out of the way, let's look at a few simple steps that allow you to set up and configure WAF Web ACLs for safeguarding your web applications.

Getting started with WAF

In this section, we are going to look at a few simple and easy-to-follow steps for getting started with AWS WAF. For demonstration purposes, we will be leveraging the same environments and application that we deployed from our previous chapter here, so, if you haven't gone through the use case, this might be a good time for a quick revisit!

In the previous chapter, we leveraged Elastic Beanstalk as well as Elastic File System services to deploy a scalable and highly available WordPress application over the internet. In this section, we will leverage the same setup and secure it even further by introducing AWS WAF into it. Why use WAF for our WordPress application? Well, the simplest answer is to completely abstract the security checks from the underlying web server instance(s), and instead place the security checks at the point of entry of our application, as depicted in the following diagram:

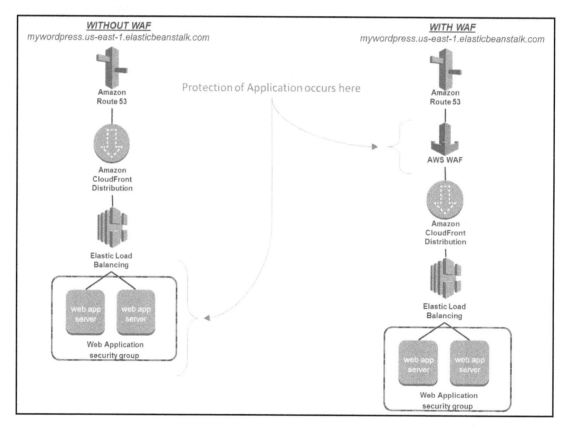

To get started, you will first need to ensure that your WordPress application has a CloudFront CDN attached to it, or alternatively an Application Load Balancer frontend its requests. This is a crucial step, as without a CloudFront CDN or an Application Load Balancer, WAF will simply not work! In my case, I have configured and deployed a simple CloudFront CDN for my production-grade WordPress application. You can refer to the following step-by-step guide for setting up your own CDN using CloudFront, at `http://docs.aws.amazon.com/AmazonCloudFront/latest/DeveloperGuide/`.

Creating the web ACL

Once you are done with your CDN, head over to the AWS Management Console and filter out WAF and Shield services using the dashboard, or alternatively, navigate to this URL `https://console.aws.amazon.com/waf/home` to bring up the WAF dashboard:

1. Assuming that this is the first time you are configuring WAF, you will be prompted by a welcome screen to either opt for AWS WAF or AWS Shield services. Select the **Go to AWS WAF** option. This will redirect you to the WAF dashboard, where we select the **Configure web ACL** option to get started.

2. Selecting the **Configure web ACL** option will bring up a **Set up a web access control list (web ACL)** wizard that will guide you through your first web ACL setup.

3. The first page on the wizard basically covers the concepts of conditions, rules, and ACLs, so simply select the **Next** option to proceed further.

4. In the **Name web ACL** page, provide a suitable **Web ACL Name** for your new ACL. You will notice that the **CloudWatch metric name** field gets correspondingly auto-populated with a matching name. You can change the name as per your requirements. This metric name will be later used to monitor our web ACLs using CloudWatch's dashboards.

5. Moving on, from the **Region** drop-down list, select either **Global (CloudFront)** or an alternative **Region** name, based on whether you want to secure a CDN or an Application Load Balancer. In my case, since I already have a CDN set up, I've opted for the **Global (CloudFront)** option.

 WAF for the Application Load Balancer is currently supported only for the following regions: US East (N. Virginia), US West (N. California), US West (Oregon), EU (Ireland), and Asia Pacific (Tokyo).

6. In the **AWS resource to associate** field, you can opt to select your CloudFront distribution or your Application Load Balancer using the drop-down list; however, for the sake of simplicity, do not configure this option for the time being. Remember, you can always associate your web ACLs with one or more AWS resources after completing this wizard! Once done, click **Next** to proceed:

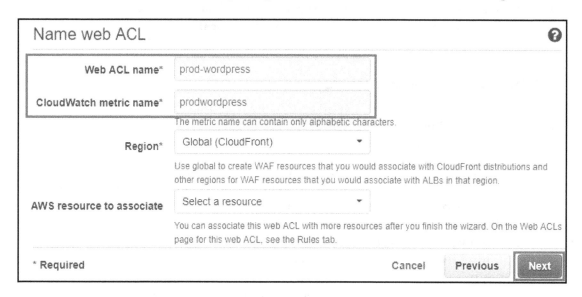

7. With the web ACL named, we move on to the next section where we can configure our conditions. On the **Create conditions** page, select an appropriate condition that you wish to configure for your web application. In this scenario, we will be configuring an IP match condition along with a string match condition. The idea here is to only grant access to our WordPress administrator login page (wp-login.php) from my local laptop's IP, and, conversely, for any other IP that wishes to access the wp-login.php page, the traffic should get dropped.

Creating the conditions

As mentioned earlier, conditions are configurable characteristics that you want WAF to monitor in each of your incoming web requests:

1. To get started with a condition, select the **Create condition** option from the **IP match conditions** tile.

2. Here, provide a suitable **Name** for your match condition and select the **IPv4** option from the **IP Version**. Provide your desktop's or laptop's public IP in the **Address** field. You can alternatively provide a range of IP addresses here using either of the supported CIDR blocks.

3. Remember to select the **Add IP address or range** option before creating the match condition:

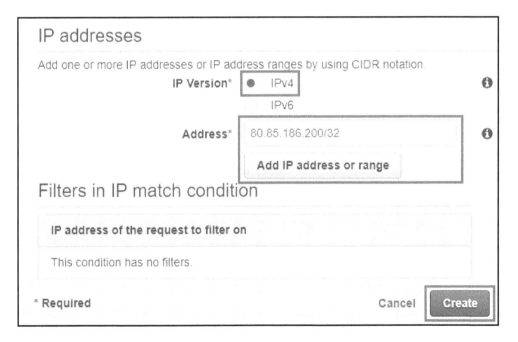

4. With the IP match condition created, let's move on to creating the second condition for our ACL as well. For this, select the **Create condition** option from the **String and regex match conditions** section.

5. Once again, we start by providing a suitable **Name** for our string match condition, followed by selecting the **Type** of string to match with. Here, select the **String match** option to begin with.

6. Next, in the **Part of the request to filter on** section, select the appropriate section of your request that you wish to filter, using the match condition. In my case, I have selected the **URI** option as we need to match the resource wp-login.php from the URI. Alternatively, you can also opt to select the following values based on your requirements:

   - Header: Used to match a specific request header, such as user-agent.
   - HTTPMethod: Used to indicate the type of operation the request intends to perform on the origin, such as PUT, GET, DELETE, and so on.
   - QueryString: Used to define a query string in a URL.
   - Body: Used to match the body of the request. In this case, WAF only inspects the first 8,192 bytes (8 KB) contained within the request's body. You can alternatively set up a **Size Constraint** condition that blocks all requests that are greater than 8 KB in size.

7. Next, in the **Match type** drop-down list, select the option **Contains**, as shown in the following screenshot. The **Contains** option means that the string to match can appear anywhere in the request. Alternatively, you can also opt to select from these options, based on your requirement:

   - **ContainsWord**: Used to specify a specific **Value to match** in the request
   - **Exactly matches**: Used to match the string and the request value exactly
   - **Starts with**: Used to check for a matching string at the beginning of a request
   - **Ends with**: Used to check for a matching string at the end of the request

8. The **Transformation** field is handy when you need to re-format the web request before WAF inspects the same. This can involve **Converting to lowercase**, **HTML decoding**, **Whitespace normalization**, **URL Decode**, and so on. For this particular use case, we don't have any particular transformation to perform on the request, and hence I've selected the **None** option.

9. Finally, in the **Value to match** field, enter the text (`wp-login`) that we want WAF to search for in the web requests. Once completed, remember to click on the **Add filter** option before you proceed with the `Create` command.

10. With this step completed, our basic conditions are in place. Alternatively, you can set up other relevant conditions based on your criteria and requirements. Once done, select the **Next** option to proceed with the wizard.

Creating rules

With your conditions defined, we now move on to the next important aspect of configuring WAF: rules. Rules basically allow you to combine one or more condition, into a logical statement, which can then be used to either allow, block, or count a particular incoming request:

1. In the **Create rules** page, you can now merge the conditions we created a while back and assign each rule a corresponding action, such as allow, block, or count. To get started, select the **Create rule** option.

2. In the **Create rule** popup, we will be creating two rules: one rule that will basically allow me to access the WordPress admin login page (`wp-login.php`) from my local laptop, and another rule that blocks traffic to the same login page. Let's first create the **Allow traffic** rule.

3. To do so, type in a suitable **Name** for your rule. You will notice the corresponding **CloudWatch metric name** field auto-populate itself with the same name as well. You can choose to change this name as per your requirements, or leave it to its default value.

4. Next, in the **Rule type** drop-down list, select whether you want this rule to be a **Regular rule** or a **Rated rule**. For this scenario, I've opted for the **Regular rule**, as shown in the following screenshot:

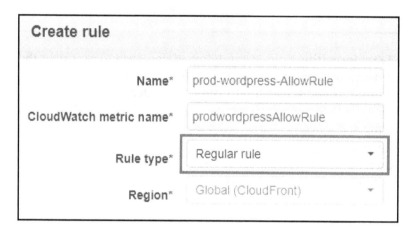

5. Once done, move on to the **Add conditions** section, where we can associate our rule with one or more conditions. Start by selecting the appropriate drop-down option to form the following rule:

```
When a request: "Does": "Originate from an IP Address in":
"<SELECT_YOUR_IP_ADDRESS_MATCH_CONDITION_HERE>"
```

Here's what your new rule should look like once it is properly set up. Click on **Create** once completed:

6. With your **Allow rule** created, we use the same steps once again to create a **Block rule** as well. Select the **Create rule** option once again, and provide a suitable **Name** for your rule. Similar to the previous case, I've opted for a **Regular rule** here as well.

7. Next, in the **Add conditions** section, we first add a condition that matches the following statement:

```
When a request: "Does not": "Originate from an IP Address in":
"<SELECT_YOUR_IP_ADDRESS_MATCH_CONDITION_HERE>"
```

8. Next, select the **Add condition** option to add the string match condition as well:

```
When a request: "Does": "Match at least one of the filters in the
string match condition":
"<SELECT_YOUR_STRING_MATCH_CONDITION_HERE>"
```

Here's what your rule should look like once both the conditions are added to it:

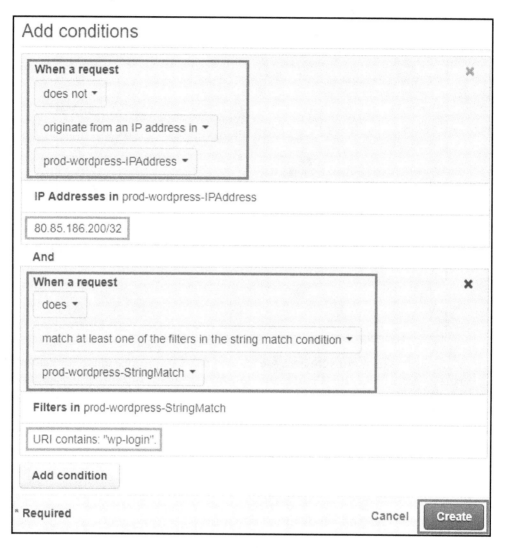

9. With the conditions in place, select the **Create** option to finally create your blocking rule.

10. Now that your two rules are created, you should see them both listed in the **Add rules to a web ACL** page, as shown in the following screenshot:

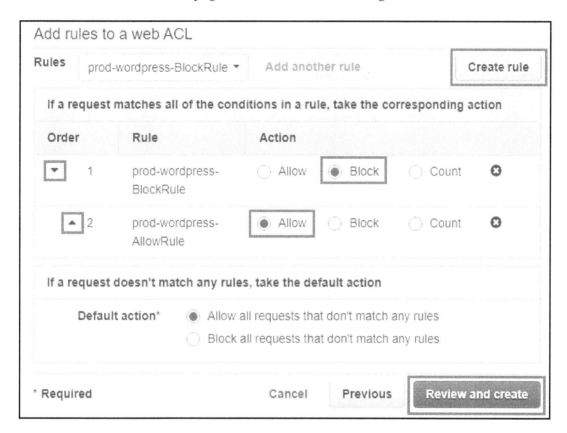

11. Here, make sure you order your rules correctly, based on their precedence, by selecting the **Order** option as required. You can additionally configure the **Default action** for your web ACL as well. This default action will only get triggered if the request does not match any of the conditions mentioned in either the *allow or the blocking rules*. Once you are confident with your configurations, select the **Review and create** option, as shown earlier. And voila! Your basic WAF is now up and running!

Assigning a WAF Web ACL to CloudFront distributions

With the web ACL created, you can now easily assign it to one or more CloudFront distributions, as per your requirements. To do so, simply log in to your AWS dashboard and filter the **CloudFront** service, or alternatively, navigate to `https://console.aws.amazon.com/cloudfront/home` to view the CloudFront dashboard directly:

1. Once logged into the CloudFront dashboard, select the appropriate **Distribution ID** for which you wish to enable the **WAF Web ACL** rules.
2. Select the **Edit** option from the **General** tab to bring up your distribution's configurations and settings.
3. Here, in the **Edit Distribution** page, select your newly created web ACL from the **AWS WAF Web ACL** drop-down list, as shown in the following screenshot:

4. Once the ACL is selected, I would also recommend that you enable the logging of your distribution in case you already haven't done that. This is just an added measure of precaution and security that is a must for any production-grade environment that you may be working on. Scroll down on the **Edit Distribution** page, and select the **On** option adjoining the **Logging** field. Provide your logging bucket's name in the **Bucket for Logs** field and click on the **Yes, Edit** option once the required fields are all filled in.

The changes will take a good few minutes to propagate through the CloudFront distribution. You can then move on to testing your WAF once the distribution's **Status** has changed to **Enabled**.

To test your WAF, simply open a browser and type in the URL of your WordPress application (`<http://YOUR_CLOUDFRONT_URL>/wp-login.php`) from your own laptop/desktop. In this case, you should be able to see the `wp-login.php` page without any issues whatsoever. However, if you try accessing the same page from a different laptop or machine, you will be thrown the following error on screen:

ERROR

The request could not be satisfied.

Request blocked.

Generated by cloudfront (CloudFront)
Request ID: CWD-tHpWMvkdw9sSIpJxBX0RVrdC-NtK9SL7FDvI4AWhHRU1yYrVfg==

At this point, your WordPress administrator login page is now protected from all IPs except those that you specified in your Web ACL's allow list! Amazing, isn't it?

> You can create a custom error page using the CloudFront distribution settings and redirect your users to this page rather than showing them the standard *error page*, as depicted in the preceding screenshot.

With this, we come towards the end of this basic web ACL configuration section. In the next section, we will be looking at how to enhance your basic ACL setup with more conditions, with more emphasis towards SQL injections and cross-site scripting.

Working with SQL injection and cross-site scripting conditions

Besides restricting access to a specific set of IP addresses, WAF additionally provides defense capabilities against more exploitative attacks, such as SQL injections and cross-site scripting. In this section, we will take a closer look at both of these conditions and how you can leverage them for protecting your own applications.

To start off, let's have a closer look at SQL injections. An SQL injection basically consists of the insertion of an SQL query within a request that is made from a client to your application.

SQL injections, if successfully implemented, can read as well as modify sensitive data from the database, and are even capable enough to execute administration operations on your database, such as restoring from a previous backed up file, shutting the database down completely, and much more.

Here's a list of some common conditions and their associated configurations that you can choose to apply in your web ACL rules:

HTTP request component to match	Relevant input transformations to apply	Justification
QUERY_STRING	URL_DECODE, HTML_ENTITY_DECODE	The most common component to match. Query string parameters are frequently used in database lookups.
URI	URL_DECODE, HTML_ENTITY_DECODE	If your application is using friendly or clean URLs, then parameters might appear as part of the URL path segment, and not the query string.
BODY	URL_DECODE, HTML_ENTITY_DECODE	A common component to match if your application accepts form input. AWS WAF only evaluates the first 8 KB of the body content.
HEADER: Cookie	URL_DECODE, HTML_ENTITY	A less common component to match. But, if your application uses cookie-based parameters in database lookups, consider matching on this component as well.
HEADER: Authorization	URL_DECODE, HTML_ENTITY_DECODE _DECODE	A less common component to match. But, if your application uses the value of this header for database validation, consider matching on this component as well.

To configure your own SQL injection conditions and rules, log in to your WAF dashboard once again by navigating to `https://console.aws.amazon.com/waf/home`.

1. Next, select the **SQL Injection** option from the navigation pane and, within that, select the **Create condition** to get started.

2. In the **Create SQL injection match condition** page, start off by providing a **Name** for your new condition. You can additionally select whether you want to enable this condition for your CloudFront CDNs (Global) or for your individual Application Load Balancers. In this case, I've opted for the **Global (CloudFront)** option, as depicted in the following screenshot:

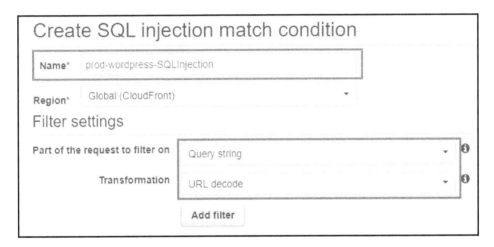

3. Next, in the **Filter settings** section, select the appropriate **Part of the request to filter on** as well as the associated **Transformation** section. You can refer to the SQL injection *common conditions* table, as discussed previously, for the same. Once the values are provided, click on the **Add filter** option to complete the process.

Now, here's a really handy tip! There will definitely be cases where you will be writing more than one filter for your SQL injection condition based on different parts of the request you wish to filter, such as URI, query string, and so on. In such cases, it is always recommended to create multiple filters within the same SQL injection condition and then attach that one condition to a web ACL rule. The reason? A web request needs only to match one of the filters in the SQL injection match condition for WAF to allow or block the request based on that condition. On the other hand, if you add only one filter per SQL injection match condition, and you create more than one such SQL injection condition, the request has to match all the conditions in order for WAF to allow or block it.

The same can also be applied for protection against cross-site scripting or XSS. Cross-site scripting generally occurs when web applications include user-provided data in web pages that is sent to the browser without proper sanitization. If the data isn't properly validated or escaped, an attacker can use those vectors to embed scripts, inline frames, or other objects into the rendered page. These, in turn, can be used for a variety of malicious purposes, including stealing user credentials by using keyloggers, installing system malware, and much more. The impact of the attack is magnified if that user data persists on the server side in a data store and is then delivered to a larger set of users.

Here's a list of some common conditions and their associated configurations that you can choose to apply in your web ACL rules:

HTTP request component to match	Relevant input transformations to apply	Justification
BODY	URL_DECODE, HTML_ENTITY_DECODE	A very common component to match if your application accepts form input. AWS WAF only evaluates the first 8 KB of the body content.
QUERY_STRING	URL_DECODE, HTML_ENTITY_DECODE	Recommended if query string parameters are reflected back into the web page. An example is the current page number in a paginated list.
HEADER: Cookie	URL_DECODE, HTML_ENTITY_DECODE	A common component to match if your application accepts form input. Recommended if your application uses cookie-based parameters that are reflected back on the web page. For example, the name of the user who is currently logged in is stored in a cookie and embedded in the page header. WAF only evaluates the first 8 KB of the body content.
URI	URL_DECODE, HTML_ENTITY_DECODE	Less common, but if your application is using friendly URLs, then parameters might appear as part of the URL path segment, not the query string (they are later rewritten server side). There are similar concerns as with query strings.

To configure your own cross-site scripting conditions and rules, log in to your WAF dashboard once again by visiting `https://console.aws.amazon.com/waf/home`.

1. Next, select the **Cross-site scripting** option from the navigation pane and, within that, select the **Create condition** to get started.
2. In the **Create cross-site scripting match condition** page, start off by providing a **Name** for your new condition. You can additionally select whether you want to enable this condition for your CloudFront CDNs (Global) or for your individual Application Load Balancers. In this case, I've opted for the **Global (CloudFront)** option for now.
3. Next, from the **Part of the request to filter on** section, select the part of the request you wish WAF to filter on. You can choose between **Header**, **HTTP method**, **Query string**, **URI**, and **Body** as valid parameters. Note, however, that by selecting the **Header** option, you will be provided with an additional field in which you can either select the header from a list of headers or, alternatively, type in the name of the header.
4. Finally, select the appropriate **Transformation** operation you wish WAF to perform over the request before it is actually inspected. Once done, remember to select the **Add filter** option before completing the condition's creation process.

You now have two additional conditions that you can add to your existing web ACL, or even, go ahead and create a new web ACL. In this way, you can create different filters and conditions based on your requirements and keep attaching them to your web ACL as and when required. But this manual way of setting up rules and conditions can get a bit tricky after some time, especially when you don't have a dedicated security team and need to deploy the ACLs a lot faster into your environment. That's precisely what we are going to cover in the next section.

Automating WAF Web ACL deployments using CloudFormation

Working with web ACLs can be really difficult at times, especially when you have a large, distributed environment and don't necessarily have a dedicated security team to create and manage the rules on a regular basis. Luckily for us, AWS makes things far simpler by providing easy to use and customize CloudFormation templates that can spin up a single web ACL, with all the basic security conditions configured, in a mere matter of minutes! The collective solution is called AWS WAF Security Automations, and, is available free of charge for all to use. All the end user has to do is specify which security feature is required, configure that, and deploy the solution! The rest is completely taken care of by AWS itself!

The architecture of the AWS WAF Security Automation solution is relatively simple, and comprises of a few more AWS services than AWS WAF, such as AWS Lambda, Amazon CloudWatch, Amazon API Gateway, and Amazon S3, as depicted in the diagram later in this section.

At the core of the solution is the WAF service that acts as the central point for making all security-related decisions and filtering. Based on the inputs specified by the user during the CloudFormation template's configuration, the respective solution components get activated accordingly. These components are further explained here:

- **Honeypot for bad bots and scraper protection (A)**: This security component automatically sets up a *honeypot* to lure and deflect a possible attack on your application. The solution provides you with an API Gateway endpoint that you need to insert into your web application as a trap to detect and lure inbound requests from various bots and scrapers. If a source accesses the trap request, an associated Lambda function intercepts that request, gathers its source IP address, and adds the same to the WAF's web ACL block list.
- **SQL injection protection (B) and cross-site scripting protection (C)**: Selecting this solution enables the creation of two AWS WAF rules that provide protection against commonly occurring SQL injection or cross-site scripting patterns:

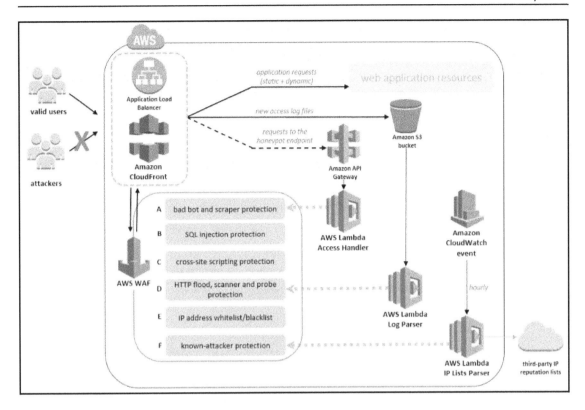

- **HTTP flood, scanner and probe protection (D)**: Also called **log parsing protection**, this solution comes in handy when you want to analyze your web application's access logs for any abnormalities that can cause a potential threat. This is performed by a dedicated AWS Lambda function that does the parsing of the access logs which get stored in a S3 bucket created by the CloudFormation template itself.
- **IP address whitelist/blacklist (E)**: Similar to the SQL injection and cross-site scripting solution, WAF creates two rules to allow you to manually enter IP addresses that you wish to either allow or block to your application.
- **Known-attacker protection (F)**: This solution also leverages a simple Lambda function that monitors certain third-party sites for a list of potential IP addresses to block against threats. The sites include *Spamhaus* (`https://www.spamhaus.org/drop/`), *Proofpoint* (`https://rules.emergingthreats.net/fwrules/emerging-Block-IPs.txt`), and *TOR* (`https://check.torproject.org/exit-addresses`), to name a few.

With these basics in mind, let's quickly move on to deploying these solutions using the CloudFormation templates. At the time of writing this book, AWS WAF Security Automations provides two templates for use: one intended for the CloudFront CDN based deployments and the other for the Application Load Balancer. Both of the templates provide a default configuration that consists of a web ACL with eight pre-configured sets of rules that you can always change or extend as required. The following are the links to download the respective templates:

- **CloudFront CDN-based template**: `https://s3.amazonaws.com/solutions-reference/aws-waf-security-automations/latest/aws-waf-security-automations.template`
- **Application Load Balancer-based template**: `https://s3.amazonaws.com/solutions-reference/aws-waf-security-automations/latest/aws-waf-security-automations-alb.template`

 You can alternatively copy the links and deploy the stacks in CloudFormation.

With the correct template downloaded, we can now move on to configuring and deploying the solution using CloudFormation:

1. To do so, first log in to your CloudFormation dashboard by navigating to `https://console.aws.amazon.com/cloudformation/home`. Note that in this case, we will be deploying the CloudFront CDN-based template in the **N.Virginia** region.
2. In the CloudFormation dashboard, select the option **Create new stack** to get started. Here, in the **Select Template** page, you can either choose to *upload* your downloaded template, or simply copy the template's URL in the **Specify an Amazon S3 template URL** field, as shown in the following screenshot. Click on **Next** to continue with the setup:

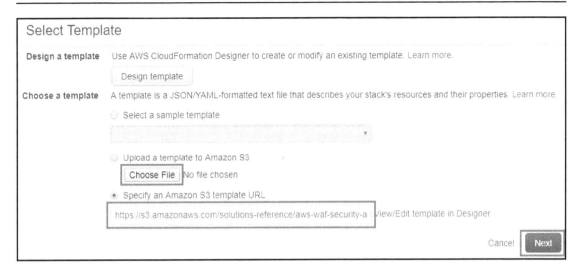

3. In the **Specify Details** page, you can start off by providing a suitable **Stack name** for your CloudFormation stack.

4. Next, in the **Parameters** section, select the **Protection services** that you wish to opt for. Remember, these are the same services that we discussed at the beginning of this section. In this case, I've opted for a rather simple setup that involves activating protection against SQL injection, cross-site scripting, and bad bots. You can alternatively select your own protection services, as required.

5. Moving on, in the **CloudFront Access Log Bucket Name** field, provide a unique name for the S3 bucket that will store your Amazon CloudFront's access logs. You can either provide the name of an existing bucket or a new one.

6. Finally, in the **Advanced Settings** section, you can additionally opt to modify a few parameters, such as **Request Threshold**, **Error Threshold**, and the **WAF Block Period**, as per your requirements. These parameters would come in handy especially if you select the **HTTP Flood Protection** or the **Activate Scanners & Probes Protection**, otherwise, you can leave these values to their defaults, as I have done in my case. Select **Next** to continue with the deployment process.

7. In the **Options** page, you can specify **Tags** for the resources that will be created by the CloudFormation template, as well as opt to provide any special *IAM Role* to allow CloudFormation to create, modify, or delete the resources in the stack. Click on **Next** to review the changes made and, finally, go ahead with the stack's creation by selecting the **Create** option on the **Review** page.

8. The stack takes a good few minutes to deploy successfully. Once done, you can verify the status of your stack's completion by checking the **Status** column, as depicted in the following screenshot:

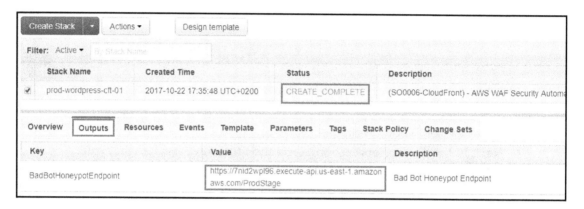

9. Additionally, based on your **Protection service** selection, you can also verify the additional outputs created by the template for your application, such as the **Honeypot Endpoint**, that's actually an Amazon API Gateway endpoint that you need to insert somewhere in your application to capture bots and scrapers. In my case, the template created a Lambda function for bad bots scraping, WAF rules for SQL injections, IP whitelisting, and XSS detection, along with an API Gateway as well.

10. With the stack up and running, you can additionally go back to the WAF dashboard and check out the individual rules that the template auto-populated against some of the protection services. In this case, the *SQL injection* and *cross-site scripting* conditions were auto-populated; however, the *IP Whitelist* and *Bad Bot* rules still require you to manually provide the IP ranges and addresses to start off with, or allow the Lambda function to inject the IP addresses into the lists at runtime as well. Here is a snapshot of the list of rules created for the SQL injection condition:

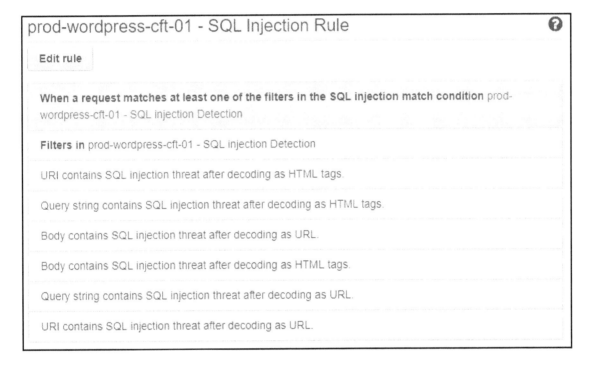

With this we come to the end of this particular section. You can additionally use these templates to spin up newer web ACLs for your Application Load Balancers. Just remember to delete your stack once your testing is completed, to avoid incurring any unnecessary charges. In the next section, we will be briefly looking at how to effectively monitor your WAF rules using a few essential monitoring tools provided by AWS.

Monitoring WAF using CloudWatch

Monitoring of your WAF rules, conditions, as well as your application's web traffic, plays an important part towards identifying and mitigating possible attacks and exploits. AWS provides a wide assortment of tools and services that you, as an administrator, can leverage for the monitoring and reporting of such activities. The following are the list of services briefly explained:

- **AWS WAF dashboard**: Yes, you read it right! AWS WAF also provides a simple monitoring dashboard that lists the total requests made to your application via either the CloudFront CDN or the Application Load Balancer, as well as the number of requests that actually match to your specified rules. To view the dashboard, all you need to do is log in to your AWS WAF, select the **Web ACLs** page, and click on the **Requests** tab, as shown in the following screenshot:

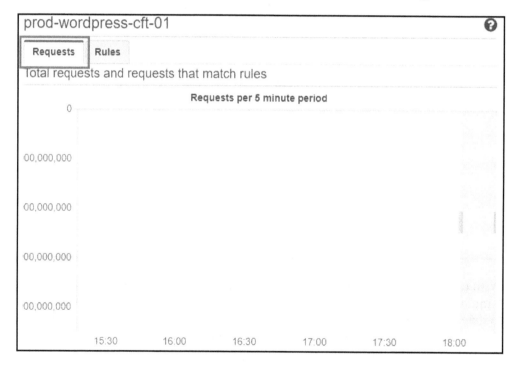

The graph aggregates and displays the requests on a five-minute period basis. You can alternatively open the same graph using Amazon CloudWatch for further analysis.

- **Amazon CloudWatch**: Amazon CloudWatch has been around for some time, and definitely provides various metrics that you can select and configure as a part of a customized requests monitoring dashboard. Here is a list of the supported WAF metrics, with a brief description:
  - `AllowedRequests`: Captures the number of allowed web requests. The valid dimensions for this metric are **Rule** and **WebACL**.
  - `BlockedRequests`: Captures the number of blocked web requests. The valid dimensions for this metric are **Rule** and **WebACL**.
  - `CountedRequests`: Typically used to test your web ACLs and rules, this metric provides a count of the web requests that match all of the conditions in a particular rule.

  You can use these metrics to monitor your WAF rules, and even configure CloudWatch alarms to trigger and send notifications in case their threshold values are crossed. Based on your requirements, you can additionally take things a step further and configure CloudWatch events that trigger an appropriate Lambda function to mitigate against a possible attack, as we performed during the Security Automations solutions. You can even leverage Amazon CloudWatch to monitor the traffic flowing into the CloudFront CDNs as well as your Application Load Balancers.

- **AWSCloudTrail**: AWS CloudTrail is yet another service that you can and should leverage for parsing and analyzing your application's access and error logs, as well as logs generated by the AWS services' logs themselves. Here is a sample of few **Log Groups**, created automatically by the Security Automations Solution, for capturing WAF traffic flow and events. We will be exploring more on AWS CloudTrail in the next chapter:

With this, we come towards the end of yet another chapter, but before we sign off, here's some interesting things that I feel you ought to try out as a part of AWS WAF.

Introduction to AWS Shield

AWS Shield is an extension of AWS WAF, but is targeted to provide security around potential DDoS attacks. It is a fully managed service that provides **Always-on** detection and automatic mitigations that minimize application downtime and latency. AWS Shield provides two tiers of services: **Standard** and **Advanced**:

- **AWS Shield Standard**: Provided at no additional costs, this service is enabled on your account and AWS services by default, and is designed to protect your web applications against the most common and frequently occurring DDoS attacks.

- **AWS Shield Advanced**: Designed for providing a higher level of protection for your web applications, AWS Shield Advanced is intended to work with applications that are currently running on Elastic or Application Load Balancers, Amazon CloudFront, and Amazon Route 53 resources. AWS Shield Advanced also provides near real-time visibility into potential attacks, along with mitigation capabilities as well. To top it all, you also get access to a dedicated 24x7 **DDoS Response Team** (**DRT**) that looks into potential DDoS attacks occurring on your web application, and provides quick resolutions against the same.

 AWS Shield Advanced is priced at $ 3,000 per month.

Here's a brief comparison between the various services offered by AWS Shield Standard and Advanced tiers:

Features	AWS Shield Standard	AWS Shield Advanced
Network flow monitoring	Yes	Yes
Automated application (layer 7) traffic monitoring	No	Yes
Helps protect from common DDoS attacks, such as SYN floods and UDP reflection attacks	Yes	Yes
Access to additional DDoS mitigation capacity	No	Yes
Layer 3/4 attack notification and attack forensic and history reports	No	Yes
Incident management during high-severity events	No	Yes
Custom mitigations during attacks	No	Yes
Post-attack analysis	No	Yes
Reimburse related Route 53, CloudFront, and ELB DDoS charges	No	Yes

To activate AWS Shield Advanced for your environments, simply log in to your AWS WAF dashboard and select the **Protected resources** option present under the **AWS Shield** section in the navigation pane. Here, click on the **Activate AWS Shield Advanced** button to start your Shield Advanced protection plan. Here, you will be asked to select a particular **Resource** to protect against DDoS attacks. Select your CloudFront CDN or the Elastic/Application Load Balancer, based on the resource you wish to protect, and provide a suitable **Name** for the resources that you are specifying for protection. Finally, remember to select the **Enable** checkbox to associate your resources with a web ACL, if you have one created already. Once done, select the **Add DDoS protection** option, and voila! You are up and running with AWS Shield Advanced! Simple isn't it?

Governing Your Environments Using AWS CloudTrail and AWS Config

5

In the previous chapter, we learned how to leverage and utilize AWS WAF for protecting your web applications against commonly occurring web attacks and exploitations. In this chapter, we will be exploring two really useful and must-have security and governance services in the form of AWS CloudTrail and AWS Config!

Keeping this in mind, let's have a quick look at the various topics that we will be covering in this chapter:

- Introducing AWS CloudTrail, its concepts, and how it works
- Enabling CloudTrail for your AWS environment by creating your very own Trail
- Integrating and managing CloudTrail Logs using Amazon CloudWatch
- Automating Amazon CloudWatch alarms for CloudTrail using CloudFormation
- Viewing CloudTrail Logs using Amazon Elasticsearch
- Introducing Amazon Config and how it works

There is so much to do, so let's get started right away!

Introducing AWS CloudTrail

As we learned in the previous chapter, AWS provides a wide variety of tools and managed services which allow you to safeguard your applications running on the cloud, such as AWS WAF and AWS Shield. But this, however, just forms one important piece in a much larger jigsaw puzzle! What about compliance monitoring, risk auditing, and overall governance of your environments? How do you effectively analyze events occurring in your environment and mitigate against the same? Well, luckily for us, AWS has the answer to our problems in the form of AWS CloudTrail.

AWS CloudTrail provides you with the ability to log every single action taken by a user, service, role, or even API, from within your AWS account. Each action recorded is treated as an event which can then be analyzed for enhancing the security of your AWS environment. The following are some of the key benefits that you can obtain by enabling CloudTrail for your AWS accounts:

- **In-depth visibility**: Using CloudTrail, you can easily gain better insights into your account's usage by recording each user's activities, such as which user initiated a new resource creation, from which IP address was this request initiated, which resources were created and at what time, and much more!
- **Easier compliance monitoring**: With CloudTrail, you can easily record and log events occurring within your AWS account, whether they may originate from the Management Console, or the AWS CLI, or even from other AWS tools and services. The best thing about this is that you can integrate CloudTrail with another AWS service, such as Amazon CloudWatch, to alert and respond to out-of-compliance events.
- **Security automations**: As we saw in the previous chapter, automating responses to security threats not only enables you to mitigate the potential threats faster, but also provides you with a mechanism to stop all further attacks. The same can be applied to AWS CloudTrail as well! With its easy integration with Amazon CloudWatch events, you can now create corresponding Lambda functions that trigger automatically each time a compliance is not met, all in a matter of seconds!

With these key points in mind, let's have a quick look at some of CloudTrail's essential concepts and terminologies:

- **Events**: Events are the basic unit of measurement in CloudTrail. Essentially, an event is nothing more than a record of a particular activity either initiated by the AWS services, roles, or even an AWS user. These activities are all logged as API calls that can originate from the Management Console, the AWS SDK, or even the AWS CLI as well. By default, events are stored by CloudTrail with S3 buckets for a period of 7 days. You can view, search, and even download these events by leveraging the events history feature provided by CloudTrail.

- **Trails**: Trails are essentially the delivery mechanism, using which events are dumped to S3 buckets. You can use these trails to log specific events within specific buckets, as well as to filter events and encrypt the transmitted log files. By default, you can have a maximum of *five trails* created per AWS region, and this limit cannot by increased.

- **CloudTrail Logs**: Once your CloudTrail starts capturing events, it sends these events to an S3 bucket in the form of a CloudTrail Log file. The log files are JSON text files that are compressed using the `.gzip` format. Each file can contain one or more events within itself. Here is a simple representation of what a CloudTrail Log looks like. In this case, the event was created when I tried to add an existing user by the name of `Mike` to an *administrator* group using the AWS Management Console:

```
{"Records": [{
    "eventVersion": "1.0",
    "userIdentity": {
        "type": "IAMUser",
        "principalId": "12345678",
        "arn": "arn:aws:iam::012345678910:user/yohan",
        "accountId": "012345678910",
        "accessKeyId": "AA34FG67GH89",
        "userName": "Alice",
        "sessionContext": {"attributes": {
            "mfaAuthenticated": "false",
            "creationDate": "2017-11-08T13:01:44Z"
        }}
    },
    "eventTime": "2017-11-08T13:09:44Z",
    "eventSource": "iam.amazonaws.com",
    "eventName": "AddUserToGroup",
    "awsRegion": "us-east-1",
    "sourceIPAddress": "127.0.0.1",
    "userAgent": "AWSConsole",
    "requestParameters": {
```

```
            "userName": "Mike",
            "groupName": "administrator"
        },
        "responseElements": null
}]}
```

You can view your own CloudTrail Log files by visiting the S3 bucket that you specify during the trail's creation. Each log file is named uniquely using the following format:

```
AccountID_CloudTrail_RegionName_YYYYMMDDTHHmmZ_UniqueString.json.gz
```

Where:

- `AccountID`: Your AWS account ID.
- `RegionName`: AWS region where the event was captured: **us-east-1**, and so on.
- `YYYYMMDDTTHHmmz`: Specifies the year, month, day, hour (24 hours), minutes, and seconds. The `z` indicates time in UTC.
- `UniqueString`: A randomly generated 16-character-long string that is simply used so that there is no overwriting of the log files.

With the basics in mind, let's quickly have a look at how you can get started with CloudTrail for your own AWS environments!

Working with AWS CloudTrail

AWS CloudTrail is a fairly simple and easy to use service that you can get started with in a couple of minutes. In this section, we will be walking through a simple setup of a CloudTrail Trail using the AWS Management Console itself.

Creating your first CloudTrail Trail

To get started, log in to your AWS Management Console and filter the **CloudTrail** service from the **AWS services** filter. On the CloudTrail dashboard, select the **Create Trail** option to get started:

1. This will bring up the **Create Trail** wizard. Using this wizard, you can create a maximum of five-trails per region. Type a suitable name for the Trail in to the **Trail name** field to begin with.

2. Next, you can either opt to **Apply trail to all regions** or only to the region out of which you are currently operating. Selecting all regions enables CloudTrail to record events from each region and dump the corresponding log files into an S3 bucket that you specify. Alternatively, selecting to record out of one region will only capture the events that occur from the region out of which you are currently operating. In my case, I have opted to enable the Trail only for the region I'm currently working out of. In the subsequent sections, we will learn how to change this value using the AWS CLI:

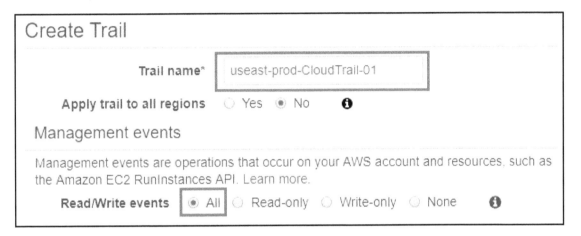

3. Next, in the **Management events** section, select the *type* of events you wish to capture from your AWS environment. By default, CloudTrail records all management events that occur within your AWS account. These events can be API operations, such as events caused due to the invocation of an EC2 **RunInstances** or **TerminateInstances** operation, or even non-API based events, such as a user logging into the AWS Management Console, and so on. For this particular use case, I've opted to record **All** management events.

Selecting the **Read-only** option will capture all the `GET` API operations, whereas the `Write-only` option will capture only the `PUT` API operations that occur within your AWS environment.

4. Moving on, in the **Storage location** section, provide a suitable name for the S3 bucket that will store your CloudTrail Log files. This bucket will store all your CloudTrail Log files, irrespective of the regions the logs originated from. You can alternatively select an existing bucket from the **S3 bucket** selection field:

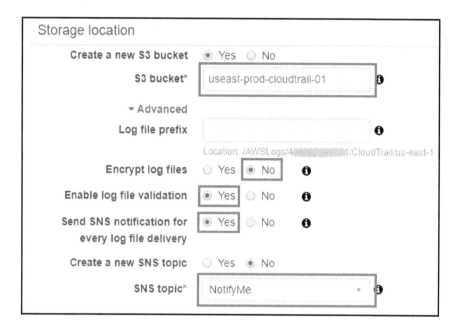

5. Next, from the **Advanced** section, you can optionally configure a **Log file prefix**. By default, the logs will automatically get stored under a folder-like hierarchy that is usually of the form `AWSLogs/ACCOUNT_ID/CloudTrail/REGION`.

6. You can also opt to **Encrypt log files** with the help of an AWS KMS key. Enabling this feature is highly recommended for production use.

7. Selecting **Yes** in the **Enable log file validation** field enables you to verify the integrity of the delivered log files once they are delivered to the S3 bucket.

8. Finally, you can even enable CloudTrail to send you notifications each time a new log file is delivered to your S3 bucket by selecting **Yes** against the **Send SNS notification for every log file delivery** option. This will provide you with an additional option to either select a predefined SNS topic or alternatively create a new one specifically for this particular CloudTrail. Once all the required fields are filled in, click on **Create** to continue.

With this, you should be able to see the newly created Trail by selecting the **Trails** option from the CloudTrail dashboard's navigation pane, as shown in the following screenshot:

Viewing and filtering captured CloudTrail Logs and Events

With the Trail created, you can now view the captured events and filter them using the *event history* option from the CloudTrail dashboard's navigation pane. Here, you can view the last 7 days of captured events, and even filter specific ones by using one or more supporting filter attributes.

Here's a quick look at the **Filter** attributes that you can use in conjunction with the **Time range** to extract the required events and logs:

- **Event ID**: Each event captured by CloudTrail has a unique ID that you can filter and view.
- **Event name**: The name of the event. For example, EC2 events **RunInstances**, **DescribeInstances**, and so on.

- **Event source**: The AWS service to which the request was made. For example, `iam.amazonaws.com` or `ec2.amazonaws.com`.
- **Resource name**: The name or ID of the resource referenced by the event. For example, a bucket named `useast-prod-wordpress-code` or an instance ID `i-1234567` for an EC2 instance.
- **Resource type**: The type of resource referenced by the event. For example, a resource type can be a **Bucket** for S3, an **Instance** for EC2, and so on.
- **User name**: The name of the user that created or performed an action on the said event. For example, an IAM user logging into the AWS Management Console, and so on:

Once you have selected a particular filter and provided its associated attribute value, you can use the **Time range** to narrow your search results based on a predefined time window. To analyze further, you can select the **View event** option present in the details pane of an **Event** as well. Selecting this option will view the event in a JSON format, as shown in the following code:

```
{
    "eventVersion": "1.05",
    "userIdentity": {
        "type": "IAMUser",
        "principalId": "AIDAIZZ25SDDZAQTF2K3I",
        "arn": "arn:aws:iam::01234567890:user/yohan",
        "accountId": "01234567890",
        "accessKeyId": "ASDF56HJERW9PQRST",
        "userName": "yohan",
        "sessionContext": {
            "attributes": {
                "mfaAuthenticated": "false",
                "creationDate": "2017-11-07T08:13:26Z"
            }
        },
        "invokedBy": "signin.amazonaws.com"
    },
    "eventTime": "2017-11-07T08:25:32Z",
```

```
    "eventSource": "s3.amazonaws.com",
    "eventName": "CreateBucket",
    "awsRegion": "us-east-1",
    "sourceIPAddress": "80.82.129.191",
    "userAgent": "signin.amazonaws.com",
    "requestParameters": {
        "bucketName": "sometempbucketname"
    },
    "responseElements": null,
    "requestID": "163A30A312B21AB2",
    "eventID": "e7b7dff6-f196-4358-be64-aae1f5e7fed6",
    "eventType": "AwsApiCall",
    "recipientAccountId": "01234567890"
}
```

 You can additionally select the Download icon and select whether you wish to export all the logs using the **Export to CSV** or **Export to JSON** option.

You can alternatively even download the log files by accessing your CloudTrail S3 bucket and downloading the individual compressed JSON files, as per your requirements.

With this, we come towards the end of this section. You can use these same steps and create different Trails for capturing data as well as management activities. In the next section, we will see how we can leverage the AWS CLI and update our newly-created Trail.

Modifying a CloudTrail Trail using the AWS CLI

With the Trail in place, you can now use either the AWS Management Console or the AWS CLI to modify its settings. In this case, we will look at how to perform simple changes to the newly created Trail using the AWS CLI itself. Before proceeding with this section, however, it is important that you have installed and configured the AWS CLI on your desktop/laptop, based on the guides provided at http://docs.aws.amazon.com/cli/latest/userguide/installing.html.

Once the CLI is installed and configured, we can now run some simple commands to verify its validity. To start off, let's first check the status of our newly-created Trail by using the `describe-trails` command, as shown in the following command:

```
# aws cloudtrail describe-trails
```

```
yoyo@YoYoNux:~$
yoyo@YoYoNux:~$ aws cloudtrail describe-trails
{
    "trailList": [
        {
            "IncludeGlobalServiceEvents": true,
            "Name": "useast-prod-CloudTrail-01",
            "TrailARN": "arn:aws:cloudtrail:us-east-1:          :trail/useast-prod-CloudTrail-01",
            "LogFileValidationEnabled": true,
            "SnsTopicARN": "arn:aws:sns:us-east-1:          :NotifyMe",
            "IsMultiRegionTrail": false,
            "HasCustomEventSelectors": false,
            "S3BucketName": "useast-prod-cloudtrail-01",
            "SnsTopicName": "arn:aws:sns:us-east-1:          :NotifyMe",
            "HomeRegion": "us-east-1"
        }
    ]
}
```

This will display the essential properties of your CloudTrail Trails, such as the `Name`, the `TrailARN`, whether the log file validation is enabled or not, and whether the Trail is a multi-regional Trail or it belongs to a single region. In this case, the `IsMultiRegionTrail` value is set to `false`, which means that the Trail will only record events for its current region, that is, `us-east-1`. Let's go ahead and modify this using the AWS CLI.

To do so, we will be using the `update-trail` command:

```
# aws cloudtrail update-trail \
--name useast-prod-CloudTrail-01 \
--is-multi-region-trail
```

The following code will simply change the `IsMultiRegionTrail` value from `false` to `true`. You can verify the same by using the `describe-trails` command, as performed earlier. Similarly, you can use the `update-trail` command to change other settings for your CloudTrail Trail, such as enabling the log file validation feature, as described in the following command:

```
# aws cloudtrail update-trail \
--name useast-prod-CloudTrail-01 \
--enable-log-file-validation
```

Finally, you can even use the AWS CLI to check the current status of your Trail by executing the `get-trail-status` command, as shown in the following command:

```
# aws cloudtrail get-trail-status \
--name useast-prod-CloudTrail-01
```

```
yoyo@YoYoNux:~$
yoyo@YoYoNux:~$ aws cloudtrail get-trail-status --name useast-prod-CloudTrail-01
{
    "LatestNotificationTime": 1510046990.498,
    "LatestNotificationAttemptSucceeded": "2017-11-07T09:29:50Z",
    "LatestDeliveryAttemptTime": "2017-11-07T09:29:50Z",
    "LatestDeliveryTime": 1510046990.498,
    "LatestDeliveryAttemptSucceeded": "2017-11-07T09:29:50Z",
    "IsLogging": true,
    "TimeLoggingStarted": "2017-11-07T08:22:21Z",
    "StartLoggingTime": 1510042941.069,
    "LatestDigestDeliveryTime": 1510047188.094,
    "LatestNotificationAttemptTime": "2017-11-07T09:29:50Z",
    "TimeLoggingStopped": ""
}
```

Apart from these values, the `get-trail-status` command will additionally show two more fields (`LatestNotificationError` and `LatestDeliveryError`) in case an Amazon SNS subscription fails or if a CloudTrail Trail was unsuccessful at writing the events to an S3 bucket.

With this completed, we will now move on to the next section of this chapter, in which we will learn how you can effectively monitor your Trails with the help of CloudWatch Logs.

Monitoring CloudTrail Logs using CloudWatch

One of the best features of using CloudTrail is that you can easily integrate it with other AWS services for an enhanced security auditing and governance experience. One such service that we are going to use and explore here with CloudTrail is Amazon CloudWatch.

Using CloudWatch, you can easily set up custom metric filters and an array of alarms that can send notifications to the right set of people in case a specific security or governance issue occurs in your AWS environment. To get started with CloudWatch using CloudTrail, you will first need to configure your Trail to send the captured log events to CloudWatch Logs. This can be easily configured using both the AWS Management Console and the AWS CLI. Next, once this is done, you will be required to define custom CloudWatch metric filters to evaluate the log events for specific matches. Once a match is made, you can then additionally configure CloudWatch to trigger corresponding alarms, send notifications, and even perform a remediation action based on the type of alarm generated.

Here is a diagrammatic representation of CloudTrail's integration with CloudWatch:

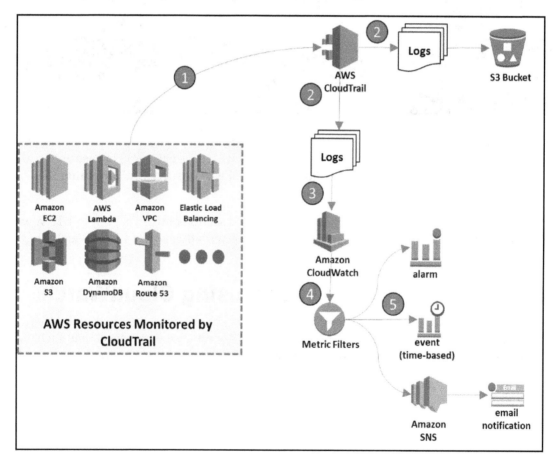

In this section, we will be using the AWS CLI to integrate the Trail's logs with Amazon CloudWatch Logs:

1. First, we will need to create a new CloudWatch Log Group using the following command:

   ```
   # aws logs create-log-group --log-group-name useast-prod-
   CloudTrail-LG-01
   ```

2. Next, you will need to extract and maintain the newly created Log Group's ARN for the forthcoming steps. To do so, type in the following command and make a note of the Log Group's ARN, as shown here:

   ```
   # aws logs describe-log-groups
   ```

3. With the Log Group successfully created, we will now need to create a new IAM Role that will essentially enable CloudTrail to send its logs over to the CloudWatch Log Group. To do so, we first need to create a policy document that assigns the AssumeRole permission to our CloudTrail Trail. Create a new file and paste the following contents into that file. Remember to to create the file with a .json extension:

   ```
   # vi policy.json
   {
     "Version": "2012-10-17",
     "Statement": [
       {
         "Sid": "",
         "Effect": "Allow",
         "Principal": {
           "Service": "cloudtrail.amazonaws.com"
         },
         "Action": "sts:AssumeRole"
   ```

```
        }
    ]
}
```

4. With the file created, use the `create-role` command to create the role with the required permissions for CloudTrail:

```
# aws iam create-role --role-name useast-prod-CloudTrail-Role-01 \
--assume-role-policy-document file://policy.json
```

5. Once this command executed, make a note of the newly created role's ARN. Next, copy and paste the following role policy document into a new file. This policy document grants CloudTrail the necessary permissions to create a CloudWatch Logs log stream in the Log Group that you created a while back, so as to deliver the CloudTrail events to that particular log stream:

```
# vi permissions.json
{
  "Version": "2012-10-17",
  "Statement": [
    {
      "Sid": "CloudTrailCreateLogStream",
      "Effect": "Allow",
      "Action": [
        "logs:CreateLogStream"
      ],
      "Resource": [
        "<YOUR_LOG_GROUP_ARN>"
      ]
    },
    {
      "Sid": "CloudTrailPutLogEventsToCloudWatch",
      "Effect": "Allow",
      "Action": [
        "logs:PutLogEvents"
      ],
      "Resource": [
        "<YOUR_LOG_GROUP_ARN>"
      ]
    }
  ]
}
```

6. Next, run the following command to apply the permissions to the role. Remember to provide the name of the policy that we created during the earlier steps here:

```
# aws iam put-role-policy --role-name useast-prod-CloudTrail-
Role-01 \

--policy-name cloudtrail-policy \
--policy-document file://permissions.json
```

7. The final step is to update the Trail with the Log Group ARN as well as the CloudWatch Logs role ARN, using the following command snippet:

```
# aws cloudtrail update-trail --name useast-prod-CloudTrail-01 \
  --cloud-watch-logs-log-group-arn <YOUR_LOG_GROUP_ARN> \
  --cloud-watch-logs-role-arn <YOUR_ROLE_ARN>
```

With this you have now integrated your CloudTrail Logs to seamlessly flow into the CloudWatch Log Group that we created. You can verify this by viewing the **Log Groups** provided under the **CloudWatch Logs** section of your CloudWatch dashboard.

In the next section, we will be leveraging this newly created Log Group and assign a custom metric as well as an alarm for monitoring and alerting purposes.

Creating custom metric filters and alarms for monitoring CloudTrail Logs

With the Log Group created and integrated with the CloudTrail Trail, we can now continue to create and assign custom metric filters as well as alarms. These alarms can be leveraged to trigger notifications whenever a particular compliance or governance issue is identified by CloudTrail.

To begin with, let's first create a custom metric filter using CloudWatch Logs. In this case, we will be creating a simple filter that triggers a CloudWatch alarm each time an S3 bucket API call is made. This API call can be either a simple PUT or DELETE operation on the bucket's policies, life cycle, and so on:

1. Log in to your Amazon CloudWatch dashboard or, alternatively, select the link provided here to get started, at https://console.aws.amazon.com/cloudwatch/.

2. Once logged in, select the **Logs** option from the navigation pane. Select the newly created Log Group that we created a while back, and opt for the **Create Metric Filter** option, as depicted in the following screenshot:

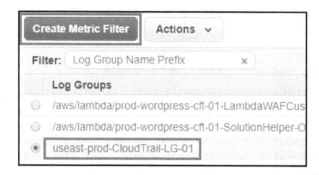

3. Here, in the **Create Metric Filter and Assign a Metric** page, start off by providing a suitable **Filter Name** for the new metric, followed by populating the **Filter Pattern** option with the following snippet:

```
{($.eventSource = s3.amazonaws.com) && (($.eventName =
PutBucketAcl) || ($.eventName = PutBucketPolicy) || ($.eventName =
PutBucketLifecycle) || ($.eventName = DeleteBucketPolicy) ||
($.eventName = DeleteBucketLifecycle))}
```

4. Once done, type in a suitable **Metric Namespace** value followed by a **Metric Name** as well. Leave the rest of the values to their defaults, and select the option **Create filter** to complete the process.

5. With this step completed, you now have a working CloudWatch filter up and running. In order to assign this particular filter an alarm, simply select the **Create Alarm** option adjacent to the filter, as depicted in the following screenshot:

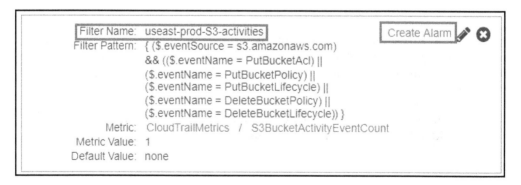

6. Creating an alarm is a fairly straightforward and simple process, and I'm sure you would be more than qualified enough to set it up. Start off by providing a **Name** and an optional **Description** to your alarm, followed by configuring the trigger by setting the event count as >= 1 for 1 consecutive period. Consequently, also remember to set up the **Actions** section by selecting an SNS **Notification List** or, alternatively, creating a new one. With all the settings configured, select the **Create Alarm** option to complete the process.

With this step completed, the only thing remaining is to give the filter a try! Log in to your S3 dashboard and create a new bucket, or alternatively, update the bucket policy of an existing one. The CloudTrail Trail will pick up this change and send the logs to your CloudWatch Log Group, where our newly created metric filter triggers an alarm by notifying the respective cloud administrator! Simply awesome isn't it? You can use more custom filters and alarms for configuring CloudWatch's notifications, as per your requirements.

In the next section, we will be looking at a fairly simple and automated method for creating and deploying multiple CloudWatch alarms using a single CloudFormation template.

Automating deployment of CloudWatch alarms for AWS CloudTrail

As discussed in the previous section, you can easily create different CloudWatch metrics and alarms for monitoring your CloudTrail Log files. Luckily for us, AWS provides a really simple and easy to use CloudFormation template, which allows you to get up and running with a few essential alarms in a matter of minutes! The best part of this template is that you can extend the same by adding your own custom alarms and notifications as well. So without any further ado, let's get started with it.

The template itself is fairly simple and easy to work with. You can download a version at `https://s3-us-west-2.amazonaws.com/awscloudtrail/cloudwatch-alarms-for-cloudtrail-api-activity/CloudWatch_Alarms_for_CloudTrail_API_Activity.json`.

At the time of writing this book, this template supports the creation of metric filters for the following set of AWS resources:

- Amazon EC2 instances
- IAM policies
- Internet gateways
- Network ACLs
- Security groups

1. To create and launch this CloudFormation stack, head over to the CloudFormation dashboard by navigating to `https://console.aws.amazon.com/cloudformation`.

2. Next, select the option **Create Stack** to bring up the CloudFormation template selector page. Paste `https://s3-us-west-2.amazonaws.com/awscloudtrail/cloudwatch-alarms-for-cloudtrail-api-activity/CloudWatch_Alarms_for_CloudTrail_API_Activity.json` in the **Specify an Amazon S3 template URL** field, and click on **Next** to continue.

3. In the **Specify Details** page, provide a suitable **Stack name** and fill out the following required parameters:
   - **Email**: A valid email address that will receive all SNS notifications. You will have to confirm this email subscription once the template is successfully deployed.
   - **LogGroupName**: The name of the Log Group that we created earlier in this chapter.

4. Once the required values are filled in, click on **Next** to proceed. Review the settings of the template on the **Review** page and finally select the **Create** option to complete the process.

The template takes a few minutes to completely finish the creation and configuration of the required alarms. Here is a snapshot of the alarms and metrics that get created for your environment:

Logical ID of resources created	Type of resource
`AlarmNotificationTopic`	`AWS::SNS::Topic`
`AuthorizationFailuresAlarm`	`AWS::CloudWatch::Alarm`
`CloudTrailChangesAlarm`	`AWS::CloudWatch::Alarm`
`CloudTrailChangesMetricFilter`	`AWS::Logs::MetricFilter`
`ConsoleSignInFailuresAlarm`	`AWS::CloudWatch::Alarm`
`ConsoleSignInFailuresMetricFilter`	`AWS::Logs::MetricFilter`
`EC2InstanceChangesAlarm`	`AWS::CloudWatch::Alarm`
`EC2InstanceChangesMetricFilter`	`AWS::Logs::MetricFilter`
`EC2LargeInstanceChangesAlarm`	`AWS::CloudWatch::Alarm`
`EC2LargeInstanceChangesMetricFilter`	`AWS::Logs::MetricFilter`
`GatewayChangesAlarm`	`AWS::CloudWatch::Alarm`
`GatewayChangesMetricFilter`	`AWS::Logs::MetricFilter`
`IAMPolicyChangesAlarm`	`AWS::CloudWatch::Alarm`
`IAMPolicyChangesMetricFilter`	`AWS::Logs::MetricFilter`
`NetworkAclChangesAlarm`	`AWS::CloudWatch::Alarm`
`NetworkAclChangesMetricFilter`	`AWS::Logs::MetricFilter`
`SecurityGroupChangesAlarm`	`AWS::CloudWatch::Alarm`
`SecurityGroupChangesMetricFilter`	`AWS::Logs::MetricFilter`
`VpcChangesAlarm`	`AWS::CloudWatch::Alarm`
`VpcChangesMetricFilter`	`AWS::Logs::MetricFilter`

So far, we have seen how to integrate CloudTrail's Log files with CloudWatch Log Groups for configuring custom metrics as well as alarms for notifications. But how do you effectively analyze and manage these logs, especially if you have extremely large volumes to deal with? This is exactly what we will be learning about in the next section, along with the help of yet another awesome AWS service called **Amazon Elasticsearch**!

Analyzing CloudTrail Logs using Amazon Elasticsearch

Log management and analysis for many organizations starts and ends with just three letters: *E*, *L*, and *K*, which stands for Elasticsearch, Logstash, and Kibana. These three open-sourced products are essentially used together to aggregate, parse, search, and visualize logs at an enterprise scale:

- **Logstash**: Logstash is primarily used as a log collection tool. It is designed to collect, parse, and store logs originating from multiple sources, such as applications, infrastructure, operating systems, tools, services, and so on.
- **Elasticsearch**: With all the logs collected in one place, you now need a query engine to filter and search through these logs for particular events. That's exactly where Elasticsearch comes into play. Elasticsearch is basically a search server based on the popular information retrieval software library, Lucene. It provides a distributed, full-text search engine along with a RESTful web interface for querying your logs.
- **Kibana**: Kibana is an open source data visualization plugin, used in conjunction with Elasticsearch. It provides you with the ability to create and export your logs into various visual graphs, such as bar charts, scatter graphs, pie charts, and so on.

You can easily download and install each of these components in your AWS environment, and get up and running with your very own ELK stack in a matter of hours! Alternatively, you can also leverage AWS own Elasticsearch service! Amazon Elasticsearch is a managed ELK service that enables you to quickly deploy operate, and scale an ELK stack as per your requirements. Using Amazon Elasticsearch, you eliminate the need for installing and managing the ELK stack's components on your own, which in the long run can be a painful experience.

For this particular use case, we will leverage a simple CloudFormation template that will essentially set up an Amazon Elasticsearch domain to filter and visualize the captured CloudTrail Log files, as depicted in the following diagram:

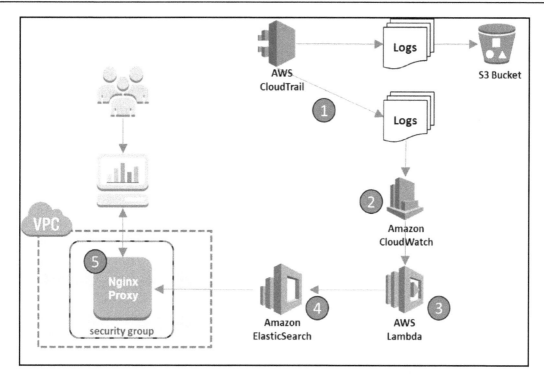

1. To get started, log in to the CloudFormation dashboard, at `https://console.aws.amazon.com/cloudformation`.

2. Next, select the option **Create Stack** to bring up the CloudFormation template selector page. Paste `http://s3.amazonaws.com/concurrencylabs-cfn-templates/cloudtrail-es-cluster/cloudtrail-es-cluster.json` in, the **Specify an Amazon S3 template URL** field, and click on **Next** to continue.

3. In the **Specify Details** page, provide a suitable **Stack name** and fill out the following required parameters:

- **AllowedIPForEsCluster**: Provide the IP address that will have access to the nginx proxy and, in turn, have access to your Elasticsearch cluster. In my case, I've provided my laptop's IP. Note that you can change this IP at a later stage, by visiting the security group of the nginx proxy once it has been created by the CloudFormation template.
- **CloudTrailName**: Name of the CloudTrail that we set up at the beginning of this chapter.
- **KeyName**: You can select a key-pair for obtaining SSH to your nginx proxy instance:

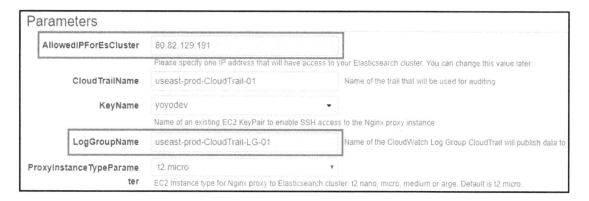

- **LogGroupName**: The name of the CloudWatch Log Group that will act as the input to our Elasticsearch cluster.
- **ProxyInstanceTypeParameter**: The EC2 instance type for your proxy instance. Since this is a demonstration, I've opted for the **t2.micro** instance type. Alternatively, you can select a different instance type as well.

4. Once done, click on **Next** to continue. Review the settings of your stack and hit **Create** to complete the process.

The stack takes a good few minutes to deploy as a new Elasticsearch domain is created. You can monitor the progress of the deployment by either viewing the CloudFormation's **Output** tab or, alternatively, by viewing the Elasticsearch dashboard. Note that, for this deployment, a default **t2.micro.elasticsearch** instance type is selected for deploying Elasticsearch. You should change this value to a larger instance type before deploying the stack for production use.

You can view information on Elasticsearch *Supported Instance Types* at `http://docs.aws.amazon.com/elasticsearch-service/latest/developerguide/aes-supported-instance-types.html`.

With the stack deployed successfully, copy the Kibana URL from the CloudFormation **Output** tab:

```
"KibanaProxyEndpoint": "http://<NGINX_PROXY>/_plugin/kibana/"
```

The Kibana UI may take a few minutes to load. Once it is up and running, you will need to configure a few essential parameters before you can actually proceed. Select **Settings** and hit the **Indices** option. Here, fill in the following details:

- **Index contains time-based events**: Enable this checkbox to index time-based events
- **Use event times to create index names**: Enable this checkbox as well
- **Index pattern interval**: Set the **Index pattern interval** to **Daily** from the drop-down list
- **Index name of pattern**: Type `[cwl-]YYYY.MM.DD` in to this field
- **Time-field name**: Select the **@timestamp** value from the drop-down list

Once completed, hit **Create** to complete the process. With this, you should now start seeing logs populate on to Kibana's dashboard. Feel free to have a look around and try out the various options and filters provided by Kibana:

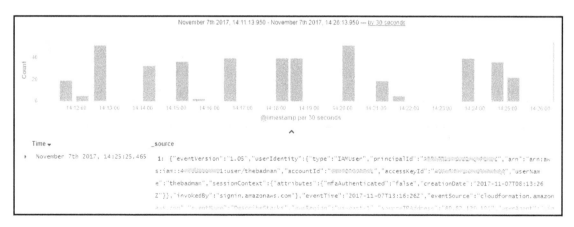

Phew! That was definitely a lot to cover! But wait, there's more! AWS provides yet another extremely useful governance and configuration management service that we need to learn about as well, so without any further ado, here's introducing AWS Config!

Introducing AWS Config

AWS Config is yet another managed service, under the security and governance wing of services, that provides a detailed view of the configurational settings of each of your AWS resources. Configurational settings here can be anything, from simple settings made to your EC2 instances or VPC subnets, to how one resource is related to another, such as how an EC2 instance is related with an EBS volume, an ENI, and so on. Using AWS Config, you can actually view and compare such configurational changes that were made to your resource in the past, and take the necessary preventative actions if needed.

Here's a list of things that you can basically achieve by using AWS Config:

- Evaluate your AWS resource configurations against a desired setting
- Retrieve and view historical configurations of one or more resources
- Send notifications whenever a particular resource is created, modified, or deleted
- Obtain a configuration snapshot of your resource that you can later use as a blueprint or template
- View relationships and hierarchies between resources, such as all the instances that are part of a particular network subnet, and so on

Using AWS Config enables you to manage your resources more effectively by setting governing policies and standardizing configurations for your resources. Each time a configuration change is violated, you can trigger off notifications or even perform a remediation against the change. Furthermore, AWS Config also provides out-of-the-box integration capabilities with the likes of AWS CloudTrail, as well to providing you with a complete end-to-end auditing and compliance monitoring solution for your AWS environment.

Before we get started by setting up AWS Config for our own scenario, let's first take a quick look at some of its important concepts and terminologies.

Concepts and terminologies

The following are some of the key concepts and terminologies that you ought to keep in mind when working with AWS Config:

- **Config rules**: Config rules form the heart of operations at AWS Config. These are essentially rules that represent the desired configuration settings for a particular AWS resource. While the service monitors your resources for any changes, these changes get mapped to one or more set of config rules, that in turn flag the resource against any non-compliances. AWS Config provides you with some rules out of the box that you can use as-is or even customize as per your requirements. Alternatively, you can also create custom rules completely from scratch.

- **Configuration items**: Configuration items are basically a point-in-time representation of a particular AWS resource's configuration. The item can include various metadata about your resource, such as its current configuration attributes, and its relationships with other AWS resources, if any, its events, such as when it was created, last updated, and so on. Configuration items are created by AWS Config automatically each time it detects a change in a particular resource's configuration.

- **Configuration history**: A collection of configuration items of a resource over a particular period of time is called its **configuration history**. You can use this feature to compare the changes that a resource may undergo overtime, and then decide to take necessary actions. Configuration history is stored in an Amazon S3 bucket that you specify.

- **Configuration snapshot**: A configuration snapshot is also a collection of configuration items of a particular resource over time. This snapshot acts as a template or benchmark that can then be used to compare and validate your resource's current configurational settings.

With this in mind, let's look at some simple steps which allow you to get started with your own AWS Config setup in a matter of minutes!

Getting started with AWS Config

Getting started with AWS Config is a very simple process, and it usually takes about a minute or two to complete. Overall, you start off by specifying the resources that you want AWS Config to record, configure an Amazon SNS topic, and Amazon S3 bucket for notifications and storing the configuration history, and, finally, add some config rules to evaluate your resources:

1. To begin, access the AWS Config dashboard by filtering the service from the AWS Management Console or by navigating to `https://console.aws.amazon.com/config/`.

2. Since this is our first time configuring this, select the **Get Started** option to commence the Config's creation process.

3. In the **Resource types to record** section, select the type of AWS resource that you wish config to monitor. By default, config will record the activities of all supported AWS resources. You can optionally specify only the services which you want to monitor by typing in the **Specific types** field, as shown in the following screenshot. In this case, I've opted to go for the default values: **Record all resources supported in this region** and **Include global resources**:

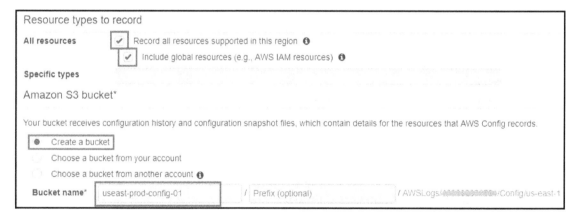

4. Next, select a location to store your configuration history as well as your configuration snapshots. In this case, I've opted to create a new S3 bucket for AWS Config by providing a unique **Bucket name**.

5. Moving on, in the **Amazon SNS topic** section, you can choose to create a new SNS topic that will send email notifications to your specified mailbox, or choose a pre-existing topic from your account.

6. Finally, you will need to provide config with a **Read-only** access role so that it can record the particular configuration information as well as send that over to S3 and SNS. Based on your requirements, you can either **Create a role** or, alternatively, **Choose a role from your account**. Click **Save** to complete the basic configuration for your AWS Config.

> With this step completed, we can now go ahead and add Config rules to our setup. To do so, from the AWS Config dashboard's navigation pane, select the **Rules** and click on the **Add rule** option.

7. In the **AWS Config rules** page, you can filter and view predefined rules using the *filter* provided. For this particular scenario, let's go ahead and add two rules for checking whether any of the account's S3 buckets have either public read prohibited or public write prohibited on them or not. To do so, simply type in `S3-bucket` in the filter and select either of the two config rules, as shown in the following screenshot:

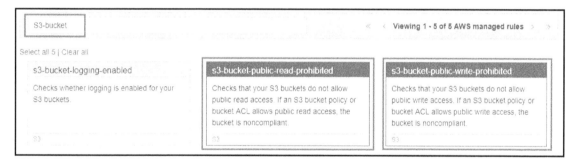

- **Resources**: When any resource that matches the evaluation criteria is either created, modified, or deleted
- **Tags**: When any resource with the specified tag is created, modified, or deleted
- **All changes**: When any resource recorded by AWS Config is created, modified, or deleted

8. Selecting a particular rule will pop up that rule's configuration page, where you can define the rule's trigger as well as its scope. Let's pick the **s3-bucket-public-read-prohibited** rule for starters and work with that.

9. In the **Configure rule** page, provide a suitable **Name** and **Description** for your new rule. Now, since this is a managed rule, you will not be provided with an option to change the **Trigger type**; however, when you create your own custom rules, you can specify whether you wish to trigger the rule based on a **Configuration change** event or using a **Periodic** check approach that uses a time frequency that you specify to evaluate the rules.

10. Next, you can also specify when you want the rule's evaluations to occur by selecting the appropriate options provided under the **Scope of changes** section. In this case, I've opted for the **Resources** scope and selected **S3: Bucket** as the resource, as depicted in the following screenshot:

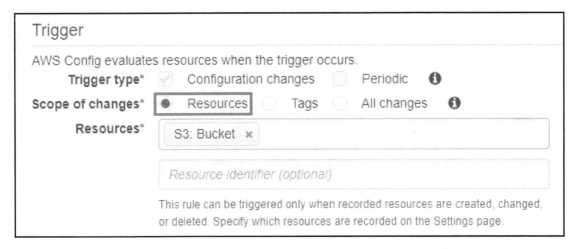

11. Optionally, you can also provide the ARN of the resource that you wish config to monitor using the **Resource identifier** field. Click on **Save** once done.

Similarly, using the aforementioned steps, create another managed config rule called **s3-bucket-public-write-prohibited**.

With the rules in place, select the **Resources** option from the config's navigation pane to view the current set of resources that have been evaluated against the set compliance.

In my case, I have two S3 buckets present in my AWS environment: one that has public read enabled on it while the other doesn't. Here's what the **Resources evaluated** dashboard should look like for you:

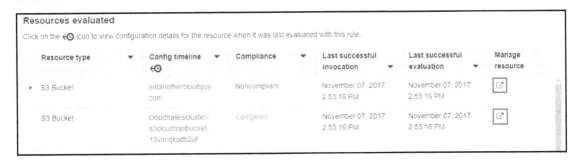

Here, you can view the evaluated resources against a **Config timeline** by simply selecting the name of the resource from the column with the same name. This will bring up a time series of your particular resource's configuration state. You can choose between the different time series options to view the state changes, as well as toggle between the time periods using the Calendar icon. The best part of using this feature of config is that you can simultaneously change your resource's configuration by selecting the **Manage resource** option. Doing so will automatically open the S3 buckets configuration page, as in this case. You can alternatively select the **Dashboard** option from AWS Config navigation pane and obtain a visual summary of the current status of your overall compliance, as depicted in the following screenshot:

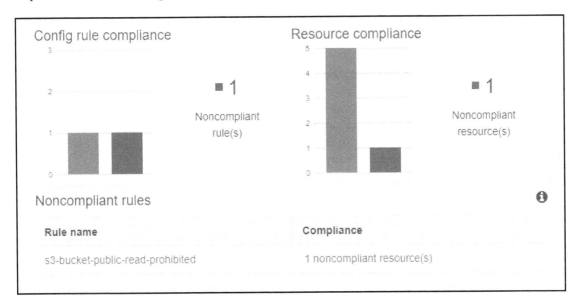

You can use the same concepts to create more such managed config rules for a variety of other AWS services, including EC2, EBS, Auto Scaling, DynamoDB, RDS, Redshift, CloudWatch, IAM, and much more! For a complete list of managed rules, check out `http:/`
`/docs.aws.amazon.com/config/latest/developerguide/managed-rules-by-aws-config.`
`html.`

With the managed config rules done, the last thing left to do is create a customized config rule, which is exactly what we will be covering in the next section.

Creating custom config rules

The process for creating a custom config rule remains more or less similar to the earlier process, apart from a few changes here and there. In this section, we will be exploring how to create a simple compliance rule that will essentially trigger a config compliance alert if a user launches an EC2 instance other than the **t2.micro** instance type:

1. To get started, select the **Rules** option from the AWS Config navigation pane, then select the **Add custom rule** button present on the **Add rule** page. The creation of the custom rule starts off like any other, by providing a suitable **Name** and **Description** for the rule. Now, here's where the actual change occurs. Custom config rules rely on AWS Lambda to monitor and trigger the compliance checks. And this is actually perfect, as Lambda functions are event driven and perfect for hosting the business logic for our custom rules.

2. Select the **Create AWS Lambda function** to get things started. Here, I'm going to make use of a pre-defined Lambda blueprint that was essentially created to work in conjunction with AWS Config. Alternatively, you can create your config rule's business logic from scratch, and deploy the same in a fresh function. For now, type in the following text in the **Blueprints** filter, as shown in the following screenshot (**config-rule-change-triggered**):

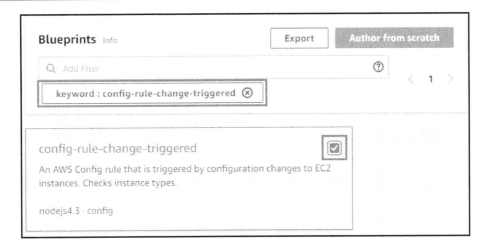

3. Ensure that the blueprint is selected, and click on **Next** to continue.

4. In the function's **Basic Information** page, provide a **Name** for your function followed by selecting the **Create new role from template(s)** option from the **Role** drop-down list. The role will essentially provide the Lambda function with the necessary permissions to read from EC2 and write the output back to AWS Config as well as to Amazon CloudWatch.

5. Type in a suitable **Role name** and select the **Create function** option to complete the process. Once the function is deployed, make a note of its ARN, as we will be requiring the same in the next step.

6. Return back to the AWS Config **Add custom rule** page and paste the newly created function's ARN in the **AWS Lambda function ARN** file, as shown in the following screenshot:

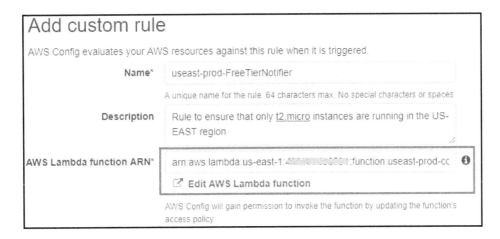

7. With the function's ARN pasted, the rest of the configuration for the custom rule remains the same. Unlike the managed rules, you can opt to change the **Trigger type** between **Configuration changes** or **Periodic**, as per your requirements. In this case, I've opted to go for the **Condition changes** as my trigger mechanism, followed by **EC2: Instance** as the **Resource** type.

8. Last, but not least, we also need to specify the **Rule parameters**, which is basically a key-value pair that defines an attribute against which your resources will be validated. In this case, **desiredInstanceType** is the **Key** and t2.micro is the **Value**. Click **Save** to complete the setup process:

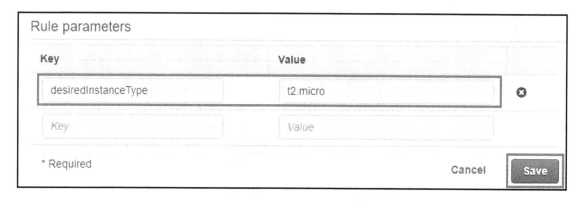

9. With the rule in place, all you need to do now is take it for a small test run! Go ahead and launch a new EC2 instance that is other than **t2.micro**. Remember that the instance has to be launched in the same region as that of your Lambda function! Sure enough, once the instance is launched, the change gets immediately reflected in AWS Config's dashboard:

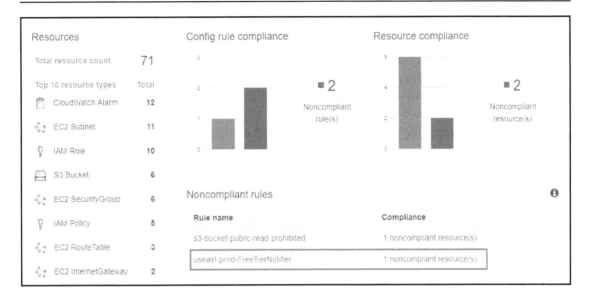

With this, we come towards the end of this section as well as the chapter! However, before we conclude, here's a quick look at some interesting best practices and next steps that you ought to keep in mind when working with AWS CloudTrail and AWS Config!

Tips and best practices

Here's a list of a few essential tips and best practices that you ought to keep in mind when working with AWS CloudTrail, AWS Config, and security in general:

- **Analyze and audit security configurations periodically**: Although AWS provides a variety of services for safeguarding your cloud environment, it is the organization's mandate to ensure that the security rules are enforced and periodically verified against any potential misconfigurations.
- **Complete audit trail for all users**: Ensure that all resource creation, modifications, and terminations are tracked minutely for each user, including root, IAM, and federated users.

- **Enable CloudTrail globally**: By enabling logging at a global level, CloudTrail can essentially capture logs for all AWS services, including the global ones such as IAM, CloudFront, and so on.
- **Enable CloudTrail Log file validation**: An optional setting, however it is always recommended to enable CloudTrail Log file validations for an added layer of integrity and security.
- **Enable access logging for CloudTrail and config buckets**: Since both CloudTrail and config leverage S3 buckets to store the captured logs, it is always recommended that you enable access tracking for them to log unwarranted and unauthorized access. Alternatively, you can also restrict access to the logs and buckets to a specialized group of users as well.
- **Encrypt log files at rest**: Encrypting the log files at rest provides an additional layer of protection from unauthorized viewing or editing of the logged data.

6

Access Control Using AWS IAM and AWS Organizations

In the previous chapter, we learnt and explored about how you can leverage two AWS services, namely AWS Config and AWS CloudTrail, to govern your Cloud environments. In this chapter, we will be continuing on the security journey by revisiting AWS IAM along with a few useful features as well as learning a bit about yet another service in the form of AWS Organizations!

Keeping this in mind, let us have a quick look at the various topics that we will be covering in this chapter:

- What's new with AWS IAM
- Creating policies using the IAM visual editor
- Testing your IAM policies using the IAM Policy Simulator
- Introducing AWS Organizations with a few essential concepts and terminologies
- Creating your own organizations using the AWS Management Console as well as the AWS CLI

What's new with AWS IAM

Before we look at some of the recent enhancements made to IAM, here is a quick crash course on IAM for the uninitiated. AWS Identity and Access Management or IAM is a web service that provides secured access control mechanisms for all AWS services. You can use IAM to create users and groups, assigning users specific permissions and policies, and a lot more. The best part of all this is that IAM is completely FREE. Yup! Not a penny is required to use it.

Let's quickly look at some interesting features provided by AWS IAM:

- **Multi-factor authentication**: IAM allows you to provide two-factor authentications to users for added security. This means that now, along with your password, you will also have to provide a secret key/pin from a special hardware device, such as a hard token, or even from software apps such as Google Authenticator.
- **Integration with other AWS products**: IAM integrates with almost all AWS products and services and can be used to provide granular access rights and permissions to each service as required.
- **Identity federation**: Do you have an on-premise Active Directory already that has users and groups created? Not a problem, as IAM can be integrated with an on-premise AD to provide access to your AWS account using a few simple steps.
- **Access mechanisms**: IAM can be accessed using a variety of different tools, the most common and frequently used being the AWS Management Console. Apart from this, IAM can also be accessed via the AWS CLI, via SDKs that support different platforms and programming languages such as Java, .NET, Python, Ruby, and so on, and programmatically via a secured HTTPS API as well.

With the basics in mind, let us now look at some interesting and useful enhancements made to IAM in recent years.

Using the visual editor to create IAM policies

IAM policies are used to define permissions for your IAM entities such as users, groups, and roles. Each policy that you create consists of one or more statements that include the following elements:

- **Effect**: This element determines whether a policy statement allows or explicitly denies access to a particular IAM resource.
- **Action**: Actions are used to define AWS service actions within a policy, for example; you can specify Amazon S3 related actions such as list buckets, read or write to buckets, and so on.
- **Resource**: Resources are the AWS services or individual entities to which the actions apply.
- **Condition**: Conditions are used to define when a particular permission is allowed or denied on a resource. You can leverage one or more conditions to provide additional granular security to your AWS resources.

Once a policy is created, you essentially attach it to your resource which can be an IAM user, group or even a role. However, creating custom and granular IAM policies can prove to be a challenge at times especially if you are just getting started with AWS. To address this, AWS has provided a new and improved visual editor using which you can easily create customized policies on your own:

1. To get started with the visual editor, first log in to the IAM Management Console by selecting this URL `https://console.aws.amazon.com/iam/home`.
2. Once logged in, select the **Policies** option from the navigation pane. This will display a page that lists both the **AWS Managed** as well as the **Customer Managed** policies. To create a policy, simply select the **Create policy** option. For this scenario, let us create a simple S3 policy that grants full access to only a single folder present within an S3 bucket.
3. On the **Create policy** page, ensure that the **Visual editor** tab is selected and click on the **Choose a service** option to filter and pick out Amazon S3.

4. With the **Service** selected, next click on the **Select actions** options to add the appropriate actions for our policy. Here, you can select the appropriate **Access levels** for your resource by either opting to add the actions *manually* or even provide individual permissions by selecting the correct access rights from each individual **Access levels**. In this case, I have opted to select the entire **List** level for permissions and the s3:GetObject from the **Read** access level followed by the s3:PutObject, and the s3:DeleteObject permissions from the **Write** access level. Following is screenshot of the **Actions** selected for your reference:

By default, all actions selected here will be allowed. To deny actions explicitly, select the **Switch to deny permissions** option provided in the **Actions** section.

5. Once completed, you can now select the **Resources** section to add either all or specific resources to your new set of permissions. In this case, we will add the set of permissions to a specific bucket called **useast-prod-stuff-01**. To do so, select the **Add ARN** option adjoining to the bucket field.

6. In the **Add ARN(s)** dialog box, type in the name of the selected bucket in the **Bucket name** field as depicted in the following screenshot. Once done, select **Add** to complete the process:

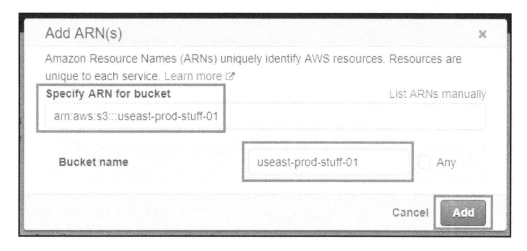

7. Once done, you can optionally choose to add permissions to an object level as well. Click on the **Add ARN** option adjoining the **object** field and fill in the required information as we performed in the previous steps. The only addition here is that you can provide an additional *folder name* in the **Object name** field for a more granular permission control. Once done, click on **Add** to complete the process. Here is a screenshot of the completed resource allocation for our policy:

8. With the permissions and the resources set, you can optionally choose to add **Conditions** as well to your policy. To do so, select the **Specify request conditions** option. Here you can opt to select and edit conditions that match your requirements. For example, for this particular policy, we want the user to access the particular S3 bucket only from within an organization's internal network. To do so, select the **Source IP** option and type in suitable IP range or a single IP address based on your organization's IP range.

9. You can also add additional conditions to your policy by selecting the **Add request condition** option. Here, you can customize and specify a granular condition using a combination of **Condition key**, **Qualifier**, and **Operator** as shown in the following screenshot:

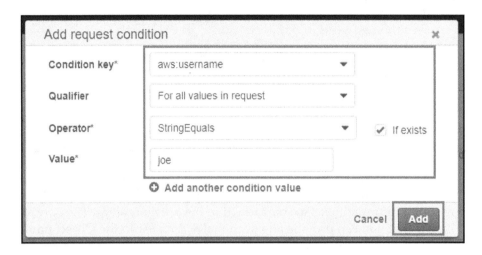

Here, the condition will check and allow only a particular AWS IAM user with the username **joe** access to the S3 bucket. You can create your own custom conditions using the same approach and once done, click on **Add** to complete the process.

10. With the permissions, resources, and conditions in place, select the **Review policy** option to complete the policy creation process. Provide a suitable **Name** and an optional **Description** for your policy before selecting the **Create policy** option.

There you have it! Simple, wasn't it! You can use the same process to create highly customized and granular policies with relative ease. However, there is still one question that remains unanswered; how do we test and troubleshoot the policies without making any actual requests? That's exactly what the IAM Policy Simulator is all about!

Testing IAM policies using the IAM Policy Simulator

With your new policy created, the next steps would be to attach it to either an IAM user or group and test it out. But how do you effectively test your new policy without having to make any actual calls or requests? That's where the new IAM Policy Simulator comes into play!

The IAM Policy Simulator is used to evaluate IAM policies in order to determine the most effective set of permissions and actions that you can specify without making any actual resource calls whatsoever. The policy simulator internally leverages the same policy evaluation engine that processes real requests to AWS resources; however, it does not make any actual service request itself. Because of this nature, the policy simulator is unable to report any responses from the generated requests. All you get as a result is whether the policy would allow or deny a particular action. Here are a few ways using which you can leverage the IAM Policy Simulator:

- You can use the IAM Policy Simulator to test policies that are attached to existing users, groups and roles.
- You can also use the simulator to test policies that are not attached yet to your resources by simply copying and executing them against the simulator
- The simulator can also be used to test policies attached to various AWS resources such as Amazon S3 buckets, Amazon EC2 instances, and so on.
- You can even use the simulator to test out real world scenarios by passing various context keys such as *IP addresses* or *usernames* that are passed alongside the conditions of a policy, and much more!

To get started with the IAM Policy Simulator, simply select this URL `https://policysim.aws.amazon.com/`. The policy simulator is a separate entity that runs outside your standard AWS Console. Use your standard AWS IAM credentials to log in to the policy simulator if asked:

1. Once logged in, you can use the simulator to test and validate your existing user, group and even role-based policies. To start with, let us test the policy we created in our earlier section of this chapter! To do so, from the **Users**, **Groups**, and **Roles** section, select the **Users** from the drop-down list. You should see a list of users present in your AWS account.

2. Select the appropriate **User** that was used to attach the policy. In my case, the username was `joe`. Once selected, you will be shown all the policies that the user is currently associated with, in this case, we should see the custom S3 access policy that we created in the earlier section as shown in the following screenshot:

3. Select the policy to view its details. You can even choose to modify and test the policy here using the inbuilt *policy editor*, however do note that changes made to the policy here are not reflected in the actual policy.

4. With the policy selected, we are now ready to test it using the **IAM Policy Simulator** section. Here's a snippet of the policy that we are going to test:

```
{
    "Sid": "VisualEditor0",
    "Effect": "Allow",
    "Action": [
        "s3:PutObject",
        "s3:GetObject",
        "s3:ListBucket",
        "s3:DeleteObject"
    ],
    "Resource": [
        "arn:aws:s3:::useast-prod-stuff-01",
        "arn:aws:s3:::useast-prod-stuff-01/Dummy"
    ],
    "Condition": {
        "IpAddress": {
            "aws:SourceIp": "10.0.0.0/24"
        },
        "ForAllValues:StringEqualsIfExists": {
            "aws:username": "joe"
        }
    }
}
```

```
    . . . . . .

        "Resource": "*",
        "Condition": {
            "IpAddress": {
                "aws:SourceIp": "10.0.0.0/24"
            },
            "ForAllValues:StringEqualsIfExists": {
                "aws:username": "joe"
            }
        }
    }
```

As per our policy, only the user `joe` has the `s3:PutObject`, `s3:GetObject`, `s3:ListBucket`, `s3:DeleteObject` rights to the `useast-prod-stuff-01` bucket and that too if Joe is accessing the bucket from his organization's internal network (`10.0.0.0/24`).

5. To test the same, from the **Select service** drop-down list, select **Amazon S3** option. Next, match either of the actions using the **Select actions** drop-down list. In this case, I've only selected the `s3:PutObject` action.

6. Once completed, from the **Global Settings** section, type in the adjacent values against the *condition keys* that appear in the policy. In this case, type in the **username** and the **sourceip** as depicted in the following screenshot:

7. Next, from the **Action Settings and Results** section, expand on the **Resource** and type in the ARN of the resource against which the policy needs to be tested. In this case, this has to be the ARN of the S3 bucket **arn:aws:s3:::useast-prod-stuff-01**. Once done, select the **Run Simulation** option.

With the simulation running, you should get either *allowed* or *denied* results based on the values you provide during the simulation. Feel free to change the *actions* as well as the *condition keys* and re-run the simulation. With each attempt, you can fine tune and troubleshoot your policy without having to actually pass any real requests to your resources.

You can also use the same policy simulator to test out new policies that are not yet attached to resources. To do so, you will first need to toggle from the current (default) mode of **Existing policies** to **New Policy** using the **Mode** option provided at the very top of the simulator.

Once the **New Policy** option is selected, you can use the **Policy Sandbox** to create new policies and test them out the same way we did a while back. Remember, however, that policies created or edited here are not reflected back in AWS IAM.

With this, we come towards the end of this section. In the next section, we will be looking at how you can leverage AWS Organizations to effectively manage multiple AWS accounts with relative ease.

Introducing AWS Organizations

So far we have been working out of a single AWS account that we use for development, testing as well as for production purposes, but this isn't the case with many organizations who end up with multiple AWS accounts for a variety of purposes such as multiple environments, compliance issues, and so on. Each account gets governed and managed in its own way with no centralized ownership or control.

AWS Organizations is a simple service that allows you to consolidate and manage multiple such AWS accounts all under one roof. It enables you to group AWS accounts into one or more collective *organizations* that you can create and manage as a whole.

Here's a quick look at some of AWS Organizations key concepts and terminologies:

- **Organizations**: Organizations are consolidated views of all your AWS accounts in one place. Using organizations, you can centrally view and manage each of your AWS accounts under one roof. Organizations provide an additional functionality using which you can determine the type of organization you wish to create. There are two such feature sets, namely:

- **Consolidated billing**: A key feature provided by AWS Organizations is the ability to view and consolidate each AWS accounts billing under one organization. This feature is selected by default when you first create an organization and only provides you with the consolidated billing views. For leveraging all of the AWS Organizations advanced features, you will have to select the **All features** option.

- **All features**: This feature set provides the full functionality of AWS Organizations, including consolidated billing and many other features that provide you with better control over your individual accounts. Using this feature set, you can restrict certain AWS services from accounts; modify access roles, and much more.

- **Root**: The root is the primary container for all your individual accounts used within AWS. AWS Organizations automatically creates a default root element for you when you first create an organization. Any changes or policies applied at the root level propagate to its subsequent child elements as well.

- **Organizational Unit (OU)**: OUs are containers for one or more AWS accounts. You can branch multiple OUs from a single OU as well, however the end of an OU is always an account. Here is a representational diagram depicting the interactions between an organization, the root element, OUs, and various AWS accounts:

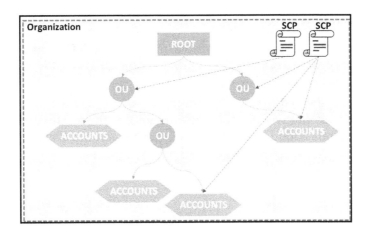

- **Accounts**: Accounts are standard AWS accounts that contain your AWS resources. When creating an organization, AWS marks the account from where the organization gets created as the *master account*. Any additional accounts added later to this organization are termed as *member accounts*. The master account is also responsible for overseeing the consolidated billing and payments for the rest member accounts as well as useful for inviting other AWS accounts into the organization, creating OUs, managing policies, and so on.
- **Service Control Policy** (**SCP**): SCPs are essentially policies that are attached to roots, accounts or OUs for specifying services and actions that the particular account's or OU's user can use. For example, you can use an SCP on an account that is created with HIPAA compliance in mind and you want to restrict all users of this account to use only HIPAA compliant AWS services, and so on.

 To know more about the HIPAA compliance and how it works along with AWS visit this URL to know more `https://aws.amazon.com/compliance/hipaa-compliance/`.

An important point to remember here is that SCPs only work when you have enabled the **All features** feature set while creating your organization.

With this basic information in hand, let us look at how you can get started with AWS Organizations using a few simple steps.

Getting started with AWS Organizations

AWS Organizations can be set up using both the AWS Management Console as well as the AWS CLI. In this section, we will be exploring simple steps using which you can get started with your own organization in a matter of minutes:

1. From the AWS Management Console, filter out **AWS Organizations** using the **Filter** option or alternatively navigating to this URL `https://console.aws.amazon.com/organizations/`.
2. Since this is the first time we are setting up an AWS Organization here, this particular account will now be transformed into the master account. Any other AWS accounts added or created to this master account will be termed as member accounts. Click on **Create organization** to get started.

3. At the time of creating an organization, you can opt to select either to **Enable all features** or **Enable only Consolidated Billing** based on your requirements. For this scenario, select **Enable all features** and click on **Create organization** once completed.

4. With the organization created, you should see your existing account listed on the accounts page as shown in the following screenshot. Select the **Add account** option to add a new AWS account to our organization:

5. As mentioned before, AWS Organizations allows you to add existing AWS accounts into a new organization as well as create new accounts as a part of your master account itself. For this particular scenario, let us go ahead and create a new account called **sandbox**. Select the **Create account** option on the **Add account** page.

6. Provide a suitable name and email address for your new account in the **Full name** and **Email** fields respectively. The email that you provide has to be globally unique so provide an email address that has not been used so far with AWS here.

7. Next, in the **IAM role name** filed, provide a suitable role name for your account. This role will enable you to access the new member account when signed in as an IAM user in the master account. Once completed, click on **Create** to complete the process.

Here is a snippet of the IAM Role that is created by AWS. The role grants full access to all AWS services and resources present in the new account:

```json
{
    "Version": "2012-10-17",
    "Statement": [
        {
            "Effect": "Allow",
            "Action": "*",
            "Resource": "*"
        }
    ]
}
```

The account creation process takes a few minutes to complete. Once done, you should see a new account created with the name **Sandbox** and a new **Account ID** as well in the **Accounts** page of AWS Organizations. Select the sandbox account to view its associated ARN and ID in the adjoining pane.

With your account created, the next step involves creation of one or more OUs and moving the newly created account into an OU. For this particular scenario, let us go ahead and create an OU called **Sandbox**:

1. Select the **Organize accounts** tab from the AWS Organizations dashboard to view the current hierarchical setup of the organization. From the **Organizational Units** section, select the **+ New Organization Unit** option to get started.

2. In the **Create organizational unit** dialog box, provide a suitable name for the new OU in the **Name of organization unit** field as shown in the following screenshot. Click on **Create organizational unit** once done:

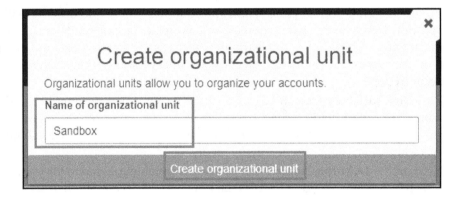

3. With the OU created, the final step in the process is to move the account into the newly created OU. To do so, from the same **Organize accounts** page, select the **Sandbox** account and click on **Move**.

4. This will bring up a simple interface using which you will need to select the new OU to which you want to move the **Sandbox** account. Select the **Sandbox** OU and click on **Move** to compete the process.

With this step, you should have a new OU and a new account listed within it. You can use the same steps to create multiple OUs and accounts based on your requirements and needs. You can additionally provide restricted access to the services present in your new account by creating and assigning a new SCP to it as well:

1. To create a new SCP, select the **Policies** tab on the AWS Organization dashboard. You should see a default policy with the name `FullAWSAccess` already present there. This is a default policy that is created by AWS the first time you create an AWS Organization. The sandbox environment too is currently referenced to the same policy.

2. To create a new SCP, select the **Create policy** option. AWS Organization provides you with two options when it comes to creating new SCPs. You can choose to leverage the **Policy generator** to select specific services and actions from a list and build your custom policy or alternatively, choose to **Copy an existing SCP** and edit the same manually. For this case, select the **Policy generator** option.

3. Next, provide a **Policy name** and **Description** followed by selecting the **Effect** the policy should have on the applied AWS account.

   AWS Organizations allows you to either whitelist (allow) or blacklist (deny) services based on your requirements. Blacklisting services will cause all services listed in the policy to be blocked by default, whereas whitelisting services will block all service APIs that are not listed in the policy. Let us go ahead and create a simple policy for our sandbox OU that allows EC2, S3, and RDS services while explicitly blocking AWS CloudTrail.

4. In the **Choose Overall Effect** section, select **Allow** to first create the whitelist of services. Use the **Statement builder** to select the correct service and its appropriate action as well. Once done, click on **Add statement** to add further services and actions as shown in the following screenshot:

5. Once you are done with adding the required statements, simply select the **Create policy** option to complete the process.

6. With the policy created, you can attach the same to an existing account, OU, or even root by simply selecting the policy from the **Policies** page and selecting either of the root, accounts, or organization units options as required. However, before you proceed further, you will first need to enable SCP policy types for your root account. To do so, select the **Root** option from the **Organize accounts** tab. In the adjoining details pane, select enable next to the **Service control policies** section.

7. With this completed, you can now proceed with attaching the newly created policy to an entity within your organization. Remember, by attaching the policy to the root domain, you effectively propagate the policy down to its members as well. This includes the sub OUs and accounts that you may have created. For this particular case however, select the **Accounts** option and click the **Attach** option below the listed **Sandbox** environment.

There you have it! A simple way using which you can create and manage your AWS accounts with utmost ease. Next, we will look at how you can achieve the same results by leveraging the AWS CLI as well.

Creating and managing AWS accounts, OUs and SCPs using the CLI has its own bit of advantages. For example, you can easily automate the entire account creation process and make it faster and easier to on-board new teams within your organization, and so on:

1. The first step involved in this exercise is to create the organization and set it to use all features, just as we performed with the AWS Management Console. To do so, type in the following command as shown:

   ```
   # aws organizations create-organization --feature-set ALL
   ```

    However this command may result in an error message for those of you who already have associated your AWS account with an organization.

   You can alternatively pass the CONSOLIDATED_BILLING value for the --feature-set parameter depending on your organization's requirements.

2. With the organization in place, let us go ahead and create an AWS account for our organization, but before we do that, we need to execute just one command that will provide us with the organization's root's ID. The ID will be in the form of r-<XY00>. Make a note of the same for later steps:

   ```
   # aws organizations list-roots
   ```

3. With the root ID noted type in the following command to create a new account. In this case, we are going to create a new account with the name of prod. Remember to substitute the <EMAIL_ID> field with a globally unique value:

   ```
   # aws organizations create-account
   --email <EMAIL_ID>
   --account-name prod
   ```

Here is a snapshot of the command's output. Make a note of the new account's status ID in the format `car-<UNIQUE_ID>` as shown in the following screenshot:

```
yoyo@YoYoNux:~$
yoyo@YoYoNux:~$ aws organizations create-account \
> --email y███████████ \
> --account-name prod
{
    "CreateAccountStatus": {
        "RequestedTimestamp": 1520255207.659,
        "State": "IN PROGRESS",
        "Id": "car-0f83b640207611e8bc03500c66ce5229",
        "AccountName": "prod"
    }
}
```

4. You can use this status ID to check whether the account creation has completed successfully or not by typing in the following command. Replace the `car-<UNIQUE_ID>` with the value copied from the earlier step:

   ```
   # aws organizations describe-create-account-status
   --create-account-request-id car-<UNIQUE_ID>
   ```

   You can view the newly created accounts ID by using the following command:
   `aws organizations list-accounts`

5. Once the new account is created, we can proceed to create a new OU and move the account over to the new OU. In this case, we are naming the new OU as `production`. Substitute the value of `r-<XY00>` with the root ID that we made a note of from our earlier steps:

   ```
   # aws organizations create-organizational-unit
   --parent-id r-<XY00>
   --name production
   ```

   The output of this command yields two important values, first is the ARN of the new OU and the second is the OU's ID which is in the form of `ou-<XY00>-<UNIQUE_ID>`. Make a note of the same for the next steps.

6. Now that the account and OU are created, we simply have to move the account into the new OU. To do so, type in the following command while substituting the correct values for the `account-id`, `parent-id`, and the `OU-id`:

```
# aws organizations move-account
--account-id <NEW_ACCOUNT_ID>
--source-parent-id r-<XY00>
--destination-parent-id ou-<XY00>-<UNIQUE_ID>
```

```
yoyo@YoYoNux:~$
yoyo@YoYoNux:~$ aws organizations move-account \
> --account-id                     \
> --source-parent-id r-            \
> --destination-parent-id ou-      -
yoyo@YoYoNux:~$
yoyo@YoYoNux:~$
```

That's it! You have just created a brand new AWS account and moved it into a new OU as well with a few simple commands! It's that easy! However, you can take things a bit further by creating a new SCP and attaching the same to our newly created OU. Let us assume for a moment that the particular OU that we have created can only allow certain AWS services to run as a part of the production environment. To do so, we first need to create a new SCP as shown in the following code block:

```
{
  "Version": "2012-10-17",
  "Statement": [{
    "Effect": "Allow",
    "Action": [
      "ec2:*",
      "rds:*",
      "dynamodb:*"
    ],
    "Resource": "*"
  }]
}
```

In this case, the SCP is whitelisting EC2, RDS, and DynamoDB however feel free to modify to suit your own requirements:

1. Paste the SQP into a new file named as `policy.json` and save it. Next, type in the following command to create it:

```
# aws organizations create-policy
--content file://policy.json
--name AllowProductionServices
--type SERVICE_CONTROL_POLICY
--description "This policy allows only certain production services"
```

2. With the policy created, you should receive a policy ID in the form of p-`<UNIQUE_ID>`. Make a note of the same. Next, use the following command to attach the newly created policy to our OU:

```
aws organizations attach-policy
--policy-id p-<UNIQUE_ID>
--target-id ou-<XY00>-<UNIQUE_ID>
```

That's it! You have just successfully attached a new policy to your OU. You can use the same syntax to attach the policy directly to each individual account as well.

7
Transforming Application Development Using the AWS Code Suite

In the previous chapter, we explored a few interesting and really useful enhancements made to the AWS **Identity and Access Management Service** (**IAM**) along with a quick deep dive into AWS Organizations as well.

In this chapter, we will be learning and exploring three extremely useful and powerful services provided by AWS that are specially catered toward enhancing a developer's experience with continuous code deployments: AWS CodeCommit, AWS CodeDeploy, and AWS CodePipeline!

Keeping this in mind, let's have a quick look at the various topics that we will be covering in this chapter:

- Introducing AWS CodeCommit, AWS CodeDeploy, and AWS CodePipeline along with each service's concepts and internal workings
- Creating your first CodeCommit repository and uploading an application to it
- Running basic Git commands against your new code repository
- Configuring the CodeDeploy agent on an EC2 instance
- Leveraging the AppSpec file for configuring application life cycle deployment
- Creating your own continuous delivery system using CodePipeline

So without any further ado, let's get started right away!

Understanding the AWS Code Suite

Besides providing a plethora of infrastructure-related services, AWS also provides a few services that are designed to help developers quickly design, develop, build, and deploy their applications on the AWS cloud platform. In this section, we will have a quick look at these services and how you can leverage them together to build your very own continuous integration and delivery pipelines:

- **AWS CodeCommit**: An important starting point for any CI/CD pipeline is a simple yet functional source control repository. Traditionally, this would be set up on one or more physical servers in the form a Git or SVN repository that developers would use to push their code and updates to; however, maintaining such code repositories and scaling them was always going to be a challenge. That's where AWS CodeCommit comes into play! AWS CodeCommit is a managed source control service that enables developers to securely store their code on the AWS cloud. It offers many of the features that you would require and use while working with different source control repositories, such as branching, commits, rollbacks, and much more.

- **AWS CodeBuild**: AWS CodeBuild is a code build service that developers can leverage to automate their source code compilations, tests, executions, and code packaging for deployments. Similar to its other counterpart services in the Code Suite, CodeBuild too is managed completely by AWS, thus eliminating any unnecessary administrative overheads, such as patching or scaling the code build software. CodeBuild is highly extensible and it also easily integrates with your existing CI/CD workflows as well.

- **AWS CodeDeploy**: With your application code stored securely and compiled, the final step requires the code to be deployed across your fleet of EC2 instances. This can be easily achieved with the help of our next Code Suite service, called AWS CodeDeploy. Using CodeDeploy, a developer can automate code deployments to any environment that runs off of either EC2 instances as well as servers that are running in an on-premise datacenter. CodeDeploy essentially eliminates deployment complexities by allowing you to automate the delivery of your code across thousands of instances without having to undergo any major downtimes.

- **AWS CodePipeline**: AWS CodePipeline is a full fledge CI/CD service provided by AWS that developers can leverage to build end-to-end CI/CD pipelines either by using the AWS Code Suite of services or even with other popular third-party tools, such as GitHub, Jenkins, and so on. Using CodePipeline, you can also create and define custom software release models using which your application gets updated with the latest set of updates, tested, and packaged as well for the next iterative set of deployments.

Here is a brief representation of how these services map together collaboratively to create a comprehensive CI/CD pipeline:

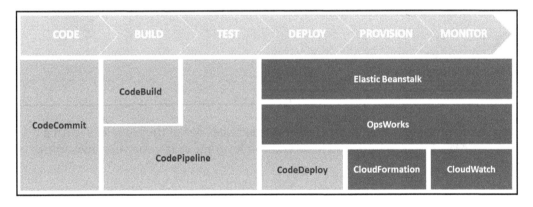

For the purpose of this chapter, however, we will be working with only three AWS Code Suite services, namely AWS **CodeCommit**, AWS **CodeDeploy**, and AWS **CodePipeline**. The chapter will showcase how these three services can be leveraged together to build your very own CI/CD pipelines for our sample WordPress application. Here is a high-level depiction of our overall use case:

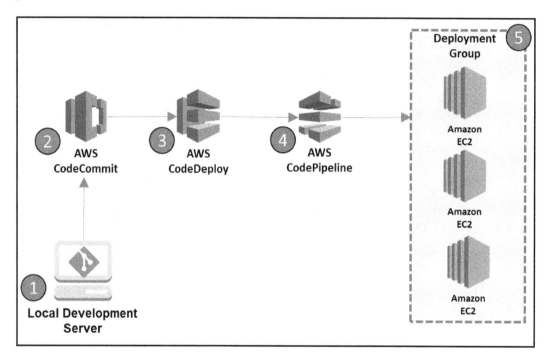

With the basic understanding of the Code Suite services out of the way, let's learn a bit more about AWS CodeCommit and how you can leverage it as your very own source code repository!

Getting Started with AWS CodeCommit

As discussed earlier, AWS CodeCommit is a secure and highly scalable source control service which allows you to create multiple private Git repositories without having to bother about any of the underlying management overheads. You can use it to store anything, from code, to application binaries, to even code packages, all using the standard Git-like functionality. This makes CodeCommit extremely easy to work with even if you have not used it before. Here is the gist of some of the most commonly used Git commands and how you can leverage them with CodeCommit:

- `git clone`: Used to clone and connect the AWS CodeCommit repository over to your local development server.
- `git add`: Once the repository is cloned locally, you can use it to add, edit, or delete files as you see fit. Once done, use the `git add` command to stage the modifications in your local Git repository.
- `git commit`: Used to commit the modifications made to the files to the local Git repository.
- `git push`: Used to push the committed files and changes over to the AWS CodeCommit repository.
- `git pull`: Used to ensure that the files you are working on are synced and are of the latest version from the AWS CodeCommit repository.

In this section, we will be looking at a few simple steps to enable you to create your very own source code repository using the AWS Management Console. However, before we move on to that, it is important to understand some of the different connections that you can use to connect to your CodeCommit repository. This can vary based on your development environments as well as security requirements:

- **Using the HTTPS connections**: Configuring Git credentials using HTTPS connections is by far the simplest and most widely used method for connecting to your Git repository. With this set up, you simply generate a static username and password using AWS IAM. Once the credentials are created, you can then use them with Git and any third-party tool, such as an IDE, for authentication.
- **Using the SSH connections**: In this case, a user will be required to create public and private key files on your local development server that Git and AWS CodeCommit can use for SSH authentication. The public key generated in this process gets associated with your IAM user, whereas the private key remains on the local development server. The generation of the keys varies from operating system to operating system and can be a tedious process at times to manage.

For this section, however, we will be leveraging the SSH connections method itself for connecting to our AWS CodeCommit repository:

1. To get started, first log in to your AWS Management Console and filter the IAM service using the **Filter** option provided. Alternatively, you can also select URL `https://console.aws.amazon.com/iam/` to view the IAM dashboard.

2. Here, we will start off by creating a dedicated user that will have full management rights to our CodeCommit repository. Select the **Users** option from the IAM dashboard's navigation pane to bring up the list of currently created IAM users.

3. Next, select the **Add user** option. This will bring up the **Add user** page where you can provide a suitable **User name** as well as opt for the user's **Access type**. In this case, the CodeCommit user will only require **Programmatic access**. Click **Next** to proceed.

4. Moving on, in the **Permissions** page, we are required to filter and attach the `AWSCodeCommitFullAccess` policy to our newly created user. To do so, select the **Attach existing policies directly** option and select the `AWSCodeCommitFullAccess` policy, as shown in the following screenshot. Alternatively, you can also provide a customized access policy here based on your requirements:

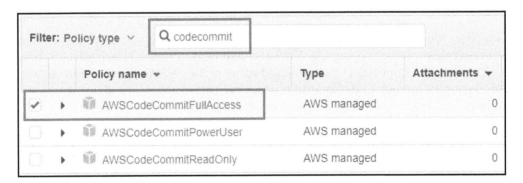

5. Complete the user creation process by reviewing the changes and making a note of the user's new access and secret keys as well.

At this point, with your CodeCommit IAM user created, we now move on to the next part of this section where we create and configure a set of public and private keys for the IAM user, using a simple Linux-based development server. Follow URL http://docs.aws. amazon.com/codecommit/latest/userguide/setting-up-ssh-windows.html if you are using a Windows operating system as your development server:

1. Log in to your development server and run the following command to generate the new set of keys:

   # **ssh-keygen**

2. When prompted, save the keys in the following directory structure:

   /home/<USER_NAME>/.ssh/<KEY_NAME>

Make a note of the public and private keys' locations, as depicted in the following screenshot:

```
yoyo@YoYoNux:~$
yoyo@YoYoNux:~$ ssh-keygen
Generating public/private rsa key pair.
Enter file in which to save the key (/home/yoyo/.ssh/id_rsa): /home/yoyo/.ssh/codecommitkey
Created directory '/home/yoyo/.ssh'.
Enter passphrase (empty for no passphrase):
Enter same passphrase again:
Your identification has been saved in /home/yoyo/.ssh/codecommitkey.
Your public key has been saved in /home/yoyo/.ssh/codecommitkey.pub.
```

3. Next, display and copy the public key's contents, using the following command. Note the public key will be saved in the file with a .pub extension:

   # **cat /home/<USER_NAME>/.ssh/<KEY_NAME>**

4. Log in to your IAM dashboard once again and select the newly created user from the **Users** page. Select the user's **Security Credentials** tab. Here, under the **SSH keys for AWS CodeCommit** section, click on **Upload SSH public key** to paste the entire copied text from the earlier step.

5. Once completed, you should now see a unique key auto-generated under the **SSH key ID** column, as shown in the following screenshot. Copy this SSH key ID as we will be requiring it in the next steps:

6. With the public key uploaded to IAM and the new SSH key ID generated, the final step is to create a simple `config` file in your local development server with the following contents pasted into it:

```
# vi ~/.ssh/config
##### SUBSTITUTE THE <VALUES> WITH YOUR ACTUAL ONES #####
    Host git-codecommit.*.amazonaws.com
      User <SSH_KEY_ID>
      IdentityFile ~/.ssh/<PRIVATE_KEY_FILENAME>
```

7. Save the file once done. Remember to modify the permissions of your `config` file before moving on to the verification step:

```
# chmod 600 config
```

8. To verify the connectivity, simply use the following command to SSH to the AWS CodeCommit endpoint. Since this will be a first connect, you will be prompted to verify the connection for authenticity. Type in `yes` when prompted:

```
# ssh git-codecommit.us-east-1.amazonaws.com
```

The endpoint you use will be specific to the AWS region that you operate out of. You can view the list of region-specific CodeCommit URLs along with the availability of the CodeCommit service at `http://docs.aws.amazon.com/codecommit/latest/userguide/regions.html`.

With this step, we have successfully validated and connected our development server with the AWS CodeCommit service! But where is our CodeCommit repository?

1. To create the repository, log in to the AWS CodeCommit service using URL `https://console.aws.amazon.com/codecommit`. Remember to change the **Region** based on what you selected during the key verification state.

2. Since this is our first time working with CodeCommit, select the **Get Started** option to begin with. This will display the **Create repository** page, as shown in the following screenshot:

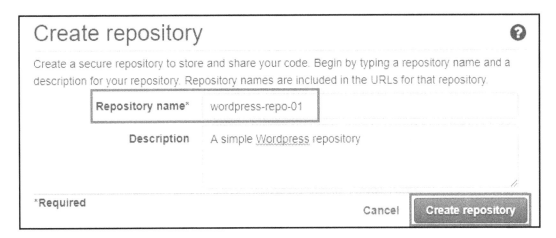

3. Provide a suitable **Repository name** and an optional **Description**. Click on **Create repository** once done.

4. You can additionally configure notifications for specific **Event types**, such as pull requests and commits made to your repo in the **Configure email notifications** page. Simply select an existing **SNS topic** or opt to **Create a new topic** based on your requirements. Once done, click on **Save** to complete the repository creation process.

With the repository created, you can now use the development server and connect to it using a simple `git clone` command. You can obtain your repository's connection URL anytime by simply selecting the **Connect** option present on the **Code** page:

```
# git clone
https://git-codecommit.us-east-1.amazonaws.com/v1/repos/<YOUR_CODECOMMIT_RE
PO>
```

Here's a snapshot of the first `git clone` command output:

```
yoyo@YoYoNux:~$
yoyo@YoYoNux:~$ git clone ssh://git-codecommit.us-east-1.amazonaws.com/v1/repos
/wordpress-repo-01
Cloning into 'wordpress-repo-01'...
Warning: Permanently added the RSA host key for IP address '54.239.20.155' to t
he list of known hosts.
warning: You appear to have cloned an empty repository.
Checking connectivity... done.
yoyo@YoYoNux:~$
yoyo@YoYoNux:~$
```

Since the repository is empty, the cloning process simply creates a folder with your repository's name on your development server. You can now use this folder as a code source control by simply adding your program files, binaries, and other application-specific data to it.

In the next section, we will be using this repository as our WordPress application source control and explore a few simple commands and features that are provided as a part of AWS CodeCommit.

Working with branches, commits, and triggers

With your CodeCommit repo created, it's now time to go ahead and use this repository as our source control repository. To do so, we will first push a standard WordPress application from our local development server to the AWS CodeCommit repository using simple Git commands and later run a few more Git commands as well as AWS actions to branch and commit our code.

 You can obtain a WordPress application ZIP file by downloading it from here:
`https://github.com/WordPress/WordPress`

To begin with, first we will need to copy the WordPress application contents over to our local repository that was cloned earlier:

1. Once the WordPress application is downloaded to your local development server, simply unzip and copy its contents over to the local repository. Your local repository should now show a folder structure similar to the following screenshot:

```
yoyo@YoYoNux:~/wordpress-repo-01$ tree -L 1
├── index.php
├── license.txt
├── readme.html
├── wp-activate.php
├── wp-admin
├── wp-blog-header.php
├── wp-comments-post.php
├── wp-config-sample.php
├── wp-content
├── wp-cron.php
├── wp-includes
├── wp-links-opml.php
├── wp-load.php
├── wp-login.php
├── wp-mail.php
├── wp-settings.php
├── wp-signup.php
├── wp-trackback.php
└── xmlrpc.php
```

2. With the code in place, simply use the following Git commands to commit and push the code over to your AWS CodeCommit repository. First up, stage the files using the git add command:

   ```
   # git add *
   ```

3. Next, commit the changes using the git commit command:

   ```
   # git commit -m "First Commit!!"
   ```

4. And, finally, push the commit over to the AWS CodeCommit repository. Here, the keyword origin is the default remote name used by Git for your AWS CodeCommit repository, whereas master is the default branch name:

   ```
   # git push -u origin master
   ```

5. You should see the code get uploaded to your AWS CodeCommit repository, as shown in the following image. You can cross-verify this by refreshing and checking the **Code** page on your AWS CodeCommit dashboard as well:

```
yoyo@YoYoNux:~/wordpress-repo-01$
yoyo@YoYoNux:~/wordpress-repo-01$ git push -u origin master
Counting objects: 1949, done.
Compressing objects: 100% (1921/1921), done.
Writing objects: 100% (1949/1949), 12.90 MiB | 471.00 KiB/s, done.0.00 KiB/s
Total 1949 (delta 248), reused 0 (delta 0)
To ssh://git-codecommit.us-east-1.amazonaws.com/v1/repos/wordpress-repo-01
 * [new branch]      master -> master
Branch master set up to track remote branch master from origin.
yoyo@YoYoNux:~/wordpress-repo-01$
yoyo@YoYoNux:~/wordpress-repo-01$
```

Similarly, you and your fellow developers can edit and commit the code back to the AWS CodeCommit repository. You can also create multiple branches of your repository so that developers can work independently on the code without affecting the master branch. Once the features are all thoroughly tested and verified, the individual developer branches can be merged into a more stable master branch of the software.

Creating a branch in CodeCommit is an extremely easy process! You can use the CodeCommit dashboard, the Git command line, or even the AWS CLI to create one of your own:

1. To create a branch using the AWS CodeCommit dashboard, simply select the **Branches** option from the navigation pane.
2. Next, select the **Create branch** option to bring up the **Create** branch page. Here, provide a suitable **Branch name** and also select where you would like this new branch to **Branch from**. In this case, since you only have the master branch created, you can select that for now. Click on **Create** once done.
3. You can also use the Git command line itself to achieve the same result. In this case, from the development server, type in the following command to create a new branch:

```
# git checkout -b <NEW_BRANCH_NAME>
```

```
yoyo@YoYoNux:~/wordpress-repo-01$
yoyo@YoYoNux:~/wordpress-repo-01$ git checkout -b dev-cli-09-12-2017
Switched to a new branch 'dev-cli-09-12-2017'
yoyo@YoYoNux:~/wordpress-repo-01$
```

With the new branch created, you can also use the **Compare** functionality provided by CodeCommit to compare the changes made to the branch against another branch. To do so, we first need to perform some changes in the application so that it can get reflected as a change.

Without changing the current branch of the repository, simply update any one of the WordPress files by adding or removing a comment. In my case, I simply made a few comment changes in the WordPress application's `index.php` file; however, feel free to modify any other file as you see fit. Once the changes are made, we once again need to stage, commit, and push the changes over to the new branch of our repository:

1. Stage the changes by using the `git add` command. You can either add all the files for staging by using * or even specify the filename you wish to stage as well:

   ```
   # git add *
   ```

2. Next, commit the changes using the `git commit` command:

   ```
   # git commit -m "<SOME_NEW_COMMIT_MESSAGE>"
   ```

3. And, finally, push the changes over to the branch using the following command:

   ```
   # git push origin <NEW_BRANCH_NAME>
   ```

4. With the changes pushed, use the **Compare** option provided under the **Commits** section in the CodeCommit dashboard. Here, select the **master** as the *source* branch and the branch that you created using the Git command line as the **Destination** branch. Click on **Compare** once done. You should see the changes compared, as shown in the following screenshot:

You can use the **Go to file** drop-down list to toggle between different files, if you have made changes in them. Alternatively, you can also use the **Unified** and **Split** views to change the visual comparison as you see fit.

CodeCommit also provides an additional feature called **triggers** that you can use to either send notifications to or run some other external code build or process. You can assign up to 10 triggers per repository that you create, however, at the time of writing this book, CodeCommit only supports AWS SNS and AWS Lambda as its trigger mechanisms:

1. To create a simple trigger, using the CodeCommit dashboard, select the **Settings** tab from the navigation pane. Here, select the **Triggers** tab to create as well as view the list of existing triggers, if any.

2. Select the **Create trigger** option to bring up the **Create trigger** page. Here, you can configure triggers in response to certain repository events, such as **Push to an existing branch**, **Create branch or tag**, **Delete branch or tag**, or **All repository events**.

3. Provide a **Trigger name** and select the appropriate **Events** and **Branch name** that you wish to associate the trigger with. Once done, you can configure the trigger to either use an existing SNS topic or a Lambda function as its **Service**. You can even test the functioning of the trigger by selecting the **Test trigger** option. This will simulate a trigger based on the *event* that you would have selected earlier.

In this way, you can configure triggers for sending notifications to your developers as well as trigger-specific Lambda functions based on your repository's requirements.

Introducing AWS CodeDeploy

With CodeCommit configured and ready to use for our WordPress application, we can now move on to yet another Code Suite service that can actually be used to deploy the code across thousands of EC2 instances! Here's introducing AWS CodeDeploy!

AWS CodeDeploy is basically a deployment service that allows you to automate the deployment of your applications to Amazon EC2 instances, Lambda functions, or even to on-premise instances. There is no limit to what an AWS CodeDeploy service can deploy. You can use it for deploying virtually anything from code, packages, binaries, scripts, files, and so on. As of writing this book, CodeDeploy only supports GitHub repositories and Amazon S3 buckets as the default application content repositories. Yes, you heard it right, CodeDeploy does not support CodeCommit as a repository source as of now.

Besides the automation, CodeDeploy also provides you with the following set of useful benefits. It allows you to:

- Quickly create new prototype software and deploy at scale without manual interventions
- Easily update to your application code without any downtime
- Rollback deployments in case of any errors
- Scale your deployment from one to a thousand instances, all without disrupting to your existing applications

In this section of the chapter, we will be looking at how to set up CodeDeploy for our own application deployments, but before we get into that, here's a quick look at some of CodeDeploy's essential concepts.

Concepts and terminologies

CodeDeploy essentially comprises two main configurable sections that can be broadly classified as deployments and applications. Here's a look at each of these concepts:

- **Applications:** Applications here imply simple names that are used by CodeDeploy to identify individual application codes targeted for specific deployments. An application can be deployed either on an EC2 instance, an on-premise instance, as well as on a serverless compute platform, such as AWS Lambda.
- **Deployments**: Deployments are a collection of deployment configurations and deployment types, including:
    - **Deployment configurations**: Deployment configurations are a set of simple rules that determine how fast an application will be deployed and the success or failure conditions for that particular deployment. For example, for an EC2 deployment, the configuration rules can dictate the required minimum number of healthy instances, whereas with a Lambda function deployment, these rules can be used to specify how the traffic is routed to the functions during a deployment.
    - **Deployment group**: This is a group of EC2 or on-premise instances that are either standalone or a part of an auto-scaling group. Since AWS Lambda is a managed service, it does not provide any deployment groups.

- **Deployment types**: Deployment types indicate the type of method used to get the latest version of your application deployed on a particular deployment group. There are two deployment types supported:
  - **In-place deployments**: In this case, the application running on each EC2 instance is stopped, updated, started, and verified. This form of deployment is only supported for EC2 and on-premise instances.
  - **Blue/green deployments**: In this scenario, the underlying instances are replaced by newer instances with the updated piece of code. The instances are registered to an **Elastic Load Balancer (ELB)** that routes traffic to the newer instances while the older instances can then be terminated. With the serverless platform, the traffic here too is shifted automatically by AWS from the current Lambda functions to the current updated ones. Note that all Lambda deployments are in fact blue/green deployments only.

- **CodeDeploy agent**: CodeDeploy agent is a simple software package that gets installed on either an EC2 or an on-premise instance and is used by CodeDeploy for setting up and working with application deployments. Once the agent is installed on an instance, an associated configuration file is created. This file contains application-specific directory paths and other settings that CodeDeploy uses to interact with the instances. The file is a simple YAML file and can be located in the following directories based on the instance's operating system:
  - **Amazon Linux, Ubuntu, RedHat Enterprise Linux**: `/etc/codedeploy-agent/conf/codedeployagent.yml`
  - **Windows Servers**: `C:ProgramDataAmazonCodeDeployconf.yml`

- **Application specification files**: Application specification files, or AppSpec files, are used to define and manage individual deployments as a series of life cycle event hooks. Each hook itself can be another file, such as a simple script to start or stop services, install dependencies, and so on. AppSpec files are supported in both JSON as well as YAML formats. At the time of the deployment, the AWS CodeDeploy agent looks up the name of the current event in the hooks section of the AppSpec file. If an event is found, the agent retrieves the list of scripts to execute and runs them sequentially in the order in which they were written in the AppSpec file.

With the basics out of the way, let's quickly look at how we can set up an EC2 instance to be used with CodeDeploy.

Installing and configuring the CodeDeploy agent

Before we begin with the actual launch of our EC2 instance with the CodeDeploy agent installed on it, we need to set up an EC2 instance profile as well as an instance role that will grant our EC2 instances the necessary permissions to interact with both CodeCommit as well as with CodeDeploy:

1. To get started, first log in to the AWS Management Console and select the **IAM** service from the services **Filter**. Alternatively, you can launch the IAM dashboard by selecting URL `https://console.aws.amazon.com/iam/`.

2. From the IAM dashboard, select the **Policies** option from the navigation pane to bring up the IAM **Policies** page. Here, click on **Create policy** to get started.

3. In the **Create policy** page, select the **JSON** tab and paste the following lines of the policy document:

```
{
    "Version": "2012-10-17",
    "Statement": [
        {
            "Action": [
                "ec2:Describe*",
                "sns:*",
                "codecommit:*",
                "codedeploy:*",
                "codepipeline:*",
                "codecommit:GetBranch",
                "codecommit:GetCommit",
                "codecommit:UploadArchive",
                "codecommit:GetUploadArchiveStatus",
                "codecommit:CancelUploadArchive",
                "s3:*"
            ],
            "Effect": "Allow",
            "Resource": "*"
        }
    ]
}
```

The policy document essentially provides the EC2 instance with the required set of permissions to interact with the likes of AWS services, such as CodeDeploy, CodeCommit, and CodePipeline.

4. Click on **Review policy** once done. In the final **Review policy** page, provide a suitable **Name** for the policy and click **Create policy** to complete the process.

5. With the policy created, we now simply assign this to a new IAM Role. To do so, select the **Roles** option from the navigation pane to bring up the IAM **Roles** page.

6. Click on **Create role** to start the wizard. From the **Select type of trusted entity** section, make sure you select **AWS service** and filter out **EC2** from there. Click on **Next: Permissions** to proceed.

7. In the **Attach permissions policy** page, filter the earlier created policy and attach it to our new role, as depicted in the following screenshot:

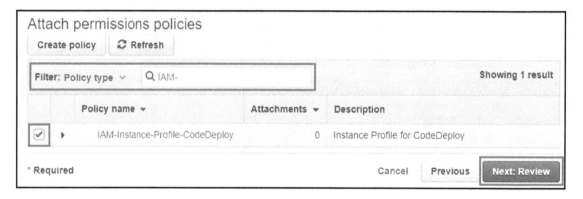

8. Finally, at the **Review** page, provide your role with a suitable **Role Name** and click on **Create role** to complete the process.

9. Before launching your EC2 instance with this newly created Role, ensure that the role's **Trust Relationship** has the following set of AWS services added in its policy document:

```
{
    "Version": "2012-10-17",
    "Statement": [
        {
            "Sid": "",
            "Effect": "Allow",
            "Principal": {
                "Service": [
                    "codecommit.us-east-1.amazonaws.com",
                    "ec2.amazonaws.com",
                    "codedeploy.us-east-1.amazonaws.com",
```

```
            "codepipeline.us-east-1.amazonaws.com"
        ]
    },
    "Action": "sts:AssumeRole"
  }
 ]
}
```

With this step completed, we are now ready to launch a simple EC2 instance and assign the newly created role:

1. From the EC2 Management Console, select the **Launch Instance** option to get started. For this particular use case, I've opted to go for the standard **Amazon Linux** AMI (`amzn-ami-hvm-2017.09.1.20171120-x86_64-gp2 - ami-55ef662f`); however, you can very well opt for a different Linux OS distribution as per your requirements.

2. Select an appropriate **Instance type** for hosting our simple WordPress application. For now, I've selected the **t2.micro** instance type itself.

3. Next, in the **Configure Instance Details** page, select the appropriate **Network**, **Subnet**, and **IAM Role** for our new EC2 instance. Paste the following set of lines as **User data** under the **Advanced Details** section, as shown in the following code. This simple user data script will copy and install the CodeDeploy agent along with a few other essential dependencies. You can find the complete copy of the following code at `https://github.com/yoyoclouds/Administering-AWS-Volume2`:

```
#!/bin/bash
yum -y update
yum install -y ruby
yum install -y aws-cli
cd /home/ec2-user
aws s3 cp s3://aws-codedeploy-us-east-1/latest/install . --region us-east-1
chmod +x ./install
./install auto
```

 Remember to change the `region` parameter as per your current operational region value.

4. Once the required storage is assigned to the instance, move on and assign a few essential tags for our EC2 instance. These tags will be used later in CodeDeploy to reference our EC2 instances, so make a note of the same.

5. Finally, create a new security group and make sure that the ports 22 (SSH) and 80 (HTTP) are open for internet traffic.

6. Review the settings of your instance and launch it. Additionally, remember to associate your instance with a key pair as well before you launch it, as it can be useful to verify or troubleshoot the AWS CodeDeploy agent.

With this, you now have successfully launched and set up a CodeDeploy agent on an EC2 instance. In the next section of this chapter, we will look at how you can take this installation further by configuring the AppSpec file for the final CodeDeploy deployment.

Setting up the AppSpec file

As mentioned earlier, the AppSpec, or the application specifications file, is basically a YAML or JSON backed file used to define life cycle hooks for a particular deployment. In this case, with our EC2 instance prepped and ready with the CodeDeploy agent, we still need the AppSpec file to define a set of dependencies that will essentially install the necessary packages on the EC2 instance, start or stop the services, change permissions, and much more.

The AppSpec file comprises the following sections:

- **Version**: The version of the AppSpec file. Currently, the version number supported with CodeDeploy is 0.0. Do not change this value.
- **OS**: Specifies the operating system of the underlying EC2/on-premise instance.
- **Files**: Specifies the files that need to be copied on the instance at the time of the deployment process. You can additionally specify a source and a destination folder as well for your applications here.
- **Hooks**: Hooks essentially specify when a particular deployment life cycle has to be triggered. There are four main types of hooks: BeforeInstall, AfterInstall, ApplicationStart, and ApplicationStop. Each hook further requires additional parameters, such as the location of the scripts to execute, a timeout value, and how the scripts should be runas.

Here is a representation of a simple AppSpec file for our WordPress deployment. Since we are using the Amazon Linux-backed instance, the os value is set to linux along with other essential parameters, such as files and hooks. Note in our case, we are configuring the WordPress application files to be copied from their default location over to /var/www/html/WordPress as well:

```
version: 0.0
os: linux
files:
  - source: /
    destination: /var/www/html/WordPress
hooks:
  BeforeInstall:
    - location: scripts/install_dependencies.sh
      timeout: 300
      runas: root
  AfterInstall:
    - location: scripts/change_permissions.sh
      timeout: 300
      runas: root
  ApplicationStart:
    - location: scripts/start_server.sh
      timeout: 300
      runas: root
  ApplicationStop:
    - location: scripts/stop_server.sh
      timeout: 300
      runas: root
```

To create this file, login to your development server and not your CodeDeploy instance. Once logged into the development server, open the WordPress application directory that we used during the CodeCommit sections of this chapter. This is the same directory that we used to sync with our master CodeCommit repository as well:

1. Here, at the application's root directory, create a blank appspec.yml, and copy-paste the appspec contents explained earlier:

   ```
   # vi appspec.yml
   ```

2. With the AppSpec file created, we now move on to create the individual files for the life cycle hooks. To do so, create a folder named scripts within the WordPress application directory and create each of these individual shell scripts within it:

   ```
   # mkdir scripts
   ```

3. Create the `install_dependencies.sh` script that will essentially install the necessary packages required to run WordPress on an instance:

```
# vi scripts/install_dependencies.sh
#!/bin/bash
sudo yum install -y httpd mysql mysql-server php
sudo yum install -y php-mysql
```

4. Similarly, create the `change_permissions.sh` script that modifies the permissions of the files present in the scripts folder to *executable*:

```
# vi scripts/change_permissions.sh
#!/bin/bash
chmod -R 755 /var/www/html/WordPress
```

5. And, finally, create the `start_server.sh` and the `stop_server.sh` scripts that will start and stop the `httpd` and `mysql` services on the deployment EC2 instances:

```
# vi scripts/start_server.sh
#!/bin/bash
service httpd start
service mysqld start

# vi scripts/stop_server.sh
#!/bin/bash
isExistApp=`pgrep httpd`
if [[ -n  $isExistApp ]]; then
    service httpd stop
fi
isExistApp=`pgrep mysqld`
if [[ -n  $isExistApp ]]; then
    service mysqld stop
fi
```

Got this far? Awesome! We are almost done with the AppSpec files, with just one small step left: uploading these changes to our CodeCommit repository!

To do so, run the following set of commands from the deployment server:

```
# git add *
# git commit -m "Added scripts directory with AppSpec file!"
# git push -u origin <NEW_BRANCH_NAME>
```

Et voila! The WordPress application and our deployment scripts are all uploaded to our CodeCommit branch and ready for deployment! In the next section, we will create and configure an application and deployment group for our CodeDeploy.

Creating a CodeDeploy application and deployment group

With our AppSpec file and scripts in place and the EC2 instance set up with the CodeDeploy agent as well, the final thing left is to configure AWS CodeDeploy and tie these things together:

1. Start off by logging into the AWS CodeDeploy service by selecting URL `https://console.aws.amazon.com/codedeploy/home`.

2. Since this is the first time we are using CodeDeploy, select the **Get Started Now** option. Here, you will be prompted to select either a **Sample deployment** that deploys a sample application on the EC2 instances or, alternatively, go for a **Custom deployment** if you have your code and EC2 instances up and running. In this case, we will select the **Custom deployment** option itself.

3. In the **Create application** page, start off by providing a suitable **Application name**, **Compute Platform**, and a **Deployment group name**. Remember to select the **EC2/On-premises** option from the **Compute Platform**, as shown in the following screenshot:

4. Next, in the **Deployment type** section, choose the **In-place deployment** option for now. This will enable CodeDeploy to update the existing instances with the revised set of application code with some amount of downtime.

5. In the **Environment configuration** section, you can specify any combination of **Auto Scaling groups**, **Amazon EC2 instances**, and **On-premises instances** to add instances to this deployment group. Since we have created an EC2 instance in our earlier steps with the CodeDeploy agent installed in it, select the **Amazon EC2 instances** tab. From the **Tag group** drop-down, select the instance's **Key** and **Value**, as shown.

Note that these are the same tags that you would have configured to your instance before its launch in our earlier sections:

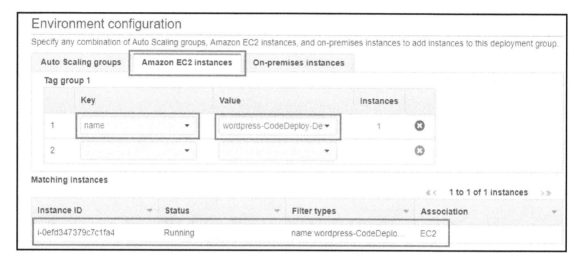

6. Moving on, in the **Deployment configuration** section, you can choose from a list of default and custom deployment configurations. As discussed earlier, a deployment configuration is a set of rules that determines how fast an application will be deployed along with the definition of success or failure conditions for a particular deployment.

There are three default configurations provided by AWS CodeDeploy itself:

- **OneAtATime**: Routes traffic to one instance in the replacement environment at a time
- **HalfAtATime**: Routes traffic to up to half the instances in the replacement environment at a time

- **AllAtOnce**: Routes traffic to all instances in the replacement environment all at once

    Since we are working with just a single EC2 instance as of now, go ahead and select the **OneAtATime** deployment configuration option.

7. Finally, select the IAM Role that we created and assigned our EC2 instance to at the time of launching, using the **Service Role** drop-down list. Once done, select the **Create application** option to complete the process!

There you have it! If you made it this far then you have successfully configured both AWS CodeCommit and AWS CodeDeploy for our WordPress application's deployment! But we are still missing the glue that ties all these services together, and that precisely is what we will be talking about in the next section with the introduction of AWS CodePipeline!

Introducing AWS CodePipeline

AWS CodePipeline is a continuous delivery service that you can use to model, visualize, and automate the steps required to release your application software. This is made possible by building *pipelines* that contain one or more *stages*. The stages can be broadly classified as *build*, where the code is compiled and built using, say, AWS CodeBuild or some other third-party tool, *staging*, and *deployment*, where the code is pushed on to compute instances using AWS CodeDeploy, and so on. Each stage internally describes a set of actions that it needs to perform in order to prepare the software for its release. This action can be anything from building your source code from a Git repository, to making changes to a file, or deploying packages, and so on. Every change made to either your code or some configurational setting within CodePipeline is considered as a *revision* and you can have multiple such revisions created within a single stage of a pipeline.

 Even changes made to a single stage within the pipeline results in all actions across all stages being re-executed.

You can use these features provided by CodePipeline to effectively manage and monitor the release of your software. In this section, we will be continuing with our use case set up earlier using CodeCommit and CodeDeploy and see how we can truly build an end-to-end continuous delivery cycle using AWS CodePipeline.

Creating your own continuous delivery pipeline

Getting started with CodePipeline is extremely easy provided you have all the necessary prerequisites met, which include setting up the CodeCommit repository with your latest piece of application code (in this case, the WordPress application), as well as configuring the application and the AppSpec file using CodeDeploy:

1. To begin with, launch the CodePipeline Management dashboard by selecting URL `https://console.aws.amazon.com/codepipeline/home`.

2. Since this is our first setup, click on the **Get Started** option to get going. This will bring up the **Getting started with AWS CodePipeline** wizard, as shown in the following screenshot. Start off by providing a suitable **Pipeline name** and click **Next step** to continue:

3. Next, in the **Source** page, we need to select and configure the source for our new pipeline. At the time of writing this book, CodePipeline supports three source code providers, namely Amazon S3, AWS CodeCommit, and GitHub. For the purpose of this use case, go ahead and select **AWS CodeCommit** from the **Source** drop-down list.

4. This will automatically prompt you to enter the subsequent CodeCommit **Repository name** as well as its corresponding **Branch name**. Make sure you provide the same branch name that contains the latest WordPress code as well as the AppSpec file. Click on **Next step** to continue.

5. The third stage of the Pipeline setup is the **Build** stage where you can specify the build provider. CodePipeline supports three build providers, namely AWS CodeBuild, Jenkins, and Solano CI. Since our WordPress installation doesn't require any compilations or build procedures, simply select the **No Build** option from the drop-down list and click on **Next step** to continue.

6. The fourth state requires the **Deployment** configurations to be set up for the pipeline. Here too you are provided with various options that you can choose to leverage based on your needs. At present, CodePipeline supports AWS Opsworks, AWS CodeDeploy, AWS CloudFormation, and AWS Elastic Beanstalk as the **Deployment providers**. Since we have already configured AWS CodeDeploy for our use case, select the same from the drop-down list.

7. Next, fill in the correct **Application name** as well as the **Deployment group** that we configured during the setup of CodeDeploy. Click on **Next step** once done:

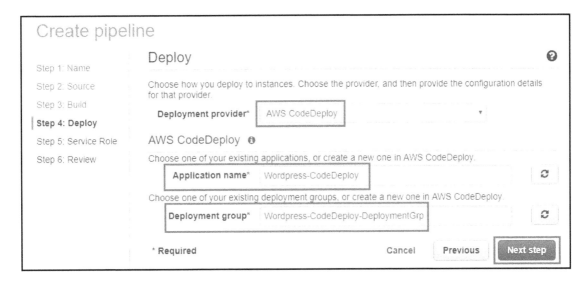

8. The final step required is to configure the **Service Role**. The service role essentially grants CodePipeline permissions to use resources in your AWS account. Provide a suitable **Role name** and click on **Next step** to review the pipeline's configuration.

9. On the **Review your pipeline** page, ensure that all the fields are correctly configured and click on **Create pipeline** when done.

Selecting this option first creates a unique S3 bucket within your environment that will contain and store all the necessary artifacts for this particular pipeline. Once the pipeline is created, you can view it on the AWS CodePipeline dashboard.

Putting it all together

With the pipeline all set up, you can now test the entire setup as one cohesive solution!

First up, ensure that there are no errors in either of the stages during the deployments. In case there are any errors, simply select the particular error link provided in the stage and follow it back to its source, which can be anywhere from issues in CodeCommit to even the setting up of CodeDeploy. Here's a screenshot of the pipeline that we created using an accumulation of all of the preceding sections:

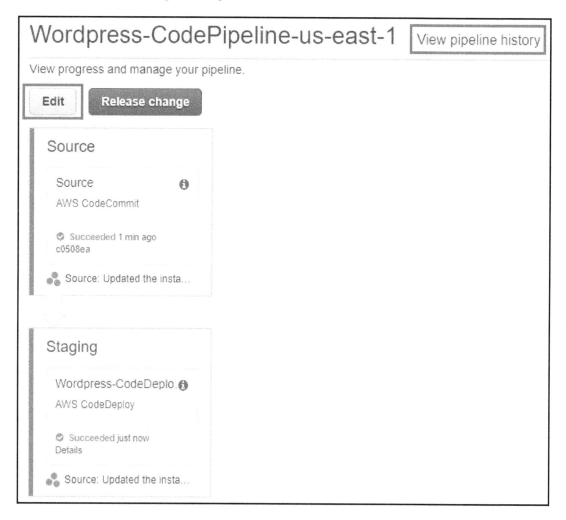

Here, you can choose to add more stages to your pipeline by simply selecting the **Edit** option, as highlighted earlier. Additionally, you can also view your pipeline's execution history by selecting the **View pipeline history** option.

In the **Edit** pipeline page, you can choose to add one or more stages to your pipeline as you see fit. Simply select the **+ Stage** option provided at the end of each existing stage. This will bring up a new dialog where you can specify the stage's **Name** as well as define one or more actions.

Consider the following use case where we need to add an approval step before the code actually gets pushed into the staging area. In that case, we need to add a new stage between the existing **Source** and **Staging** stages:

1. Click on the **+ Stage** option and provide a suitable name for this new stage. Next, select the **+ Action** option to add the rules for setting up the approval process.

2. In the **Add action** dialog box, start by selecting the type of action from the **Action category** drop-down list. The following list of actions can be added to a stage: **Approval**, **Source**, **Build**, **Test**, **Deploy**, and **Invoke**. For this use case, select **Approval**:

3. Fill in a suitable **Action name** and select an appropriate **Action type** as well. At present, only a **Manual approval configuration** option is provided by CodePipeline.

4. Finally, select either one of a pre-existing SNS topics using the **SNS topic ARN** field and click on **Add action** once completed.

5. With the new stage added, click on **Save pipeline changes** to commit the change. You should have a new stage added and visible in your pipeline, as shown in the following screenshot:

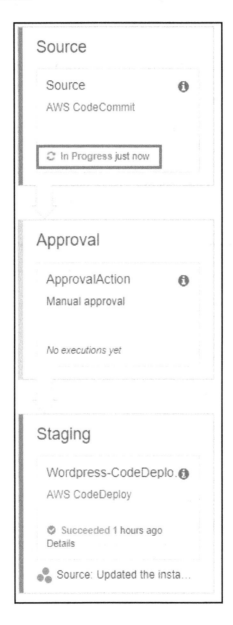

6. Once the **Source** stage is prepped, the pipeline automatically halts at the **Approval** stage, as depicted in the following screenshot. Here, you can approve the process by simply selecting the **Review** option and then selecting the `approval` command. Doing so initiates the final **Staging** stage which invokes the CodeDeploy service to deploy the WordPress code over to our awaiting EC2 instance:

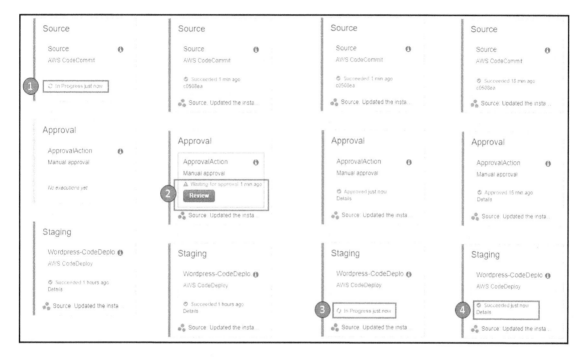

After a few minutes, the application is successfully uploaded on the instance and is up and running as well. You can verify this by making a note of your instances public IP address and typing in the following URL on a browser:

```
http:///WordPress/wp-admin/index.php
```

Remember to prefix `WordPress` in your URL since the `AppSpec` file clearly pointed to the root of the application at the `/var/www/html/WordPress` directory and not at `/var/www/html` itself.

In this way, you can easily leverage and automate the deployments of your application code using the AWS Code Suite of services! Amazing isn't it?

8
Powering Analytics Using Amazon EMR and Amazon Redshift

In this chapter, we will be turning things up a notch and exploring two amazingly powerful AWS services that are ideal for processing and running large-scale analytics and data warehousing in the cloud: Amazon EMR and Amazon Redshift.

Keeping this in mind, let's have a quick look at the various topics that we will be covering in this chapter:

- Understanding the AWS analytics suite of services with an in-depth look at Amazon EMR, along with its use cases and benefits
- Introducing a few key EMR concepts and terminologies, along with a quick getting started tour
- Running a sample workload on EMR, using steps
- Introducing Amazon Redshift
- Getting started with an Amazon Redshift cluster
- Working with Redshift databases and tables
- Loading data from Amazon EMR into Amazon Redshift

So without any further ado, let's get started right away!

Understanding the AWS analytics suite of services

With the growth of big data and its adoption across organizations on the rise, many cloud providers today provide a plethora of services that are specifically designed to run massive computations and analytics on large volumes of data. AWS is one such cloud provider that also has invested a lot into the big data and analytics paradigm with a host of services offering ready-to-use frameworks, business insights and data warehousing solutions, as well. Here is a brief explanation of the AWS analytics suite of services:

- **Amazon EMR**: Amazon **Elastic MapReduce** or **EMR** is a quick and easy to use service that provides users with a scalable, managed Hadoop ecosystem and framework. You can leverage EMR to process vast amounts of data without having to worry about configuring the underlying Hadoop platform. We will be learning and exploring more on EMR in the subsequent sections of this chapter.

- **Amazon Athena**: Amazon Athena takes big data processing up a notch by providing a standard SQL interface for querying data that is stored directly on Amazon S3. With Athena, you do not have any underlying hardware to manage or maintain; it is all managed by AWS itself. This *serverless* approach makes Athena ideal for processing data that does not require any complex ETL processing. All you need to do is create a schema, point Athena to your data on Amazon S3, and start querying it using simple SQL syntax.

- **Amazon Elasticsearch Service**: Amazon Elasticsearch Service provides a managed deployment of the popular open source search and analytics engine: Elasticsearch. This service comes in really handy when you wish to process streams of data originating from various sources such as logs generated from instances, and so on.

- **Amazon Kinesis**: Unlike the other services discussed so far, Amazon Kinesis is more of a streaming service provided by AWS. You can use Amazon Kinesis to push vast amounts of data originating from multiple sources, into one or more streams that can be consumed by other AWS services for performing analytics and other data processing processes.

- **Amazon QuickSight**: Amazon QuickSight is an extremely cost-effective business insights solution that can be used to perform fast ad hoc analysis on data.

- **Amazon Redshift**: Amazon Redshift is a petabyte-scale data warehousing solution provided by AWS that you can leverage for analyzing your data, using an existing set of tools. We will be learning more about Redshift a bit later during this chapter. The services are depicted here:

COLLECT	MOVE	STORE	ANALYZE
AWS Snowball	AWS Data Pipeline	Amazon S3	Amazon EMR / Amazon Athena
Amazon Kinesis	Amazon Kinesis	Amazon EFS	Amazon ES / AWS Glue
		Amazon DynamoDB	Amazon Redshift
			Amazon QuickSight

- **AWS Data Pipeline:** Moving large amounts of data between AWS services can be difficult to perform, especially when the data sources vary. AWS Data Pipeline makes it easier to transfer data between different AWS storage and compute services, as well as helping in the initial transformation and processing of data. You can even use Data Pipeline to transfer data reliably from an on-premise location into AWS storage services, as well.
- **AWS Glue**: AWS Glue is a managed **ETL** (**Extract**, **Transform** and **Load**) service recently launched by AWS. Using AWS Glue greatly simplifies the process of preparing, extracting, and loading data from large datasets into an AWS storage service.

With this brief overview of the AWS analytics suite of services, let's now move forward and get started with understanding a bit more about Amazon EMR!

Introducing Amazon EMR

As mentioned earlier, Amazon EMR is a managed service that provides big data analytics frameworks, such as Apache Hadoop and Apache Spark straight out of the box and ready for use. Using Amazon EMR, you can easily perform a variety of use cases such as batch processing, big data analytics, low-latency querying, data streaming, or even use EMR as a large datastore itself!

With Amazon EMR, there is very little underlying infrastructure to manage on your part. You simply have to decide the number of instances you initially want to run your EMR cluster on and start consuming the framework for analytics and processing. Amazon EMR provides you with features that enable you to scale your infrastructure based on your requirements, without affecting the existing setups. Here is a brief look at some of the benefits that you can obtain by leveraging Amazon EMR for your own workloads:

- **Pricing**: Amazon EMR relies on EC2 instances to spin up your Apache Hadoop or Apache Spark clusters. Although you can vary costs by selecting the instance types for your cluster from large to extra large and so on, the best part of EMR is that you can also opt between using a combination of on-demand EC2 instances, reserved and spot instances based on your setup, thus providing you with flexibility at significantly lower costs.
- **Scalability**: Amazon EMR provides you with a simple way of scaling running workloads, depending on their processing requirements. You can resize your cluster or its individual components as you see fit and additionally, configure one or more instance groups for a guaranteed instance availability and processing.
- **Reliability**: Although you, as an end user, have to specify the initial instances and their sizes, AWS ultimately ensures the reliability of the cluster by swapping out instances that either have failed or are going to in the due course of time.
- **Integration**: Amazon EMR integrates with the likes of other AWS services to provide your cluster with additional storage, network, and security requirements. You can use services such as Amazon S3 to store both the input as well as the output data, AWS CloudTrail for auditing the requests made to EMR, VPC to ensure the security of your launched EMR instances and much more!

With these details in mind, let's move an inch closer to launching our very own EMR cluster by first visiting some of its key concepts and terminologies.

Concepts and terminologies

Before we get started with Amazon EMR, it is important to understand some of its key concepts and terminologies, starting out with clusters and nodes:

- **Clusters**: Clusters are the core functioning component in Amazon EMR. A cluster is a group of EC2 instances that together can be used to process your workloads. Each instance within a cluster is termed as a node and each node has a different role to perform within the cluster.

- **Nodes**: Amazon EMR distinguishes between clusters instances by providing them with one of these three roles:
    - **Master node**: An instance that is responsible for the overall manageability, working and monitoring of your cluster. The *master node* takes care of all the data and task distributions that occur within the cluster.
    - **Core node**: The core nodes are very similar to the master node; however, they are primarily used to run tasks and store data on your **Hadoop Distributed File System** (**HDFS**). The core node can also contain some additional software components of Hadoop applications within itself.
    - **Task node**: Task nodes are only designed to run tasks. They do not contain any additional software components of Hadoop applications within themselves and are optional when it comes to the cluster's deployment.

- **Steps**: Steps are simple tasks or jobs that are submitted to a cluster for processing. Each step contains some instructions on how the particular job is to be performed. Steps can be ordered such that a particular step can be used to fetch the input data from Amazon S3, while a second step can be used to run a Pig or Hive query against it, and finally a third step to store output data to say Amazon DynamoDB. If one step fails, the subsequent steps are automatically cancelled from execution, however, you can choose to overwrite this behavior by selecting your steps to ignore failures and process further.

Apart from these concepts, you will additionally be required to brush up on your Apache Hadoop framework and terminologies, as well. Here's a quick look at some of the Apache frameworks and applications that you will come across while working with Amazon EMR:

- **Storage**: A big part of EMR is how the data is actually stored and retrieved. The following are some of the storage options that are provided to you while using Amazon EMR:
  - **Hadoop Distributed File System (HDFS)**: As the name suggests, HDFS is a distributed and scalable filesystem that allows data to be stored across the underlying node instances. By default, the data is duplicated and stored across the instances present in the cluster. This provides high availability and data resiliency in case of an instance failure. You can read more about HDFS at: `https://hadoop.apache.org/docs/stable/hadoop-project-dist/hadoop-hdfs/HdfsUserGuide.html`.
  - **EMR File System (EMRFS)**: EMRFS is an extension of the HDFS filesystem, using which you can access and store data directly on Amazon S3, just as a normal filesystem.
  - **Local filesystem**: Apart from HDFS, each instance within the cluster is also provided with a small block of pre-attached ephemeral disks which is also called the local filesystem. You can use this local filesystem to store additional software or applications required by your Hadoop frameworks.
- **Frameworks**: As mentioned before, Amazon EMR provides two data processing frameworks that you can leverage based on your processing needs: Apache Hadoop MapReduce and Apache Spark:
  - **Apache Hadoop MapReduce**: MapReduce is by far the most commonly used and widely known programming model when it comes to building distributed applications. The open source model relies on a `Mapper` function that maps the data to sets of key-value pairs and a `Reducer` function that combines these key-value pairs, applies some additional processing, and finally generates the desired output. To know more about MapReduce and how you can leverage it, check out this URL: `https://hadoop.apache.org/docs/r1.2.1/mapred_tutorial.html`.

- **Apache Spark**: Apache Spark is a fast, in-memory data processing model using which a developer can process streaming, machine learning or SQL workloads that require fast iterative access to datasets. It is a cluster framework similar to Apache Hadoop; however, Spark leverages graphs and in-memory databases for accessing your data. You can read more about Spark at `https://spark.apache.org/`.

- **Applications and programs**: With the standard data processing framework, Amazon EMR also provides you with additional applications and programs that you can leverage to build native distributed applications. Here's a quick look into a couple of them:

  - **YARN: Yet Another Resource Negotiator**, is a part of the Hadoop framework and provides management for your cluster's data resources

  - **Hive**: Hive is a distributed data warehousing application that leverages standard SQL to query extremely large datasets stored on the HDFS filesystem.

There are yet many other applications and programs made available for use by Amazon EMR, such as Apache Pig, Apache HBase, Apache Zookeeper, and so on. In the next section, we will be looking at how to leverage these concepts and terminologies to create our very own Amazon EMR Cluster, so let's get busy!

Getting started with Amazon EMR

With the basics covered, in this section we will be working with the Amazon EMR dashboard to create our very first cluster. However, before we get going, here's a small list of prerequisite steps that we need to complete first.

To begin with, we will need to create an Amazon S3 bucket that will be used to store the output, logs generated by EMR, as well as some additional script and software files:

1. From the AWS Management Console, filter and select the **Amazon S3** service by using the **Filter** option. Alternatively, launch the Amazon S3 dashboard by navigating to this URL: `https://s3.console.aws.amazon.com/s3/`.

2. Next, select the **Create bucket** option. In the **Create bucket** wizard, provide a suitable **Bucket name** followed by the selection of an appropriate **Region** to create the bucket in. For this use case, the EMR cluster, as well as the S3 buckets, are created in the **US East (Ohio)** region, however you can select an alternative based on your requirements. Click on **Next** to continue with the process.

3. On the **Set properties** page, you can optionally choose to provide some *tags* for your bucket for cost allocations and tracking purposes. Click **Next** to continue.

4. In the **Set permissions** page, ensure that the no public read access is granted to the bucket. Click on **Next** to review the settings and finally, select **Create bucket** to complete the process.

5. Once the bucket is created, use the **Create folder** option to create dedicated folders for storing the logs, output, as well as some additional scripts that we might use in the near future. Here is a representational screenshot of the bucket after you have completed all of the previous steps:

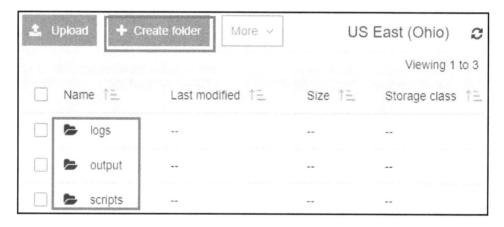

6. With the bucket created and ready for use, the next prerequisite item left to create is a key pair using which you can SSH into your EC2 instances. Ensure that the key pair is created in the same region (**US East (Ohio)** in this case) as your EMR cluster.

Now that the prerequisites are out of the way, we can finally get started with our EMR cluster setup!

1. From the AWS Management Console, filter and select the **Amazon EMR** service by using the **Filter** option. Alternatively, launch the Amazon EMR dashboard by selecting this URL: `https://us-east-2.console.aws.amazon.com/elasticmapreduce/home`.

2. Since this is the first time we've created an EMR cluster, select the **Create cluster** option to get started.

3. You can configure your EMR cluster using two ways: a fast and easy **Quick Options** which is shown to you by default, and an **Advanced options** page where you can select and configure the individual items for your cluster. In this case, we will go ahead and select **Go to advanced options**.

4. The Advanced options page provides us with a four-step wizard that essentially guides us to configuring a fully functional EMR cluster. To begin with, the first step is where you can select and customize the *software* that you wish to install on your EMR cluster.

5. From the **Release** drop-down list, select the appropriate EMR release that you would like to work with. The latest version released as of writing this book is `emr-5.11.1`. Each release contains several distributed applications available for installation on your cluster. For example, selecting emr-5.11.1 which is a 2018 release, contains Hadoop v2.7.3, Flink v1.3.2, Ganglia v3.7.2, HBase v1.3.1, and many other such applications and software.

> For a complete list of available EMR releases and their associated software versions, go to `https://docs.aws.amazon.com/emr/latest/ReleaseGuide/emr-release-components.html`.

6. In this case, I have gone ahead and selected the basic applications that we will be requiring for this scenario, including Hadoop, Hive and Hue. Feel free to select other applications as per your requirements.

7. The next couple of sections are optional, however, it is important to know their purpose:

   - **AWS Glue Data Catalog settings**: With EMR version 5.8.0 and above, you optionally have the choice to configure Spark SQL to use the AWS Glue Data Catalog (an external Hive table) as its metastore.

- **Edit software settings**: You can use this option to override the default configuration settings for certain applications. This is achieved by providing a configuration object in the form of a JSON file. You can either **Enter configuration** or **Load JSON from S3** as well:

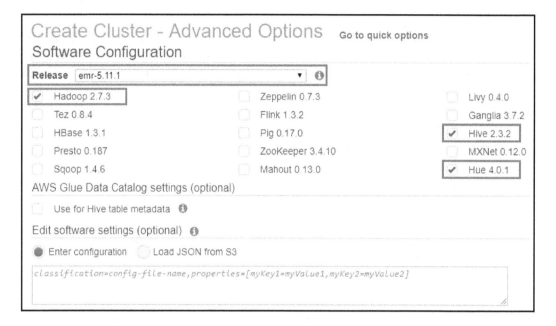

- **Add steps**: The final optional parameter left on the **Software Configuration** page is the *add steps*. As discussed briefly earlier in this chapter, steps are essentially a unit of work that we submit to the cluster. This can be something as trivial as loading input data from S3, or processing and running a MapReduce job on the data. We will be exploring steps a little more in detail a bit later in this chapter, so leave this field to its default value and select **Next** to continue with the process.

8. The second step in the **Advanced options** wizard is configuring the cluster's hardware, or the instance configurations, as well as the cluster's networking.

EMR provides two options: instance fleets and instance groups; both explained briefly here:

- **Instance fleets**: Instance fleets allows you to specify a target capacity for the instances present in a cluster. With this option, you get the widest variety of instance provisioning options where you can leverage mixed instance types for your nodes, and even go for different purchasing options for the same. With each instance fleet that created, you get to establish a target capacity for on-demand, as well as for spot instances.

 You can have only one instance fleet per node type (master, core, task).

- **Instance groups**: Instance groups on the other hand do not offer many custom configurable options per node type. In instance groups, each node consists of the same instance type and the same purchasing option, as well. Once these settings are configured during the cluster's creation, they cannot be altered; however, you can always add more instances as you see fit.

9. For this particular use case, we are going to go ahead and select **Uniform instance groups,** as depicted in the following screenshot:

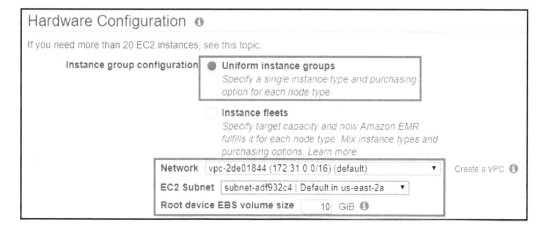

10. Next, from the **Network** drop-down list, select the appropriate *VPC* in which you wish to launch your EMR cluster. You can alternatively choose to create a new VPC specifically for EMR, using the adjoining **Create a VPC** option.

11. Similarly, select the appropriate subnet from the **EC2 Subnet** drop-down list.

12. Finally, assign a value for the **Root device EBS volume size** that will be provisioned for each instance in the cluster. You can provide values between 10 GB and 100 GB.

13. Using the edit options provided, you can additionally configure the **Instance type**, the **Instance count** as well as the **Purchasing option** for each node type, as depicted in the following screenshot. Note that these options are provided because we selected instance groups as our preferred mode of instance configurations. The options will vary if the **Instance Fleet** option is selected:

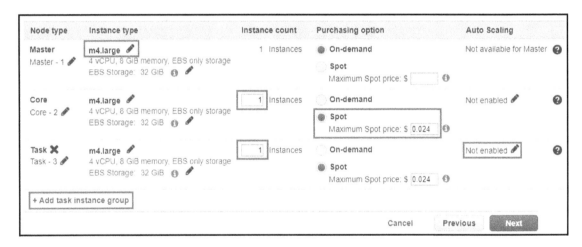

14. You can additionally choose to enable autoscaling for the **Core** and **Task** nodes by selecting the **Not enabled** option under the **Auto scaling** column. Subsequently, you can add additional task instance groups by selecting the **Add task instance group** option, as well. Once done, select the **Next** option to proceed with the set up.

15. The third step in the **Advanced options** provides general configurations that you can set, based on your requirements. To start off, provide a suitable **Cluster name** followed by selecting the **Logging** option for your EMR cluster. Use the folder option to browse to our newly created S3 bucket, as shown in the following screenshot:

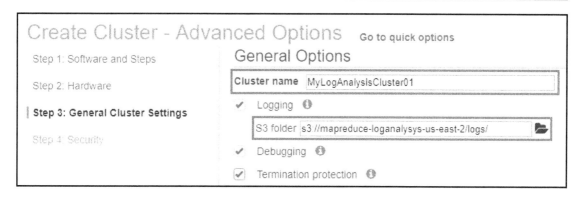

16. You can additionally enable the **Termination protection** option to prevent against accidental deletions of your cluster.

17. Moving on, the final configuration item left on the cluster's **General Options** page is the **Bootstrap Actions**. Bootstrap actions as the name implies are certain scripts or code that you wish to execute on your cluster's instances at the time of booting up. This feature thus comes in very handy when you have to add new instances to an existing running cluster.

Bootstrap actions are executed using the Hadoop user by default. You can switch to root privileges by using the `sudo` command.

There are two types of Bootstrap actions that you can execute on your instances:

- **Run if**: The **Run if** action executes an action when an *instance-specific* value is found in either the `instance.json` or the `job-flow.json` file. This is a predefined bootstrap action and comes in very handy when you only want to execute the action on a particular type of instance, for example, execute the bootstrap action only if the instance type is `master`.

- **Custom action**: Custom actions leverage your own scripts to perform a customized bootstrap action.

18. To create a bootstrap action, select the **Configure and add** option from the **Add Bootstrap Action**. Make sure the **Run if** action is selected before proceeding.

19. This will bring up the **Add Bootstrap Action** dialog as depicted in the following screenshot. Type in a suitable **Name** for your **Run if** action. Since the **Run if** action is a predefined bootstrap action, the script's location is not an editable field. You can, however, add **Optional arguments** for the script, as shown here. In this case, the **Run if** action will only echo the message if the instance is a **master**:

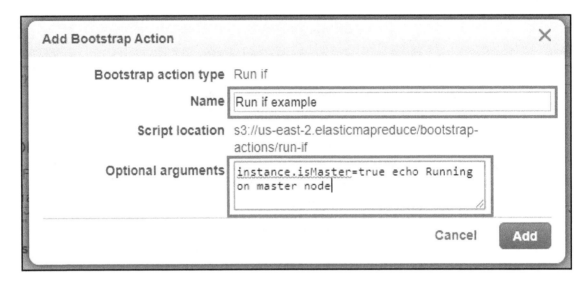

20. Click on **Add** once done. Similarly, you can add your custom bootstrap actions as well, by placing the executable scripts in the Amazon S3 bucket that we created during the prerequisite phase of this chapter and providing that path here.

21. Moving on to the final step in this cluster creation process, on the **Security Options** page, you can review the various permissions, roles, authentication, and encryption settings that the cluster will use once it's deployed. Start off by selecting the **EC2 key pair** that we created at the start of this chapter. You can additionally opt to change the **Permissions** or use the default ones provided.

22. Once done, click on **Create cluster** to complete the process.

The cluster's creation takes a couple of minutes, depending on the number of instances selected for the cluster, as well as the software identified to be installed. Once done, you can use the EMR dashboard to view the cluster's health status and other vital information.

Connecting to your EMR cluster

Once you have provisioned the EMR cluster, you should see its state change from **Starting** to **Bootstrapping** to finally into a **Running** state. If you do not have any jobs currently executing, then your cluster may go into a **Waiting** state as well. Here, you can now start using the EMR cluster for running your various jobs and analysis. But before that, here's a quick introduction of a few ways in which you can connect to your running EMR cluster.

First up, connecting to the master node using a simple SSH. Connecting to the master node via SSH can be used for monitoring the cluster, viewing Hadoop's log flies or for even running an interactive shell for Hive or Pig programming:

1. To do so, log in to your Amazon EMR dashboard and select your newly created cluster's name from the **Cluster list** page. This will display the clusters **Details** page where you can manage, as well as monitor your cluster.

2. Next, copy the **Master public DNS** address. Once copied, open up a PuTTY Terminal and paste the copied public DNS in the **Host Name (or IP Address)** field.

3. Convert the key pair that you associated with this EMR cluster into a private key and attach that private key in PuTTY by selecting the **Auth** option present under the **SSH** section.

4. Once done, click on **Open** to establish the connection. At the certificate dialog, accept the certificate and type in `Hadoop` as the username when prompted. You should get SSH access into your cluster's master node now!

The same task can be performed using the AWS CLI as well:

1. From the Terminal, first type in the following command to retrieve the running cluster's ID. The cluster's ID will be in this format `j-XXXXXXXX`:

   ```
   # aws emr list-clusters
   ```

2. To list the instances running in your cluster, use the cluster ID obtained from the previous command's output in the following command:

   ```
   # aws emr list-instances --cluster-id <CLUSTER_ID>
   ```

Copy the `PublicDnsName` value from the output of this command. You can then use the following set of commands to get access to your master node.

3. Ensure that the cluster's private key has the necessary permissions:

   `# chmod 400 <PRIVATEKEY.pem>`

4. Once done, SSH to the master node using the following command:

   `# ssh hadoop@<PUBLIC_DNS_NAME> -i <PRIVATEKEY.pem>`

You can additionally connect to the various application web interfaces, such as *Hue* or the *Hadoop HDFS NameNode,* using a few simple steps:

1. To get started, you will once again require the public DNS name of your master node. You can obtain that from the EMR dashboard or by using the CLI steps we just walked through.
2. Next, using PuTTY , paste the public DNS name in the **Host Name (or IP Address)** field as done earlier. Browse and load the private key using the **Auth** option as well.
3. Under the **SSH** option from PuTTY's navigation pane, select **Tunnels**.
4. Fill in the required details as mentioned in the following list:
   - Set source port field to 8157
   - Enable the **Dynamic** and **Auto** options
5. Once completed, select **Add** and finally **Open** the connection.

This form of tunnelling or port forwarding is essential as the web interfaces can only be viewed from the master node's local web server. Once completed, launch your favorite browser and view the respective web interfaces, as given here:

- For accessing Hue, type in the following in your web browser:

  `http://<PUBLIC_DNS_NAME>:8888/`

- For accessing the Hadoop HDFS NameNode, type in the following:

  `http:// <PUBLIC_DNS_NAME>::50070/`

| Hadoop | Overview | Datanodes | Datanode Volume Failures | Snapshot | Startup Progress | Utilities |

Overview 'ip-172-31-6-217.us-east-2.compute.internal:8020' (active)

Started:	Wed Jan 24 09:48:40 UTC 2018
Version:	2.7.3-amzn-6, rfc548a0642e795113789414490c9e59e6a8b91e4
Compiled:	2017-12-13T22:46Z by ec2-user from (HEAD detached at fc548a0642)
Cluster ID:	CID-8ddbd912-4b42-431e-bf66-0af89b3b2fe5
Block Pool ID:	BP-1404246105-172.31.6.217-1516787314975

You can even use the CLI to create a tunnel. To do so, substitute the public DNS name and the private key values in the following command:

```
# ssh -i <PRIVATEKEY.pem> -N -D 8157 hadoop@<PUBLIC_DNS_NAME>
```

The -D flag indicates that the port forwarding is dynamic.

Running a job on the cluster

With the connectivity established, you can now execute jobs as one or more steps on your cluster. In this section, we will be demonstrating the working of a step using a simple example which involves the processing of a few Amazon CloudFront logs. The details of the sample data and script can be found at: https://docs.aws.amazon.com/emr/latest/ManagementGuide/emr-gs-prepare-data-and-script.html. You can use similar techniques and bases to create and execute your own jobs as well:

1. To get started with a job, from the EMR dashboard select your cluster's name from the **Cluster list** page. This will bring up the newly created clusters details page. Here, select the **Steps** tab.

2. Since this is going to be our first step, go ahead and click on the **Add step** option. This brings up the **Add step** dialog as shown in the following screenshot. Fill in the required information as described and, once all the fields are filled in, click on **Add** to complete the step's creation:

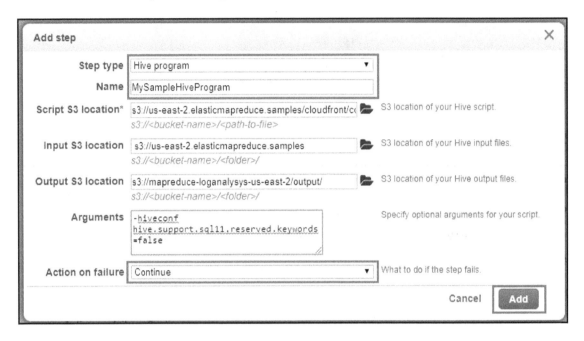

- **Step type**: You can choose between various options such as **Streaming program** which essentially will prompt you to provide Mapper and Reducer function details, or alternatively, you can also select **Hive program**, **Pig program**, **Spark program** or a **Custom application**. In this case, we select the **Hive program** option.
- **Name**: A suitable name for your step.
- **Script S3 location**: Provide the Hive script's location here. Since we are using a predefined script, simply replace the <REGION> field with your EMR's operating region:
  s3://<REGION>.elasticmapreduce.samples/cloudfront/co de/Hive_CloudFront.q.

- **Input S3 location**: Provide the input data file's location here. Replace the <REGION> placeholder with your EMR's operating region as done before:

  `s3://<REGION>.elasticmapreduce.samples.`

- **Output S3 location**: Specify where the processed output files have to be stored. In this case, I'm using the custom S3 bucket that we created as a prerequisite step during the EMR cluster creation. You can provide any other alternative bucket as well.

- **Arguments**: You can use this field to provide any optional arguments required by the script to run. In this case, copy, and paste the following `-hiveconf`

  `hive.support.sql11.reserved.keywords=false.`

- **Action on failure**: You can optionally choose what EMR should do in case the step's execution undergoes a failure. In this case, we have selected the default **Continue** value.

3. Once the required fields are filled out, click on **Add** to complete the process.

The step now starts executing the supplied script on the EMR cluster. You can view the progress by viewing the changes in the step's status from **Pending** to **Running** to **Completed,** as shown in the following screenshot:

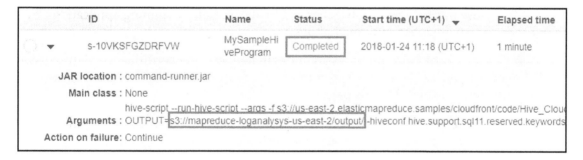

Once the job completes its execution, head back to your Amazon S3's output bucket and view the output of the processing. In this case, the output contains the number of access requests made to CloudFront, sorted by the operating system.

Monitoring EMR clusters

The EMR dashboard provides a rich feature set using which you can manage and monitor your EMR clusters all from one place. You can additionally view logs and leverage Amazon CloudWatch as well to track the performance of your cluster.

In this section, we will be looking at a few simple ways using which you can monitor your EMR clusters. To start off, let's look at how to monitor the status of your cluster using the EMR dashboard:

1. From the EMR dashboard, select your cluster name from the cluster list page. This will bring up the newly created cluster's details page. Here, select the **Events** tab, as shown in the following screenshot:

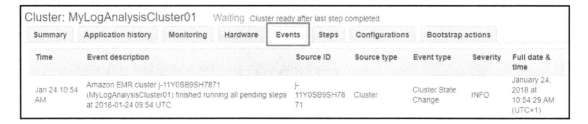

   The **Events** tab allows you to view the event logged by your cluster. You can use this to view events generated by the cluster, by running applications, by step execution and much more.

2. The dashboard also provides an in-depth look into the performance of the cluster over a period. To view the performance indicators, select the **Monitoring** tab from the cluster's **Details** page.

   Here, you can view essential details and status about your cluster, the running nodes, as well as the underlying I/O and data storage.

3. Alternatively, you can also use Amazon CloudWatch to view and monitor the cluster's various metrics. To do so, launch the Amazon CloudWatch dashboard by selecting this URL: `https://console.aws.amazon.com/cloudwatch/home`.

4. Next, from the navigation pane, select the **Metrics** option to view all the metrics associated with EMR. Use the `JobFlowID` dimension to filter the EMR cluster in case you have multiple clusters running in the same environment.

Here is a list of some important EMR metrics worth monitoring:

Metric name	Metric description
AppsFailed	The number of applications submitted to the EMR cluster that have failed to complete. This application status is monitored internally and reported by YARN.
MRUnhealthyNodes	The number of nodes available to MapReduce jobs marked in an UNHEALTHY state.
MRLostNodes	The number of nodes allocated to MapReduce that have been marked in a LOST state.
CorruptBlocks	The number of blocks that HDFS reports as corrupted.

You can view the complete list of monitored metrics at: `https://docs.aws.amazon.com/emr/latest/ManagementGuide/UsingEMR_ViewingMetrics.html`.

5. Once a Metric is identified, select the **Metric** and click on the **Graphed metrics** tab. Here, select the **Create alarm** option provided under the **Actions** column to create and set an alarm threshold, as well as its corresponding action.

In this way, you can also leverage Amazon CloudWatch events to periodically monitor the events generated by the cluster. Remember, however, that EMR tracks and records events only for a period of seven days. With this, we come to the end of this particular section and EMR, as well. In the next section, we will be learning and exploring a bit about yet another awesome analytics service called Amazon Redshift!

Introducing Amazon Redshift

Amazon Redshift is one of the **database as a service (DBaaS)** offerings from AWS that provides a massively scalable data warehouse as a managed service, at significantly lower costs. The data warehouse is based on the open source PostgreSQL database technology however; not all features offered in PostgreSQL are present in Amazon Redshift. Here's a look at some of the essential concepts and terminologies that you ought to keep in mind when working with Amazon Redshift:

- **Clusters**: Just like Amazon EMR, Amazon Redshift too relies on the concept of clusters. Clusters here are logical containers containing one or more instances or compute nodes, and one leader node that is responsible for the cluster's overall management. Here's a brief look at what each node provides:
  - **Leader node**: The leader node is a single node present in a cluster that is responsible for orchestrating and executing various database operations, as well as facilitating communication between the database and associate client programs.
  - **Compute node**: Compute nodes are responsible for executing the code provided by the leader node. Once executed, the compute nodes share the results back to the leader node for aggregation. Amazon Redshift supports two types of compute nodes: dense storage nodes and dense compute nodes. The dense storage nodes provide standard hard disk drives for creating large data warehouses; whereas, the dense compute nodes provide higher performance SSDs. You can start off by using a single node that provides 160 GB of storage and scale up to petabytes by leveraging one or more 16 TB capacity instances as well.

- **Node slices**: Each compute node is partitioned into one or more smaller chunks or slices by the leader node, based on the cluster's initial size. Each slice contains a portion of the compute nodes memory, CPU and disk resource, and uses these resources to process certain workloads that are assigned to it. The assignment of workloads is again performed by the leader node.

- **Databases**: As mentioned earlier, Amazon Redshift provides a scalable database that you can leverage for a data warehouse, as well as analytical purposes. With each cluster that you spin in Redshift, you can create one or more associated databases with it. The database is based on the open source relational database PostgreSQL (v8.0.2) and thus, can be used in conjunction with other RDBMS tools and functionalities. Applications and clients can communicate with the database using standard PostgreSQL JDBC and ODBC drivers.

Here is a representational image of a working data warehouse cluster powered by Amazon Redshift:

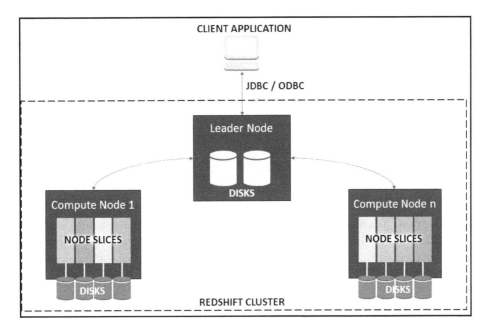

With this basic information in mind, let's look at some simple and easy to follow steps using which you can set up and get started with your Amazon Redshift cluster.

Getting started with Amazon Redshift

In this section, we will be looking at a few simple steps which you can take to have a fully functioning Amazon Redshift cluster up and running in a matter of minutes:

1. First up, we have a few prerequisite steps that need to be completed before we begin with the actual set up of the Redshift cluster. From the AWS Management Console, use the **Filter** option to filter out **IAM**. Alternatively, you can also launch the **IAM** dashboard by selecting this URL: `https://console.aws.amazon.com/iam/`.

2. Once logged in, we need to create and assign a role that will grant our Redshift cluster read-only access to Amazon S3 buckets. This role will come in handy later on in this chapter when we load some sample data on an Amazon S3 bucket and use Amazon Redshift's COPY command to copy the data locally into the Redshift cluster for processing. To create the custom role, select the **Role** option from the **IAM** dashboards' navigation pane.

3. On the **Roles** page, select the **Create role** option. This will bring up a simple wizard using which we will create and associate the required permissions to our role.

4. Select the **Redshift** option from under the **AWS Service** group section and opt for the **Redshift - Customizable** option provided under the **Select your use case** field. Click **Next** to proceed with the set up.

5. On the **Attach permissions policies** page, filter and select the **AmazonS3ReadOnlyAccess** permission. Once done, select **Next: Review**.

6. In the final **Review** page, type in a suitable name for the role and select the **Create Role** option to complete the process. Make a note of the role's ARN as we will be requiring this in the later steps. Here is snippet of the role policy for your reference:

```
{
  "Version": "2012-10-17",
  "Statement": [
    {
      "Effect": "Allow",
      "Action": [
        "s3:Get*",
        "s3:List*"
      ],
      "Resource": "*"
    }
  ]
}
```

With the role created, we can now move on to creating the Redshift cluster.

7. To do so, log in to the AWS Management Console and use the **Filter** option to filter out **Amazon Redshift**. Alternatively, you can also launch the Redshift dashboard by selecting this URL: https://console.aws.amazon.com/redshift/.

8. Select **Launch Cluster** to get started with the process.

9. Next, on the **CLUSTER DETAILS** page, fill in the required information pertaining to your cluster as mentioned in the following list:

- **Cluster identifier**: A suitable name for your new Redshift cluster. Note that this name only supports *lowercase* strings.
- **Database name**: A suitable name for your Redshift database. You can always create more databases within a single Redshift cluster at a later stage. By default, a database named `dev` is created if no value is provided:

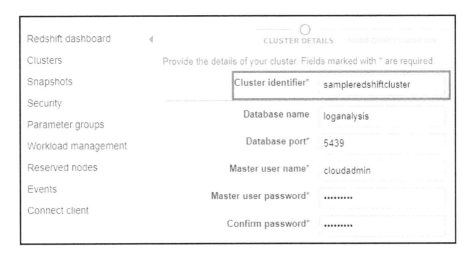

- **Database port**: The port number on which the database will accept connections. By default, the value is set to `5439,` however you can change this value based on your security requirements.
- **Master user name**: Provide a suitable username for accessing the database.
- **Master user password**: Type in a strong password with at least one uppercase character, one lowercase character and one numeric value. Confirm the password by retyping it in the **Confirm password** field.

10. Once completed, hit **Continue** to move on to the next step of the wizard.

11. On the **NODE CONFIGURATION** page, select the appropriate **Node type** for your cluster, as well as the **Cluster type** based on your functional requirements. Since this particular cluster setup is for demonstration purposes, I've opted to select the **dc2.large** as the **Node type** and a **Single Node** deployment with *1* compute node. Click **Continue** to move on the next page once done.

It is important to note here that the cluster that you are about to launch will be live and not running in a sandbox-like environment. As a result, you will incur the standard Amazon Redshift usage fees for the cluster until you delete it. You can read more about Redshift's pricing at: `https:/ /aws.amazon.com/redshift/pricing/`.

12. In the **ADDITIONAL CONFIGURATION** page, you can configure add-on settings, such as encryption enablement, selecting the default VPC for your cluster, whether or not the cluster should have direct internet access, as well as any preferences for a particular Availability Zone out of which the cluster should operate. Most of these settings do not require any changes at the moment and can be left to their default values.

13. The only changes required on this page is associating the previously created IAM role with the cluster. To do so, from the **Available Roles** drop-down list, select the custom Redshift role that we created in our prerequisite section. Once completed, click on **Continue**.

14. Review the settings and changes on the **Review** page and select the **Launch Cluster** option when completed.

The cluster takes a few minutes to spin up depending on whether or not you have opted for a single instance deployment or multiple instances. Once completed, you should see your cluster listed on the **Clusters** page, as shown in the following screenshot. Ensure that the status of your cluster is shown as **healthy** under the **DB Health** column. You can additionally make a note of the cluster's endpoint as well, for accessing it programmatically:

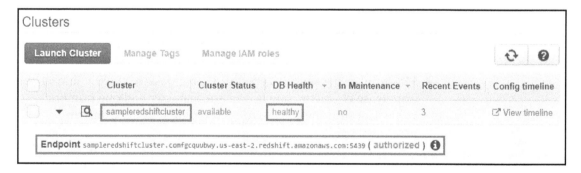

With the cluster all set up, the next thing to do is connect to the same. In the next section, we will be looking at a few simple steps you can take to connect to your newly deployed Redshift cluster.

Connecting to your Redshift cluster

You can use a number of tools to connect to your Redshift cluster once its up and running. Most of these tools are PostgreSQL compliant and easily available off the shelf. In this case, we are going to install and use an open source SQL client tool called **SQL Workbench/J**.

To begin with, you will need to have Java runtime installed on your local workstation. The Java runtime version will have to *match* the requirements of SQL Workbench/J, otherwise it simply won't work. You can check the version of the installed Java runtime on your local desktop by either locating the Java configuration on the **Control Panel** or by typing in the following command in a Terminal if you are working with a Linux distribution:

```
# java --version
```

In this case, we are using a simple Windows desktop for installing SQL Workbench/J. Download the correct version of the software from here: `http://www.sql-workbench.net/downloads.html`.

With the software downloaded, the installation is pretty straightforward. Accept the end user license agreement, select a path for the software's installation and that's it! You should have the SQL Workbench/J up and running now:

1. To connect SQL Workbench/J with your Redshift cluster, you will need your newly created database's JDBC URL. You can copy it by selecting the **Connect client** option from Redshift's navigation pane and selecting your newly deployed cluster from the **Get cluster connection URL** section, as shown in the following screenshot:

2. You will also need to download the correct version of the associated Amazon Redshift **JDBC Driver** JAR using the same page as well.

3. Once completed, from the SQL Workbench/J client, select **File**, followed by the **Connect window** option.

4. Here, click on **Create a new connection profile** to get started. This will pop up a **New profile** box where you will need to enter a name for this new profile.

5. Once the profile is created; select the **Manage drivers** option. This will display the **Manage drivers** dialog box, as shown in the following screenshot. Select the **Amazon Redshift** option and provide a suitable **Name** for your connection driver, as well. Click on the browse icon and select the downloaded Amazon Redshift driver JAR that we downloaded from Redshift a while back. Click on **OK** to complete the driver settings:

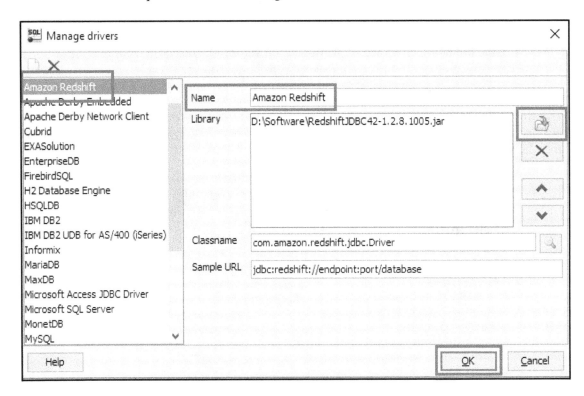

6. With the driver in place, the final thing left to do is connect to the database and test it. For that, select the newly created **Connection profile** from SQL Workbench/J and paste the copied database JDBC URL in the **URL** field as shown. Provide the database's **Username** and **Password** as configured during the cluster's setup. Additionally, ensure that the **Autocommit** option is checked as shown here:

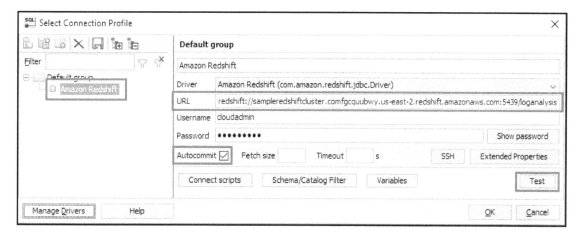

7. You can also test the connection by selecting the **Test** option on the SQL Workbench/J screen. Once completed, click **OK** to establish and open the SQL prompt.

With this step completed, you should have a running Redshift cluster connected to the SQL Workbench/J client as well. The next and final step left for us is to run a few sample queries and test the cluster's functionality, so let's get started with that right away!

Working with Redshift databases and tables

Before we start querying the Redshift database, we will first need to upload some same data to it. For this particular scenario, we are going to use a small subset of HTTP request logs that originated from a web server at the NASA Kennedy Space Center in Florida. This data is available for public use and can be downloaded from here: `http://ita.ee.lbl.gov/html/contrib/NASA-HTTP.html`.

The log file essentially contains the following set of columns:

- **Host**: The host that is making the web request to the web server. This field contains fully qualified hostnames or IP addresses as well.
- **Timestamp**: The timestamp of the particular web request. The format is DAY MON DD HH:MM:SS YYYY. This timestamp uses a 24-hour clock.
- **Request**: The method used to request the server (GET/HEAD/POST).
- **URL**: The URL of the resource that was requested by the client.
- **Response**: This contains the HTTP response code (200, 302, 304, and 404).
- **Bytes**: The size of the reply in bytes.

Here's a snippet of the data for your reference:

```
pppa006.compuserve.com,807256800,GET,/images/launch-logo.gif,200,1713
vcc7.langara.bc.ca,807256804,GET,/shuttle/missions/missions.html,200,8677
pppa006.compuserve.com,807256806,GET,/history/apollo/images/apollo-
logo1.gif,200,1173
```

You can download the sample CSV file (2.14 MB containing 30,970 entries) used for this scenario using the following link: https://github.com/yoyoclouds/Administering-AWS-Volume2.

With the file downloaded, all you need to do is upload it to one of your Amazon S3 buckets. Remember, that this bucket should be accessible by Amazon Redshift otherwise you may get a S3ServiceException: Access Denied exception during execution.

Next, from the SQL Workbench/J client, type in the following code to create a new table within our Redshift database:

```
create table apachelogs(
host varchar(100),
time varchar(20),
method varchar(8),
url varchar(200),
response varchar(10),
bytes varchar(10));
```

You can find the complete copy of the previous code at: https://github. com/yoyoclouds/Administering-AWS-Volume2.

Select the **Execute Query** button. You should receive an output stating that the table is created, as shown in the following screenshot:

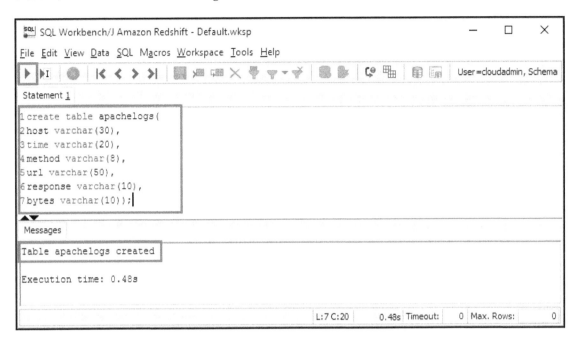

Next, use the COPY command to load the contents of the data file stored in Amazon S3 into the newly created Redshift table. The COPY command is a very versatile command and can be used to load data residing in Amazon S3, Amazon EMR, or even from an Amazon DynamoDB table into Amazon Redshift. To know more about the COPY command, navigate to this URL: https://docs.aws.amazon.com/redshift/latest/dg/r_COPY.html.

Substitute the values of <REDSHIFT_TABLE_NAME> with the name of the newly created table, the <BUCKET_NAME> with the name of the S3 bucket that contains the data file, and <REDSHIFT_IAM_ROLE_ARN> with the ARN of the IAM read-only access role that we created as a part of Amazon Redshift's prerequisite process:

```
copy <REDSHIFT_TABLE_NAME> from 's3://<BUCKET_NAME>/data.csv'
credentials 'aws_iam_role=<REDSHIFT_IAM_ROLE_ARN>'
csv;
```

Once the code is pasted into the SQL Workbench/J, click on the **Execute Query** button. Here is a snapshot of the command execution from SQL Workbench/J:

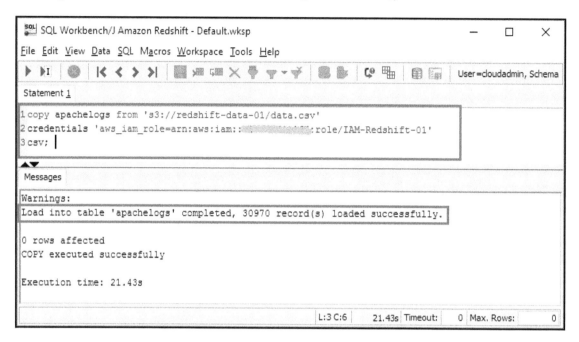

With the data loaded, you can now use simple queries to query the dataset, as described in this section. The following command will list all 30,970 records from the table:

```
select * from apachelogs;
```

The following command will list only those records whose response value was 404:

```
select * from apachelogs where response=404;
```

The following command will list all the hosts that have requested for the particular resource:

```
select host from apachelogs where url='/images/NASA-logosmall.gif';
```

You can also use the Redshift dashboard to view the performance and runtime of each individual query by first selecting your Redshift cluster name from the **Cluster** page. Next, select the **Queries** tab to bring up the list of the most recently executed queries, as shown in the following screenshot:

You can drill down into each query by further selecting the *query identification number* as well.

Orchestrating Data using AWS Data Pipeline

9

In the previous chapter, we explored the AWS analytics suite of services by deep diving into Amazon EMR and Amazon Redshift services.

In this chapter, we will be continuing the trend and learning about an extremely versatile and powerful data orchestration and transformation service called AWS Data Pipeline.

Let's have a quick look at the various topics that we will be covering in this chapter:

- Introducing AWS Data Pipeline along with a quick look at some of its concepts and terminologies
- Getting started with Data Pipeline using a simple Hello World example
- Working with the Data Pipeline definition file
- Executing scripts and commands on remote EC2 instances using a data pipeline
- Backing up data from one S3 bucket to another using a simple, parameterized data pipeline
- Building pipelines using the AWS CLI

So without any further ado, let's get started right away!

Introducing AWS Data Pipeline

AWS Data Pipeline is an extremely versatile web service that allows you to move data back and forth between various AWS services, as well as on-premise data sources. The service is designed specifically to provide you with an in-built fault tolerance and highly available platform, using which you can define and build your very own custom data migration workflows. AWS Data Pipeline also provides add-on features such as scheduling, dependency tracking, and error handling, so that you do not have to waste extra time and effort in writing them on your own. This easy-to-use and flexible service, accompanied by its low operating costs, make the AWS Data Pipeline service ideal for use cases such as:

- Migrating data on a periodic basis from an Amazon EMR cluster over to Amazon Redshift for data warehousing
- Incrementally loading data from files stored in Amazon S3 directly into an Amazon RDS database
- Copying data from an Amazon MySQL database into an Amazon Redshift cluster
- Backing up data from an Amazon DynamoDB table to Amazon S3
- Backing up files stored in an Amazon S3 bucket on a periodic basis, and much more

In this section, we will be understanding and learning a bit more about AWS Data Pipeline by first getting to know some of its internal components, concepts and terminologies.

The core foundation of AWS Data Pipeline is, as the name suggests, a pipeline. You can create pipelines to schedule and run your data migration or transformation tasks. Each pipeline relies on a pipeline definition that essentially contains the business logic required to drive the data migration activities. We will be learning more about the data pipeline definition in the upcoming sections. For now, let's dive a bit into a few essential pipeline concepts and components:

- **Pipeline components**: A single pipeline can comprise of multiple sections, each having its own specific place in the overall functioning of the pipeline. For example, a pipeline can contain sections for specifying the input data source from where the data has to be collected, the activity that needs to be performed on this data along with a few necessary conditions, the time at which the activity has to be triggered, and so on. Each of these sections, individually, are called the pipeline's components and are used together to build a pipeline definition.

- **Task runners**: Task runners are special applications or agents that carry out the task assigned in a pipeline. The task runners poll AWS Data Pipeline for any active tasks available. If found, the task is assigned to a task runner and executed. Once the execution completes, the task runner will report the status (either success or failure) back to AWS Data Pipeline. By default, AWS provides a default task runner for resources that are launched and managed by AWS Data Pipeline. You can also install the task runner on instances or on-premise servers that you manage:

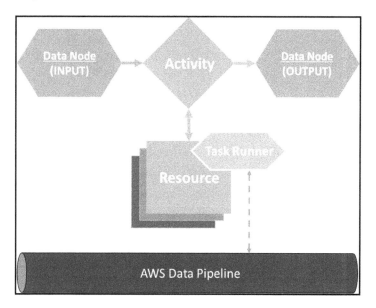

- **Data nodes**: Data nodes are used to define the location and the type of input as well as output data for the pipeline. As of now, the following data nodes are provided by AWS Data Pipeline:
    - `S3DataNode`: Used to define an Amazon S3 location as an input or output for storing data
    - `SqlDataNode`: Defines a SQL table or a database query for use in the pipeline
    - `RedshiftDataNode`: Used to define an Amazon Redshift table as input or output for the pipeline
    - `DynamoDBDataNode`: Used to specify a DynamoDB table as input or output for the pipeline

- **Activities**: With the data's location and type selected using the data nodes, the next component left to define is the type of activity to be performed on that data. AWS Data Pipeline provides the following set of pre-packaged activities that you can use and extend as per your requirements:
    - `CopyActivity`: Used to copy data from one data node to another
    - `ShellCommandActivity`: Used to run a shell command as an activity
    - `SqlActivity`: Executes a SQL query on a data node such as `SqlDataNode` or `RedshiftDataNode`
    - `RedshiftCopyActivity`: A specific activity that leverages the `COPY` command to copy data between Redshift tables
    - `EmrActivity`: Used to run an EMR cluster
    - `PigActivity`: Used to run a custom Pig script on an EMR cluster
    - `HiveActivity`: Runs a Hive query on an EMR cluster
    - `HiveCopyActivity`: Used to run a Hive `COPY` query for copying the data from the EMR cluster to an Amazon S3 bucket or an Amazon DynamoDB table
- **Resources**: With the data nodes and activities selected, the next step in configuring a pipeline is selecting the right resource for executing the activity. AWS Data Pipeline supports two types of resources:
    - `Ec2Resource`: An EC2 instance is leveraged to execute the activity selected in the pipeline. This resource type is common for activities, such as `CopyActivity`, `ShellCommandActivity`, and so on.
    - `EmrCluster`: An Amazon EMR cluster is used to execute the activity selected in the pipeline. This resource is best suited for activities such as `EmrActivity`, `PigActivity`, `HiveActivity`, and so on.
- **Actions**: Actions are certain steps that a pipeline takes whenever a *success*, *failure* or *late activity* event occurs. You can use actions as a way to monitor and notify the execution status of your pipeline; for example, send an SNS notification in case a `CopyActivity` fails, and so on.

With these concepts and terms done and dusted, let's move on to some hands-on action where we will be creating our very first simple and minimalistic pipeline.

Getting started with AWS Data Pipeline

Creating your own pipeline is a fairly simple process, once you get to know the intricacies of working with the pipeline dashboard. In this section, we will be exploring the AWS Data Pipeline dashboard, its various functions, and editor to create a simple Hello World example pipeline. To start off, here are a few necessary prerequisite steps that you need to complete first, starting with a simple Amazon S3 bucket for storing all our data pipeline logs.

 AWS Data Pipeline is only available in the EU (Ireland), Asia Pacific (Sydney), Asia Pacific (Tokyo), US East (N. Virginia), and the US West (Oregon) regions. For the purpose of the scenarios in this chapter, we will be using the US East (N. Virginia) region only.

From the AWS Management Console, launch the Amazon S3 console by either filtering the service name from the **Filter** option or navigating to this URL: `https://s3.console.aws.amazon.com/s3/home?region=us-east-1`.

Next, select the **Create bucket** option and provide a suitable value in the **Bucket name** field. Leave the rest of the fields to their default values and select **Create** to complete the process.

With the log bucket created, the next prerequisite step involves the creation of a couple of IAM Roles that are required by AWS Data Pipeline for accessing resources, as well as what particular action it can perform over them. Since we are going to use the AWS Data Pipeline console for our first pipeline build, Data Pipeline provides two default IAM Roles that you can leverage out of the box:

- `DataPipelineDefaultRole`: An IAM Role that grants AWS Data Pipeline access to all your AWS resources, including EC2, IAM, Redshift, S3, SNS, SQS and EMR. You can customize it to restrict the AWS services that Data Pipeline can access. Here is a snippet of the policy that is created:

```
{
    "Version": "2012-10-17",
    "Statement": [
        {
            "Effect": "Allow",
            "Action": [
                "cloudwatch:*",
                "datapipeline:DescribeObjects",
                "datapipeline:EvaluateExpression",
                "dynamodb:BatchGetItem",
                "dynamodb:DescribeTable",
```

```
                    "dynamodb:GetItem",
                    ...
                    "ec2:RunInstances",
                    "ec2:StartInstances",
                    "ec2:StopInstances",
                    ...
                    "elasticmapreduce:*",
                    "iam:GetInstanceProfile",
                    "iam:GetRole",
                    "iam:GetRolePolicy",
                    ...
                    "rds:DescribeDBInstances",
                    "rds:DescribeDBSecurityGroups",
                    "redshift:DescribeClusters",
                    "redshift:DescribeClusterSecurityGroups",
                    "s3:CreateBucket",
                    "s3:DeleteObject",
                    "s3:Get*",
                    "s3:List*",
                    "s3:Put*",
                    ...
                    "sns:ListTopics",
                    "sns:Publish",
                    "sns:Subscribe",
                    ...
                    "sqs:GetQueue*",
                    "sqs:PurgeQueue",
                    "sqs:ReceiveMessage"
                ],
                "Resource": [
                    "*"
                ]
            },
            {
                "Effect": "Allow",
                "Action": "iam:CreateServiceLinkedRole",
                "Resource": "*",
                "Condition": {
                    "StringLike": {
                        "iam:AWSServiceName": [
                            "elasticmapreduce.amazonaws.com",
                            "spot.amazonaws.com"
                        ]
                    }
                }
            }
        ]
    }
```

- `DataPipelineDefaultResourceRole`: This Role allows applications, scripts, or code executed on the Data Pipeline resources' (EC2/EMR instances) access to your AWS resources:

```
{
    "Version": "2012-10-17",
    "Statement": [
        {
            "Effect": "Allow",
            "Action": [
                "cloudwatch:*",
                "datapipeline:*",
                "dynamodb:*",
                "ec2:Describe*",
                "elasticmapreduce:AddJobFlowSteps",
                "elasticmapreduce:Describe*",
                "elasticmapreduce:ListInstance*",
                "elasticmapreduce:ModifyInstanceGroups",
                "rds:Describe*",
                "redshift:DescribeClusters",
                "redshift:DescribeClusterSecurityGroups",
                "s3:*",
                "sdb:*",
                "sns:*",
                "sqs:*"
            ],
            "Resource": [
                "*"
            ]
        }
    ]
}
```

With the prerequisites out of the way, let's now move on to creating our very first pipeline:

1. From the AWS Management Console, filter out **Data Pipeline** using the **Filter** option or alternatively, selecting this URL provided here `https://console.aws.amazon.com/datapipeline/home?region=us-east-1`. Select the **Get started now** option.

2. This will bring up the **Create Pipeline** wizard as displayed. Start by providing a suitable name for the pipeline using the **Name** field followed by an optional **Description**.

3. Next, select the **Build using Architect** option from the **Source** field.

   AWS Data Pipeline provides different ways for creating pipelines. You can leverage either one of the several pre-built templates using the **Build using a template** option, or opt for a more customized approach by selecting the **Import a definition** option, where you can create and upload your own data pipeline definitions. Finally, you can use the data pipeline architect mode to drag-drop and customize your pipeline using a simple intuitive dashboard, which is what we are going to do in this use case:

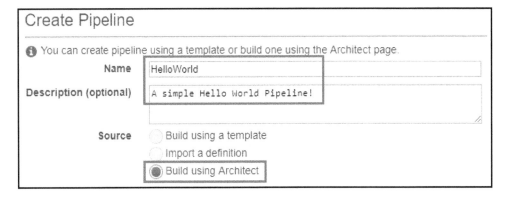

4. Moving on, you can also schedule the run of your pipeline by selecting the correct option, provided under the **Schedule** section. For now, select the **On pipeline activation** option, as we want our pipeline to start its execution only when it is first activated.

5. Next, browse and select the correct *S3 bucket* for logging the data pipelines' logs using the **S3 location for logs** option. This should be the same bucket that was created during the prerequisite section of this scenario.

6. Optionally, you can also provide your custom IAM Roles for Data Pipeline by selecting the **Custom** option provided under the **Security/Access** section. In this case, we have gone ahead and selected the **Default** IAM Roles themselves.

7. Once all the required fields are populated, select the **Edit in Architect** option to continue.

   With this step completed, you should see the *architect* view of your current pipeline as depicted. By default, you will only have a single box called **Configuration** displayed.

8. Select the **Configuration** box to view the various configuration options required by your pipeline to run. This information should be visible on the right-hand side navigation pane under the **Others** section, as shown in the following screenshot:

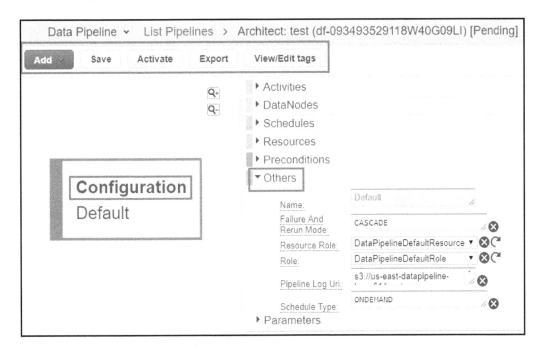

You can use this **Configuration** to edit your pipeline's **Resource Role**, **Pipeline Log Uri**, **Schedule Type,** and many other such settings as well.

9. To add **Resources** and **Activities** to your pipeline, select the **Add** drop-down list as shown. Here, select ShellCommandActivity to get started. We will use this activity to echo a simple Hello World message for starters.

10. Once the ShellCommandActivity option is selected, you should be able to see its corresponding configuration items in the adjoining navigation pane under the **Activities** tab.

11. Type in a suitable **Name** for your activity. Next, from the **Type** section, select the **Add an optional field** drop-down list and select the **Command** option as shown. In the new **Command** field, type echo "This is just a Hello World message!".

12. With the activity in place, the final step left is to provide and associate a resource to the pipeline. The resource will execute the `ShellCommandActivity` on either an EC2 instance or an EMR instance.

13. To create and associate a resource, from the **Activities** section, select the **Add an optional field** option once again and from the drop-down list, select the **Runs On** option. Using the **Runs On** option, you can create and select **Resources** for executing the task for your pipeline.

14. Select the **Create new: Resource** option to get started. This will create a new resource named `DefaultResource1`, as depicted in the following screenshot:

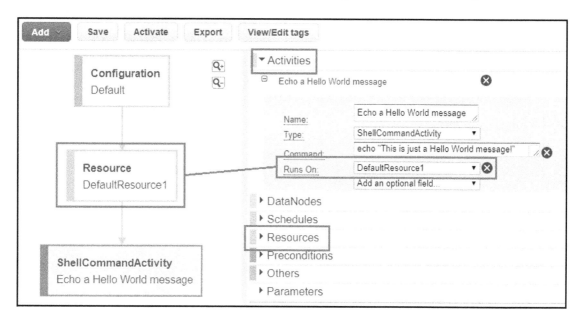

15. Select the newly created resource or alternatively, select the **Resources** option from the navigation pane to view and add resource specific configurations.

16. Fill in the following information as depicted in the previous screenshot in the **Resources** section of your pipeline:
    - **Name**: Provide a suitable name for your new resource.
    - **Type**: Select the **Ec2Resource** option from the drop-down list.
    - **Role/Resource Role**: You can choose to provide different IAM Roles, however I have opted to go for the default pipeline roles itself.

- **Instance Type**: Type in `t1.micro` in the adjoining field. If you do not provide or select the instance type field, the resource will launch a **m1.medium** instance by default.
- **Terminate After**: Select the appropriate time after which the instance should be terminated. In this case, I have selected to terminate after `10` minutes.

Here's a screenshot of what the final pipeline would look like once the **Resources** section is filled out:

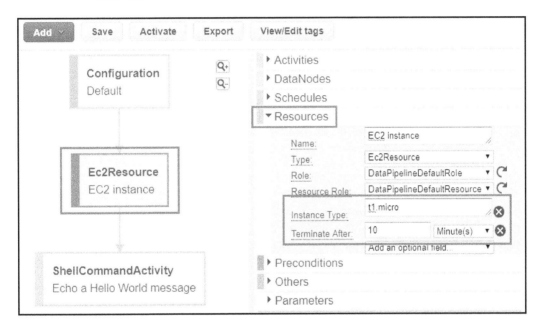

17. Once the pipeline is ready, click on **Save** to save the changes made. Selecting the **Save** option automatically compiles your pipeline and checks for any errors as well. If any errors are found, they will be displayed in the **Errors/Warnings** section. If no errors are reported, click on **Activate** to finally activate your pipeline.

The pipeline takes a few minutes to transition from **WAITING_FOR_RUNNER** state to a **FINISHED** state. This process involves first spinning up the EC2 instance or resource, which we defined in the pipeline. Once the resource is up and running, Data Pipeline will automatically install the *task runner* on this particular resource, as Data Pipeline itself manages it. With the task runner installed, it starts polling the data pipeline for pending activities and executes them.

Once the pipeline's status turns to **FINISHED**, expand the pipeline's component name and select the **Attempts** tab, as shown. If not specified, Data Pipeline will try and execute your pipeline for a default three attempts before it finally stops the execution.

For each attempt, you can view the corresponding **Activity Logs**, **Stdout** as well as the **Stderr** messages:

Select the **Stdout** option to view your Hello World message! Et voila! Your first pipeline is up and running!

Feel free to try out a few other options for your pipeline by simply selecting the pipeline name and click on the **Edit Pipeline** option. You can also export your pipeline's definition by selecting the pipeline name and from the **Actions** tab, opting for the **Export** option.

Pipeline definitions are a far better and easier way of creating pipelines if you are a fan of working with JSON and CLI interfaces. They offer better flexibility and usability as compared to the standard pipeline dashboard which can take time to get used to for beginners. With this in mind, in the next section we will be exploring a few basics on how you can get started by creating your very own pipeline definition file.

Working with data pipeline definition Files

The AWS Data Pipeline console provides us with three different options to get started with creating a new pipeline. You could use the architect mode, which is exactly what we ended up working with in the earlier section, or alternatively, use any one of the pre-defined templates as a boilerplate and build your pipeline fro them. Last but not the least, the console also provides you with an ability to upload your very own pipeline definition file, which is basically a collection of various pipeline objects and conditions written in a JSON format. In this section, we will be learning how to write our very own pipeline definitions and later, use the same for building a custom pipeline as well.

To start, you will need two components to build up a pipeline definition file: objects and fields:

- **Objects**: An object is an individual component required to build a pipeline. These can be data nodes, conditions, activities, resources, schedules, and so on.
- **Fields**: Each object is described by one or more fields. The fields are made up of key-value pairs that are enclosed in double quotes and separated by a colon.

Here is a skeleton structure of a pipeline definition file:

```
{
  "objects" : [
    {
      "key1" : "value1",
      "key2" : "value2"
    },
    {
      "key3" : "value3"
    }
  ]
}
```

Here is a look at the pipeline definition file obtained by exporting the **Hello World** pipeline example that we performed a while back:

```
{
  "objects": [
    {
      "failureAndRerunMode": "CASCADE",
      "resourceRole": "DataPipelineDefaultResourceRole",
      "role": "DataPipelineDefaultRole",
      "pipelineLogUri": "s3://us-east-datapipeline-logs-01/logs/",
      "scheduleType": "ONDEMAND",
      "name": "Default",
      "id": "Default"
    },
    {
      "name": "myActivity",
      "id": "ShellCommandActivityId_2viZe",
      "runsOn": {
        "ref": "ResourceId_EhxAF"
      },
      "type": "ShellCommandActivity",
      "command": "echo "This is just a Hello World message!""
    },
    {
      "resourceRole": "DataPipelineDefaultResourceRole",
```

```
        "role": "DataPipelineDefaultRole",
        "name": "myEC2Resource",
        "id": "ResourceId_EhxAF",
        "type": "Ec2Resource",
        "terminateAfter": "10 Minutes"
    }
  ],
  "parameters": []
}
```

 You can find the complete copy of code at https://github.com/yoyoclouds/Administering-AWS-Volume2.

Each object generally contains an id, name, and type fields that are used to describe it and its functionality. For example, the Resource object in the Hello World scenario contains the following values:

```
{
        "name": "myEC2Resource",
        "id": "ResourceId_EhxAF",
        "type": "Ec2Resource",
        ...
}
```

You can also find the same fields in both the ShellCommandActivity, as well as the default configurations objects.

A pipeline object can refer to other objects within the same pipeline using the "ref" : "ID_of_referred_resource" field. Here is an example of the ShellCommandActivity referencing to the EC2 resource, using the resource ID:

```
{
        "name": "myActivity",
        "id": "ShellCommandActivityId_2viZe",
        "runsOn": {
          "ref": "ResourceId_EhxAF"
        },
        "type": "ShellCommandActivity",
        "command": "echo "This is just a Hello World message!""
    },
    {
        "resourceRole": "DataPipelineDefaultResourceRole",
        "role": "DataPipelineDefaultRole",
        "name": "myEC2Resource",
        "id": "ResourceId_EhxAF",
```

```
    "type": "Ec2Resource",
    "terminateAfter": "10 Minutes"
  }
```

You can additionally create custom or user-defined fields and refer them to other pipeline components, using the same syntax as described in the previous code:

```
{
  "id": " ResourceId_EhxAF",
  "type": "Ec2Resource",
  "myCustomField": "This is a custom field.",
  "myCustomReference": {"ref":" ShellCommandActivityId_2vi"}
  },
```

 You can find the detailed references for data nodes, resources, activities, and other objects at https://docs.aws.amazon.com/datapipeline/latest/DeveloperGuide/dp-pipeline-objects.html.

Last but not the least; you can also leverage a parameterized template to customize the pipeline definition. Using this method, you can basically have one common pipeline definition and pass different values to it at the time of pipeline creation.

To parametrize a pipeline definition you need to specify a variable using the following syntax:

```
"#{VARIABLE_NAME}"
```

With the variable created, you can define its value in a separate parameters object which can be stored in the same pipeline definition file, or in a separate JSON file altogether as well. Consider the following example where we pass the same Hello World message in the ShellCommandActivity however, this time using a variable definition:

```
{
        "name": "myActivity",
        "id": "ShellCommandActivityId_2viZe",
        "runsOn": {
          "ref": "ResourceId_EhxAF"
        },
        "type": "ShellCommandActivity",
        "command": "#{myVariable}"
}
```

Once the variable is defined, we pass its corresponding values and expression in a separate `parameters` object, as shown in the following code:

```
{
  "parameters": [
    {
      "id": "myVariable",
      "description": "Shell command to run",
      "type": "String",
      "default": "echo "Default message!""
    }
  ]
}
```

In this case, the variable `myVariable` is a simple string type and we have also provided it with a default value, in case a value is not provided to this variable at the time of the pipeline's creation.

 To know more about how to leverage and use variable and parameters in your pipeline definitions, visit `https://docs.aws.amazon.com/ datapipeline/latest/DeveloperGuide/dp-custom-templates.html`.

With this, we come towards the end of this section. In the next section, we will look at how you can leverage the AWS Data Pipeline to execute scripts and commands on remote EC2 instances using a parameterized pipeline definition.

Executing remote commands using AWS Data Pipeline

One of the best parts of working with Data Pipeline is that versatility of tasks that you can achieve by just using this one tool. In this section, we will be looking at a relatively simple pipeline definition using which you can execute remote scripts and commands on EC2 instances.

How does this setup work? Well, to start with, we will be requiring one S3 bucket (can be present in any AWS region) to be created that will store and act as a repository for all our shell scripts. Once the bucket is created, simply create and upload the following shell script to the bucket. Note however that in this case, the shell script is named simplescript.sh and the same name is used in the following pipeline definition, as well:

```
#!/bin/bash
echo "---------------------------------"
echo "Your username is: $(echo $USER)"
echo "---------------------------------"
echo "The current date and time : $(date)"
echo "---------------------------------"
echo "Users currently logged on this system: "
echo "$(who)"
echo "---------------------------------"
echo "AWS CLI installed at: "
echo "$(aws --version)"
echo "---------------------------------"
```

The script is pretty self-explanatory. It will print out a series of messages based on the EC2 instance it is launched from. You can substitute this script with any other shell script that can either be used to take backups of particular files, or archive existing files into a tar.gz and push it over to an awaiting S3 bucket for archiving, and so on.

With the script file uploaded to the correct S3 bucket, the final step is to copy and paste the following pipeline definition in a file and upload it to Data Pipeline for execution:

```
{
  "objects": [
    {
      "failureAndRerunMode": "CASCADE",
      "resourceRole": "DataPipelineDefaultResourceRole",
      "role": "DataPipelineDefaultRole",
      "pipelineLogUri": "s3://<DATAPIPELINE_LOG_BUCKET>",
      "scheduleType": "ONDEMAND",
      "name": "Default",
      "id": "Default"
    },
    {
      "name": "CliActivity",
      "id": "CliActivity",
      "runsOn": {
        "ref": "Ec2Instance"
      },
      "type": "ShellCommandActivity",
      "command": "(sudo yum -y update aws-cli) && (#{myCustomScriptCmd})"
    },
```

```
      {
        "instanceType": "t1.micro",
        "name": "Ec2Instance",
        "id": "Ec2Instance",
        "type": "Ec2Resource",
        "terminateAfter": "15 Minutes"
      }
    ],
    "parameters": [
      {
        "watermark": "aws [options] <command> <subcommand> [parameters]",
        "description": "AWS CLI command",
        "id": "myCustomScriptCmd",
        "type": "String"
      }
    ],
    "values": {
      "myCustomScriptCmd": "aws s3 cp
  s3://<S3_BUCKET_SCRIPT_LOCATION>/simplescript.sh . && sh simplescript.sh"
    }
  }
```

Remember to swap out the values for <DATAPIPELINE_LOG_BUCKET> and
<S3_BUCKET_SCRIPT_LOCATION> with their corresponding actual values, and to save the
file with a JSON extension.

This particular pipeline definition relies on the ShellCommandActivity to first install the
AWS CLI on the remote EC2 instance and then execute the shell script by copying it locally
from the S3 bucket.

To upload the pipeline definition, use the AWS Data Pipeline console to create a new
pipeline. In the **Create Pipeline** wizard, provide a suitable **Name** and **Description** for the
new pipeline. Once done, select the **Import a definition** option from the **Source** field, as
shown in the following screenshot:

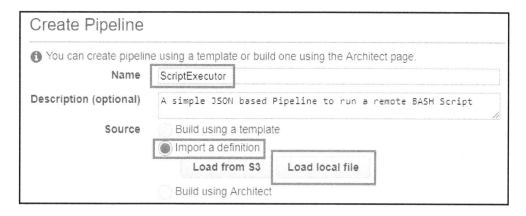

Once the script loads, you should see the custom AWS CLI command in the
Parameters section. With the pipeline definition successfully loaded, you can now choose to
run the pipeline, either on a schedule or on activation. In my case, I have select to run the
pipeline on activation itself, as this is for demo purposes.

Ensure that the *logging* is enabled for the new pipeline and the correct S3 bucket for storing
the pipeline's logs is mentioned. With all necessary fields filled, click on **Activate** to start up
the pipeline.

Once again, the pipeline will transition from **WAITING_FOR_RUNNER** state to the
FINISHED state. This usually takes a good minute or two to complete.

From the Data Pipeline console, expand on the existing pipeline and select the **Attempts** tab
as shown in the following screenshot. Here, click on **Stdout** to view the output of the
script's execution:

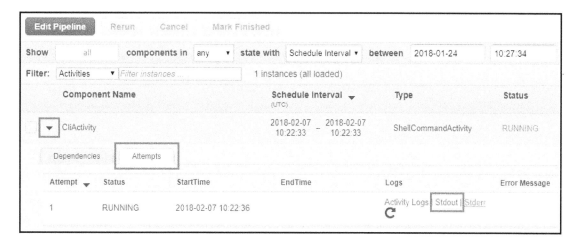

Once the output is viewed, you can optionally select the pipeline and click on **Mark Finished** option, as well. This will stop the pipeline from undertaking any further attempts on executions.

Simple, isn't it! You can use a similar method and approach to back up your files and execute some commands over managed instances. In the next section, we will be looking at one last pipeline definition example as well, that essentially helps us take periodic backups of content stored in one Amazon S3 bucket to another using both the Data Pipeline console, as well as the AWS CLI!

Backing up data using AWS Data Pipeline

One of the most widely used use cases for AWS Data Pipeline is its ability to synchronize and schedule backup jobs. You can use Data Pipeline to take backups of data stored within EC2 instances, EBS volumes, databases and even S3 buckets. In this section, we will walk through a simple, parameterized pipeline definition using which you can effectively schedule and perform backups of files stored within an Amazon S3 bucket.

First up, let's have a look at the pipeline definition file itself:

 You can find the complete copy of code at https://github.com/ yoyoclouds/Administering-AWS-Volume2.

To start with, we once again provide a list of *objects* that describe the pipeline components starting with a pipeline configuration object, as highlighted in the following code:

```
"objects": [
  {
    "failureAndRerunMode": "CASCADE",
    "resourceRole": "DataPipelineDefaultResourceRole",
    "role": "DataPipelineDefaultRole",
    "pipelineLogUri": "#{myDataPipelineLogs}",
    "scheduleType": "ONDEMAND",
    "name": "Default",
    "id": "Default"
  },
```

Next, we provide the definition for other pipeline objects, including the data nodes:

```
{
  "filePath": "#{myInputS3FilePath}",
  "name": "inputS3Bucket",
  "id": "InputS3FilePath",
  "type": "S3DataNode"
},
{
  "filePath": "#{myOutputS3FilePath}/#{format(@scheduledStartTime,
'YYYY-MM-dd-HH-mm-ss')}.bak",
  "name": "outputS3Bucket",
  "id": "OutputS3FilePath",
  "type": "S3DataNode"
},
```

In this case, we are using the #{VARIABLE_NAMES} to declare a set of variables to make the pipeline definition more reusable. Once the data nodes are configured, we also have to define a set of actions that will trigger SNS alerts based on the pipeline's success or failure. Here is a snippet of the same:

```
{
    "role": "DataPipelineDefaultRole",
    "subject": "Failure",
    "name": "SNSAlertonFailure",
    "id": "OnFailSNSAlert",
    "message": "File was not copied over successfully. Pls check with Data
Pipeline Logs",
    "type": "SnsAlarm",
    "topicArn": "#{mySNSTopicARN}"
},
```

With the objects defined, the second section requires the `parameters` to be set up, where each of the variables declared in the objects section are detailed and defined:

```
"parameters": [
  {
    "watermark": "s3://mysourcebucket/filename",
    "description": "Source File Path:",
    "id": "myInputS3FilePath",
    "type": "AWS::S3::ObjectKey",
    "myComment": "The File path from the Input S3 Bucket"
  },
  {
    "watermark": "s3://mydestinationbucket/filename",
    "description": "Destination (Backup) File Path:",
    "id": "myOutputS3FilePath",
    "myComment": "The File path for the Output S3 Bucket",
```

```
        "type": "AWS::S3::ObjectKey"
    },
    {
        "watermark": "arn:aws:sns:us-east-1:28619EXAMPLE:ExampleTopic",
        "description": "SNS Topic ARN:",
        "id": "mySNSTopicARN",
        "type": "string",
        "myComment": "The SNS Topic's ARN for notifications"
    },
    . . . .
    ]
}
```

With this in mind, let us first look at uploading this definition to AWS Data Pipeline using the web console:

1. Log in to the AWS Data Pipeline console by navigating to this URL: `https://console.aws.amazon.com/datapipeline/home?region=us-east-1`.

We have deployed all of our pipelines so far in the US East (N. Virginia) region itself. You can opt to change the region, as per your requirements.

2. Once done, select the **Create Pipeline** option to get started. In the **Create Pipeline** page, fill in a suitable **Name** and **Description** for the new pipeline:

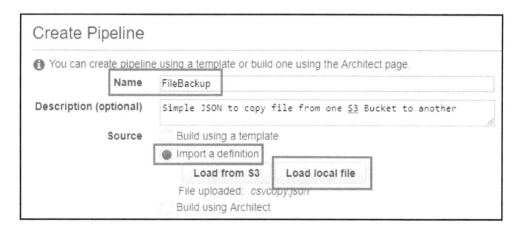

3. Next, select the **Import a definition** option and click on the **Load local file** as shown. Copy and upload the JSON file definition here.
4. With the file uploaded, fill out the **Parameters** section as explained here:

   - **S3 bucket path to data pipeline logs**: Browse and provide the bucket path for storing the pipeline's logs.

   - **Source file path**: Browse and select a file that you wish to backup from an Amazon S3 bucket.

   - **Destination (backup) file path**: Browse and select an Amazon S3 bucket path where you store the backed up file. You can optionally provide a backup folder name as well. Each file backed up to this location will follow a standard naming convention: `YYYY-MM-dd-HH-mm-ss.bak`.

   - **SNS Topic ARN**: Provide a valid SNS Topic ARN here. This ARN will be used to notify the user whether the pipeline's execution was a success or a failure.

   - **EC2 instance type**: You can optionally provide a different EC2 instance type as a resource here. By default, it will take the **t1.micro** instance type.

   - **EC2 instance termination:** Once again, you can provide a different instance termination value here. By default, it is set to 20 minutes. The termination time should be changed based on the approximate time taken to back up a file. The larger the file, the more time required to copy it and vice versa.

5. Once the parameter fields are populated, select the Edit in Architect option to view the overall components of the pipeline definition. You should see the following depiction:

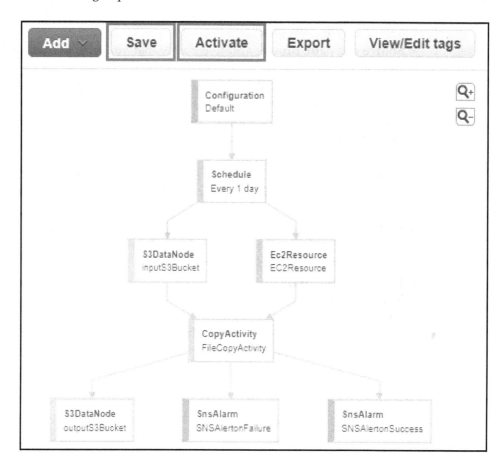

6. Click on **Save** to validate the pipeline for any errors. Once done, select **Activate** to start the pipeline's execution process.

7. The pipeline takes a few minutes to transition from the WAITING_FOR_RUNNER state to the **FINISHED** state. Once done, check for the backed up file in your destination S3 folder.

You can further tweak this particular pipeline definition to include entire S3 folder paths rather than just an individual file as performed now. Additionally, you can also change the start of the pipeline's execution by changing the `scheduleType` from `ONDEMAND` to `Schedule`, as depicted in the following code snippet:

```
{
    "id" : "Default",
    "type" : "Schedule",
    "period" : "1 hours",
    "startDateTime" : "2018-03-01T00:00:00",
    "endDateTime" : "2018-04-01T00:00:00"
}
```

The following snippet will execute the pipeline every hour starting from March 1, 2018 at 00:00:00 until April 1, 2018 00:00:00.

> To know more on how you can use the `Schedule` object, visit `https://docs.aws.amazon.com/datapipeline/latest/DeveloperGuide/dp-object-schedule.html`.

Now that the pipeline is up and running using the console, let us also have a look at a few simple AWS CLI commands using which you can achieve the same results:

1. To start with, create a blank pipeline using the following command:

   ```
   # aws datapipeline create-pipeline
   --name <NAME_OF_PIPELINE>
   --unique-id <UNIQUE_TOKEN>
   ```

   The `<UNIQUE_TOKEN>` can be any string of characters and is used to ensure idempotency during repeated calls to the `create-pipeline` command.

2. Once the pipeline is created, you will be presented with the pipeline's ID, as depicted in the following screenshot. Make a note of this ID as it will be required in the next steps:

```
yoyo@YoYoNux:~$ aws datapipeline create-pipeline --name CopyActivityPipeline \
> --unique-id SOm#Uniqu#TOkEn
{
    "pipelineId": "df-07900892NQ4TP65JLDRW"
}
yoyo@YoYoNux:~$
```

3. Next, we need to create three separate JSON files with the following content in them:

- `pipeline.json`: Copy and paste only the object definitions in this file.
- `parameters.json`: Copy and paste the parameter definitions here.
- `values.json`: Create a new file that contains the values for the parameters ,as shown in the following code snippet. Remember to substitute the values in <> with those of your own:

```
{
  "values":
    {
      "myDataPipelineLogs": "s3://<BUCKET_NAME>",
      "myOutputS3FilePath": "s3://<BUCKET_NAME>/<FOLDER>",
      "myInputS3FilePath":
  "s3://<BUCKET_NAME>/<FILE_NAME>",
      "mySNSTopicARN": "<SNS_ARN_FOR_NOTIFICATIONS>",
      "myEC2InstanceType": "t1.micro",
      "myEC2InstanceTermination": "20"
    }
}
```

4. Once done, save all three files and type in the following command to attach the pipeline definition to the newly created pipeline:

```
# aws datapipeline put-pipeline-definition
--pipeline-id <PIPELINE_ID>
--pipeline-definition file://pipeline.json
--parameter-objects file://parameters.json
--parameter-values-uri file://values.json
```

Here is a screenshot of the command's output for your reference:

```
yoyo@YoYoNux:~$
yoyo@YoYoNux:~$ aws datapipeline put-pipeline-definition \
> --pipeline-id df-07900892NQ4TP65JLDRW \
> --pipeline-definition file://pipeline.json \
> --parameter-objects file://parameters.json \
> --parameter-values-uri file://values.json
{
    "validationErrors": [],
    "errored": false,
    "validationWarnings": []
}
yoyo@YoYoNux:~$
```

5. With the pipeline definition uploaded, the final step left is to activate the pipeline using the following command:

```
# aws datapipeline activate-pipeline
--pipeline-id <PIPELINE_ID>
```

6. Once the pipeline is activated, you can view its status and last runtimes, using the following command:

```
# aws datapipeline list-runs
--pipeline-id <PIPELINE_ID>
```

7. Once the pipeline's execution completes, you can deactivate and delete the pipeline using the following set of commands:

```
# aws datapipeline deactivate-pipeline
--pipeline-id <PIPELINE_ID>
# aws datapipeline delete-pipeline
--pipeline-id <PIPELINE_ID>
```

Here is a screenshot of the command's output for your reference:

```
yoyo@YoYoNux:~$
yoyo@YoYoNux:~$ aws datapipeline deactivate-pipeline \
> --pipeline-id df-07900892NQ4TP65JLDRW
yoyo@YoYoNux:~$
yoyo@YoYoNux:~$ aws datapipeline delete-pipeline \
> --pipeline-id df-07900892NQ4TP65JLDRW
yoyo@YoYoNux:~$
```

With this, we come towards the end of yet another interesting chapter.

Managing AWS Accounts

10

In this chapter, we will cover the following topics:

- Setting up a master account
- Creating a member account
- Inviting an account
- Managing your accounts
- Adding a service control policy

Introduction

We work with a lot of companies who maintain a large, ever-growing number of AWS accounts. Keeping a handle on all these accounts has typically been quite difficult to do—even for the most seasoned AWS users.

With the release of AWS Organizations, you now have the ability to centrally manage your AWS accounts, to arrange them into logical groupings and hierarchies, and to apply controls to them in ways which haven't previously been possible on the AWS platform.

Setting up a master account

All accounts that use AWS Organizations for billing and control purposes must have a *master account*. This account controls membership to the organization, and pays the bills of all the members (someone's got to do it).

How to do it...

To set up a master account, perform the following steps:

1. Go to the **My Organization** section of the account you want to become the master. You must be logged in with your root credentials (that is, those you created the account with):

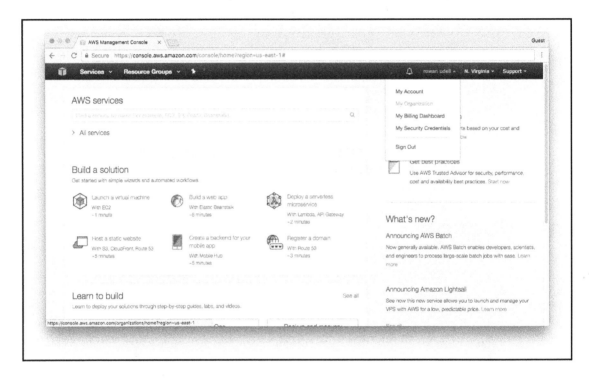

2. In the **AWS Organizations** section of the AWS console, click on **Create organization**, as shown in the following screenshot:

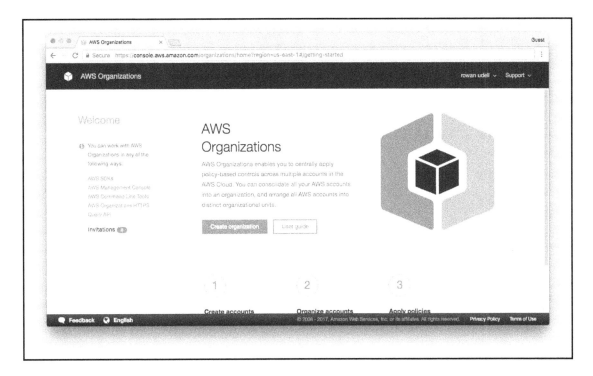

3. Unless you have a specific requirement, choose **ENABLE ALL FEATURES** to get the full benefit of organizations, as shown in the following screenshot:

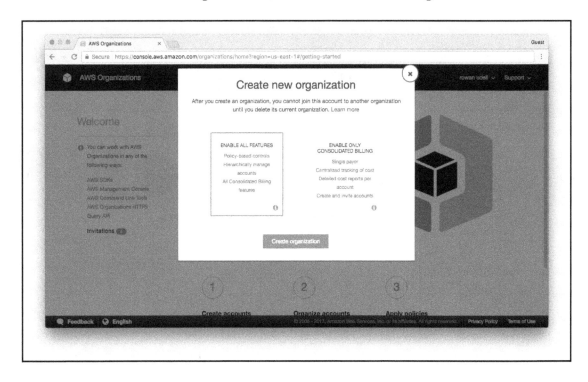

4. Now that your account has been converted, you can return to the **AWS Organizations** page to see a list of all your accounts:

How it works...

While this is a very simple recipe, it's the first thing you must do before you can use any of the useful features of AWS Organizations.

Here you can see a high-level diagram of the relationships between master accounts, members, and **organizational units** (**OUs**):

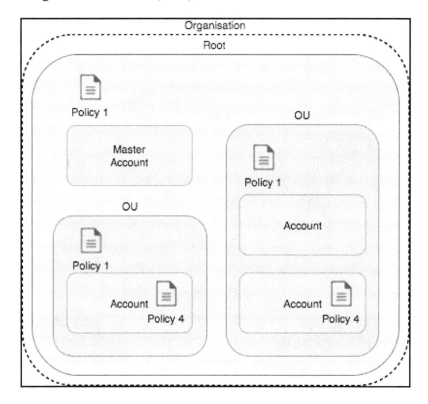

We deliberately enable all the features of organizations. The consolidated billing option is available for backward compatibility—before organizations, consolidated billing was your only option to link accounts.

Do not use your master account for day-to-day tasks. Since it is so important, it doesn't make sense to risk using it and/or having access keys for it. If your master account was to become compromised somehow, it would impact all of your member accounts. Just don't do it.

The master account will always have a star next to its name.

There's more...

All of the organizations functionality is exposed via the API. This means you can use the AWS SDKs or the CLI tool to do the same things you would in the web console.

Multi-factor authentication

As mentioned in the consolidated billing confirmation e-mail, it is advisable to configure **multi-factor authentication** (**MFA**) on your console. To do this, log in as your root user (that is, the credentials you used when first creating your account), go to the **Identity and Access Management** (**IAM**) console, and follow the **Activate MFA on your root account** prompts.

Using the CLI

You can easily create your master account with the CLI tool. The following command will turn your account into a master account, with all organizations features enabled:

```
aws organizations create-organization
```

See also

- The *Inviting an account* recipe
- The *Creating a member account* recipe

Creating a member account

Once your organization is up and running, the most common use you will have for it is automating the account creation process. Accounts created inside an organization are referred to as **member accounts**.

All charges incurred by a member account will be billed to the master account.

Getting ready

Obviously, you will need an organization to perform this recipe. See the other recipes in this chapter to get started.

How to do it...

1. Run the CLI tool command to create a new account, with appropriate values:

```
aws organizations create-account \
   --email <member-account-owners@email.com> \
   --account-name <member-account-name> \
   --query 'CreateAccountStatus.Id'
```

2. This command will return a create account status request ID value that you can use to check the status:

```
aws organizations describe-create-account-status \
   --create-account-request-id <your-create-account-status-id>
```

How it works...

The command to create a member account in your organization is extremely simple.

 The e-mail address used cannot be associated with any other AWS accounts.

The account creating process takes some time, so it is done *asynchronously*. This means that you won't receive an immediate status to your create-account command. Instead, the command in this recipe will return a request ID.

This ID is then passed to another account to check the status of the creation. When the status is CREATED, you can start to use the new account.

There's more...

While this functionality is definitely useful, the AWS Organizations service is relatively new. This means there are a few *features* you should be aware of.

Accessing the member account

Once you've created your member account, it's time to put it to work!

An IAM role will be present in the new account, with a default name of `OrganizationAccountAccessRole`. This is so you can assume the role (from your master account) and administer the member account. While this name is as good as any, it can be configured by passing the `--role-name` argument when creating the account.

In order to assume the role, you need to know its **Amazon Resource Name** (**ARN**). Working out the ARN is a multi-step process:

1. List your member accounts by running the following command in your master account:

   ```
   aws organizations list-accounts
   ```

2. Find the account you created (by its name) and note the ID value in the record. Using that ID, generate the role's ARN by following this pattern:

   ```
   arn:aws:iam::<your-member-account-
   id>:role/OrganizationAccountAccessRole
   ```

3. If you have changed the created role's name, update the last part of the ARN accordingly.

Service control policies

The **service control policies** (**SCPs**) are another major feature of AWS Organizations. You can apply them at multiple levels/resources, including accounts (both member accounts and invited accounts). Check the other recipes in this chapter for more details.

Root credentials

Some activities still require the root credentials of the account. An example activity would be closing (or deleting) an account (see the next section for more details).

In order to do this, you will need to do the password recovery process for the e-mail that was associated with the account when the `create-account` request was sent.

Deleting accounts

At the time of writing, *there is no way to delete an account created in your organization via the API*. We can only imagine that being able to programmatically delete a member account created in an organization will be a *highly requested* feature, and will be addressed soon. You can still go into the member account and close it using the root credentials, but these don't exist by default.

 While you can technically delete your *organization* via the API, you cannot do it if you have created any member accounts in your organization (because you can't delete them, your organization will never be empty). This should improve in the near future, but is still worth being aware of now.

See also

- The *Setting up a master account* recipe
- The *Adding a service control policy* recipe
- The *Cross-account user roles* recipe

Inviting an account

While it makes sense to create new accounts in your organization, what do you do with all the other accounts you have now?

You can invite existing accounts to your organization, which means you can treat them just like a member account from an administrative point of view. This greatly simplifies the administrative overhead of your accounts, as there isn't a separate process for *old* and *new* accounts.

As this is generally performed once for each existing account, we will use the console.

 All the AWS organizations functionality is available via the SDKs and AWS CLI tool. If you need to automate this process, you can.

Getting ready

You must have enabled AWS Organizations for one of your accounts (your master account), and have another account that has not been made part of an organization yet (that you will invite).

How to do it...

1. From the AWS console of the master account, click on your username, and select **My Organization** from the drop-down menu:

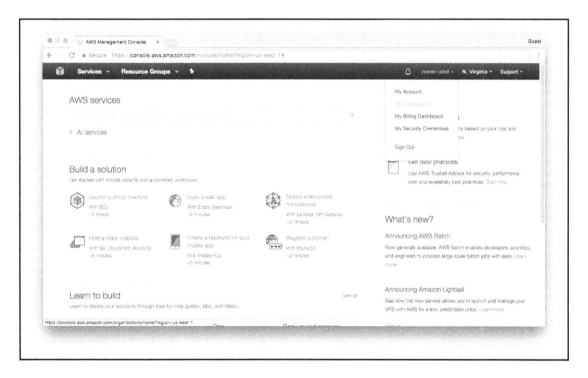

2. You will be taken to the **AWS Organizations** console, where you will see your current account:

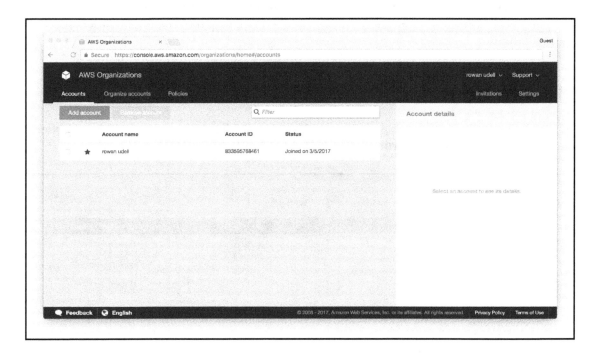

3. Click on the **Invitations** tab in the top-right of the console:

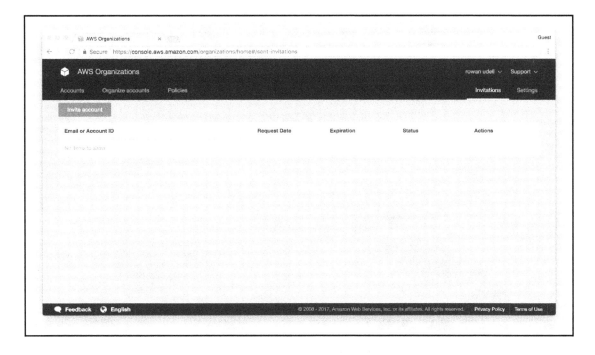

4. Click on the **Invite account** button. Specify the account ID (or main e-mail address) of the account to invite:

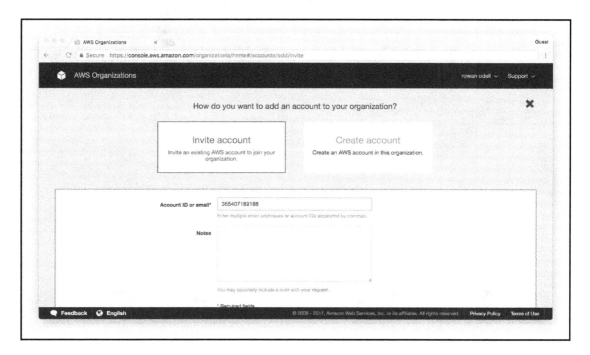

5. Once you click **Invite**, you will be taken to a list of invitations where you can view the status:

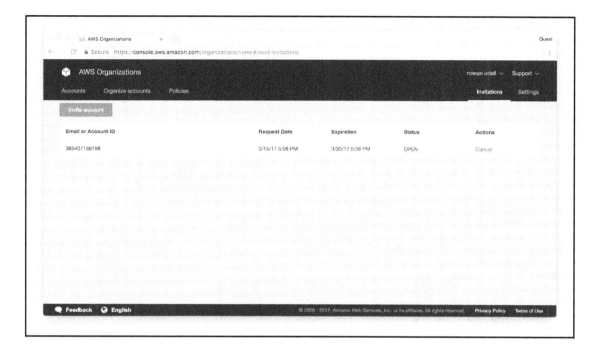

6. At this stage, the target/invited account will receive an e-mail notifying them of the invite:

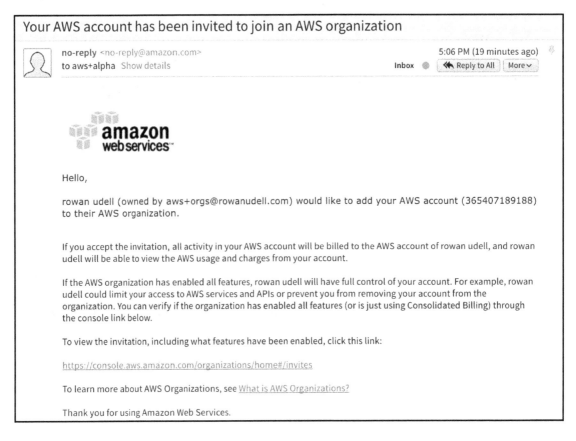

7. Log in to the invited account and go to the **My Organization** link under the user menu:

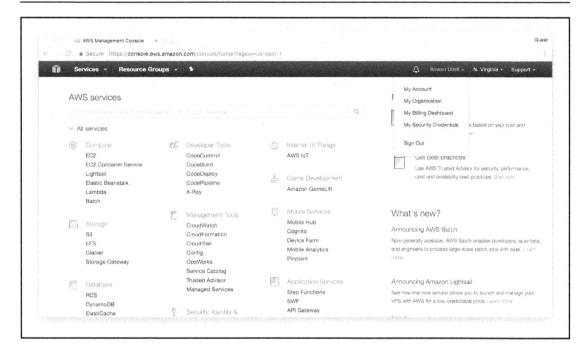

8. In the **AWS Organizations** console, you can see the pending invite on the left:

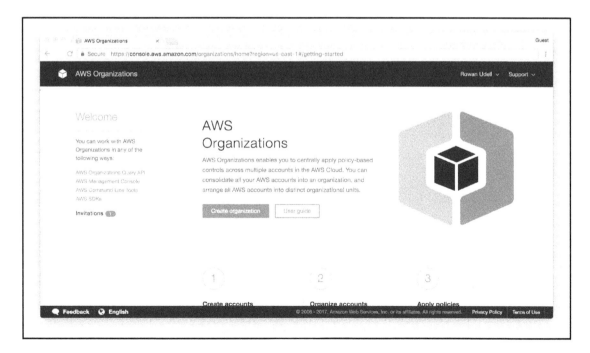

9. Clicking on the invite, you can see its details:

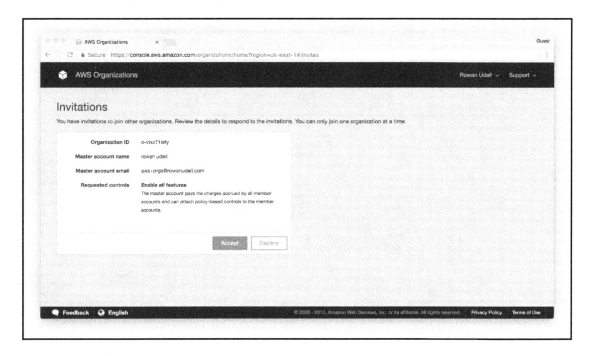

10. When the invite includes all features, you will be asked to confirm your acceptance:

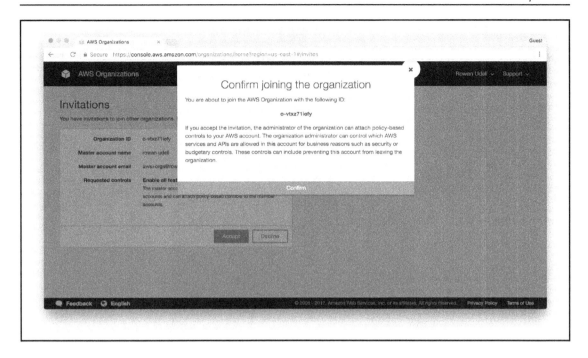

11. Once confirmed, you can now see the details of the organization you have joined:

12. At this stage, the master account will be notified of the accepted invite:

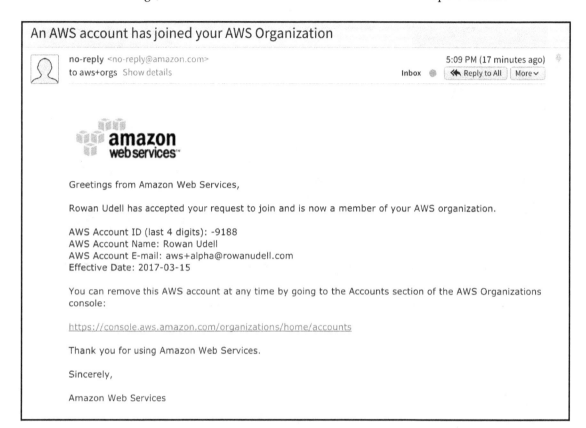

13. Back in the master account, you can now see the new account alongside the master:

How it works...

While there are many steps involved, the process of inviting an existing account is a relatively simple *handshake* process. This means that both sides must actively initiate/accept the invite, in order for it to succeed—an invite cannot be forced.

After specifying the target account's account ID (or e-mail address), the e-mail address associated will be notified.

As part of the handshake process, the invited account must explicitly accept the invite.

 It is important to note that the default invite type (and what we have used in the recipe) is to use the full feature set for AWS Organizations. As noted in the console, this means that the invited account *could be prevented from leaving the organization* if the relevant policies are configured.

After confirmation, both parties will receive an e-mail detailing the membership. From this point forward, the bill for the invited account will be paid by the master account.

There's more...

Invited accounts are treated differently to accounts created via the organizations functionality.

Removing accounts

Unlike *member accounts* (which are created via the AWS Organizations API), invited accounts can be removed from an organization.

Consolidated billing

As an alternative to the *full feature* invite, it is possible to specify just *consolidated billing* mode for an organization. In this mode, no OUs or policies will be available, only the billing relationship will be shared between the accounts (that is, the master account will pay the bill of the member accounts).

Any pre-existing accounts that were configured to use consolidated billing will have been *automatically* migrated to AWS Organizations *in consolidated billing mode*.

See also

- The *Creating a member account* recipe

Managing your accounts

There are a number of ways to group and arrange your AWS accounts. How you do this is completely up to you, but here are a few examples to consider:

- **Business unit (BU) or location**: You may wish to allow each BU to work in isolation on their own products or services, on their own schedule, without impacting other parts of the business
- **Cost center**: Grouping according to cost may help you track spend versus allocated budget

- **Environment type**: It may make sense to group your development, test, and production environments together in a way which helps you manage the controls across each environment
- **Workload type or data classification**: Your company may want to isolate workload types from each other, or ensure that particular controls are applied to all accounts containing a particular kind of data

In the following fictitious example, we have isolated the **Sitwell Enterprises Account** from the rest of the organization by placing it in an OU called **Sudden Valley**. Perhaps they operate in a different geographical location and have different regulatory requirements around controls and access.

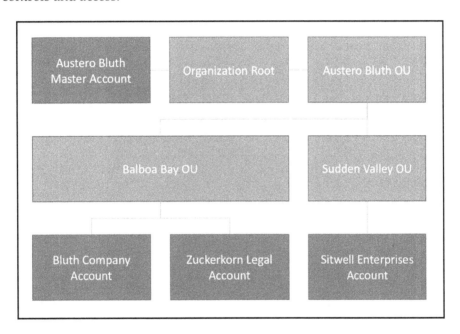

Organization hierarchy

Note that while it's also technically possible for us to put the master account inside an OU, we avoid doing this to make it obvious that:

- It's the master account and has control over the entire organization
- The rules we set, using SCPs for the member accounts in our organization, do not apply to the master account (because they can't)

Learn more about SCPs in the *Adding a service control policy* recipe in this chapter.

Getting ready

Before we can proceed, you should have already done the following:

- Set up a master AWS account
- Created an organization
- Created member accounts in your organization, or manually added member accounts (by invitation) to your organization

How to do it...

We'll now cover the one-line commands you'll need to perform the common tasks required to manage your OU. These commands can only be performed in your master account.

Getting the root ID for your organization

You can run this command to get the ID of the root for your organization. The root is created automatically for you when you create your organization in your master account. The ID returned to you will look something like this: r-bmdw.

```
aws organizations list-roots
```

Creating an OU

To create an OU, perform the following steps:

1. Determine where you'd like this OU to live. If it lives directly underneath the root, then your root ID will be the parent. Alternatively, if this OU is going to be a child of another OU, use the ID of the OU instead. Obviously, if this is the first OU you're creating, the root will be the parent.

2. Use the CLI to create your OU like so:

```
aws organizations create-organizational-unit \
  --parent-id <root-id or parent-ou-id> \
  --name <desired-ou-name>
```

Getting the ID of an OU

If you need to fetch the ID of an OU, you can use the CLI to do so; note that you'll need to know the parent of the OU. Here is how you'd get a list of all the OUs and their IDs in a root or OU:

```
aws organizations list-organizational-units-for-parent \
  --parent-id <root-id or parent-ou-id>
```

Adding an account to an OU

To add an account to an OU, perform the following steps:

1. When an account is initially added to your organization, it will be a child of the organization root. To add it to the OU you just created, you need to move it using the following CLI command:

```
aws organizations move-account \
  --account-id <twelve-digit-account-id> \
  --source-parent-id <root-id> \
  --destination-parent-id <new-parent-ou-id>
```

2. If you wish to move an account from one OU to another, simply use the same command but use the existing parent OU ID instead of the root ID.

Removing an account from an OU

To remove an account from an OU, perform the following steps:

1. If you wish to remove an account from an OU, you have two options. You can move it to another OU, or you can move it back to the root. If you decide you want to delete an OU, you'll need to make sure no accounts exist inside it first (we'll show you how to do this next).

2. Run the following command to move an account back to the root:

```
aws organizations move-account \
  --account-id <twelve-digit-account-id> \
  --source-parent-id <existing-parent-ou-id> \
  --destination-parent-id <root-id>
```

Deleting an OU

To delete an OU, you'll first need to make sure it's empty by removing its child accounts (as mentioned previously). You can then go ahead and delete the OU like so:

```
aws organizations delete-organizational-unit \
  --organizational-unit-id <ou-id>
```

How it works...

If done right, grouping your accounts together using OUs will help you simplify the way you manage and administer them. Try to use only *just enough* OUs to get the job done. The idea is to use OUs to make your life easier, not harder.

There's more...

- The **organizational control policies (OCPs)** can be attached to your root, OU, or AWS accounts. At this time, only one kind of OCP is supported: SCP.
- Accounts can only belong to one OU or root.
- Similarly, OUs can only belong to one OU or root.
- It's best to avoid deploying resources in the master account because this account can't be controlled with SCPs. The master account should be treated as a management account for audit, control, and billing purposes only.

See also

- The *Adding a service control policy* recipe

Adding a service control policy

Before we begin, we should talk through what SCPs are and how they apply to your organization.

An SCP consists of a policy document which defines (by way of filtering) the services and actions which are able to be used and performed within an OU or in an AWS account. If you've previously configured an IAM policy, then you will have more than enough background knowledge to get started with SCPs. Apart from a couple of minor exceptions, they look exactly the same.

SCPs can be applied at different levels throughout an organization. These are the levels, starting from the bottom and going up:

- **AWS account level**: An SCP applied to an AWS account takes effect on only that account. It's important to note that the SCP is very separate from the IAM policies which live inside the account. For example, an SCP might allow full access to S3 for an AWS account but the IAM policies inside the account may deny it (for certain roles and/or users).
- **OU level**: An SCP applied at the OU level will apply to all the AWS accounts which live inside the OU as well as any child OUs (remember that an OU can by a member of an OU).
- **Root level**: If an SCP is applied at this level, it will apply to all AWS accounts inside the organization.

Things can start to get really interesting when you have an SCP applied at multiple levels. The *intersection* of the polices at the root, OU, account, and IAM levels is evaluated and will determine whether or not an API call is allowed to be made. For example, someone belonging to an IAM role which has full administrator access to an account still won't be able to call any EC2 APIs if any of the SCPs above it (account, OU, root) deny EC2 access.

In the following example, we have a top-level OU, Austero Bluth, with an SCP which allows access to all AWS resources for all OUs and accounts underneath it:

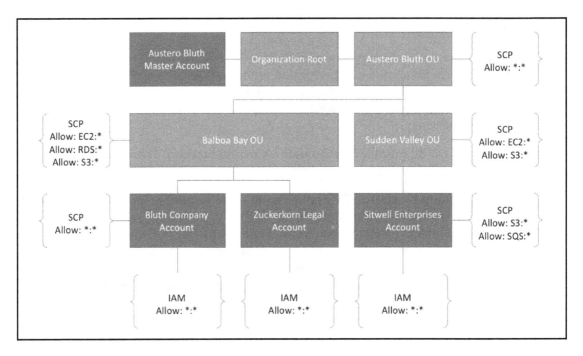

Organization hierarchy and policies

Austero Bluth has two child OUs; let's focus on Sudden Valley. It has an SCP which allows only EC2 and S3. By using a whitelisting approach, anything except these two services will be denied. Remembering that SCPs act like a filter, any OU or AWS accounts living underneath the Sudden Valley OU will, at most, have access to EC2 and S3.

The **Sitwell Enterprises Account** also has an SCP attached to it. This particular SCP allows S3 and SQS. Note that the SQS statement will have no effect here because the Sitwell account is inside an OU which does not allow SQS. Also note that this account has no access to EC2 despite the **Sudden Valley OU** allowing it; this is because EC2 wasn't explicitly allowed in the SCP attached to the account.

At the IAM level, we have a role in the Sitwell AWS account which allows full administrator privileges. But, because the intersection of the SCPs governing this account will only allow S3, anyone using this role will be denied access if they attempt to use EC2 or SQS, for example.

Let's also take a look at the **Bluth Company Account**. The SCP which is attached to it allows full AWS access; however, it lives inside an OU (Balboa Bay) which only allows EC2, RDS, and S3. There is an IAM role inside this account which also allows full admin access but, again, administrators in this account will be limited to EC2, RDS, and S3.

Getting ready

We're going to step through creating an SCP and adding it to an OU.

You're going to need the ID of the OU in question; you can fetch it from the organizations web console or use the CLI. It will look something like this: `ou-bmdw-omzypry7`.

We'll be preparing a policy document as well. In this example, we're going to add an SCP to the Sudden Valley OU to allow access to EC2 and S3. Here's what our SCP looks like:

```
{
    "Version":"2012-10-17",
    "Statement":[
        {
            "Effect":"Allow",
            "Action":["EC2:*","S3:*"],
            "Resource":"*"
        }
    ]
}
```

How to do it...

1. Open a new file in your text editor, add your JSON policy document, and save it.
2. Run the `create-policy` CLI command like so. We're getting a little tricky with the `tr` command here: we're using it to remove the carriage returns from the policy document, so pay close attention to the syntax in the example provided. Unfortunately, the organizations CLI doesn't allow us to provide the path to the policy document directly:

```
aws organizations create-policy \
  --content "$(tr -d '\n' < my-policy-file.json)" \
  --description "A policy description goes here" \
  --name "My policy" \
  --type SERVICE_CONTROL_POLICY
```

3. If the preceding CLI command works successfully, some JSON will be returned to you containing the ID of the policy we just added. It will look something like this: `p-o9to04s7`.

4. You can now go ahead and attach this policy to the OU. Use the following CLI command to do this:

```
aws organizations attach-policy \
  --target-id <ou-or-aws-account-id> \
  --policy-id <policy-id>
```

5. Unfortunately, the preceding command does not output anything if it ran successfully. You can double-check your handiwork in the AWS web console or use the following CLI command to verify that it worked:

```
aws organizations list-targets-for-policy \
  --policy-id <policy-id>
```

How it works...

Again, the policies you add will act as a filter at each level of your organizational structure. With this in mind, it might be a good time to point out that testing your policies on a single account before applying them organization-wide will save you a lot of heartache. Making sweeping changes to an SCP living at the top of your organization may create an unforeseen situation at the AWS account level at the bottom of the chain. A local admin in an AWS account is not able to override SCPs.

There's more...

- At the time of publishing, you are only able to have a single root inside an organization (it's created automatically for you when you create an organization).
- For obvious reasons, the master account is not affected by any SCPs which are attached to it. You may also notice that it's technically possible to place the master account in an OU; again, it will be unaffected by any SCPs which have been attached to that OU.
- Since the master account is unaffected by SCPs, it's a good idea to leave it as empty as possible and to not create any resources in it. Use child AWS accounts instead so you can apply fine-grained controls to them.
- SCPs are required on each OU and account but shouldn't be considered the only form of access control for your AWS accounts. Apply IAM where appropriate.

- When creating our policy, we have to specify a `--type` parameter. At the time of publishing, AWS only supports one variant of OCP: `SERVICE_CONTROL_POLICY`.

- As much as possible, follow the principle of least privilege. You want to give your AWS accounts access to only the services they need. This helps you mitigate damage caused by misclicks, programming errors, or compromised accounts.

- In the long run, you may find it advantageous to not assign controls at the root level. Instead, you may be better off adding *all* accounts to an OU and applying your controls to the OU instead.

- Your policies can take a whitelisting or blacklisting approach. In this recipe, we've used a whitelist approach, but you may instead prefer to allow your OUs and accounts to use all services except the ones you explicitly disallow. You should choose one of these approaches and stick with it, as mixing the two will cause you lots of confusion down the road.

- Unlike IAM policies, you can't specify conditions in SCP documents and `Resource` *must* be `*`.

11
Using AWS Compute

In this chapter, we will cover:

- Creating a key pair
- Launching an instance
- Attaching storage
- Securely accessing private instances
- Auto scaling an application server
- Creating machine images
- Creating security groups
- Creating a load balancer

Introduction

Elastic Cloud Compute (**EC2**) is by far the most utilized and complex service in the AWS catalogue. More than *just virtual machines*, EC2 provides a framework of sub-services to help you secure and manage your instances elastically.

Creating a key pair

A key pair is used to access your instances via SSH. This is the quickest and easiest way to access your instances.

Getting ready

To perform this recipe, you must have your AWS CLI tool configured correctly.

How to do it...

1. Create the key pair, and save it to disk:

```
aws ec2 create-key-pair \
  --key-name MyEC2KeyPair \
  --query 'KeyMaterial' \
  --output text > ec2keypair.pem
```

2. Change the permissions on the created file:

```
chmod 600 ec2keypair.pem
```

How it works...

This call requests a new private key from EC2. The response is then parsed using a JMESPath query, and the private key (in the `KeyMaterial` property) is saved to a new key file with the `.pem` extension.

Finally, we change the permissions on the key file so that it cannot be read by other users—this is required before SSH will allow you to use it.

Launching an instance

There will be scenarios—usually when testing and developing your infrastructure code—when you need quick access to an instance. Creating it via the AWS CLI is the quickest and most consistent way to create one-off instances.

There are other recipes in the book that will require a running instance. This recipe will get you started.

Getting ready

For this recipe, you must have an existing key pair.

In this recipe, we are launching an instance of AWS Linux using an AMI ID in the us-east-1 region. If you are working in a different region, you will need to update your image-id parameter.

You must have configured your AWS CLI tool with working credentials.

How to do it...

Run the following AWS CLI command, using your own key-pair name:

```
aws ec2 run-instances \
  --image-id ami-9be6f38c \
  --instance-type t2.micro \
  --key-name <your-key-pair-name>
```

How it works...

While you can create an instance via the AWS web console, it involves many distracting options. When developing and testing, the CLI tool is the best way to provision instances.

While the key-name argument is optional, you will not be able to connect to your instance unless you have pre-configured some other way of logging in.

 The t2.micro instance type used in this recipe is included in the AWS free tier. You can run one micro instance per month for free during the first 12 months of your usage. See https://aws.amazon.com/free for more information.

As no VPC or security groups are specified, the instance will be launched in your account's default VPC and security group. The default security group allows access from anywhere, on all ports, and so is not suitable for long-lived instances. You can modify an instance's security groups after it is launched, without stopping it.

There's more...

If you have created your own AMI, then you can change the `image-id` argument to quickly launch your specific AMI.

You may also want to take note of the `InstanceId` value in the response from the API, as you may need it for future commands.

See also

- The *Creating a key pair* recipe
- The *Creating machine images* recipe

Attaching storage

Ideally, you will have defined all your storage requirements up-front as code using a service such as CloudFormation. However, sometimes that is not possible due to application restrictions or changing requirements.

You can easily add additional storage to your instances while they are running by attaching a new volume.

Getting ready

For this recipe, you will need the following:

- A running instance's ID. It will start with `i-` followed by alphanumeric characters.
- The AZ the instance is running in. This looks like the region name with a letter after it; for example, `us-east-1a`.

In this recipe, we are using an AWS Linux instance. If you are using a different operating system, the steps to mount the volume will be different. We will be running an instance in the AZ us-east-1a.

You must have configured your AWS CLI tool with working credentials.

How to do it...

1. Create a volume:

```
aws ec2 create-volume --availability-zone us-east-1a
```

 Take note of the returned VolumeId in the response. It will start with vol- followed by alphanumeric characters.

2. Attach the volume to the instance, using the volume ID noted in the last step and the instance ID you started with:

```
aws ec2 attach-volume \
  --volume-id <your-volume-id> \
  --instance-id <your-instance-id> \
  --device /dev/sdf
```

3. On the instance itself, mount the volume device:

```
mount /dev/xvdf /mnt/volume
```

How it works...

In this recipe, we start by creating a volume. Volumes are created from snapshots. If you do not specify a snapshot ID it uses a blank snapshot, and you get a blank volume.

While volumes are hosted redundantly, they are only hosted in a single AZ, so must be provisioned in the same AZ the instance is running in.

The `create-volume` command returns a response that includes the newly created volume's `VolumeId`. We then use this ID in the next step.

It can sometimes take a few seconds for a volume to become available. If you are scripting these commands, use the `aws ec2 wait` command to wait for the volume to become available.

In step 3, we attach a volume to the instance. When attaching to an instance, you must specify the name of the device that it will be presented to the operating system as. Unfortunately, this does not guarantee what the device will appear as. In the case of AWS Linux, `/dev/sdf` becomes `/dev/xvdf`.

Device naming is kernel-specific, so if you are using something other than AWS Linux, the device name may be different. See `http://docs.aws.amazon.com/AWSEC2/latest/UserGuide/device_naming .html` for full details.

Securely accessing private instances

Any instance or resource living in a private subnet in your VPC will be inaccessible from the Internet. This makes good sense from a security perspective because it gives your instances a higher level of protection.

Of course, if they can't be accessed from the Internet, then they're not going to be easy to administer.

One common pattern is to use a VPN server as a single, highly controlled, entry point to your private network. This is what we're going to show you in this recipe, as pictured in the following diagram:

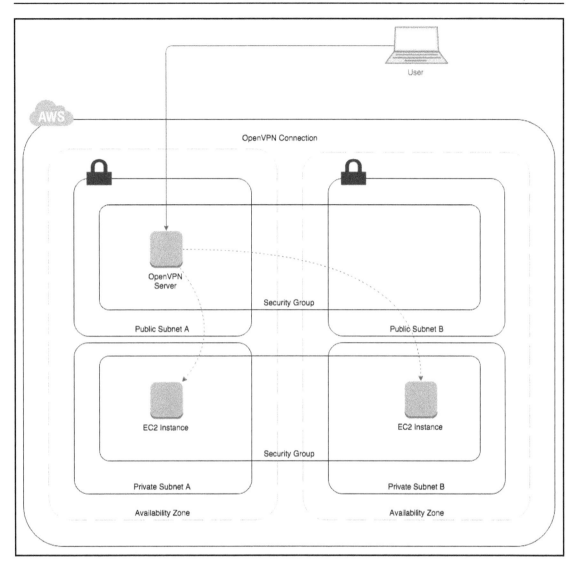

Accessing private instances securely

Getting ready

We're going to use OpenVPN for this example. They provide a free (for up to two users)
AMI in the AWS marketplace, which has OpenVPN already installed and configured.
You'll need to accept the terms and conditions for using this AMI. You can do so by visiting
the AMI's marketplace page at `https://aws.amazon.com/marketplace/pp/B00MI40CAE/`.

You need to decide on a password, which will be your *temporary* admin password. We'll feed this password into a CloudFormation template and then change it after we create our stack.

You can use the default VPC for this example.

How to do it...

1. Create a new CloudFormation template and add the following Mappings. This is a list of all the latest OpenVPN AMIs in each region. We're adding these to maximize region portability for our template—you can omit the regions you have no intention of using:

```
Mappings:
  AWSRegion2AMI: # Latest OpenVPN AMI at time of publishing: 2.1.4
    us-east-1:
      AMI: ami-bc3566ab
    us-east-2:
      AMI: ami-10306a75
    us-west-2:
      AMI: ami-d3e743b3
    us-west-1:
      AMI: ami-4a02492a
    eu-west-1:
      AMI: ami-f53d7386
    eu-central-1:
      AMI: ami-ad1fe6c2
    ap-southeast-1:
      AMI: ami-a859ffcb
    ap-northeast-1:
      AMI: ami-e9da7c88
    ap-southeast-2:
      AMI: ami-89477aea
    sa-east-1:
      AMI: ami-0c069b60
```

2. We now need to define some `Parameters`. Firstly we'll need to know which VPC and subnet to deploy our VPN instance to. Note that you need to specify a *public* subnet here, otherwise you won't be able to access your OpenVPN server:

```
VpcId:
  Type: AWS::EC2::VPC::Id
  Description: VPC where load balancer and instance will launch
SubnetId:
  Type: List<AWS::EC2::Subnet::Id>
  Description: Subnet where OpenVPN server will launch
    (pick at least 1)
```

3. We also need to define `InstanceType` and `KeyName`. These are the EC2 instance class and SSH key pair to use to launch our OpenVPN server:

```
InstanceType:
  Type: String
  Description: OpenVPN server instance type
  Default: m3.medium
KeyName:
  Type: AWS::EC2::KeyPair::KeyName
  Description: EC2 KeyPair for SSH access
```

4. We need a parameter for `AdminPassword`. This is the temporary password which will be given to the `openvpn` user (administrator) when the server starts up:

```
AdminPassword:
  Type: String
  Description: Password for 'openvpn' user
  Default: openvpn
  NoEcho: true
```

5. The last parameter is the CIDR block, which we wish to allow to connect to our VPN server. You may wish to lock this down to the public IP range of your corporate network, for example:

```
AllowAccessFromCIDR:
  Type: String
  Description: IP range/address to allow VPN connections from
  Default: "0.0.0.0/0"
```

6. The first `Resource` we need to define is the security group our OpenVPN server will live in. You'll also use this security group to allow access to other resources in your network. Add it to your template as follows:

```
VPNSecurityGroup:
  Type: AWS::EC2::SecurityGroup
  Properties:
    GroupDescription: Inbound access to OpenVPN server
    VpcId: !Ref VpcId
    SecurityGroupIngress:
    - CidrIp: !Ref AllowAccessFromCIDR
      FromPort: 443
      IpProtocol: tcp
      ToPort: 443
    - CidrIp: !Ref AllowAccessFromCIDR
      FromPort: 22
      IpProtocol: tcp
      ToPort: 22
    - CidrIp: !Ref AllowAccessFromCIDR
      FromPort: 1194
      IpProtocol: udp
      ToPort: 1194
```

7. We can now define the actual OpenVPN instance itself. You'll notice that we are explicitly configuring the network interface. This is required, because we want to declare that this instance must get a public IP address (otherwise you won't be able to access it). In the `UserData`, we declare some variables that the OpenVPN software will pick up when it starts so that it can configure itself:

```
OpenVPNInstance:
  Type: AWS::EC2::Instance
  Properties:
    ImageId: !FindInMap [ AWSRegion2AMI, !Ref "AWS::Region", AMI ]
    InstanceType: !Ref InstanceType
    KeyName: !Ref KeyName
    NetworkInterfaces:
      - AssociatePublicIpAddress: true
        DeviceIndex: "0"
        GroupSet:
          - !Ref VPNSecurityGroup
        SubnetId: !Select [ 0, Ref: SubnetId ]
    Tags:
      - Key: Name
        Value: example-openvpn-server
    UserData:
      Fn::Base64: !Sub
        - |
```

```
               public_hostname=openvpn
               admin_user=openvpn
               admin_pw=${admin_pw}
               reroute_gw=1
               reroute_dns=1
         - admin_pw: !Ref AdminPassword
```

8. Finally, we add some helpful `Outputs`:

```
Outputs:
  OpenVPNAdministration:
    Value:
      Fn::Join:
        - ""
        - - https://
          - !GetAtt OpenVPNInstance.PublicIp
          - /admin/
    Description: Admin URL for OpenVPN server
  OpenVPNClientLogin:
    Value:
      Fn::Join:
        - ""
        - - https://
          - !GetAtt OpenVPNInstance.PublicIp
          - /
    Description: Client login URL for OpenVPN server
  OpenVPNServerIPAddress:
    Value: !GetAtt OpenVPNInstance.PublicIp
    Description: IP address for OpenVPN server
```

9. Go ahead and launch this stack in the CloudFormation web console, or via the CLI, with the following command:

```
aws cloudformation create-stack \
  --template-body file://04-securely-access-private-instances.yaml \
  --stack-name example-vpn \
  --parameters \
  ParameterKey=KeyName,ParameterValue=<key-pair-name> \
  ParameterKey=VpcId,ParameterValue=<your-vpc-id> \
  ParameterKey=SubnetId,ParameterValue=<your-public-subnet-id>
```

Configuration

1. Once your stack is created, you'll want to change the password for the `openvpn` user (administrator). Go to the admin control panel and do this now: `https://<ip-or-hostname-of-vpn-server>/admin`. If your VPN server is operating as expected you'll be greeted with a status page after logging in, as pictured in the following screenshot:

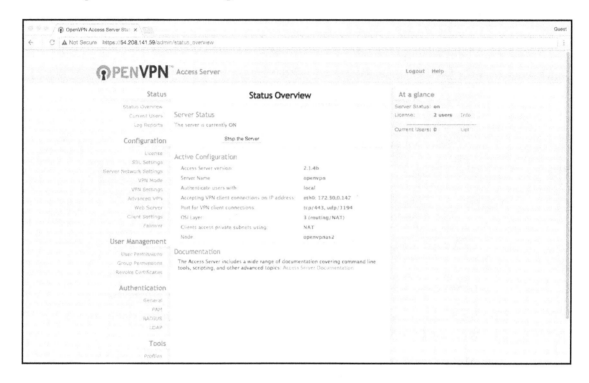

While you're there, you should create a non-administrator user account. This will be the account you'll use to connect to the VPN. Add this account on the **User Permissions** page as pictured in the following screenshot:

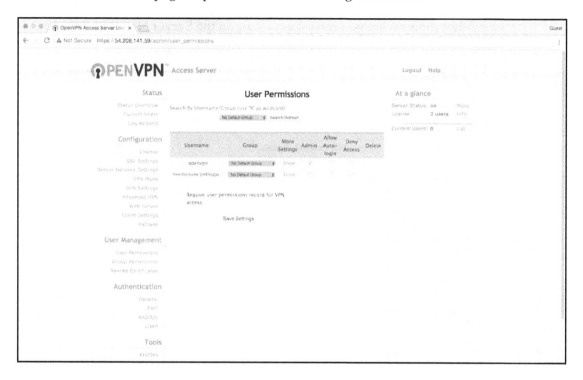

2. Under **Server Network Settings**, in the **Hostname or IP address** field, enter the hostname or IP address of the server. This step is important, and when you download your OpenVPN config file from the server (next step), it will make your life much easier if it has the correct hostname or IP address in it. The next screenshot shows what you can expect to see on the **Server Network Settings** page:

How it works...

You should now be able to connect to your VPN server. Go to the user login page and log in with the credentials you gave to the previously mentioned non-administrator user:

```
https://<ip-or-hostname-of-vpn-server>/
```

After logging in, you will have the option to download the OpenVPN client with configuration which is specific to your account. Alternatively, if you already have a VPN client installed, you can just download the configuration on its own.

There's more...

There are a couple of important points you'll need to keep in mind now that you are up and running with an OpenVPN server:

- If you need to SSH to the instance, you must connect with the username `openvpnas`
- To access your other instances, you'll need to allow connections from the VPN security group created in this recipe

Auto scaling an application server

Auto scaling is a fundamental component of compute in the cloud. It provides not only the ability to scale up and down in response to application load, but also redundancy, by ensuring that capacity is always available. Even in the unlikely event of an AZ outage, the auto scaling group will ensure that instances are available to run your application.

Auto scaling also allows you to pay for only the EC2 capacity you need, because underutilized servers can be automatically de-provisioned.

Getting ready

You must supply two or more subnet IDs for this recipe to work.

The following example uses an AWS Linux AMI in the `us-east-1` region. Update the parameters as required if you are working in a different region.

How to do it...

1. Start by defining the template version and description:

   ```
   AWSTemplateFormatVersion: "2010-09-09"
   Description: Create an Auto Scaling Group
   ```

2. Add a `Parameters` section with the required parameters that will be used later in the template:

   ```
   Parameters:
     SubnetIds:
       Description: Subnet IDs where instances can be launched
   ```

```
                          Type: List<AWS::EC2::Subnet::Id>
```

3. Still under the `Parameters` section, add the optional instance configuration parameters:

```
AmiId:
  Description: The application server's AMI ID
  Type: AWS::EC2::Image::Id
  Default: ami-9be6f38c # AWS Linux in us-east-1
InstanceType:
  Description: The type of instance to launch
  Type: String
  Default: t2.micro
```

4. Still under the `Parameters` section, add the optional auto scaling group-configuration parameters:

```
MinSize:
  Description: Minimum number of instances in the group
  Type: Number
  Default: 1
MaxSize:
  Description: Maximum number of instances in the group
  Type: Number
  Default: 4

ThresholdCPUHigh:
  Description: Launch new instances when CPU utilization
    is over this threshold
  Type: Number
  Default: 60

ThresholdCPULow:
  Description: Remove instances when CPU utilization
    is under this threshold
  Type: Number
  Default: 40

ThresholdMinutes:
  Description: Launch new instances when over the CPU
    threshold for this many minutes
  Type: Number
  Default: 5
```

5. Add a `Resources` section, and define the auto scaling group resource:

```
Resources:
  AutoScalingGroup:
    Type: AWS::AutoScaling::AutoScalingGroup
    Properties:
      MinSize: !Ref MinSize
      MaxSize: !Ref MaxSize
      LaunchConfigurationName: !Ref LaunchConfiguration
      Tags:
        - Key: Name
          Value: !Sub "${AWS::StackName} server"
          PropagateAtLaunch: true
      VPCZoneIdentifier: !Ref SubnetIds
```

6. Still under the `Resources` section, define the launch configuration used by the auto scaling group:

```
LaunchConfiguration:
  Type: AWS::AutoScaling::LaunchConfiguration
  Properties:
    ImageId: !Ref AmiId
    InstanceType: !Ref InstanceType
    UserData:
      Fn::Base64: !Sub |
        #!/bin/bash -xe
        # This will be run on startup, launch your application here
```

7. Next, define two scaling policy resources—one to scale up and the other to scale down:

```
ScaleUpPolicy:
  Type: AWS::AutoScaling::ScalingPolicy
  Properties:
    AdjustmentType: ChangeInCapacity
    AutoScalingGroupName: !Ref AutoScalingGroup
    Cooldown: 60
    ScalingAdjustment: 1

ScaleDownPolicy:
  Type: AWS::AutoScaling::ScalingPolicy
  Properties:
    AdjustmentType: ChangeInCapacity
    AutoScalingGroupName: !Ref AutoScalingGroup
    Cooldown: 60
    ScalingAdjustment: -1
```

8. Define an alarm that will alert when the CPU goes *over* the `ThresholdCPUHigh` parameter:

```
CPUHighAlarm:
  Type: AWS::CloudWatch::Alarm
  Properties:
    ActionsEnabled: true
    AlarmActions:
      - !Ref ScaleUpPolicy
    AlarmDescription: Scale up on CPU load
    ComparisonOperator: GreaterThanThreshold
    Dimensions:
      - Name: AutoScalingGroupName
        Value: !Ref AutoScalingGroup
    EvaluationPeriods: !Ref ThresholdMinutes
    MetricName: CPUUtilization
    Namespace: AWS/EC2
    Period: 60
    Statistic: Average
    Threshold: !Ref ThresholdCPUHigh
```

9. Finally, define an alarm that will alert when the CPU goes *under* the `ThresholdCPULow` parameter:

```
CPULowAlarm:
  Type: AWS::CloudWatch::Alarm
  Properties:
    ActionsEnabled: true
    AlarmActions:
      - !Ref ScaleDownPolicy
    AlarmDescription: Scale down on CPU load
    ComparisonOperator: LessThanThreshold
    Dimensions:
      - Name: AutoScalingGroupName
        Value: !Ref AutoScalingGroup
    EvaluationPeriods: !Ref ThresholdMinutes
    MetricName: CPUUtilization
    Namespace: AWS/EC2
    Period: 60
    Statistic: Average
    Threshold: !Ref ThresholdCPULow
```

10. Save the template with the filename `04-auto-scaling-an-application-server.yaml`.

11. Launch the template with the following AWS CLI command, supplying your subnet IDs:

```
aws cloudformation create-stack \
  --stack-name asg \
  --template-body file://04-auto-scaling-an-application-server.yaml \
  --parameters \
  ParameterKey=SubnetIds,ParameterValue='<subnet-id-1>\, \
    <subnet-id-2>'
```

How it works...

This example defines an auto scaling group and the dependent resources. These include the following:

- A launch configuration to use when launching new instances
- Two scaling policies, one to scale the number of instances up, and an inverse policy to scale back down
- An alarm to alert when the CPU crosses a certain threshold, for a certain number of minutes

The auto scaling group and launch-configuration resource objects in this example use mostly default values. You will need to specify your own `SecurityGroups` and a `KeyName` parameter in the `LaunchConfiguration` resource configuration if you want to be able to connect to the instances (for example, via SSH).

AWS will automatically take care of spreading your instances evenly over the subnets you have configured, so make sure they are in different AZs! When scaling down, the oldest instances will be removed before the newer ones.

Scaling policies

The scaling policies detail how many instances to create or delete when they are triggered. It also defines a `Cooldown` value, which helps prevent *flapping* servers—when servers are created and deleted before they have finished starting and are useful.

While the scaling policies in this example use equal values, you might want to change that so your application can scale *up* quickly, and scale *down* slowly for the best user experience.

Alarms

The `CPUHighAlarm` parameter will alert when the average CPU utilization goes over the value set in the `ThresholdCPUHigh` parameter. This alert will be sent to the `ScaleUpPolicy` resource provisioning more instances, which will bring the average CPU utilization down across the whole auto scaling group. As the name suggests, the `CPULowAlarm` parameter does the reverse when the average CPU utilization goes under the `ThresholdCPULow` parameter.

This means that new instances will be launched until the CPU utilization across the auto scaling group stabilizes somewhere between 40-60% (based on the default parameter values), or the `MaxSize` of instances is reached.

 It is very important to leave a gap between the high and low alarms thresholds. If they are too close together, the alarms will not stabilize and you will see instances created and destroyed almost continually.

The minimum charge for an instance is *one hour*, so creating and destroying them multiple times in one hour may result in higher than expected charges.

Creating machine images

Creating or *baking* your own **Amazon Machine Images** (**AMIs**) is a key part of systems administration in AWS. Having a pre-baked image helps you provision your servers faster, easier, and more consistently than configuring it by hand.

Packer is the de facto standard tool that helps you make your own AMIs. By automating the launch, configuration, and clean-up of your instances, it makes sure you get a repeatable image every time.

In this recipe, we will create an image with the Apache web server pre-installed and configured. While this is a simple example, it is also a very common use-case.

By baking-in your web server, you can scale up your web serving layer to dynamically match the demands on your websites. Having the software already installed and configured means you get the fastest and most reliable start-up possible.

Getting ready

For this recipe, you must have the Packer tool available on your system. Download and install Packer from the project's website `https://www.packer.io/downloads.html`.

How to do it...

1. Create a new Packer template file, and start by defining an `amazon-ebs` builder in the `builders` section:

```
"builders": [
  {
    "type": "amazon-ebs",
    "instance_type": "t2.micro",
    "region": "us-east-1",
    "source_ami": "ami-9be6f38c",
    "ssh_username": "ec2-user",
    "ami_name": "aws-linux-apache {{timestamp}}"
  }
],
```

The entire template file must be a valid JSON object. Remember to enclose the sections in curly braces: { ... }.

2. Create a `provisioners` section, and include the following snippet to install and activate Apache:

```
"provisioners": [
  {
    "type": "shell",
    "inline": [
      "sudo yum install -y httpd",
      "sudo chkconfig httpd on"
    ]
  }
]
```

3. Save the file with a specific name, such as `04-creating-machine-images.json`.

4. Validate the configuration file you've created with the following `packer validate` command:

```
packer validate 04-creating-machine-images.json
```

5. When valid, build the AMI with the following command:

```
packer build 04-creating-machine-images.json
```

6. Wait until the process is complete. While it is running, you will see an output similar to the following:

```
                         awsac — packer • packer build src/04-creating-machine-images.json — 114×31
$ packer build src/04-creating-machine-images.json
amazon-ebs output will be in this color.

==> amazon-ebs: Prevalidating AMI Name...
    amazon-ebs: Found Image ID: ami-9be6f38c
==> amazon-ebs: Creating temporary keypair: packer_587a9f63-1bcc-7e85-b9c9-eeec160cc172
==> amazon-ebs: Creating temporary security group for this instance...
==> amazon-ebs: Authorizing access to port 22 the temporary security group...
==> amazon-ebs: Launching a source AWS instance...
    amazon-ebs: Instance ID: i-0c249b526d0cabe9b
==> amazon-ebs: Waiting for instance (i-0c249b526d0cabe9b) to become ready...
==> amazon-ebs: Waiting for SSH to become available...
==> amazon-ebs: Connected to SSH!
==> amazon-ebs: Provisioning with shell script: /var/folders/vt/1kw7w5ns6h16vt8j_tk08pzm0000gn/T/packer-shell21831
1435
    amazon-ebs: Loaded plugins: priorities, update-motd, upgrade-helper
    amazon-ebs: Resolving Dependencies
    amazon-ebs: --> Running transaction check
    amazon-ebs: ---> Package httpd.x86_64 0:2.2.31-1.8.amzn1 will be installed
```

7. Take note of the AMI ID returned by Packer so that you can use it when launching instances in the future:

```
  amazon-ebs: Verifying   : httpd-tools-2.2.31-1.8.amzn1.x86_64              1/5
  amazon-ebs: Verifying   : apr-1.5.1-1.12.amzn1.x86_64                      2/5
  amazon-ebs: Verifying   : httpd-2.2.31-1.8.amzn1.x86_64                    3/5
  amazon-ebs: Verifying   : apr-util-ldap-1.4.1-4.17.amzn1.x86_64           4/5
  amazon-ebs: Verifying   : apr-util-1.4.1-4.17.amzn1.x86_64                5/5
  amazon-ebs:
  amazon-ebs: Installed:
  amazon-ebs: httpd.x86_64 0:2.2.31-1.8.amzn1
  amazon-ebs:
  amazon-ebs: Dependency Installed:
  amazon-ebs: apr.x86_64 0:1.5.1-1.12.amzn1           apr-util.x86_64 0:1.4.1-4.17.amzn1
  amazon-ebs: apr-util-ldap.x86_64 0:1.4.1-4.17.amzn1 httpd-tools.x86_64 0:2.2.31-1.8.amzn1
  amazon-ebs:
  amazon-ebs: Complete!
==> amazon-ebs: Stopping the source instance...
==> amazon-ebs: Waiting for the instance to stop...
==> amazon-ebs: Creating the AMI: aws-linux-apache 1484431202
  amazon-ebs: AMI: ami-fb816ded
==> amazon-ebs: Waiting for AMI to become ready...
==> amazon-ebs: Terminating the source AWS instance...
==> amazon-ebs: Cleaning up any extra volumes...
==> amazon-ebs: No volumes to clean up, skipping
==> amazon-ebs: Deleting temporary security group...
==> amazon-ebs: Deleting temporary keypair...
Build 'amazon-ebs' finished.

==> Builds finished. The artifacts of successful builds are:
--> amazon-ebs: AMIs were created:

us-east-1: ami-fb816ded
$
```

How it works...

While this is a very simple recipe, there is a lot going on behind the scenes. This is why we recommend you use Packer to create your machine images.

Template

In the `builders` section of the template, we define our build details.

We are using the most common type of AMI builder: `amazon-ebs`. There are other types of AWS builders, for instance, storage-backed instance types.

Next, we define the type of instance to use when baking.

 Make sure that you can often decrease the time it takes to bake your instance by using a larger instance size. Remember that the minimum price paid for an instance is one hour of billable time.

The `source_ami` property in this recipe is an AWS Linux AMI ID in the `region` we have specified. The `ssh_username` allows you to set the username used to connect and run `provisioners` on the instance. This will be determined by your operating system, which in our case is `ec2-user`.

Finally, the `ami_name` field includes the built-in Packer variable `{{timestamp}}`. This ensures the AMI you create will always have a unique name.

Validate the template

The `packer validate` command is a quick way to ensure your template is free of syntax errors before you launch any instances.

Build the AMI

Once you have created and validated your template, the `packer build` command does the following for you:

- Creates a one-time key pair for SSH access to the instance
- Creates a dedicated security group to control access to the instance
- Launches an instance
- Waits until SSH is ready to receive connections
- Runs the provisioner steps on the instance
- Stops the instance
- Generates an AMI from the stopped instance
- Terminates the instance

 Check the Packer documentation for more provisioners and functionality at `https://www.packer.io/docs/`.

There's more...

While Packer makes the administration of images much easier on AWS, there are still a few things to watch out for.

Debugging

Obviously, with so many steps being automated for you, there are many things that can potentially go wrong. Packer gives you a few different ways to debug issues with your builds.

One of the most useful arguments to use with Packer is the `-debug` flag. This will force you to manually confirm each step *before* it takes place. Doing this makes it easy to work out exactly which step in the command is failing, which in turn usually makes it obvious what needs to be changed.

Another useful thing to do is to raise the level of logging output during a Packer command. You can do this by setting the `PACKER_LOG` variable to `true`. The easiest way to do this is with `PACKER_LOG=1` at the beginning of your Packer command line. This will mean you get a lot more information printed to the console (for example, SSH logs, AWS API calls, and so on) during the command. You may even want to run with this level of logging normally in your builds, for auditing purposes.

Orphaned resources

Packer does a great job of managing and cleaning up the resource it uses, but it can only do that while it is running.

If your Packer job aborts for any reason (most likely network issues) then there may be some resources left **orphaned**, or **unmanaged**. It is good practice to check for any Packer instances (they will have *Packer* in their name), and stop them if there are no active Packer jobs running.

You may also need to clean up any leftover key pairs and security groups, but this is less of an issue as there is no cost associated with them (unlike instances).

Deregistering AMIs

As it becomes easier to create AMIs, you may find you end up with more than you need!

AMIs are made up of EC2 snapshots, which are stored in S3. There is a cost associated with storing snapshots, so you will want to clean them up periodically. Given the size of most AMIs (usually a few GBs), it is unlikely to be one of your major costs.

An even greater cost is the administrative overhead of managing too many AMIs. As your images improve and fixes are applied (especially security fixes), you may want to prevent people from using them.

To remove an AMI, you must first *deregister* it, and then remove the underlying snapshots.

 Make sure you do not deregister AMIs that are currently in use. For example, an auto scaling group that references a deregistered AMI will fail to launch new instances!

You can easily deregister snapshots through the web console or using the AWS CLI tool.

Once an AMI is no longer registered, you can remove the associated snapshots. Packer automatically adds the AMI ID to the snapshots' description. By searching your snapshots for the deregistered AMI ID, you can find which ones need to be deleted.

You will not be able to delete snapshots if the AMI has not been deregistered, or if the deregistration is still taking place (it can take a few minutes).

Other platforms

It is also worth noting that Packer can build for more platforms that just AWS. You can also build images for VMWare, Docker, and many others.

This means you could build almost exactly the same machine image locally (for example, using Docker) as you do in AWS. This makes it much more convenient when setting up local development environments, for example.

Check the `builders` section of the Packer documentation for details.

Creating security groups

AWS describes security groups as *virtual firewalls*. While this analogy helps newcomers to the EC2 platform understand their purpose and function, it's probably more accurate to describe them as a *firewall-like* method of authorizing traffic. They don't offer all the functionality you'd find in a traditional firewall, but this simplification also makes them extremely powerful, particularly when combined with Infrastructure as Code and modern SDLC practices.

We're going to go through a basic scenario involving a web server and load balancer. We want the load balancer to respond to HTTP requests from everywhere, and we want to isolate the web server from everything except the load balancer.

Getting ready

Before we get started there's a small list of things you'll need to have ready:

- `AmiId` This is the ID of an AMI in your region. For this recipe, we'd recommend using an AWS Linux AMI because our instance will attempt to run some `yum` commands on startup.
- `VPCID`: This is the ID of the VPC you wish to launch the EC2 server into.
- `SubnetIDs`: These are the subnets which our EC2 instance can launch in.

How to do it...

1. Open up your text editor and create a new CloudFormation template. We're going to start by adding a few `Parameters` as follows:

```
AWSTemplateFormatVersion: '2010-09-09'
Parameters:
  AmiId:
    Type: AWS::EC2::AMI::Id
    Description: AMI ID to launch instances from
  VPCID:
    Type: AWS::EC2::VPC::Id
    Description: VPC where load balancer and instance will launch
  SubnetIDs:
    Type: List<AWS::EC2::Subnet::Id>
    Description: Subnets where load balancer and instance will launch
      (pick at least 2)
```

2. Let's take a look at a security group we'll apply to a public load balancer:

```
ExampleELBSecurityGroup:
  Type: AWS::EC2::SecurityGroup
  Properties:
    GroupDescription: Security Group for example ELB
    SecurityGroupIngress:
      - IpProtocol: tcp
        CidrIp: 0.0.0.0/0
        FromPort: 80
        ToPort: 80
```

Anything which resides in this security group will allow inbound TCP connections on port 80 from anywhere (0.0.0.0/0). Note that a security group can contain more than one rule; we'd almost certainly want to also allow HTTPS (443), but we've left it out to simplify this recipe.

3. Now let's look at a security group for a web server sitting behind our load balancer:

```
ExampleEC2InstanceSecurityGroup:
  Type: AWS::EC2::SecurityGroup
  Properties:
    GroupDescription: Security Group for example Instance
    SecurityGroupIngress:
      - IpProtocol: tcp
        SourceSecurityGroupName:
          Ref: ExampleELBSecurityGroup
        FromPort: 80
        ToPort: 80
```

Here you can see we are not specifying a source IP range. Instead, we're specifying a source security group, which we will accept connections from. In this case, we're saying that we want to allow anything from our ELB security group to connect to anything in our EC2 instance security group on port 80.
Since this is the only rule we're specifying, our web server will not accept connections from anywhere except our load balancer, to port 80 or otherwise. Our web server isn't wide open to the Internet, and it is even isolated from other instances in our VPC

 Remember that multiple instances can reside in a security group. In a scenario where you have multiple web servers attached to this load balancer it would be unnecessary, inefficient, and somewhat of an anti-pattern to create a new security group for each web server. Given that all web servers attached to this load balancer would be serving the same role or function, it makes sense to apply the same security group to them.

This is where the power of security groups really comes in. If an EC2 instance is serving multiple roles—let's say you have an outbound HTTP proxy server in your VPC which you also want to act as an SMTP relay—then you can simply apply multiple security groups to it.

4. Next, we need to add our load balancer. This is probably the most basic load balancer configuration you'll come across. The following code will give you a load balancer, a listener and a target group containing our EC2 instance.

```
ExampleLoadBalancer:
  Type: AWS::ElasticLoadBalancingV2::LoadBalancer
  Properties:
    Subnets:
      - Fn::Select: [ 0, Ref: SubnetIDs ]
      - Fn::Select: [ 1, Ref: SubnetIDs ]
    SecurityGroups:
      - Fn::GetAtt: ExampleELBSecurityGroup.GroupId
ExampleListener:
  Type: AWS::ElasticLoadBalancingV2::Listener
  Properties:
    LoadBalancerArn:
      Ref: ExampleLoadBalancer
    DefaultActions:
      - Type: forward
        TargetGroupArn:
          Ref: ExampleTargetGroup
    Port: 80
    Protocol: HTTP
ExampleTargetGroup:
  Type: AWS::ElasticLoadBalancingV2::TargetGroup
  Properties:
    Port: 80
    Protocol: HTTP
    VpcId:
      Ref: VPCID
    Targets:
      - Id:
          Ref: ExampleEC2Instance
```

5. The last resource we'll add to our template is an EC2 server. This server will install and start nginx when it boots.

```
ExampleEC2Instance:
  Type: AWS::EC2::Instance
  Properties:
    InstanceType: t2.nano
    UserData:
      Fn::Base64:
        Fn::Sub: |
          #!/bin/bash -ex
          yum install -y nginx
          service nginx start
          exit 0
```

```
ImageId:
  Ref: AmiId
SecurityGroupIds:
  - Fn::GetAtt: ExampleEC2InstanceSecurityGroup.GroupId
SubnetId:
  Fn::Select: [ 0, Ref: SubnetIDs ]
```

6. Lastly, we're going to add some Outputs to the template to make it a little more convenient to use our ELB and EC2 instance after the stack is created.

```
Outputs:
  ExampleEC2InstanceHostname:
    Value:
      Fn::GetAtt: [ ExampleEC2Instance, PublicDnsName ]
  ExampleELBURL:
    Value:
      Fn::Join:
        - ''
        - [ 'http://', { 'Fn::GetAtt': [ ExampleLoadBalancer,
            DNSName ] }, '/' ]
```

7. Go ahead and launch this template using the CloudFormation web console or the AWS CLI.

There's more...

You'll eventually run into circular dependency issues when configuring security groups using CloudFormation. Let's say you want all servers in our ExampleEC2InstanceSecurityGroup to be able to access each other on port 22 (SSH). In order to achieve this, you would need to add this rule as the separate resource type AWS::EC2::SecurityGroupIngress. This is because a security group can't refer to itself in CloudFormation when it is yet to be created. This is what the extra resource type looks like:

```
ExampleEC2InstanceIngress:
  Type: AWS::EC2::SecurityGroupIngress
  Properties:
    IpProtocol: tcp
    SourceSecurityGroupName:
      Ref: ExampleEC2InstanceSecurityGroup
    GroupName:
      Ref: ExampleEC2InstanceSecurityGroup
    FromPort: 22
    ToPort: 22
```

Differences from traditional firewalls

- Security groups can't be used to explicitly block traffic. Only rules of a permissive kind can be added; deny style rules are not supported. Essentially, all inbound traffic is denied unless you explicitly allow it.
- Your rules also may not refer to source ports; only destination ports are supported.
- When security groups are created, they will contain a rule which allows all outbound connections. If you remove this rule, new outbound connections will be dropped. It's a common pattern to leave this rule in place and filter all your traffic using inbound rules only.
- If you do replace the default outbound rule, it's important to note that only new outbound connections will be filtered. Any outbound traffic being sent in response to an inbound connection will still be allowed. This is because security groups are *stateful*.
- Unlike security groups, network ACLs are not stateful and do support DENY rules. You can use them as a complementary layer of security inside your VPC, especially if you need to control traffic flow between subnets.

Creating a load balancer

AWS offers two kinds of load balancers:

- Classic load balancer
- Application load balancer

We're going to focus on the application load balancer. It's effectively an upgraded, second generation of the ELB service, and it offers a lot more functionality than the classic load balancer. HTTP/2 and WebSockets are supported natively, for example. The hourly rate also happens to be cheaper.

 Application load balancers do not support layer-4 load balancing. For this kind of functionality, you'll need to use a classic load balancer.

How to do it...

1. Open up your text editor and create a new CloudFormation template. We're going to require a VPC ID and some subnet IDs as `Parameters`. Add them to your template like this:

```
AWSTemplateFormatVersion: '2010-09-09'
Parameters:
  VPCID:
    Type: AWS::EC2::VPC::Id
    Description: VPC where load balancer and instance will launch
  SubnetIDs:
    Type: List<AWS::EC2::Subnet::Id>
    Description: Subnets where load balancer and instance will launch
      (pick at least 2)
```

2. Next we need to add some `Mappings` of ELB account IDs. These will make it easier for us to give the load balancer permission to write logs to an S3 bucket. Your mappings should look like this:

 You can find the complete list of ELB account IDs here http://docs.aws. amazon.com/elasticloadbalancing/latest/classic/enable-access-logs.html#attach-bucket-policy.

```
Mappings:
  ELBAccountMap:
    us-east-1:
    ELBAccountID: 127311923021
    ap-southeast-2:
    ELBAccountID: 783225319266
```

3. We can now start adding `Resources` to our template. First we're going to create an S3 bucket and bucket policy for storing our load balancer logs. In order to make this template portable, we'll omit a bucket name, but for convenience we'll include the bucket name in our outputs so that CloudFormation will echo the name back to us.

```
Resources:
  ExampleLogBucket:
    Type: AWS::S3::Bucket
  ExampleBucketPolicy:
    Type: AWS::S3::BucketPolicy
    Properties:
      Bucket:
```

```
        Ref: ExampleLogBucket
    PolicyDocument:
      Statement:
        -
          Action:
            - "s3:PutObject"
          Effect: "Allow"
          Resource:
            Fn::Join:
              - ""
              -
                - "arn:aws:s3:::"
                - Ref: ExampleLogBucket
                - "/*"
          Principal:
            AWS:
              Fn::FindInMap: [ ELBAccountMap, Ref: "AWS::Region",
                ELBAccountID ]
```

4. Next, we need to create a security group for our load balancer to reside in. This security group will allow inbound connections to port 80 (HTTP). To simplify this recipe, we'll leave out port 443 (HTTPS), but we'll briefly cover how to add this functionality later in this section. Since we're adding a public load balancer, we want to allow connections to it from everywhere (0.0.0.0/0). This is what our security group looks like:

```
ExampleELBSecurityGroup:
  Type: AWS::EC2::SecurityGroup
  Properties:
    GroupDescription: Security Group for example ELB
    SecurityGroupIngress:
      -
        IpProtocol: tcp
        CidrIp: 0.0.0.0/0
        FromPort: 80
        ToPort: 80
```

5. We now need to define a target group. Upon completion of this recipe, you can go ahead and register your instances in this group so that HTTP requests will be forwarded to it. Alternatively, you can attach the target group to an auto scaling group and AWS will take care of the instance registration and de-registration for you.

6. The target group is where we specify the health checks our load balancer should perform against the target instances. This health check is necessary to determine if a registered instance should receive traffic. The example provided with this recipe includes these health-check parameters with the values all set to their defaults. Go ahead and tweak these to suit your needs, or, optionally, remove them if the defaults work for you.

```
ExampleTargetGroup:
  Type: AWS::ElasticLoadBalancingV2::TargetGroup
  Properties:
    Port: 80
    Protocol: HTTP
    HealthCheckIntervalSeconds: 30
    HealthCheckProtocol: HTTP
    HealthCheckPort: 80
    HealthCheckPath: /
    HealthCheckTimeoutSeconds: 5
    HealthyThresholdCount: 5
    UnhealthyThresholdCount: 2
    Matcher:
      HttpCode: '200'
    VpcId:
      Ref: VPCID
```

7. We need to define at least one listener to be added to our load balancer. A listener will *listen* for incoming requests to the load balancer on the port and protocol we configure for it. Requests matching the port and protocol will be forwarded through to our target group.

   The configuration of our listener is going to be reasonably simple. We're listening for HTTP requests on port 80. We're also setting up a default action for this listener, which will forward our requests to the target group we've defined before. There is a limit of 10 listeners per load balancer.

 Currently, AWS only supports one action: forward.

```
ExampleListener:
  Type: AWS::ElasticLoadBalancingV2::Listener
  Properties:
    LoadBalancerArn:
      Ref: ExampleLoadBalancer
    DefaultActions:
      - Type: forward
```

```
      TargetGroupArn:
         Ref: ExampleTargetGroup
   Port: 80
   Protocol: HTTP
```

8. Finally, now that we have all `Resources` we need, we can go ahead and set up our load balancer. We'll need to define at least two subnets for it to live in—these are included as `Parameters` in our example template:

```
ExampleLoadBalancer:
  Type: AWS::ElasticLoadBalancingV2::LoadBalancer
  Properties:
    LoadBalancerAttributes:
      - Key: access_logs.s3.enabled
       Value: true
      - Key: access_logs.s3.bucket
       Value:
          Ref: ExampleLogBucket
      - Key: idle_timeout.timeout_seconds
        Value: 60
    Scheme: internet-facing
    Subnets:
      - Fn::Select: [ 0, Ref: SubnetIDs ]
      - Fn::Select: [ 1, Ref: SubnetIDs ]
    SecurityGroups:
      - Fn::GetAtt: ExampleELBSecurityGroup.GroupId
```

9. Lastly, we're going to add some `Outputs` to our template for convenience. We're particularly interested in the name of the S3 bucket we created and the URL of the load balancer.

```
Outputs:
  ExampleELBURL:
    Value:
      Fn::Join:
        - ''
        - [ 'http://', { 'Fn::GetAtt': [ ExampleLoadBalancer,
            DNSName ] }, '/' ]
  ExampleLogBucket:
    Value:
      Ref: ExampleLogBucket
```

How it works...

As you can see, we're applying a logging configuration which points to the S3 bucket we've created. We're configuring this load balancer to be Internet-facing, with an idle timeout of 60 seconds (the default).

All load balancers are Internet-facing by default, so it's not strictly necessary to define a Scheme in our example; however, it can be handy to include this anyway. This is especially the case if your CloudFormation template contains a mix of public and private load balancers.

 If you specify a logging configuration but the load balancer can't access the S3 bucket, your CloudFormation stack will fail to complete.

Private ELBs are not Internet-facing and are available only to resources which live inside your VPC.

That's it! You now have a working application load balancer configured to ship logs to an S3 bucket.

There's more...

Load balancers on AWS are highly configurable and there are many options available to you. Here are some of the more frequent ELB options you'll encounter:

HTTPS/SSL

If you wish to accept HTTPS requests, you'll need to configure an additional listener. It will look something like the following:

```
ExampleHTTPSListener:
  Type: AWS::ElasticLoadBalancingV2::Listener
  Properties:
    Certificates:
      - CertificateArn:
          arn:aws:acm:ap-southeast-2:123456789012:
          certificate/12345678-1234-1234-1234-123456789012
    LoadBalancerArn:
      Ref: ExampleLoadBalancer
    DefaultActions:
      - Type: forward
```

```
        TargetGroupArn:
            Ref: ExampleTargetGroup
    Port: 443
    Protocol: HTTPS
```

The listener will need to reference a valid **Amazon Resource Name** (**ARN**) for the certificate you wish to use. It's really easy to have AWS Certificate Manager create a certificate for you, but it does require validation of the domain name you're generating the certificate for. You can, of course, bring your own certificate if you wish. You'll need to import it in to AWS Certificate Manager before you can use it with your ELB (or CloudFront distribution).

Unless you have specific requirements around ciphers, a good starting approach is to not define an SSL Policy and let AWS choose what is currently *best of breed*.

Path-based routing

Once you are comfortable with ELB configuration, you can start to experiment with path-based routing. In a nutshell, it provides a way to inspect a request and proxy it to different targets based on the path requested.

One common scenario you might encounter is needing to route requests for /blog to a different set of servers running WordPress, instead of to your main server pool, which is running your Ruby on Rails application.

12
Management Tools

In this chapter, we will cover:

- Auditing your AWS account
- Recommendations with Trusted Advisor
- Creating e-mail alarms
- Publishing custom metrics in CloudWatch
- Creating monitoring dashboards
- Creating a budget
- Feeding log files into CloudWatch logs

Introduction

As with all administration, monitoring and alerting is a critical part of using AWS-based infrastructure. If anything, due to the ephemeral nature of cloud resources, keeping track and measuring your usage is even more important than when using on-premises systems.

Auditing your AWS account

We're now going to show you how to set up CloudTrail in your AWS account. Once CloudTrail has been enabled, it will start to record all of the API calls made in your account to the AWS service and then deliver them to you as log files in an S3 bucket.
When we talk about API calls we mean things like:

- Actions performed in the AWS console.
- Calls made to AWS APIs using the CLI or SDKs.
- Calls made on your behalf by AWS services. Think CloudFormation or the auto scaling service.

Each entry in the log will contain useful information, such as:

- The service that was called
- The action that was requested
- The parameters sent with the request
- The response that was returned by AWS
- The identity of the caller (including IP address)
- The date and time of the request

How to do it...

1. Create a new CloudFormation template file; we're going to define the following `Resources`:
   - An S3 bucket for our CloudTrail log files to be stored in
   - A policy for our S3 bucket that allows the CloudTrail service to write to our bucket
   - A CloudTrail *trail*

2. Define an S3 bucket like so. We don't need to give it a name; we'll add the bucket name to the list of `Outputs` later:

```
ExampleTrailBucket:
  Type: AWS::S3::Bucket
```

3. Next, we need to define a policy for our bucket. This section is a little wordy so you may prefer to get this from the code samples instead. This policy essentially allows CloudTrail to do two things to our bucket: `s3:GetBucketAcl` and `s3:PutObject`.

```
ExampleBucketPolicy:
  Type: AWS::S3::BucketPolicy
  Properties:
    Bucket: !Ref ExampleTrailBucket
    PolicyDocument:
      Statement:
      - Sid: AWSCloudTrailAclCheck20150319
        Effect: Allow
        Principal:
          Service: cloudtrail.amazonaws.com
          Action: s3:GetBucketAcl
          Resource: !Join
            - ""
            -
              - "arn:aws:s3:::"
              - !Ref ExampleTrailBucket
      - Sid: AWSCloudTrailWrite20150319
        Effect: Allow
        Principal:
          Service: cloudtrail.amazonaws.com
        Action: s3:PutObject
        Resource: !Join
          - ""
          -
            - "arn:aws:s3:::"
            - !Ref ExampleTrailBucket
            - "/AWSLogs/"
            - !Ref AWS::AccountId
            - "/*"
        Condition:
          StringEquals:
            s3:x-amz-acl: bucket-owner-full-control
```

4. Now we can set up our trail.

One thing to note here is that we use `DependsOn` to make CloudFormation create this trail after it has created the S3 bucket and policy. If you don't do this you'll likely encounter an error when you create the stack because CloudTrail won't be able to access the bucket.

5. Add the `Trail` to your template like so:

```
ExampleTrail:
  Type: AWS::CloudTrail::Trail
  Properties:
    EnableLogFileValidation: true
    IncludeGlobalServiceEvents: true
    IsLogging: true
    IsMultiRegionTrail: true
    S3BucketName: !Ref ExampleTrailBucket
  DependsOn:
    - ExampleTrailBucket
    - ExampleBucketPolicy
```

6. Finally, we're going to output the name of the S3 bucket where our CloudTrail logs will be stored:

```
Outputs:
  ExampleBucketName:
    Value: !Ref ExampleTrailBucket
    Description: Bucket where CloudTrail logs will be stored
```

7. You can go ahead and run your CloudFormation stack using the following command:

```
aws cloudformation create-stack \
  --template-body file://05-auditing-your-aws-account.yaml \
  --stack-name example-cloudtrail
```

How it works...

This template will set up CloudTrail with the following configuration:

- CloudTrail will be turned on for all regions in your account. This is a sensible place to start because it gives you visibility over where your AWS resources are being created. Even if you are the sole user of your AWS account it can be handy to know if you are making API calls to other regions by mistake (it's easy to do). When you create a multi region trail, new regions will automatically be included when they come online with no additional effort on your part.
- Global service events will also be logged. Again this is a sensible default because it includes services that aren't region-specific. CloudFront and IAM are two examples of AWS services that aren't region-specific.

- Log file validation is turned on. With this feature enabled, CloudTrail will deliver a digest file on an hourly basis that you can use to determine if your CloudTrail logs have been tampered with. CloudTrail uses SHA-256 for hashing and signing (RSA). The AWS CLI can be used to perform ad hoc validation of CloudTrail logs.

For a quick view of your CloudTrial logs, with some basic search and filter functionality, you can head to the AWS web console:

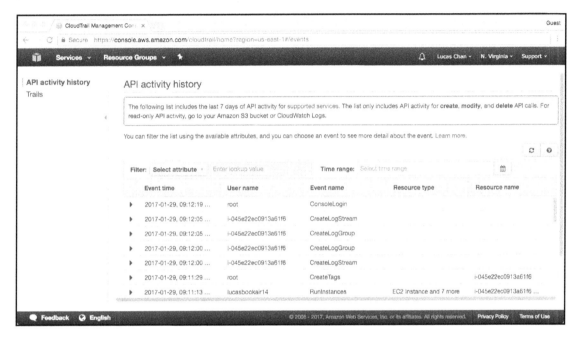

CloudTrail web console

There's more...

- Log files are encrypted using server side encryption in S3. This encryption is transparent to you, but you can opt to encrypt these files with your own **customer master key** (**CMK**) if you wish.
- API calls are logged by CloudTrail in under 15 minutes.
- Logs are shipping to your S3 bucket every five minutes.

- It's possible to aggregate CloudTrail events across many accounts into a single bucket. This is a pattern often used to log AWS activity into a *SecOps* or similar account for auditing.
- Logging aside, CloudTrail keeps your API activity for seven days.
- You can create more than one trail. You might consider creating a trail for your developers that is separate from the trail consumed by security.
- If a CloudFormation stack creates an S3 bucket and that S3 bucket has objects in it the delete operation will fail if and when you choose to delete the stack. You can manually delete the S3 bucket in the S3 web console if you wish to work around this.

Recommendations with Trusted Advisor

Trusted Advisor covers four main areas and it is designed to give you some guidance around what are considered best practices for your cloud deployment. The areas covered are:

- **Cost Optimization**
- **Performance**
- **Security**
- **Fault Tolerance**

It's available to everyone and free to use—with one fairly large catch. Unless you are paying for Business or Enterprise level support with AWS you only get access to four checks. At the time of publishing there are 55 possible checks.

How to do it...

The good news is you don't need to do anything at all to turn on Trusted Advisor. It's automatically enabled when your AWS account is created and will continue to update for the lifetime of your account.

Go ahead and navigate to the **Trusted Advisor** section of the AWS web console.

How it works...

The four checks provided for free with this service are:

- **Unrestricted ports**: This is a check on the highest risk ports in your security groups. They'll be flagged if they're open to everyone (0.0.0.0/0).
- **IAM usage**: This is a fairly rudimentary check. If there isn't at least one IAM user in your account this check won't pass. It's considered good practice to not use your root login credentials for your AWS account and instead create IAM users with least privilege access.
- **MFA on root account**: This is also a fairly rudimentary check. You need to have MFA enabled for your root login in order for this check to pass. It's obviously a good idea to enable MFA for your IAM users too.
- **Service limits**: This one is quite handy: if you're approaching 80% of your service limits, this check won't pass. For example, it's nice to know if you're about to hit the cap of CloudFormation stacks or EC2 instances before you attempt to create them.

Even though there's only four checks here, these are some of the more useful ones so we'd encourage you to pay attention to them.

The console uses a color scheme to denote the status of each check:

- **Red**: It's recommended that you take action to remedy this check
- **Yellow**: This check requires investigation and possible remediation
- **Green**: This check is passing and needs no attention

Visit the **Preferences** page in the **Trusted Advisor** web console if you'd like to have a weekly report e-mailed to you.

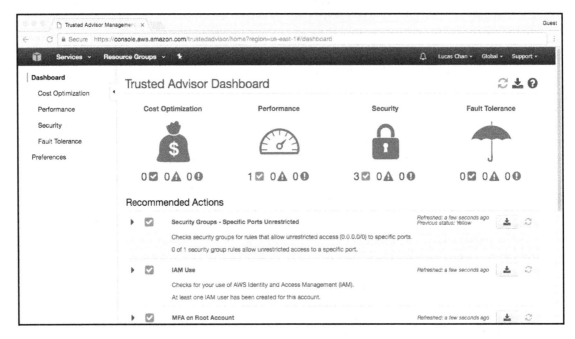

Trusted Advisor console

There's more...

As well as opening up the entire suite of Trusted Advisor checks, a Business or Enterprise level support arrangement gives you access to the following:

- **Notifications**: You are able to have notifications delivered to you at a higher frequency using a number of delivery methods. Since Trusted Advisor is an available source in CloudWatch Events you'll be able to create notifications that can be handled by SNS (e-mail, push, SMS) or even notifications that will trigger Lambda functions.

- **API access**: You'll have access to a number of Trusted Advisor API methods such as `DescribeTrustedAdvisorCheckResult` and `DescribeTrustedAdvisorCheckSummaries`. You can use these to integrate the results from checks into your own dashboards or monitoring systems. You'll also be able to use the APIs to refresh Trusted Advisor checks (after you've taken corrective action on them, for example).
- **Exclusion**: You can selectively mute checks that are failing. You'll sometimes want to do this for things such as RDS instances in your development environments that aren't in multi-AZ mode or don't have backups enabled.

Finally, some of the more useful checks we see for our Business and Enterprise level support customers are:

- **Reserved Instances**: A nice cost optimization if you have a reasonably static workload.
- **Unassociated Elastic IPs**: If IP addresses are not associated with a network interface (on an EC2 instance for example) you will still be charged for them. Also if there are unassociated IPs floating around, that is usually a sign that they are being allocated manually instead of with CloudFormation. Remember that the goal here is for more automation, not less.
- **Idle load balancers**: Again, these cost money and are often easily orphaned in low automation environments.
- **S3 bucket permissions**: It's not always obvious if the permissions on an S3 bucket have been misconfigured. This check helps you avoid unintentionally leaking data.

Creating e-mail alarms

While e-mail alarms may not be the most scalable of all alarms (due to the amount of e-mail most people get), they are the easiest to integrate—almost everyone has an e-mail address!

This recipe uses two AWS services:

- **CloudWatch** (**CW**)
- **Simple Notification Service** (**SNS**)

As you will often want to create alarms for metrics after viewing them through the CloudWatch dashboard, this recipe will use the console to create the alarms.

How to do it...

1. In the CloudWatch console, go to the **Alarms** section:

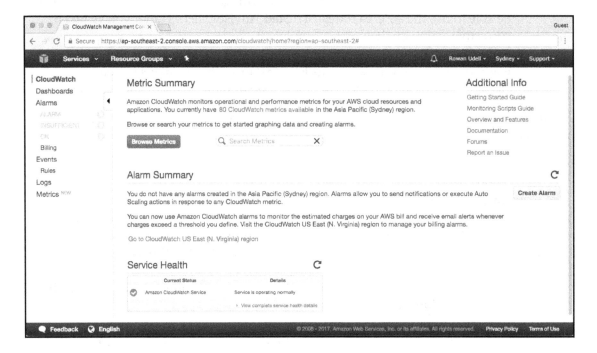

2. Click **Create Alarm** to start the wizard:

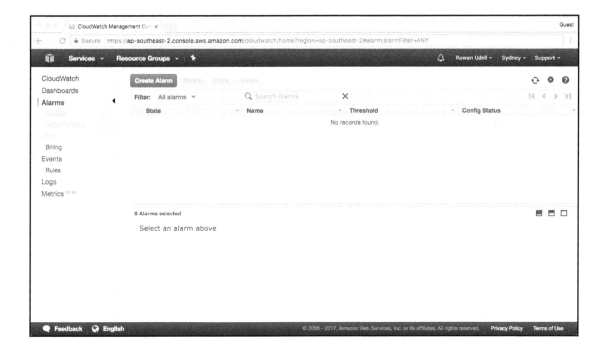

3. Select the metric you are interested in alerting on. In this case, we will choose **By Function Name** under **Lambda Metrics**:

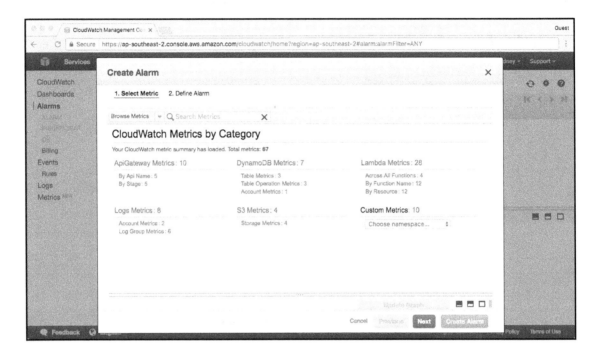

4. Select the specific metric. You can filter by any of the values in the table. In this case, we will select **Errors** and click **Next**:

5. Define the alarm, giving at least a name and a threshold. In this case, we will alert if there are ever *any* errors (such as > 0):

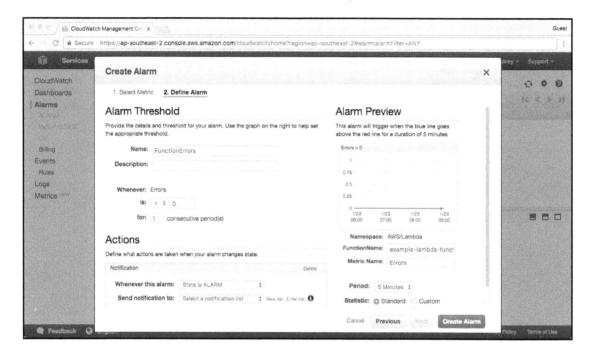

6. In the **Actions** section, create a new list by giving the e-mail address you want to be notified on of a breach, and a topic name (in this example, we use `EmailMe`), and then click **Create Alarm**:

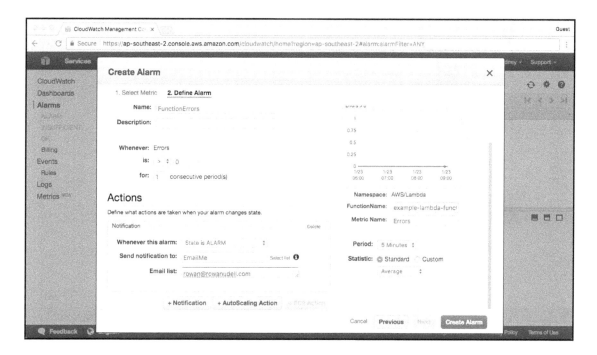

7. You will be asked to confirm the e-mail address, and no notifications will be given until it is verified.

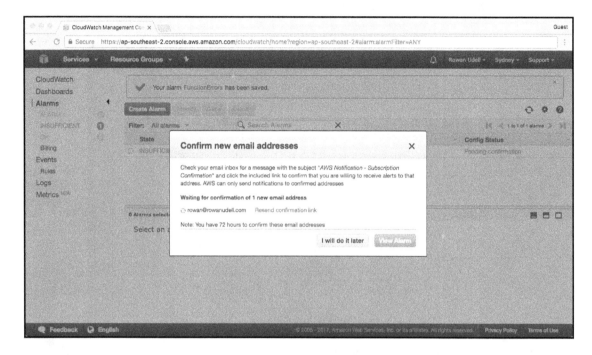

8. The confirmation e-mail will look like this:

9. Once you have clicked on the **Confirm subscription** link in the e-mail, you will
   see a confirmation message as follows:

10. Back in the console the status will update, showing that you have successfully
    confirmed your subscription:

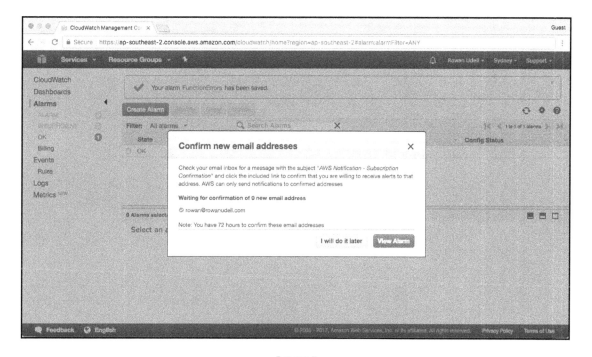

11. You will then see your newly created alarm in the console, and can view its status and history:

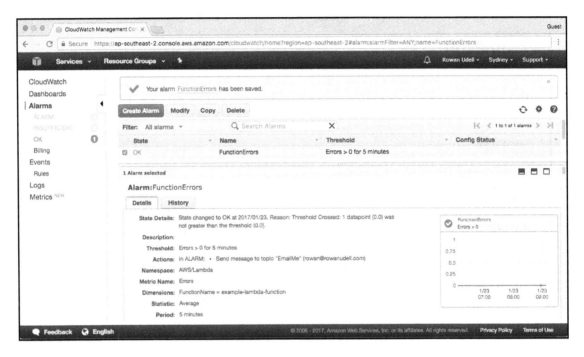

12. In the SNS console, you can see the topic that was created for you as follows:

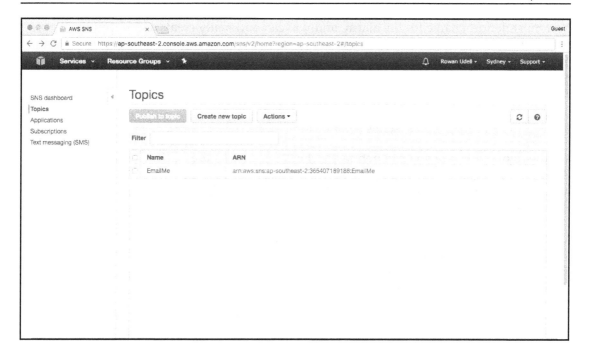

How it works...

While we normally prefer the CLI (or CloudFormation) for creating AWS resources the wizard for creating alarms does a lot of work for you, so it is a good place to start. Once you know what kinds of alarms you are interested in, you can automate them.

The CloudWatch console is a great place to keep an eye on the performance of your resources. Often when looking at the metrics you might find a scenario that you would want to be notified of, and quickly create an alarm on it.

 While e-mail is probably the easiest way to get started with alarms, it doesn't scale all that well (Do you really want more e-mail?). For very important metrics you might want a CloudWatch dashboard instead, or a different notification protocol/target.

We start by selecting the metric we are interested in; in this case, it is errors from the **example-lambda-function**, but the process would work the same regardless of the metric you select.

You must define a name for the alarm, and you can optionally create a description. One of the most important parts of the alarm is how you define the threshold that will trigger it. You can choose not only the value and comparison operator used (for example, greater than (>), less than (<), greater than or equal to (>=), and so on), but also the number of failing data points that must occur before the alarm is triggered. This can stop you being alerted unnecessarily for temporary *spikes* in metric values. In this scenario we want to know if there are *any* errors, so we set the value to 1.

On the right-hand side you can define the check period and the statistic used (for example, **Average**, **Maximum**, **Minimum**, and so on). You can also see the recent history of the selected metric in the top-right corner. The red line on the graph is where the currently defined threshold will sit, so you can quickly see if the alarm would have been triggered.

In the **Actions** section of the alarm, you define what action will be taken when triggered. While you can select an existing SNS topic, we will define a new one by clicking on **New list**. You are then prompted for the details of the new topic; you must give both a name and an e-mail address to subscribe to the topic.

When you click **Create Alarm,** you will see the status of the subscription. After receiving the e-mail and clicking on the confirmation link, the status will automatically update. It doesn't matter if you navigate away from the window before you confirm the subscription. Just remember that your target e-mail address won't receive any notifications if you do not confirm the subscription.

Viewing the newly created alarm shows its current state, and its recent history. An alarm has three possible states:

- **ALARM**: The metric is over the defined threshold
- **INSUFFICIENT_DATA**: There were not enough data points to determine if the metric is under or over the threshold
- **OK**: The metric is under the defined threshold

You can filter alarms by their state by the links on the side menu, which also show an updated view of how many alarms are in each state.

Behind the scenes, the wizard has created an SNS topic for you. The topic is what handles converting the alarm message to an e-mail, and sending it. Without the SNS topic the alarm would still alert (that is change state), but there would be no way to tell without looking at the metric in the CloudWatch dashboard.

There's more...

This recipe represents the simplest useful configuration of SNS topics and CW alarms, but there is a lot more depth available to you in this pattern.

Existing topics

Instead of choosing **New list** in the wizard, you can use the **Select list** functionality. You then give the name of an existing SNS topic to use, rather than creating a new one.

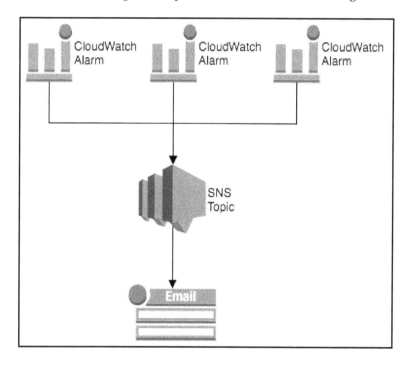

This means you can set up a single topic to push multiple alarms to. In addition to being simpler it also means you only need to confirm the subscription *once*, instead of doing it for each alarm.

Other subscriptions

An SNS topic that notifies an e-mail is the most common subscription, but not the only option. SNS topics can also send notifications to:

- HTTP(S) endpoints
- Amazon SQS
- AWS Lambda
- SMS

Publishing custom metrics in CloudWatch

Once you get used to using CloudWatch, it is highly likely that you will want to see more than just the built-in AWS metrics.

One of the most common metrics users ask for after starting to run servers in EC2 is memory usage; the built-in metrics for EC2 instances are CPU utilization, network in/out, disk reads/writes, and status—memory is not included by default!

This recipe will show you how to feed the amount of memory inuse on your Linux instances to CloudWatch, so that you can see them alongside the other instance metrics.

 Knowing how utilized (or not) your instances are is a key component in choosing the right instance type to use for your workloads. Getting it wrong can cost you a lot of money!

Getting ready

You will need an EC2 instance running Linux, with the AWS CLI tool installed to perform this recipe. If you use an instance based on AWS Linux, you will have the AWS CLI tool installed for you.

The instance role or credentials you use to run the following commands must have permission to submit metrics to CloudWatch. This is the `CloudWatch:PutMetricData` permission.

How to do it...

1. On the instance, run the following AWS CLI command:

```
aws cloudwatch put-metric-data \
  --metric-name MemoryUsagePercent \
  --namespace CustomMetrics \
  --dimensions InstanceId=`curl -s \
    http://169.254.169.254/latest/meta-data/instance-id` \
  --unit Percent \
  --value `free | grep Mem | awk '{print $3/$2 * 100.0}'`
```

2. Go to the CloudWatch console, and navigate to the **Metrics** dashboard. Your metric will appear under the namespace **CustomMetrics**, **InstanceId**, and the unique ID for the instance, with the metric name **MemoryUsagePercent**.

It can take *up to* 15 minutes for a custom metric to appear in the CloudWatch dashboard (although it usually takes less). Even for the built-in metrics, it may take a minute or two for the metric data to appear in the console.

How it works...

In this recipe, we use the built-in `put-metric-data` AWS CLI command to send our metric to CloudWatch.

We start by defining the metric name and namespace that the values will appear under. This is important because it defines how we will see the metric in the console and dashboards. Names should identify and describe the metric. They do not need to be unique, as the dimension(s) we add will take care of that (we will discuss this later). Namespaces are used to group similar metrics together, like a category. The built-in metrics appear under the namespace `AWS/`. For example, EC2 metrics appear under the `AWS/EC2` namespace.

We then specify a dimension for the metric. A **dimension** is a way to uniquely identify similar metrics. In this case we are using the instance's ID to identify the metric, because the metric is unique to that instance, but we will likely have many instances of the `MemoryUsagePercent` metric (across many EC2 instances). We are obtaining the instance ID by querying (via the `curl` command) the instance metadata service, which is accessed over HTTP on the special IP address `169.254.169.254`.

 There's a lot of other useful information in the instance metadata. See the AWS documentation on instance metadata for more details `http://docs.aws.amazon.com/AWSEC2/latest/UserGuide/ec2-instance-metadata.html`.

Next we specify a percent, because we know what kind of data we are dealing with. This argument can be leftoff if you don't know (or care), as CloudWatch attaches no significance to it (although some other applications may be able to use it, for example, for display).

Finally we specify the value to send. We work this value out dynamically from the output of the `free` command and use `awk` to convert it to a percentage of memory inuse.

Once the metric is being sent to CloudWatch, we can view it in the console. The easiest way is to select your specific metric and view it in the **Metrics** section of the CloudWatch console.

There's more...

This is a good real-world use-case to get started with your own custom metrics, but there's a lot more you can do with them.

Cron

One-off metric values are rarely useful on their own. The real value comes when you can plot and see them over time; how they change, how fast they change, what their range is, and so on.

On Linux you can schedule a command easily with the `cron` command. By putting the AWS CLI commands in a script, and scheduling it with `cron` to run periodically, you can feed metrics consistently to CloudWatch, without the overhead of running a dedicated agent on your instances.

Auto scaling

Instance-based metrics like memory usage become especially useful when collected from all the instances in an auto scaling group.

By collecting instance or even application-specific metrics (for example: number of threads used, internal request duration, and so on) you can make your auto scaling groups increase and decrease in size at the most appropriate times to your workload and performance profile.

To do this, make the auto scaling group name one of the dimensions (you can define multiple dimensions) sent along with your metric value.

Backfilling

You can backfill metrics by running the same command and supplying an additional `--timestamp` argument. The timestamp argument accepts an ISO 8601 date and time stamp in UTC time for example: `2017-01-01T12:00:00.000Z`

Keep in mind that CloudWatch will only retain your metrics for a certain period, decided by the granularity of your metrics. The retention period is:

- Data points with a period of 60 seconds (1 minute) are available for 15 days
- Data points with a period of 300 seconds (5 minute) are available for 63 days
- Data points with a period of 3600 seconds (1 hour) are available for 455 days (15 months)

While you can send metrics with millisecond precision, the minimum value CloudWatch will store is at the 1 minute level. Anything less than the 1 minute level and CloudWatch will aggregate the values. When aggregated, you can see some additional information about your metric; namely the sample size, minimum and maximum value, and the average of the values.

Creating monitoring dashboards

The real value of collecting metrics is the ability to spot trends and relationships (often unknown or unexpected) between disparate systems. With this kind of visibility, you are able to identify and troubleshoot issues before they become an incident.

In addition to providing a way to aggregate and view metrics from your systems, the CloudWatch service also makes it easy to create monitoring dashboards so that you can quickly and clearly view the most important metrics.

This recipe uses the AWS console because you cannot create dashboards via CloudFormation or the AWS CLI tool yet.

Getting ready

You will need to have some metrics already present in CloudWatch in order to create a dashboard.

If you have been using AWS services (for example: EC2, RDS, DDB, and so on), then you should have plenty—almost all the AWS services populate metrics in CloudWatch by default.

How to do it...

1. Navigate to the CloudWatch section of the AWS console:

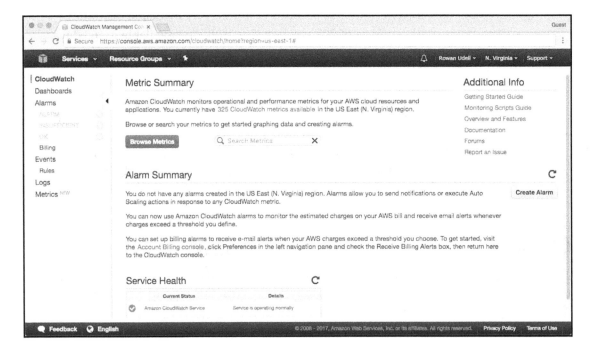

2. Go to the **Dashboards** section of the console via the link on the left-hand menu:

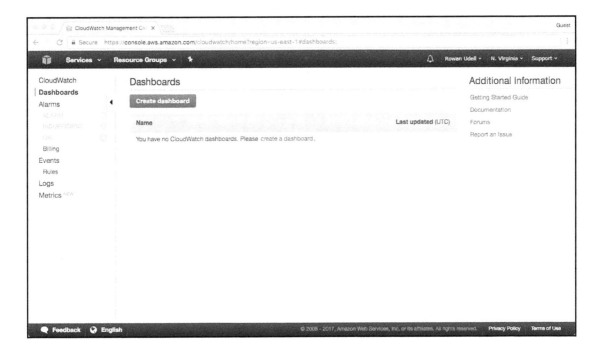

3. Click the **Create Dashboard** button:

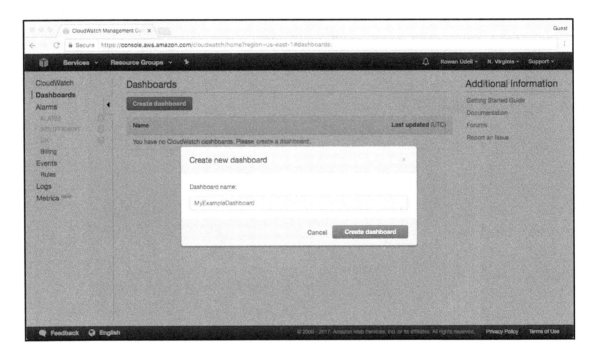

4. Choose the type of widget you want to use to display your metric. In this example, we will choose the most versatile, **Line**:

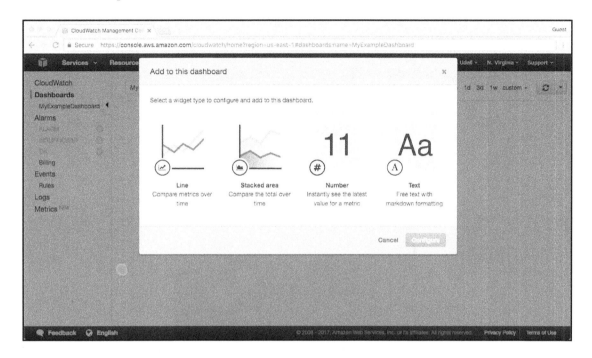

5. Navigate the **All metrics** tab to find the metric(s) you want to include, selecting it by clicking the tick box on the left of the metric details. You will see a preview of the metric(s) and how they will look:

6. Once selected, you can modify how the metric is displayed via the settings on the **Graphed metrics** tab. In this case we have given the widget a name, and changed the **Period** setting for our metric to **1 Minute** to reflect the additional granularity available (You can see that the metric line appears *smoother* because of it).

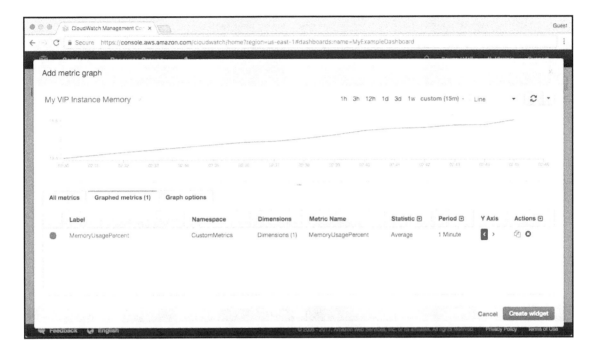

7. Once you click **Create widget,** you will see your widget on the dashboard. Once you click **Save dashboard,** it will appear under the **Dashboards** heading on the left-hand menu:

8. At a dashboard level, you can turn on **Auto refresh** and the refresh frequency interval:

9. You can resize and rearrange your widgets by dragging them. Just remember to click **Save dashboard** to persist any changes:

There's more...

CloudWatch dashboard's value is the ease and simplicity that it allows you to publicize your most important metrics.

As with any dashboard, make sure that the metrics you choose to display are relevant and actionable. There's no point in displaying a metric if there's no action required when it changes.

Widget types

Line graphs are not the only type of widget that can be displayed in a dashboard. There is also:

- **Stacked area**
- **Number**
- **Text**

Depending on the type of metrics you are collecting or are interested in, you should experiment with different types of widgets to display them. Not all metrics are suited to line graphs.

Creating a budget

One of the main attractions of using AWS, is its pay-as-you-go model. You only pay for what you use, no more and no less.

Unfortunately, this can sometimes result in what's known as **bill shock** at the end of the month. This happens when you do something that you might not know is a charged service, or you do not know how much is charged for it, and you don't find out until it's too late. Especially when getting started, users may not fully appreciate the cost of the activities they're undertaking.

There are also ways to optimize your costs on AWS, for example, by transferring at slower speeds, removing external access, and so on. All this means that you should be aware of your cost obligations, and manage them in real time. To this end, you can create budgets that help you be aware of your usage and spending.

While you can create budgets via the AWS CLI tool, it is useful to know how the **Billing** dashboard works for administration purposes, so we will use the AWS console for this recipe.

Getting ready

By default, IAM Users do not have access to the billing section of the AWS console. You must perform these steps using the root login details for your account, or enable IAM access for other users, which is a one-off step.

While you should not generally use the root credentials for your AWS account when administering, creating budgets (which should happen only infrequently) is an exception.

> You *should not* be creating access keys for your root account under any circumstances, which is another reason why we use the console (and not the CLI) for this recipe.

How to do it...

1. Log in to the AWS console with your root credentials, and navigate to the **My Billing Dashboard** via the user menu accessed by clicking on your name in the top right:

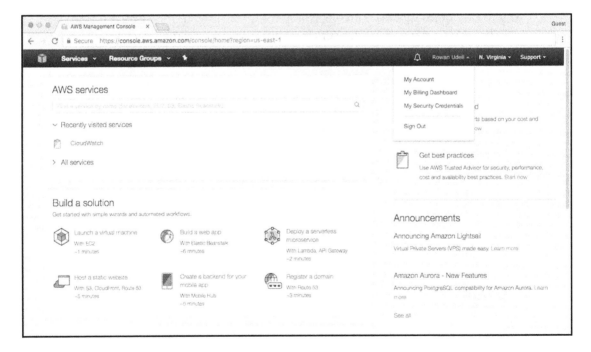

2. The **Billing** dashboard displays your up-to-date usage for the month. Click on **Budgets** in the left-hand menu:

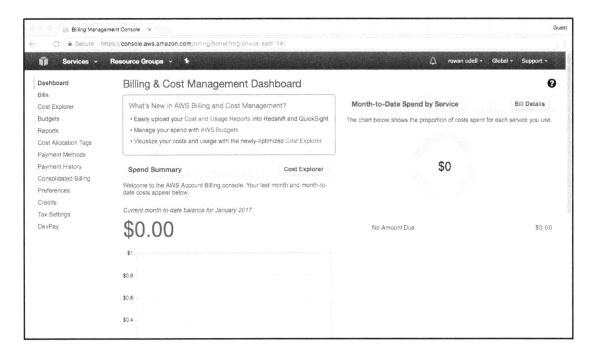

3. When you first arrive at the **Budgets** console, there will be no budgets to display. Click on the **Create budget** button to get started:

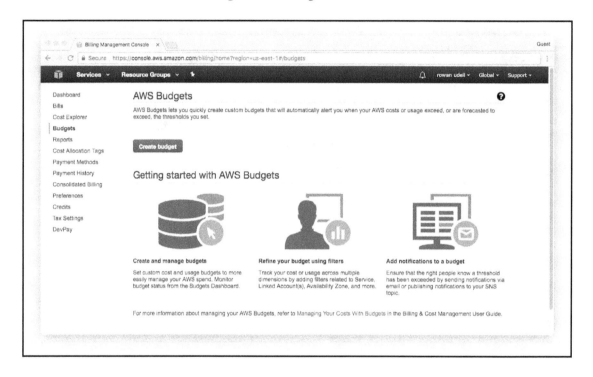

4. Start by filling out the budget details, such as `Cost` for the measurement type, `Monthly` for the period, and the budget amount. Select the **Start date** (which defaults to the first of the current month), and optionally the **End date**. Leave the **End date** field blank to create a rolling budget that is reset each month:

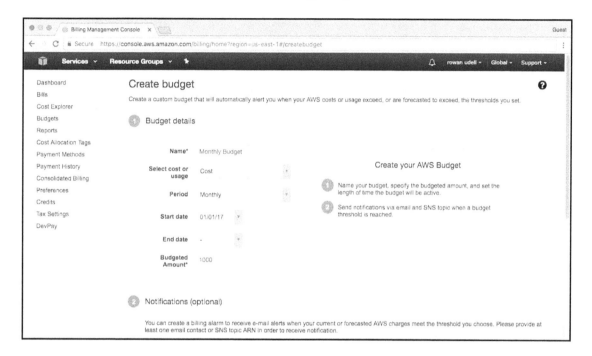

5. Next enter the notification details. This includes the threshold for notification, which we will set to be 80% (of our budget) in forecasted use. For e-mail notifications, simply enter the e-mail addresses you want to receive the notifications. Click **Create** when finished:

6. You will be returned to the **Budgets** section of the **Billing** dashboard, and you can see your newly created budget:

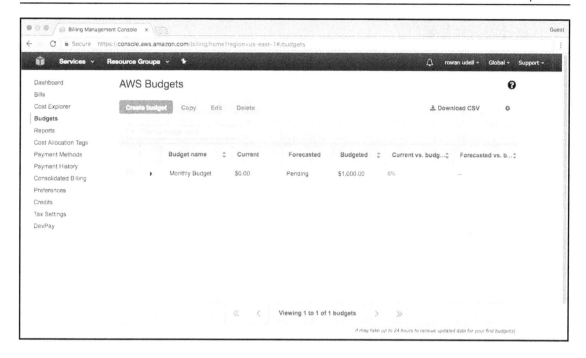

7. For each of the budgets you create, you can select it to view the full details:

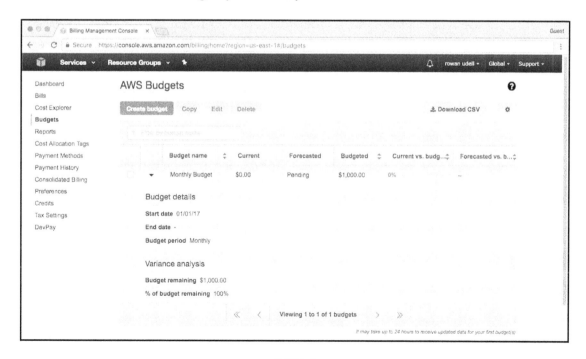

How it works...

The **Billing** dashboard is closely tied to the account itself, which is why it is not part of the regular services in the console. Accessing it via the user menu hints at the special access it requires. Generally, you would configure a budget when you first open a new AWS account, so you don't get any surprises in your bill at the end of the month.

If you get access denied messages in the **Billing** dashboard, it is most likely because you are using an IAM user and IAM access has not been enabled. You must use your root account credentials (such as that you used to create the account), or enable IAM access. IAM access can only be enabled by the root user.

When you first arrive at the billing section, you will see a high-level summary of your usage and expenses. As I performed this example in a new account, there's not much to see at this point. The **Month-to-Date Spend by Service** graph on the right can be particularly useful to find out what the most popular services you use are. This is a great place to start when trying to reduce or optimize your AWS spending.

We then navigate to the budgets section and create a new budget. Most of the details should be self-explanatory, and obvious for the purposes of budgeting. Your main choice is to decide if you want to alert on usage or costs. Cost budgets work against the dollar (or appropriate billing currency) amount you will be charged. Usage budgets work against a selected unit of usage, for example, instance hours or data transfer for EC2. A usage budget can only track one type of usage unit, so you will need to create multiple budgets to track the various units that you might be charged for. This is one reason why we prefer a cost budget, as it takes into account multiple forms of usage.

Specifying e-mail addresses to alert is the simplest way to send any alerts from the budget. For more advanced use cases, you can specify an SNS topic to receive notifications. An example might be if you wanted to receive budget alerts on your phone via an SMS message, or send the alert to a different system automatically (via HTTP/JSON).

Once finished, you can view all your budgets in the dashboard. You can repeat the process to create multiple budgets. This means you can create budgets for forecast usage and actual usage, as well as different time periods.

Feeding log files into CloudWatch logs

CloudWatch logs is a managed, highly durable, log storage system in AWS. It's capable of ingesting logs from many sources. We're going to focus on what is probably the most common use case which is shipping logs off your EC2 instances into CloudWatch logs.

This capability is particularly important in highly dynamic auto scaling environments. Since the lifetime of your EC2 instances can be quite short, any logs which are written only to a local disk will be lost upon instance termination. You'll inevitably find yourself wishing you had access to server logs after an instance has disappeared.

The following pattern we're about to show you allows you to aggregate, search and filter log entries across a number of sources. You can then create custom metrics and trigger alarms based on log activity. Super handy!

In this recipe we're going to:

- Launch an EC2 instance
- Configure it to send logs to CloudWatch logs
- Create a filter based on SSH logins to the instance
- Send ourselves an e-mail alert on filter matches

This might be something you'd consider doing on your bastion boxes since they will typically be the sole point of SSH access to your environments and it can be a good idea to make a lot of noise if people are logging in to production servers.

Getting ready

We're going to do all of this in `us-east-1` with the AWS Linux AMI. If you wish to do this in a different region you'll simply need to provide a different AMI ID to the template we're going to create.

Let's get in to it; you'll need the following:

- The VPC ID of your default VPC in `us-east-1`. You don't have to use the default VPC, you'll just need to make sure you choose a VPC which has a public subnet (which is configured to assign public IP addresses)
- The subnet ID of the public subnet
- An SSH key pair configured in `us-east-1`
- An e-mail address we can send alerts to

How to do it...

1. Create a new CloudFormation template. Add the following `Parameters` to it:

```
AmiId:
  Type: AWS::EC2::Image::Id
  Description: AMI ID to launch instances from
  Default: ami-0b33d91d
VpcId:
  Type: AWS::EC2::VPC::Id
  Description: VPC where load balancer and instance will launch
SubnetIDs:
  Type: List<AWS::EC2::Subnet::Id>
  Description: Public subnet where the instance will launch
    (pick at least 1)
KeyPair:
  Type: AWS::EC2::KeyPair::KeyName
  Description: Key to launch EC2 instance with
AlertEmail:
  Type: String
  Description: Email Address which alert emails will be sent to
```

2. Now for the `Resources`, we need to define a `Role` and `InstanceProfile` for our EC2 instance. This will give our server the appropriate permissions to send logs to CloudWatch.

```
ExampleRole:
  Type: AWS::IAM::Role
  Properties:
    AssumeRolePolicyDocument:
      Version: "2012-10-17"
      Statement:
        -
          Effect: Allow
          Principal:
            Service:
              - ec2.amazonaws.com
          Action:
            - sts:AssumeRole
    Path: /
    Policies:
      -
        PolicyName: WriteToCloudWatchLogs
        PolicyDocument:
          Version: "2012-10-17"
          Statement:
            -
```

```
              Effect: Allow
                Action:
                  - logs:CreateLogGroup
                  - logs:CreateLogStream
                  - logs:PutLogEvents
                  - logs:DescribeLogStreams
                Resource: "*"
  ExampleInstanceProfile:
    Type: AWS::IAM::InstanceProfile
    Properties:
      Roles:
        - !Ref ExampleRole
      Path: /
```

3. Our instance will need to live in a security group which allows SSH access, so let's add that now:

```
ExampleEC2InstanceSecurityGroup:
  Type: AWS::EC2::SecurityGroup
  Properties:
    GroupDescription: Security Group for example Instance
    SecurityGroupIngress:
      - IpProtocol: tcp
        CidrIp: "0.0.0.0/0"
        FromPort: 22
        ToPort: 22
    VpcId: !Ref VpcId
```

4. Next we can define our instance. We make sure to use the profile and security group we just created and we also add a small amount of user-data which does the following:

    1. Install the `awslogs` package.

    2. Writes a configuration file which will ship `/var/log/secure` to CloudWatch logs.

    3. Starts the `awslogs` service.

    4. Make the `awslogs` service start on boot (in case of reboot).

```
ExampleEC2Instance:
  Type: AWS::EC2::Instance
  Properties:
    IamInstanceProfile: !Ref ExampleInstanceProfile
    InstanceType: t2.nano
    KeyName: !Ref KeyPair
    UserData:
      Fn::Base64:
        Fn::Sub: |
```

```
                              #!/bin/bash -ex
                              yum update -y
                              yum install -y awslogs
                              cat << EOF >
                              /etc/awslogs/config/var-log-secure.conf
                              [/var/log/secure]
                              datetime_format = %b %d %H:%M:%S
                              file = /var/log/secure
                              buffer_duration = 5000
                              log_stream_name = {instance_id}
                              initial_position = start_of_file
                              log_group_name = /var/log/secure
                              EOF
                              service awslogs start
                              chkconfig awslogs on
              ImageId: !Ref AmiId
              SecurityGroupIds:
                - Fn::GetAtt: ExampleEC2InstanceSecurityGroup.GroupId
              SubnetId: !Select [ 0, Ref: SubnetIDs ]
```

5. We're now going to add an SNS topic. This topic will receive alerts and forward them to the e-mail address we're using for alerts:

```
ExampleSNSTopic:
  Type: AWS::SNS::Topic
  Properties:
    Subscription:
      -
        Endpoint: !Ref AlertEmail
        Protocol: email
```

6. Next, we need to filter our /var/log/secure logs for logins. A MetricFilter resource allows us to do this. CloudFormation will throw an error if we refer to a log group which doesn't yet exist, so we add that here too (with a DependsOn reference):

```
ExampleLogGroup:
  Type: AWS::Logs::LogGroup
  Properties:
    LogGroupName: /var/log/secure
    RetentionInDays: 7
ExampleLogsMetricFilter:
  Type: AWS::Logs::MetricFilter
  Properties:
    FilterPattern: '"Accepted publickey for ec2-user from"'
    LogGroupName: /var/log/secure
    MetricTransformations:
```

```
       MetricValue: "1"
       MetricNamespace: SSH/Logins
       MetricName: LoginCount
    DependsOn: ExampleLogGroup
```

7. The last `Resource` we need is the actual `Alarm`. Add it like so:

```
ExampleLoginAlarm:
  Type: AWS::CloudWatch::Alarm
  Properties:
    AlarmDescription: SSH Login Alarm
    AlarmActions:
    - Ref: ExampleSNSTopic
    MetricName: LoginCount
    Namespace: SSH/Logins
    Statistic: Sum
    Period: 60
    EvaluationPeriods: 1
    Threshold: 0
    ComparisonOperator: GreaterThanThreshold
```

8. Lastly, we'll add the public IP address of our instance to the `Outputs` so we don't need to go to the EC2 web console to look it up:

```
Outputs:
  ExampleEC2InstancePublicIp:
    Value: !GetAtt [ ExampleEC2Instance, PublicIp ]
```

9. Go ahead and launch this CloudFormation stack. You can do it from the AWS CLI like this:

```
aws cloudformation create-stack \
  --template-body \
  file://05-feed-log-files-in-to-cloudwatch-logs.yaml \
  --stack-name example-cloudwatchlogs \
  --capabilities CAPABILITY_IAM \
  --parameters \
  ParameterKey=VpcId,ParameterValue=<your-vpc-id> \
  ParameterKey=SubnetIDs,ParameterValue='<your-subnet-id>' \
  ParameterKey=KeyPair,ParameterValue=<your-ssh-key-name> \
  ParameterKey=AlertEmail,ParameterValue=<your-email-address>
```

10. Before proceeding you'll need to check your e-mail and confirm your subscription to the SNS topic. If you don't do this you won't receive any alerts from CloudWatch:

In the following screenshot, an example of confirmed subscription is illustrated:

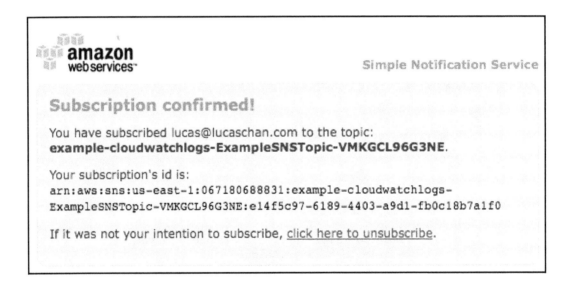

11. Go ahead and SSH to your instance. If your login is successful, you'll see your alarm triggered in the CloudWatch web console:

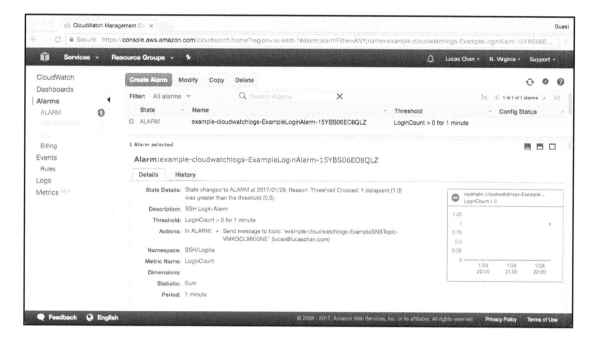

An e-mail will land in your inbox as shown in the following screenshot:

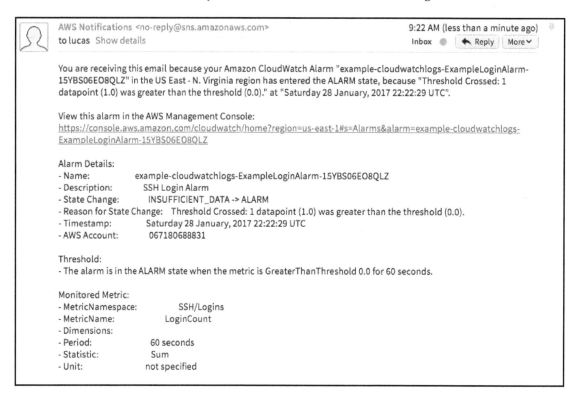

How it works...

It's important that you understand the difference between log streams and log groups.

Log streams are log sequences which come from a single source. This could be an EC2 instance, an application process, or another source within AWS. In our case the name of our log stream is the ID of our EC2 instance. In fact, the CloudWatch logs agent will set the `log_stream_name` to the instance ID by default.

Log groups are collections of log streams with the same properties. In our previous example, the log groups will correspond to `/var/log/secure`. So, we end up with a configuration which looks like:

```
log_group_name = /var/log/secure
log_stream_name = {instance_id}
```

When you install the CloudWatch logs agent, it actually sets up `/var/log/messages` in exactly the same manner as we've just described:

```
log_group_name = /var/log/messages
log_stream_name = {instance_id}
```

Once the agent has started, it will ship new log entries off the box to CloudWatch logs approximately every 5 seconds.

There's more...

- CloudWatch logs supports ingestion of traditional text-based log entries as well as JSON formatted logs.
- Logs can be ingested from other sources including CloudTrail, IAM, Kinesis Streams and Lambda.
- By default, logs are stored indefinitely. You can customize this time period to suit your needs however.
- Metric filters, like the one we created previously, can be used to graph and chart in the CloudWatch console. Add them to your dashboards as well as your alerting system.
- The CloudWatch web console allows you to test metric filters before you add them. Using this feature will save you a lot of trial and error with CloudFormation. Don't rely on the web console completely however: you should move these metric filters to CloudFormation as soon as you get them right.
- There is a one-one relationship between a log stream and a log source. For example, you can't have multiple instances sending `/var/log/secure` to the same log stream.
- The non-alarm state for the alarm we've created, will be **INSUFFICIENT_DATA**. This is because our metric filter outputs a value only if a login is detected.

13
Database Services

In this chapter, we will cover:

- Creating a database with automatic failover
- Creating a NAT gateway
- Creating a database read-replica
- Promoting a read-replica to master
- Creating a one-time database backup
- Restoring a database from a snapshot
- Migrating a database
- Calculating DynamoDB performance

Introduction

Having a persistent storage service is a key component of effectively using the AWS cloud for your systems. By ensuring that you have a highly available, fault-tolerant location to store your application state in, you can stop depending on individual servers for your data.

Creating a database with automatic failover

In this recipe, we're going to create a MySQL RDS database instance configured in multi-AZ mode to facilitate automatic failover.

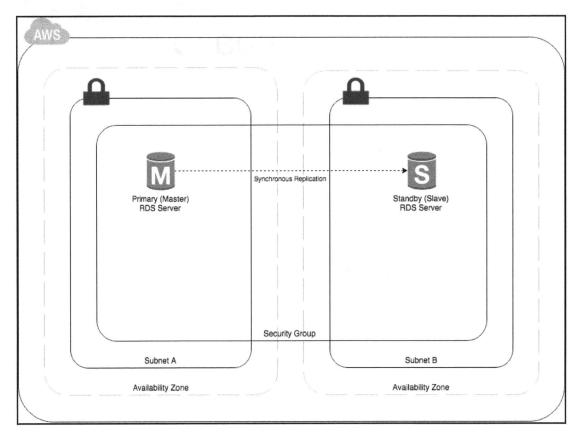

Database with automatic failover

Getting ready

The default VPC will work fine for this example. Once you are comfortable with creating databases, you may want to consider a VPC containing private subnets that you can use to segment your database away from the Internet and other resources (in the style of a three tier application). Either way, you'll need to note down the following:

- The ID of the VPC

- The CIDR range of the VPC
- The IDs of at least two subnets in your VPC. These subnets need to be in different Availability Zones, for example, `us-east-1a` and `us-east-1b`

How to do it...

Create a new CloudFormation template. We're going to add a total of 12 parameters to it:

1. The first three parameters will contain the values we mentioned in the *Getting ready* section:

```
VPCId:
  Type: AWS::EC2::VPC::Id
  Description: VPC where DB will launch
SubnetIds:
  Type: List<AWS::EC2::Subnet::Id>
  Description: Subnets where the DB will launch (pick at least 2)
SecurityGroupAllowCidr:
  Type: String
  Description: Allow this CIDR block to access the DB
  Default: "172.30.0.0/16"
```

2. We're also going to add the database credentials as parameters. This is good practice as it means we're not storing any credentials in our infrastructure source code. Note that the password contains the `NoEcho` parameter set to `true`. This stops CloudFormation from outputting the password wherever the CloudFormation stack details are displayed:

```
DBUsername:
  Type: String
  Description: Username to access the database
  MinLength: 1
  AllowedPattern: "[a-zA-Z][a-zA-Z0-9]*"
  ConstraintDescription: must start with a letter, must
    be alphanumeric
DBPassword:
  Type: String
  Description: Password to access the database
  MinLength: 1
  AllowedPattern: "[a-zA-Z0-9]*"
  NoEcho: true
  ConstraintDescription: must be alphanumeric
```

3. The next block of parameters pertains to cost and performance. They should be mostly self-explanatory. Refer to the AWS documentation on database instance types should you wish to change the instance class for this example. We're supplying a default value of 10 GB for the storage size and choosing a magnetic (`standard`) volume for the storage type. `gp2` offers better performance, but it costs a little more:

```
DBInstanceClass:
  Type: String
  Description: The instance type to use for this database
  Default: db.t2.micro
DBStorageAmount:
  Type: Number
  Description: Amount of storage to allocate (in GB)
  Default: 10
DBStorageType:
  Type: String
  Description: Type of storage volume to use
    (standard [magnetic] or gp2)
  Default: standard
  AllowedValues:
    - standard
    - gp2
```

4. We need to set some additional parameters for our database. These are the MySQL engine version and port. Refer to the AWS documentation for a list of all the available versions. We are setting a default value for this parameter as the latest version of MySQL at the time of writing:

```
DBEngineVersion:
  Type: String
  Description: DB engine version
  Default: "5.7.11"
DBPort:
  Type: Number
  Description: Port number to allocate
  Default: 3306
  MinValue: 1150
  MaxValue: 65535
```

5. Finally, we are going to define some parameters relating to backup and availability. We want our database to run in *multi-AZ* mode, we set this to true by default. We also set a backup retention period of 1 day by default; you might want to choose a period larger than this. If you set this value to 0, backups will be disabled (not recommended!):

```
DBMultiAZ:
  Type: String
  Description: Should this DB be deployed in Multi-AZ configuration?
  Default: true
  AllowedValues:
    - true
    - false
DBBackupRetentionPeriod:
  Type: Number
  Description: How many days to keep backups (0 disables backups)
  Default: 1
  MinValue: 0
  MaxValue: 35
```

6. We're done with the parameters for this template; we can now go ahead and start defining our Resources. First of all, we want a security group for our DB to reside in. This security group allows inbound access to the database port from the CIDR range we've defined:

```
ExampleDBSecurityGroup:
  Type: AWS::EC2::SecurityGroup
  Properties:
    GroupDescription: Example security group for inbound access to DB
    SecurityGroupIngress:
      - IpProtocol: tcp
        CidrIp: !Ref SecurityGroupAllowCidr
        FromPort: !Ref DBPort
        ToPort: !Ref DBPort
    VpcId: !Ref VPCId
```

7. Next, we need to define a DBSubnetGroup resource. This resource is used to declare which subnet(s) our DB will reside in. We define two subnets for this resource so that the primary and standby servers will reside in separate Availability Zones:

```
ExampleDBSubnetGroup:
  Type: AWS::RDS::DBSubnetGroup
  Properties:
    DBSubnetGroupDescription: Example subnet group for example DB
    SubnetIds:
```

```
- Fn::Select: [ 0, Ref: SubnetIds ]
- Fn::Select: [ 1, Ref: SubnetIds ]
```

8. Finally, we define our RDS instance resource. We specify it as being a MySQL database and the rest of the properties are made up of the parameters and resources that we've defined previously. Lots of `!Ref` is required here:

```
ExampleDBInstance:
  Type: AWS::RDS::DBInstance
  Properties:
    AllocatedStorage: !Ref DBStorageAmount
    BackupRetentionPeriod: !Ref DBBackupRetentionPeriod
    DBInstanceClass: !Ref DBInstanceClass
    DBSubnetGroupName: !Ref ExampleDBSubnetGroup
    Engine: mysql
    EngineVersion: !Ref DBEngineVersion
    MasterUsername: !Ref DBUsername
    MasterUserPassword: !Ref DBPassword
    MultiAZ: !Ref DBMultiAZ
    StorageType: !Ref DBStorageType
    VPCSecurityGroups:
      - !GetAtt ExampleDBSecurityGroup.GroupId
```

9. For good measure, we can add an output to this template that will return the hostname for this RDS database:

```
Outputs:
  ExampleDbHostname:
    Value: !GetAtt ExampleDBInstance.Endpoint.Address
```

10. You can provision the database via the CloudFormation web console or use a CLI command like so:

```
aws cloudformation create-stack \
  --stack-name rds1 \
  --template-body \
  file://06-create-database-with-automatic-failover.yaml \
  --parameters \
  ParameterKey=DBUsername,ParameterValue=<username> \
  ParameterKey=DBPassword,ParameterValue=<password>  \
  ParameterKey=SubnetIds,"ParameterValue='<subnet-id-a>, \
  <subnet-id-b>'" \
  ParameterKey=VPCId,ParameterValue=<vpc-id>
```

How it works...

In a multi-AZ configuration, AWS will provision a standby MySQL instance in a separate Availability Zone. Changes to your database will be replicated to the standby DB instance in a synchronous fashion. If there is a problem with your primary DB instance AWS will automatically failover to the standby, promote it to be the primary DB, and provision a new standby.

You don't have access to query standby databases directly. So you can't use it to handle all of your read queries, for example. If you wish to use additional database instances to increase read capacity, you'll need to provision a *read-replica*. We'll cover those in a separate recipe.

Backups will always be taken from the standby instance, which means there is no interruption to your DB availability. This is not the case if you opted against deploying your DB in multi-AZ mode.

When you deploy this example it will take roughly 20 minutes or more for the stack to report completion. This is because the RDS service needs to go through the following process in order to provision a fully working multi-AZ database:

- Provision the primary database
- Back up the primary database
- Provision the standby database using the backup from the primary
- Configure both databases for synchronous replication

WARNING

Be careful about making changes to your RDS configuration after you've started writing data to it, especially when using CloudFormation updates. Some RDS configuration changes require the database to be re-provisioned, which can result in data loss. We'd recommend using CloudFormation change sets, which will give you an opportunity to see which changes are about to cause destructive behavior. The CloudFormation RDS docs also provide some information on this.

There's more...

- You can define a maintenance window for your RDS instance. This is the time period when AWS will perform maintenance tasks such as security patches or minor version upgrades. If you don't specify a maintenance window (which we don't in this example), one is chosen for you.

Creating a NAT gateway

Unless required, your instances should not be publicly exposed to the Internet. When your instances are on the Internet, you have to assume that they will be attacked at some stage.

This means most of your workloads should run on instances in private subnets. Private subnets are those that are not connected directly to the Internet.

In order to give your private instances access to the Internet you use **network address translation** (**NAT**). A NAT gateway allows your instances to initiate a connection to the Internet, without allowing connections from the Internet.

Getting ready

For this recipe, you must have the following resources:

- A VPC with an **Internet gateway** (**IGW**)
- A public subnet
- A private subnet route table

You will need the IDs for the public subnet and private subnet route table. Both of these resources should be in the same AZ.

How to do it...

1. Start with the usual CloudFormation template version and description:

```
AWSTemplateFormatVersion: "2010-09-09"
Description: Create NAT Gateway and associated route.
```

2. The template must take the following required parameters:

```
Parameters:
  PublicSubnetId:
    Description: Public Subnet ID to add the NAT Gateway to
    Type: AWS::EC2::Subnet::Id
  RouteTableId:
    Description: The private subnet route table to add the NAT
      Gateway route to
    Type: String
```

3. In the `Resources` section, define an Elastic IP that will be assigned to the NAT gateway:

```
Resources:
  EIP:
    Type: AWS::EC2::EIP
    Properties:
      Domain: vpc
```

4. Create the NAT gateway resource, assigning it the EIP you just defined in the public subnet:

```
NatGateway:
  Type: AWS::EC2::NatGateway
  Properties:
    AllocationId: !GetAtt EIP.AllocationId
    SubnetId: !Ref PublicSubnetId
```

5. Finally, define the route to the NAT gateway and associate it with the private subnet's route table:

```
Route:
  Type: AWS::EC2::Route
  Properties:
    RouteTableId: !Ref RouteTableId
    DestinationCidrBlock: 0.0.0.0/0
    NatGatewayId: !Ref NatGateway
```

How it works...

The parameters required for this recipe are as follows:

- A public subnet ID
- A private subnet route table ID

The public subnet ID is needed to host the NAT gateway, as it must have Internet access. The private subnet route table will be updated with a route to the NAT gateway.

Using the AWS NAT gateway service means that AWS takes care of hosting and securing the service for you. The service will be hosted redundantly in a single AZ.

 You can use the recipe multiple times to deploy NAT gateways in each of your private subnets. Just make sure the public subnet and the private subnet are in the same AZ.

To cater for the unlikely event of an AZ outage (unlikely, but possible) you should deploy a NAT gateway per subnet. This means if one NAT gateway goes offline, instances in the other AZ can continue to access the Internet as normal. You *are* deploying your application in multiple AZs, aren't you?

This recipe will only work if you have created your own private subnets, as the default subnets in a new AWS account are all *public*. Instances in a public subnet have direct access to the Internet (via an IGW), so they do not need a NAT gateway.

Creating a database read-replica

This recipe will show you how to create an RDS read-replica. You can use read-replicas in order to increase the performance of your application by off-loading database reads to a separate database instance. You can provision up to five read-replicas per source DB.

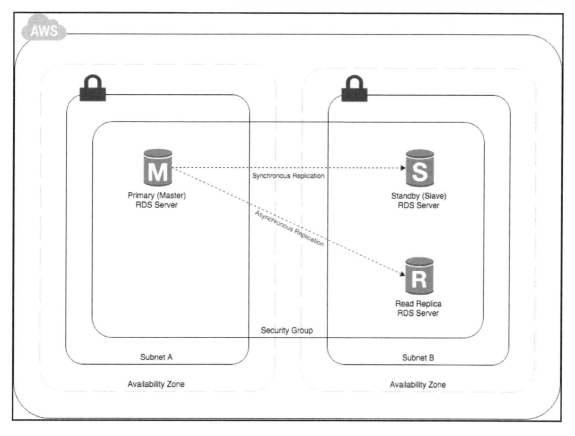

Read-only database slaves

Getting ready

You will need an RDS DB deployed with backup retention enabled. We are going to build upon the DB deployed in the previous *Creating a database with automatic failover* recipe.

You're going to need the following values:

- The identifier for your source RDS instance, for example, `eexocwv5k5kv5z`
- A unique identifier for the read-replicate we're going to create, for example, `read-replica-1`

How to do it...

In the AWS CLI, type this command:

```
aws rds create-db-instance-read-replica \
  --source-db-instance-identifier <source-db-identifier> \
  --db-instance-identifier <unique-identifier-for-replica>
```

How it works...

RDS will now go ahead and create a new read-replica for you.

Some parameters are inherited from the source instance and can't be defined at the time of creation:

- Storage engine
- Storage size
- Security group

The CLI command accepts some parameters that we could have defined, but didn't to keep things simple. They will instead be inherited from the source database. The main two are as follows:

- `--db-instance-class`: The same class as the source instance is used
- `--db-subnet-group-name`: The source instance's subnet group will be used and a subnet is chosen at random (hence, an Availability Zone is chosen at random)

There's more...

- Read-replicas are deployed in a single Availability Zone; there is no standby read-replica.
- It's not possible to enable backups on read-replicas during time of creation. This must be configured afterwards.
- The default storage type is `standard` (magnetic). You can increase performance by choosing `gp2` or using provisioned IOPS.
- It's possible to add MySQL indexes directly to a read-replica to further increase read performance. These indexes are not required to be present on the primary DB.

- Using read-replicas for availability purposes is more of a complimentary DR strategy and shouldn't be used in place of multi-AZ RDS. A multi-AZ configuration gives you the benefit of failure detection and automatic failover.
- It is possible to deploy a read-replica in an entirely different region.
- Unlike the replication between a primary and standby DB (which is synchronous), replication to a read-replica is asynchronous. This means that it's possible for a read-replica to fall behind the primary. Keep this in mind when sending time sensitive read queries to your read-replicas.

Promoting a read-replica to master

We're going to show you how to promote an RDS read-replica to be a primary instance. There are a few reasons you might like to do this:

- To handle a table migration that would typically cause a large amount of downtime, especially when messing with columns or indexes
- Because you need to implement sharding
- Recovery from failure, should you choose not to deploy your existing primary in multi-AZ mode (not recommended)

Getting ready

You're going to need the unique ID, which has been assigned to an RDS read-replica. If you followed the previous *Creating a database with automatic failover*, and *Creating a database read-replica* recipes, then you'll be all set.

It's also a good idea to have backups enabled on this read-replica prior to promoting it. This shortens the promotion process because you won't need to wait for a backup to be taken. You'll want to set the backup retention period to a value between 1 and 8.

 Enabling backups on your read-replica will cause it to reboot!

In order to enable backups, you can use the following CLI command:

```
aws rds modify-db-instance \
   --db-instance-identifier <identifier-for-read-replica> \
   --backup-retention-period <days-to-keep-backups-for> \
   --apply-immediately
```

You can drop the `--apply-immediately` parameter if you prefer to wait for the reboot to happen during the configured maintenance window. But you'll still want to wait until after the reboot happens before you continue with the promotion process.

To ensure that you have the most up-to-date data before promotion you'll want to stop all write traffic to the current source primary DB before going ahead. It's also a good idea to make sure that the replication lag on your read-replica is 0 (you can check this in CloudWatch).

How to do it...

1. Run the following command to promote your read-replica to a primary DB instance. This command will cause your read-replica to reboot:

```
aws rds promote-read-replica \
   --db-instance-identifier <identifier-for-read-replica>
```

2. If you wish to then go ahead and configure your new primary RDS instance to run in a multi-AZ configuration then you'll need to run this additional command. Expect to wait a while for this operation to complete:

```
aws rds modify-db-instance \
   --db-instance-identifier <identifier-for-new-primary> \
   --multi-az \
   --apply-immediately
```

Creating a one-time database backup

We're now going to show you how to make a one-off snapshot of your database. You might opt to do this if you have a specific requirement around keeping a point in time backup of your DB. You might also want to take a snapshot for the purpose of creating a new working copy of your dataset.

Getting ready

In order to proceed you're going to need the following:

- The identifier for the RDS instance you wish to back up
- A unique identifier that you'd like to assign to this snapshot

The snapshot identifier has some constraints:

- It needs to start with a letter
- It must not be longer than 255 characters

 If your primary database isn't running in a multi-AZ configuration then be aware that creating a snapshot will cause an outage. In a multi-AZ configuration the snapshot is taken on the standby instance so no outage occurs.

How to do it...

Type the following AWS CLI command to initiate the creation of a snapshot. You'll need to wait for a few minutes for the snapshot to complete before you can use it:

```
aws rds create-db-snapshot \
  --db-instance-identifier <primary-rds-id> \
  --db-snapshot-identifier <unique-id-for-snapshot>
```

Restoring a database from a snapshot

We'll now talk through how to restore a database from a snapshot. This process creates a new database that will retain a majority of the configuration of the database that the snapshot was taken from.

Getting ready

You'll need the following pieces of information:

- The ID of the snapshot you wish to restore from
- A name or identifier that you wish to give to the database we're about to create

AWS does not allow RDS services in your account to share the same identifier. If the source database is still online you'll need to make sure to choose a different identifier (or rename the source database).

How to do it...

1. Type the following command:

```
aws rds restore-db-instance-from-db-snapshot \
    --db-snapshot-identifier <name-of-snapshot-to-restore > \
    --db-instance-identifier <name-for-new-db> \
    --db-subnet-group-name <your-db-subnet-group> \
    --multi-az
```

2. You may have noticed that this command creates a new database in the default security group. This happens because the `restore-db-instance-from-db-snapshot` doesn't accept a security group ID as a parameter. You'll have to run a second command to assign a nondefault security group to the new database:

```
aws rds modify-db-instance \
    --db-instance-identifier <name-of-newly-restored-db> \
    --vpc-security-group-ids <id-of-security-group>
```

The `modify-db-instance` command will return an error unless the state of the target database is `available`.
Also, security group names aren't valid with this command; you'll need to use a security group ID instead, for example, `sg-7603d50a`.

There's more...

The previous command includes the parameter for enabling multi-AZ on the new DB. If you'd like the new DB to be running in single-AZ mode only then can you simply remove this flag.

Migrating a database

In this recipe, we will use **Database Migration Service** (**DMS**) to move an external database into **Relational Database Service** (**RDS**).

Unlike many of the other recipes, this will be performed manually through the web console.

Most database migrations are one-off, and there are many steps involved. We suggest that you first perform the process manually via the console before automating it, if required (which you can do with the AWS CLI tool or SDKs).

Getting ready

For this recipe you will need the following:

- An external database
- An RDS database instance

The source database in this example is called **employees**, so substitute your own database name as required.

Both databases must be accessible from the replication instance that will be created as part of the recipe. The simplest way to do this is to allow access to the databases from the Internet, but obviously this has security implications.

How to do it...

1. Navigate to the DMS console:

2. Click on **Create Migration** to start the migration wizard:

3. Specify the details for your replication instance. Unless you have a specific VPC configuration, the defaults will be fine:

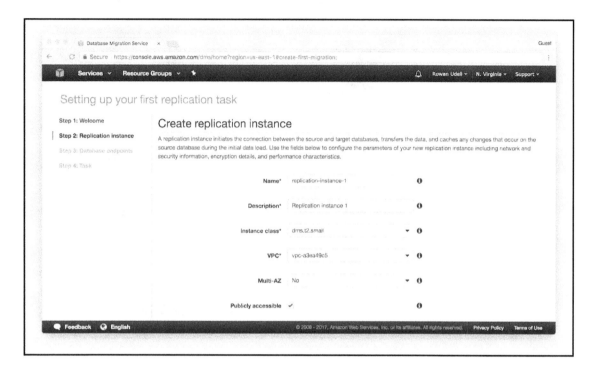

4. While waiting for the replication instance to be ready, fill out the source and target endpoint information, including server hostname and port, and the username and password to use when connecting:

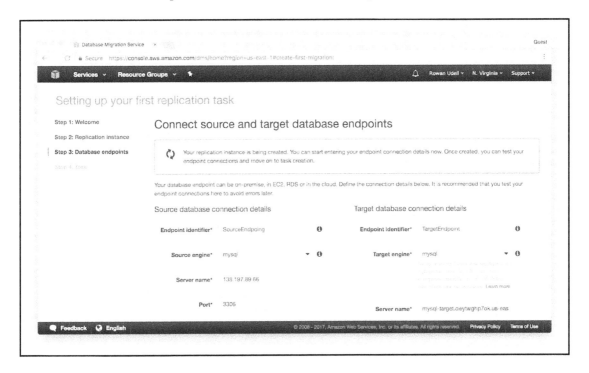

5. Once the instance is ready, the interface will update and you can proceed:

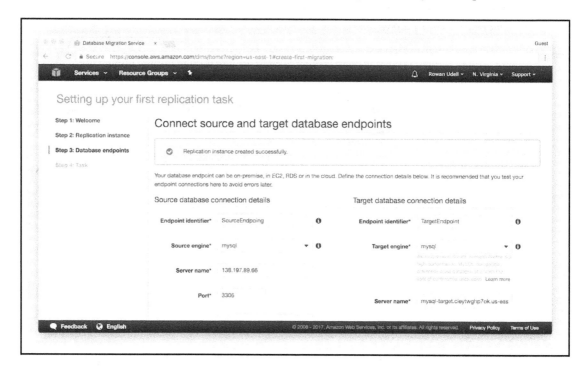

6. In order to confirm and create the source and target endpoints, click on the **Run test** button for each of your databases:

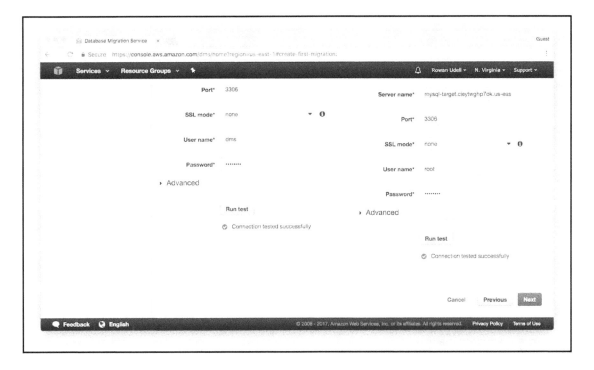

7. After the endpoints have been successfully tested and created, define your task. In this recipe, we will simply migrate the data (without ongoing replication):

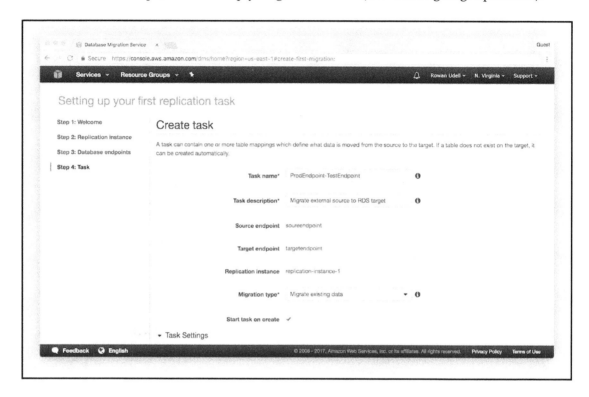

8. For simplicity, drop the tables in the target database (which should be empty) to ensure parity between the databases:

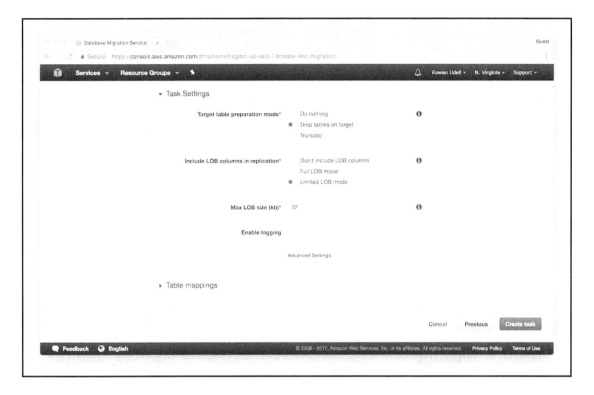

9. Finally, define the mappings between the two databases. In this case, we will migrate all the tables (by using the wildcard %) in the **employees** database on the source:

10. Once you click **Add selection rule** you will see your rule in the selection rules list:

11. Once the task is defined you have finished the wizard. You will then see the task being created:

12. Once the status of the task is **Ready** you can select it and click on the **Start/Resume** button:

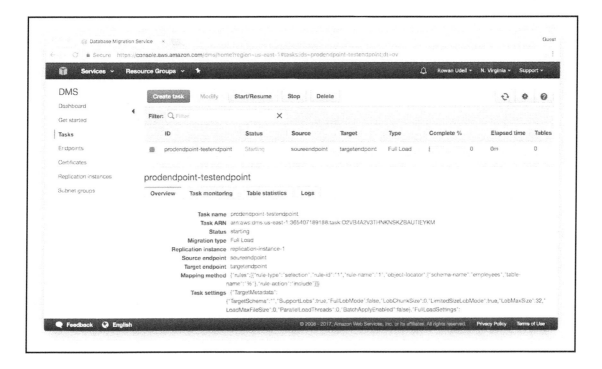

13. When complete, you will see the task's details updated in the console:

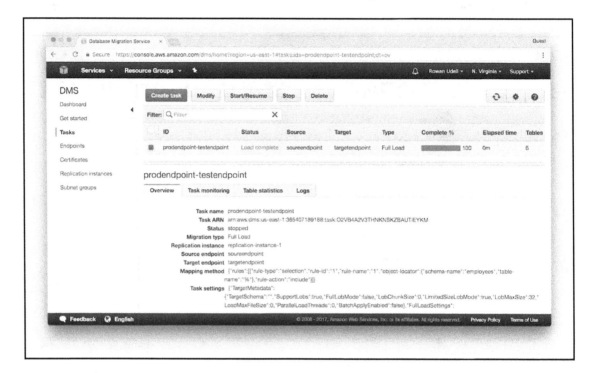

How it works...

At a high level, this is what the DMS architecture looks like:

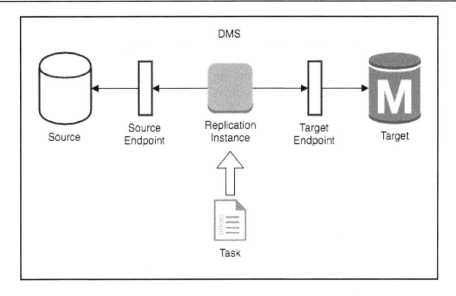

Both the **Source** and **Target** databases are external to **DMS**. They are represented internally by endpoint resources that are references to the databases. Endpoints can be reused between different tasks if needed.

This recipe starts by defining the replication instance details. Keep in mind that the DMS migration process works best when the migration/transform between the two databases is kept *in memory*. This means that for larger jobs you should allocate a more powerful instance. If the process needs to temporarily write data to disk (such as swap) then the performance and throughput will be much lower. This can have flow-on effects, particularly for tasks that include ongoing replication.

Next, the two endpoints are defined. It is very important to verify your endpoint configuration by using the built-in testing feature so that your tasks do not fail later in the process. Generally, if the connectivity test fails, it is one of two main issues:

- Network connectivity issues between the replication instance and the database. This is particularly an issue for on-premise databases, which are usually specifically restricted from being accessed externally.
- User permissions issues: For example, in the case of MySQL, the root user cannot be used to connect to the database externally, so this default user cannot be used.

Defining the task involves defining your migration type. The recipe uses the simplest type; migrate tables. This means that the data will be copied between the two databases, and will be complete when the data is propagated. We also get to define the behavior on the target database. For simplicity, we have configured the task to drop the tables in the target database ensuring that the two databases look as similar as possible, even if the tables are renamed, or the table mappings change. For the task table mappings we use the wildcard symbol % to match all tables in the source database. Obviously, you could be more selective if you only wanted to match a subset of your data.

Once the replication instance, endpoints, and task are defined the wizard ends and you are returned to the DMS console. After the task is finished creating it can be started.

As it is a *migrate existing data-type* task, it will complete once all the data has been propagated to the target database.

There's more...

This is obviously a simple example of what DMS can do. There are other features and performance aspects that you should consider in more advanced scenarios.

Database engines

While this example uses two MySQL databases, it is possible to migrate from one database engine to a complete database engine, for example, Oracle to MySQL. Unfortunately, this can be a complex process, and while this functionality is very useful it is beyond the scope of this recipe. Due to the differences in the various engines, there are some limitations on what you can migrate and transform.

See the *AWS Schema Conversion Tool* documentation for more details on what can be migrated between different database engines.

Ongoing replication

There are also some limits around the ongoing propagation of data—only table data can be migrated. Things such as indexes, users, and permissions cannot be replicated continually.

Multi-AZ

For ongoing replication tasks, you may want to create a multi-AZ replication instance so that the impact of any interruptions of services are minimized. Obviously you will need to have a similarly configured (such as multi-AZ) RDS instance as your target to get the full benefit!

 For best performance, when setting up your replication instance you should make sure it is in the *same* AZ as your target RDS instance.

Calculating DyanmoDB performance

DynamoDB (**DDB**) is the managed NoSQL database service from AWS.

As DDB pricing is based on the amount of read and write capacity units provisioned, it is important to be able to calculate the requirements for your use case.

This recipe uses a written formula to estimate the required **read capacity units** (**RCU**) and **write capacity units** (**WCU**) that should be allocated to you DDB table.

It is also crucial to remember that while new partitions will be automatically added to a DDB table, they cannot be automatically taken away. This means that excessive partitioning can cause long-term impacts to your performance, so you should be aware of them.

Getting ready

All of these calculations assume that you have chosen a good partition key for your data. A good partition key ensures the following:

- Data is evenly spread across all the available partitions
- Read and write activity is spread evenly in time

Unfortunately, choosing a good partition key is very data-specific, and beyond the scope of this recipe.

All reads are assumed to be strongly consistent.

How to do it...

1. Start with the size of the items, in **kilobytes** (**KB**):

   ItemSize = Size of the items (rows) in KB

2. Work out the required number of RCUs required by dividing the number by 4, and rounding up:

   RCU Per Item = ItemSize / 4 (rounded up)

3. Define the expected number of read operations per second. This is one of the numbers you will use to provision your table with:

   *Required RCU = Expected Number of Reads * RCU Per Item*

4. Divide the number by *3,000* to calculate the number of DDB partitions required to reach the capacity:

   Read Partitions = Required RCU / 3,000

5. Next, work out the write capacity required by dividing the item size by *1*, and rounding up:

   WCU Per Item = ItemSize / 1 (rounded up)

6. Define the expected number of write operations per second. This is one of the numbers you will use to provision your table with:

   *Required WCU = Expected Number of Writes * WCU Per Item*

7. Divide the number by *1,000* to calculate the number of DDB partitions required to reach the capacity:

   Write Partitions = Required WCU / 1,000

8. Add these two values to get the capacity partitions required (rounding up to a whole number):

   Capacity Partitions = Read Partitions + Write Partitions (rounded up)

9. Work out the minimum number of partitions required by the amount of data you plan to store:

Size Partitions = Total Size in GB / 10 (rounded up)

10. Once you have the partition requirements for your use case, take the maximum of your previous calculations:

Required Partitions = Maximum value between Capacity Partitions and Size Partitions

11. Since your allocated capacity is spread evenly across partitions, divide the RCU and WCU values to get the per-partition performance of your table:

Partition Read Throughput = Required RCU / Required Partitions

Partition Write Throughput = Required WCU / Required Partitions

How it works...

Behind the scenes, DDB throughput is controlled by the number of partitions that are allocated to your table. It is important to consider how your data will be spread across these partitions to ensure you get the performance you expect *and have paid for*.

We start this recipe by calculating the size of the items in your database, for throughput purposes. DDB has a minimum size it will consider, and even if an operation uses less than this size, it is rounded up in terms of allocated throughput used. The minimum size depends on the type of operation:

- Read operations are calculated in 4-K blocks
- Write operations are calculated in 1-K blocks

We then work out what the required RCU and WCU is, based on the expected number of operations. These values are what can then be used to provision the DDB table, as they represent the minimum required throughput (in optimal conditions).

Once you have these values, you can use them to provision your table.

Next, we calculate the throughput per partition key. These calculations rely on knowing what the performance of each partition is expected to be. The numbers 3,000 (for RCUs) and 1,000 (for WCUs) represent the capacity of a single DDB partition. By expressing the capacity in terms of partition performance (reads and writes) and adding them together we get the minimum number of partitions required from a capacity point of view.

We then do the same calculation for total data size. Each DDB partition can handle up to 10 GB of data. Any more than that will need to be split between multiple partitions.

 The specific values for partition capacity (for reads, writes, and size) have been stable for a while, but may change in the future. Double-check that the current values are the same as used here for complete accuracy.

Once we have the minimum partitions for both capacity and size, we take the highest value and work with that. This ensures we meet both the capacity and size requirements.

Finally, we take the provisioned capacity and divide it by the number of partitions. This gives us the throughput performance for each partition key, which we can then use to confirm against our use case.

There's more...

There are many nuances to using DDB efficiently and effectively. Here are some of the more important/impactful things to note.

Burst capacity

There is a burst capacity available to tables that go over their allocated capacity. Unused read and write capacity can be retained for up to five minutes (such as 300 seconds, for calculation purposes). Relying on this capacity is not good practice, and it will undoubtedly cause issues at some stage in the future.

Metrics

DDB tables automatically send data to CloudWatch metrics. This is the quickest and easiest way to confirm that your calculations and provision capacity are meeting your needs. It also helps you keep an eye on your usage to track your throughput needs over time. All metrics appear in the *AWS/DynamoDB* namespace. Some of the most interesting metrics for throughput calculations are as follows:

- `ConsumedReadCapacityUnits`
- `ConsumedWriteCapacityUnits`
- `ReadThrottleEvents`
- `WriteThrottleEvents`

There are other metrics available; see the *Amazon DynamoDB Metrics and Dimensions* documentation for more details.

Eventually consistent reads

Using eventually consistent reads (as opposed to strongly consistent reads) *halves* the RCU requirements for calculation purposes. In this recipe, we have used strongly consistent reads because it works with all workloads, but you should confirm that your use case actually requires it. Use eventually consistent reads if it does not.

By reducing the required provisioned capacity for reads, you effectively reduce your *cost* for using DDB.

14
Introducing AWS Lambda

I still remember the days when there was a clear demarcation between IT developers and system administrators; so much so that, each time a developer wanted a simple software platform or environment to be set up on their workstations, they would have to log one or more change requests, then dubiously wait for an IT admin to come along, who would more often than not provide you with an incorrect version of the software that you requested. Basically, you would end up wasting a week's effort just to get some simple software like Java or Tomcat to be setup, right? Many of us have sometime or the other been through this so called **vicious cycle** in IT and some still do, even today. But what if I told you that there is some ray of light around the corner! What if you, as a developer had the flexibility to simply write your code and put it up for execution; without having to worry about the underlying software platform, the OS or the hardware on which your code will run? Sounds too good to be true? Well fret no more, because that is what this book is all about! How you, as a developer start leveraging certain cloud-based services to develop, test, and host applications without having to even manage anything! Welcome to the amazing world of serverless computing!

In this chapter, we are going to get an understanding of the following topics:

- What serverless computing is, along with its pros and cons
- Introduction of AWS Lambda as a service and how it works
- Getting started with AWS Lambda using the AWS Management Console, as well as the CLI
- Pricing and a few of Lambda's limitations

So, without further ado, let's get started!

What is serverless computing?

To understand what serverless computing is all about and how it came to be, we first need to travel back in time to the era of mainframes and traditional data centers! Sounds like a long-lost time, right? Don't worry, we are not going that far back. This is probably in the time when most IT organizations had massive in-house data centers for hosting almost all enterprise applications and services. First, these applications were hosted directly on physical servers, and then eventually migrated onto the virtualized environments that provided a better utilization of resources as well as helped to slash down the overall costs and time for deployments from months to days. With the advent of the virtualization era, we also started to develop and use more convenient deployment tools that helped to deploy our applications with more ease, but it still meant managing the application's underlying operating system, software platform, and so on:

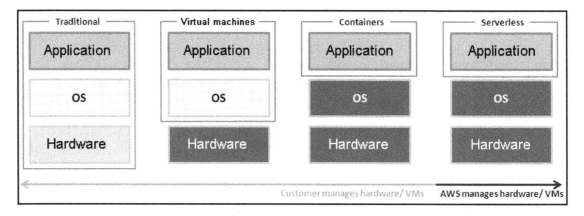

With virtualization clearly not having all the answers, we started looking for a much simpler application deployment model and, in return, found **Containers**. Unlike their earlier counterparts, **Virtual Machines**, **Containers** don't require a lot of resources or overhead to run. They are far easier and quicker to deploy, hence, reduce the overall application deployment time from days to minutes! You could now easily roll out a new patch for your application, scale your application dynamically based on incoming requests, and even orchestrate various other functions using a vast variety of container management products. However, the question of managing the **Containers** still remains, and trust me, managing a fleet of thousands of **Containers** and their underlying physical servers is no easy task. A better, more efficient, deployment model was needed; something that provided us with the agility and flexibility of containers, but without all the hassle and trouble of managing them. Enter serverless computing!

Serverless computing is all about running your application code on small ingots of some CPU and memory without having to worry about the OS type, the software platform, or any of the underlying hardware either. Just take your code and run it! Yes! It's that simple! Serverless computing today is offered by most public cloud providers, such as Amazon Web Services, Google Cloud Platform, Microsoft Azure, and even by IBM as a managed service. This essentially means that all you need to do is write your code or functions that perform a very specific task, select the quantity of resources (in this case RAM) required to run your code and submit it to the serverless cloud computing service to execute on. The service makes sure that your code gets the required amount of memory and CPU cycles it needs to execute. Hence, the collective term **Function as a Service** (**FaaS**).

Pros and cons of serverless computing

Here is a quick look at some of the key benefits that you, as a developer, can attain with the help of serverless computing:

- **No ware to manage**: Perhaps one of the biggest reasons for the hype about serverless computing is the fact there is absolutely no hardware or software to manage. The management of the serverless computing environment all the way from the underlying hardware to the OS, to even the application's platform layer, is managed by the cloud provider itself.
- **Faster execution time**: Unlike your standard cloud instances, which generally take a good minute or two to boot up, functions, on the other hand, spin up very quickly, mostly in a matter of seconds. This could be due to the fact that the functions are made to run on top of a containerized platform.
- **Really low costs**: Since there is virtually no opex involved with serverless computing, it is fairly cheap, even when compared to hosting and managing instances in the cloud. Also, the pricing model for serverless computing is a little different from that of your traditional cloud pricing model. Here, you are generally billed on the duration of your function's execution and the amount of memory it consumed during its execution period. The duration is calculated from the time your code begins executing until it returns or otherwise terminates and is rounded up to the nearest 100 ms.
- **Support of popular programming languages**: Most cloud providers that provide serverless computing frameworks today, support a variety of programming languages, such as Java, Node.js, Python, and even C#. Azure functions allows the use of F#, PHP, Bash, Batch and PowerShell scripts in addition to the few mentioned.

- **Microservices compatible**: Since serverless computing functions are small, independent chunks of code that are designed to perform a very specific set of roles or activities, they can be used as a delivery medium for microservices as well. This comes as a huge advantage as compared to hosting your monolithic applications on the cloud, which do not scale that effectively.
- **Event-driven applications**: Serverless functions are an ideal choice for designing and running event-driven applications that react to certain events and take some action against them. For example, an image upload operation to a cloud storage triggers a function that creates associated thumbnail images for the same.

Feeling excited already about giving serverless computing a try? Hold on! There are a few cons to serverless computing as well that you should be aware of before we proceed further:

- **Execution duration**: Serverless functions are designed to run for short durations of time, ideally somewhere under 300 seconds only. This is a hard limit set by most cloud providers, however, there are a few workarounds to this as well.
- **Stateless**: Serverless functions are purely stateless, which means that once the function completes its execution or is terminated for some reason, it won't store any data locally on its disk.
- **Complexity**: The smaller you make things, the more complex it's going to become. Although writing functions that perform very particular tasks is a good idea, it can cause complexity issues when you view your application as a whole system. A simple example can break one large application into some ten different functions such that each perform a specific task. Now you need to manage ten different entities rather than just one. Imagine if you had a thousand functions instead.
- **Lack of tools**: Although serverless computing is all at its hype, it still doesn't provide a lot of out-of-the-box tools for management, deployment, and even monitoring. Most of your monitoring tools that you use today were designed for long-running, complex applications; not for simple functions that execute in a mere seconds.
- **Vendor lock-in**: With each cloud provider providing its own unique tool sets and services around serverless computing, you often tend to get tied down to a particular vendor. This means that you cannot change your cloud provider without making some changes to your functions as well.

With these key points in mind, let us get to understanding and learning a bit more about the core serverless computing service that this book is all about--AWS Lambda.

Introducing AWS Lambda

So, here we are, finally to the fun part! In this section, we will learn what Lambda is actually all about, what some of its salient features are, how it works and some steps on getting started with your very first Lambda invocation.

AWS Lambda was first introduced way back in 2014, at the yearly *AWS re:Invent* conference in Las Vegas. The idea back then, and which pretty much holds true even today, is that Lambda is a simple compute service that runs your code in response to certain events. These events can be anything, from an upload operation of an object to an S3 bucket, a record insertion in a DynamoDB table, or even some form of event triggered from your mobile app. The idea here is simple--you simply provide your code to AWS Lambda. Lambda will internally take care of provisioning and managing the underlying infrastructure resources, making sure your code gets deployed successfully; even things like your code's scalability and high availability are taken care of by Lambda itself! Now, that's neat!

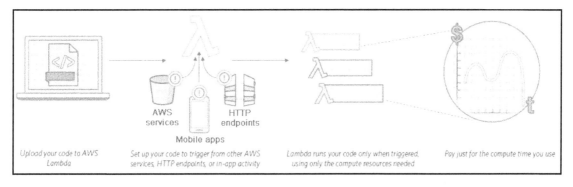

Source: https://aws.amazon.com/lambda/

Lambda was specially introduced by AWS to answer a very particular issue with EC2. Although EC2 still remains one of the most widely used core AWS services, it's still not designed to handle or respond to events; something that is required more often than not in today's applications. For example, a simple image upload activity to an S3 bucket triggers some form of operation, such as checking whether the object is actually a valid image, or whether it contains any viruses or unwanted malware. You can even have a requirement to create thumbnails of the uploaded image and put that up on your website. Now, imagine an EC2 instance doing all these activities for you. Firstly, you would have to program some mechanism for S3 to notify your EC2 instances to periodically perform checks on your S3 bucket, as EC2 has no way of telling when a new object has been uploaded.

Then again, you would have to manage the EC2 instance and handle all failovers, such as what happens if the EC2 instance fails to poll the S3 bucket, or what happens if the EC2 instance gets terminated for some reason. There's also the issue of scalability, right? Today you may be uploading just about 30-40 odd images, enough for a single EC2 instance to work on; but what happens when there is a large surge of upload operations? Will your EC2 instances scale effectively? And most important of all and by far the biggest issue for most enterprises--cost. Your EC2 instance will be running even on those days when there are no upload operations occurring in your S3 bucket. Sure there are many ways in which we can create workarounds for this, such as by creating a separate instance that polls continuously and by leveraging SQS or SNS as well, but isn't all that really overkill for something so simple? That's exactly the reason why Lambda is so popular and so widely used today. It just makes things simple!

How it works

Well, we do know for sure that Lambda powers your code on some form of container technology which explains how AWS is able to get it to spin up so quickly as compared to running your code on standard EC2 instances. These containers are spun up on underlying EC2 instances that are all created from a common image (Amazon Linux AMI: `amzn-ami-hvm-2016.03.3.x86_64-gp2`). Once again, we cannot control or see these containers or EC2 instances; they are managed by AWS itself.

 There is a short latency between the time a Lambda function is invoked. This is primarily because AWS has to bootstrap the container that runs your code and provides the necessary resources for it to run as well. This latency is generally observed when the function is either invoked for the first time or when it is updated.

At the heart of the container is your code, which, as a rule of thumb, has to be written specifically to perform a single task or a few simple processes; similar to how you would write functions in your normal code. Each Lambda project that you deploy can thus be termed as a **Lambda function**, or just a **function**. At the time of writing this book, AWS supports Java, Python, Node.js, and even C# as programming languages for your functions. Each function can be invoked either on demand or invoked dynamically based on certain types of supported events. A few event examples are listed out as follows:

- **Amazon S3**: Lambda functions can be triggered when an object is created, updated, or deleted in an S3 bucket
- **Amazon DynamoDB**: Lambda functions are triggered when any updates are made to a particular DynamoDB table, such as row insertion, deletion, and so on

- **Amazon Simple Notification Service** (SNS): Trigger a Lambda function when a message is published on a, SNS topic
- **Amazon CloudWatch Logs**: Use Lambda functions to process CloudWatch Logs as feeds
- **Scheduled events**: Run Lambda functions as scheduled events, just like a `cron` job
- **AWS CodeCommit**: Execute Lambda functions whenever new code is pushed to an existing branch, and so on

 For a complete list of the latest AWS services that are supported as Lambda invokers, refer to `http://docs.aws.amazon.com/lambda/latest/dg/invoking-lambda-function.html`.

When creating Lambda functions, you have to specify the amount of memory resource your function will require, as well as the approximate time it will take to execute before timing out. The memory can be set from 128 MB to 1.5 GB of RAM and the timeouts anywhere from one second to a max of 300 seconds. Both the memory and duration values are upper limits to your Lambda function, which means that if you have allocated 512 MB of RAM to your function, it doesn't mean the function will have to use all 512 MB, of it. It can work at any value up to 512 MB post which Lambda will simply throw you an error message stating that your function ran out of memory. The same applies for the duration of your function as well. You may set your function to timeout after 60 seconds and the function may only run for, say, 10 seconds. However, if your function fails to complete its processing by the 60th second, Lambda once again will time it out and pop you up an error message.

It is important to note, however, that varying the amount of memory for your function or the duration of the timeout also impacts the cost of your Lambda function. Let us learn a bit more on how to actually get started with deploying Lambda functions using the AWS Management Console, as well as the AWS CLI.

Getting started with AWS Lambda

In this section, we will look at how easy and effortless it is to execute a simple Lambda function using both the AWS Management Console, as well as the AWS CLI, and in the process learn a few necessary components and configurable items along the way.

Using the AWS Management Console

The AWS Management Console is by far the simplest way to getting started with AWS Lambda. Now I'm going to assume that you already have a valid AWS account and some basic hands-on knowledge with the core AWS services and products such as EC2, IAM, S3, and so on. If not, then you can always create a new account with AWS and leverage the awesome one-year Free Tier scheme as well.

 To read more about Free Tier usage, check out this link here `https://aws.amazon.com/free/`.

The following are the steps to create a new Lambda function:

1. Log in to your AWS Management Console using your IAM credentials and from the **AWS Services** filter, type in `Lambda` to get started. You should see the AWS Lambda dashboard, as shown in the following screenshot.
2. Click on the **Get Started Now** option to create a new Lambda function:

Creating a Lambda function is a straightforward four-step process and it begins with the selection of a *function blueprint*. Just the way we have AMIs for easy and fast deployments of EC2 instances, the same applies for a Lambda function as well. Blueprints are nothing more than sample code that you can use as starting points to writing your very own functions. AWS provides a cool 70-odd blueprints that you can select from, this can help you integrate S3, DynamoDB, and Kinesis with Lambda for to perform specific tasks. For this section, we are going to be using a very simple `hello-world` Lambda function blueprint from the catalog. We can do so by following the given steps:

1. First, simply type in the keyword `hello` in the filter provided. You can optionally even select the runtime for your function as Node.js from the **Select runtime** drop-down list provided to narrow your search.

2. Select the **hello-world** blueprint, as shown here:

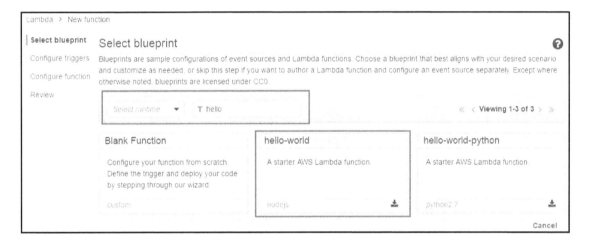

The second stage of creating your own Lambda function involves the configuration of the function's trigger mechanism. This is an optional page, however, it's worth paying attention to. Here, you can select a particular service that will trigger the Lambda function's invocation by selecting the highlighted box adjoining the Lambda function icon, as shown. To select a particular service, you will be required to populate some necessary fields pertaining to that service.

For example, if you happen to select S3 as the service, then you will be prompted with fields where you will need to provide the particular bucket name, the event type (whether to trigger the function based on an object's creation or deletion), and so on:

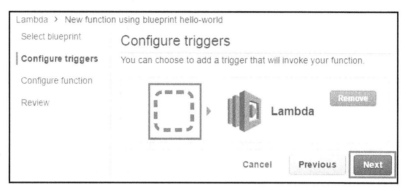

3. Select **Next** to continue with the wizard. The next page that shows up is the function's configuration page. Using this page, you can provide your function's basic configurable items, such as **Name**, **Description**, and **Runtime**.

4. Provide a suitable **Name** for your Lambda function. The **Description** field is optional, however, it is always a good practice to provide one. The **Runtime** for this scenario is already auto populated to **Node.js 4.3**. At the time of writing this book, the following runtimes are supported:

   - **Node.js 4.3**
   - **Edge Node.js 4.3**
   - **Java 8**
   - **Python 2.7**
   - **C#** (.NET Core 1.0)

 Edge Node.js is nothing but a new extension of the Lambda service called **Lambda@Edge**. This service basically allows you to run Lambda functions at various AWS Edge locations in response to CloudFront events. You can read more about it here at http://docs.aws.amazon.com/lambda/latest/dg/lambda-edge.html.

5. Post the runtime. You will also notice your Lambda code prewritten and ready for execution, shown as follows:

```
'use strict';
console.log('Loading function');
exports.handler = (event, context, callback) => {
  //console.log('Received event:',JSON.stringify(event, null,
  2));
  console.log('value1 =', event.key1);
  console.log('value2 =', event.key2);
  console.log('value3 =', event.key3);
  callback(null, event.key1);
  // Echo back the first key value
  //callback('Something went wrong');
};
```

The code itself can be broken up into three distinctive parts: the first is the invocation of the *function*. The function, in this case, is called **handler**, which gets exported from your Node.js code. This handler is then invoked by calling the function's file name (which in this case is *index*), followed by the function's name in this format: index.handler. The rest of the parameters go as follows: event is the variable where you get your function's event-related data; context is used to get some contextual information about your Lambda function, such as the function's name, how much memory it consumed, the duration it took to execute, and so on, callback is used to send back some value to your caller, such as an error or result parameter: callback(error,result).

Callbacks are optional however they are really useful when it comes to debugging errors in your function's code.

You can either edit your code inline using the code editor provided in the console or even upload a packaged code in the form of a ZIP file either from your local workstation or even from S3. We will be exploring these options later in the next chapter, for now let us continue moving forward.

The next section on the function configuration page is the **Lambda function handler and role** as shown in the following screenshot. Here you provide the **Handler*** for your code along with the necessary permissions it needs to run in the form of IAM roles. You have three options to select from the **Role*** drop-down list. The first in the list is, **Choose an existing role** that basically allows you to select an IAM role from a list of predefined one. For this scenario, I've gone ahead and selected the role `lambda_basic_execution` which as the name suggests, provides basic execution rights to your Lambda function:

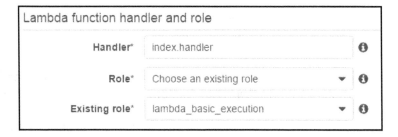

The other two options are **Create a custom role** or **Create a role from a template**. You can use either of these options to create new roles based on your requirements.

Make sure your role has the necessary permissions to view CloudWatch Logs as that's where your function's execution logs are displayed.

The final section on the function configuration page is the **Advanced settings** section. Here you can configure your function's resource requirements along with a few necessary items as well. Let us have a quick look at each one:

- **Memory (MB)**: Select the appropriate amount of memory for your function to run. There is no provision for selecting the CPU resources for your function however the more RAM that you provide to your instance, the better CPU cycle it will get as well. For instance, a 256 MB function will generally have twice the CPU than that of a 128 MB function.

- **Timeout**: The **Timeout** field is used to specify your function's maximum execution time. Once the timeout is breached, AWS will automatically terminate your function's execution. You can specify any value between 1 second and 300 seconds.
- **DLQ Resource**: This feature is quite new, but a very useful feature when it comes to building fault tolerant asynchronous applications. By default, AWS automatically queues the various asynchronous events that the function has to invoke on. It can automatically retry the invocation twice before that particular event is discarded. If you do not wish the event to be discarded, you can now leverage either AWS **SQS** or **SNS** to push those stranded events to the dead letter queue. Selecting **SNS** prompts for a valid **SNS Topic** name and selecting **SQS** prompts you to enter a valid **SQS Queue** name:

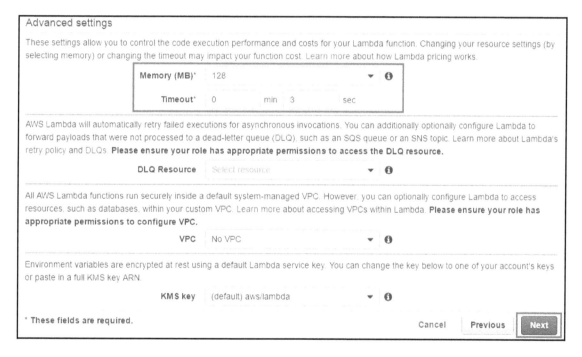

- **VPC**: By default, your Lambda functions are created and deployed in an AWS managed VPC. You can optionally toggle this setting and provide your own VPCs for the functions to run out of.

- **KMS key**: Lambda provides you to develop functions by passing environment variables as well. By default, when you create environment variables, AWS encrypts them using the KMS service. You can use this default service key or even create your own custom key using the IAM console.

6. With the **Advanced settings** out of the way, click **Next** to proceed. On the **Review** page, make sure you go through the items that you have configured during this section.

7. Once done, click on **Create function** to launch your first Lambda function. You should see your Lambda function successfully deployed as shown in the following screenshot. You can use this dashboard to edit your function's code inline, as well as change a few necessary parameters and even test it. Let's take a quick look at the tabs for a better understanding:

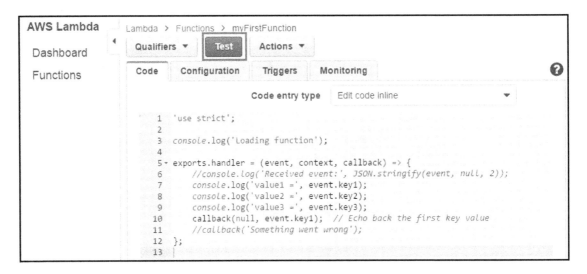

The tabs in the screenshot above are explained as follows:

- **Code**: Using this particular tab, you can edit the deployed code inline as well as upload a newer version of your code using either your local workstation or from S3. Once you have made changes to your code you will be prompted to **Save and test** the same.
- **Configuration**: This tab provides you with the same configurable items as described earlier in this very section. You mostly will use this tab to reconfigure your function's resources or change its execution duration.

- **Triggers**: Use this tab to configure your function's triggering mechanism. For this section, this would be blank anyways.
- **Monitoring**: This tab will display the function's invocation count, its duration, and whether any errors or throttling events occurred.

For now, let us run a quick and simple test to verify whether our function is working or not:

1. To do so, select the **Test** option. Here, you can select from a list of few a predefined test sample events using **Sample event template**, as shown in the following screenshot.
2. Select the template **Hello World**:

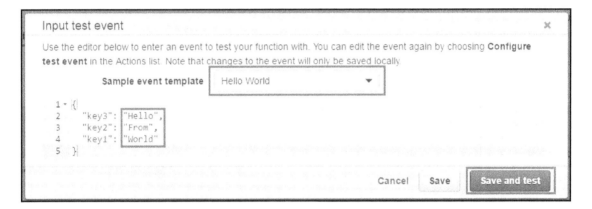

3. The function processes incoming events in the following format. Replace the `value` field with your own string values and click on **Save and test** to view the results of your function's execution:

```
{
    "key3": "value3",
    "key2": "value2",
    "key1": "value1"
}
```

4. If the execution goes well, you should see the following displayed on your dashboard. The first thing you need to notice here is the result of your code's execution, followed by the **Summary** of your function's execution. The **Summary** section displays the **Duration** the function took to execute, **Billed duration**, along with other important details such as the function's **Resources configured** and **Max memory used**.

You can always use these details to fine-tune the amount of resources you provide to your function to execute the next time:

AWS Lambda rounds the function's execution duration to the nearest 100 ms.

The second important part is **Log output**, which displays a part of the function's execution logs. You can use these logs to rectify code errors and make performance improvements as well.

Here's a handy tip! You may notice your function might have taken some 10 ms to execute on an average. That's not too, bad but still it is way too long for something as simple as this function, especially when there is no computation involved. So rerun the test again and verify the duration now. It should be significantly less, right? This is the same latency issue that we talked about earlier, and this is just a way to demonstrate the same.

So, with just a few simple clicks we were able to create, run, and test our first Lambda function, and all the while we did not bother about setting up the development platform nor managing the underlying infrastructure! That's exactly what serverless architecture is all about! There are still quite a few options available from the dashboard that we can use, however, we will keep them aside for the next chapter. For now, let us explore how the AWS CLI can be leveraged to spin up and manage Lambda functions as well.

Using the CLI

As you may be well aware of, AWS provides a rich and easy to use CLI as well for managing your cloud resources. In this section, we will be using the AWS CLI to create, package, and invoke a simple Lambda function:

1. To begin with, make sure your AWS CLI is set up and ready for use. You can install the CLI on most major Linux OSes, as well as macOS, and Windows. You can go through the following guide for the installation, as well as the configuration steps:

   http://docs.aws.amazon.com/cli/latest/userguide/installing.html.

2. Next, create a new folder (in this case, I created a folder named `lambda`) and copy the following contents into a new file:

   ```
   console.log('Loading function');
   exports.handler = function(event, context) {
     var date = new Date().toDateString();

     context.succeed("Hello " + event.username +
       "! Today's date is " + date);
   };
   ```

   The following screenshot shows the output of the preceding file:

```
[root@YoYoNUX ~]#
[root@YoYoNUX ~]# cd lambda/
[root@YoYoNUX lambda]#
[root@YoYoNUX lambda]# cat index.js
console.log('Loading function');

exports.handler = function(event, context) {
var date = new Date().toDateString();
console.log("Function Name: " + context.functionName);
console.log("Request ID: " + context.awsRequestId);
console.log('Remaining Time =', context.getRemainingTimeInMillis());
console.log("Log Group Name: " + context.logGroupName);
console.log("Log Stream Name: " + context.logStreamName);
context.succeed("Hello " + event.username + "! Today's date is " + date);
};
[root@YoYoNUX lambda]#
[root@YoYoNUX lambda]#
```

3. Name the file `index.js` and save it. This particular code is fairly straightforward. It logs the current date and prints a user-friendly message with the user's name passed as the event.

4. Now, in order for the Lambda function to execute, we need to create a minimalistic IAM role that Lambda can assume for executing the function on our behalf. Create a file named `policy.json` and paste the following content into it:

```json
{
    "Version": "2012-10-17",
    "Statement": [
        {
            "Effect": "Allow",
            "Principal": {
                "Service": "lambda.amazonaws.com"
            },
            "Action": "sts:AssumeRole"
        }
    ]
}
```

5. To create an IAM Role, we need to make use of the `create-role` command, as shown:

```
# aws iam create-role
--role-name basic-lambda-role
--assume-role-policy-document file://policy.json
```

From the output of the preceding command, copy the ARN that and keep it handy. We will be requiring the same in the coming steps.

```
[root@YoYoNUX ~]#
[root@YoYoNUX ~]# cd lambda/
[root@YoYoNUX lambda]#
[root@YoYoNUX lambda]# cat index.js
console.log('Loading function');

exports.handler = function(event, context) {
var date = new Date().toDateString();
context.succeed("Hello " + event.username + "! Today's date is " + date);
};
[root@YoYoNUX lambda]#
[root@YoYoNUX lambda]#
```

6. With the role created, we can now go ahead and create our function. First, zip the `index.js` file using the following `zip` command. This is going to be our deployment package that will be uploaded to an S3 bucket and executed as a function by Lambda itself:

```
# zip -r mySecondFunction.zip index.js
```

 Make sure you only zip the file and the folder it was created in.

7. Next, we use the `create-function` command to create our Lambda function. Type in the following command:

```
# aws lambda create-function
--region us-west-2
--function-name mySecondFunction
--zip-file fileb://mySecondFunction.zip
--role arn:aws:iam::00123456789:role/basic-lambda-role
--handler index.handler
--runtime nodejs4.3
--memory-size 128
```

Let us explore a few of the options that we just passed with the `create-function` command:

- `--function-name`: The name of the function that you will be uploading. You can optionally even provide a description for you function by passing the `--description` option.
- `--zip-file`: This is the path of the deployment package that we are uploading.
- `--role`: The ARN of the IAM role that Lambda will assume when it has to execute the function.
- `--handler`: The function name that Lambda will call to begin the execution of your code.

- `--runtime`: You can provide the runtime environment for the code that you will be executing. There are a few pre-defined values here that you can use, namely: `nodejs`, `nodejs4.3`, `nodejs4.3-edge`, `java8`, `python2.7`, and `dotnetcore1.0`.
- `--memory-size`: The amount of RAM you wish to allocate to your Lambda function. You can optionally set the timeout value as well by using the `--timeout` option.

The full list of options can be found here `https://docs.aws.amazon.com/cli/latest/reference/lambda/create-function.html`.

By default, your functions will timeout after 3 seconds if no value is provided.

Once you have created the function, you should get a response similar to the one shown in the following screenshot. This means we are now ready to invoke our function:

```
"RoleId": "AROAJOIFGVHSL2JDV6NSE",
"CreateDate": "2017-01-28T05:44:37.204Z",
"RoleName": "basic-lambda-role",
"Path": "/",
"Arn": "arn:aws:iam::8          7:role/basic-lambda-role"
```

8. To invoke the function from the command line, we need to call the `invoke` command, as shown:

```
# aws lambda invoke
--invocation-type RequestResponse
--function-name mySecondFunction
--region us-west-2
--log-type Tail
--payload '{"username":"YoYo"}'
output.txt
```

Let us explore a few of the options from the `invoke` command:

- `--invocation-type`: The type of invocation your Lambda will undertake. By default, the `RequestResponse` invocation is invoked. You can also choose between `event` meant for asynchronous executions or the `dryrun` invocation if you want to verify your function without running it.
- `--log-type`: Used to display the log of your function's execution. Do note, however, that the `Tail` parameter only works when the `-invocation-type` is set to `RequestResponse`.
- `--payload`: The data you wish to send to your Lambda function in JSON format.
- `output`: The file where you want to log the output of your function's execution.

The full specification can be found here `https://docs.aws.amazon.com/cli/latest/reference/lambda/invoke.html`.

9. Once you have successfully invoked the function, check the output of the execution in the `output.txt` file:

```
{
    "FunctionName": "mySecondFunction",
    "CodeSize": 412,
    "MemorySize": 128,
    "FunctionArn": "arn:aws:lambda:us-west-2:8        7:function:mySecondFunction",
    "Handler": "index.handler",
    "Role": "arn:aws:iam::8        7:role/basic-lambda-role",
    "Timeout": 3,
    "LastModified": "2017-01-28T05:47:48.049+0000",
    "Runtime": "nodejs4.3",
    "Description": ""
}
```

There you have it! You have now successfully created and launched a Lambda function using the AWS CLI. There are a few other important commands that you should also keep in mind when working with the CLI, here's a quick look at some of them:

- `list-functions`: A simple command to list your published Lambda functions. You can invoke it by using the following command:

```
# aws lambda list-functions
```

You can optionally use other parameters, such as `--max-items`, to return a mentioned number of functions at a time:

```
[root@YoYoNUX lambda]#
[root@YoYoNUX lambda]# cat output.txt
"Hello YoYo! Today's date is Sat Jan 28 2017"[root@YoYoNUX lambda]# []
```

- `get-function` and `get-function-configuration`: As the name suggests, both commands return the configuration information of the Lambda function that was created using the `create-function` command. The difference being that the `get-function` command also provides a unique URL to download your code's deployment package (ZIP file). The URL is pre-signed and is valid for up to 10 minutes from the time you issue the `get-function` command:

```
# aws lambda get-function <FUNCTION_NAME>
(or)
# aws lambda get-function-configuration
<FUNCTION_NAME>
```

The following screenshot shows the output for the preceding command:

```
[root@YoYoNUX lambda]#
[root@YoYoNUX lambda]# aws lambda list-functions
{
    "Functions": [
        {
            "FunctionName": "myFirstFunction",
            "MemorySize": 128,
            "CodeSize": 333,
            "FunctionArn": "arn:aws:lambda:us-west-2:          7:function:myFirstFunction",
            "Handler": "index.handler"
        },
        {
            "FunctionName": "mySecondFunction",
            "MemorySize": 128,
            "CodeSize": 412,
            "FunctionArn": "arn:aws:lambda:us-west-2:8         7:function:mySecondFunction",
            "Handler": "index.handler"
        }
    ]
}
```

To get a complete list of the CLI supported commands, click here
http://docs.aws.amazon.com/cli/latest/reference/lambda/.

15
Writing Lambda Functions

In the previous chapter, we understood serverless computing and took a quick look at how easy it is to get started with AWS Lambda functions using the AWS Management Console, as well as with the AWS CLI.

In this chapter, we are going to take things a step further by learning the anatomy of a typical Lambda function, and also how to actually write your own functions. The following topics are covered in this chapter:

- Understanding the programming model for a Lambda function using simple functions as examples
- Working with environment variables and versioning
- Leveraging third-party tools for a quick and effortless code deployment to Lambda

So no more talking, let's get coding!

The Lambda programming model

So far we have seen that certain applications can be broken down into one or more simple nuggets of code called as **functions** and uploaded to AWS Lambda for execution. Lambda then takes care of provisioning the necessary resources to run your function along with other management activities such as auto-scaling of your functions, their availability, and so on. So what exactly are we supposed to do in all this? A developer basically has three tasks to perform when it comes to working with Lambda--writing the code, packaging it for deployment, and finally monitoring its execution and fine-tuning.

In this section, we are going to explore the different components that actually make up a Lambda function by understanding what AWS calls as a **programming model** or a **programming pattern**. Currently, AWS officially supports Node.js, Java, Python, and C# as the programming languages for writing Lambda functions, with each language following a generic programming pattern that comprises of the following concepts.

Handler

As discussed briefly in the earlier chapter, the handler is basically a function that Lambda calls first for execution. A handler function is capable of processing incoming event data that is passed to it as well as invoking other functions or methods from your code.

 In this book, we will be concentrating a lot of our code and development on Node.js; however, the programming model remains more or less the same for the other supported languages as well.

A skeleton structure of a handler function is shown as follows:

```
exports.myHandler = function(event, context, callback) {
  // Your code goes here.
  callback();
}
```

Here, `myHandler` is the name of your handler function. By exporting it, we make sure that Lambda knows which function it has to invoke first. The other parameters that are passed with the handler function are:

- `event`: Lambda uses this parameter to pass any event related data back to the handler.
- `context`: Lambda again uses this parameter to provide the handler with the function's runtime information such as the name of the function, the time it took to execute, and so on.
- `callback`: This parameter is used to return any data back to its caller. The `callback` parameter is the only optional parameter that gets passed when writing handlers. If not specified, AWS Lambda will call it implicitly and return the value as `null`. The `callback` parameter also supports two optional parameters in the form of `error` and `result`; `error` will return any of the function's error information back to the caller, while `result` will return any result of your function's successful execution.

Here are a few simple examples of invoking callbacks in your handler:

- `callback()`
- `callback(null, 'Hello from Lambda')`
- `callback(error)`

> Callback is supported only in Node.js runtime v4.3. You will have to use the `context` methods in case your code supports earlier Node.js runtime (v0.10.42)

Let us try out a simple handler example with a code:

```
exports.myHandler = function(event, context, callback) {
  console.log("value = " + event.key);
  console.log("functionName = ", context.functionName);
  callback(null, "Yippee! Something worked!");
};
```

The preceding code snippet will print the value of an event (key) that we will pass to the function, print the function's name as part of the `context` object, and finally print the success message `Yippee! Something worked!` if all goes well!

Follow the given steps to create a Lambda function:

1. Login to the AWS Management Console and select **AWS Lambda** from the dashboard.
2. Select the **Create a Lambda function** option as we did in our earlier chapter.
3. From the **Select blueprint** page, select the **Blank Function** blueprint.
4. Since we are not configuring any triggers for now, simply click on **Next** at the **Configure triggers** page.

5. Provide a suitable **Name** and **Description** for your Lambda function and paste the preceding code into the inline code editor as shown:

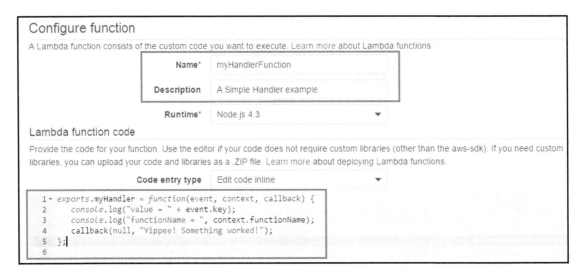

6. Next, in the **Lambda function handler and role** section on the same page, type in the correct name of your **Handler*** as shown. The handler name should match with the handler name in your function to work. Remember also to select the **basic-lambda-role** for your function's execution before selecting the **Next** button:

7. In the **Review** page, select the **Create function** option.
8. With your function now created, select the **Test** option to pass the sample event to our function.

9. In the **Sample event** section, pass the following event, and select the **Save and test** option:

```
{
    "key": "My Printed Value!!"
}
```

With your code execution completed, you should get a similar execution result as shown as follows. The important things to note here are the values for the event, context, and callback parameters. You can note the callback message being returned back to the caller as the function executed successfully. The other event and context object values are printed in the **Log output** section as highlighted:

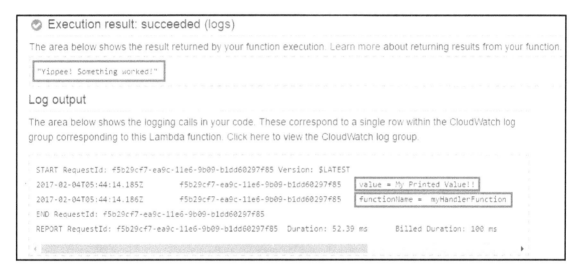

 In case you end up with any errors, make sure the handler function name matches the handler name that you passed during the function's configuration.

The context object

As discussed earlier, the context object is a really useful utility when it comes to obtaining runtime information about your function. The context object can provide information such as the executing function's name, the time remaining before Lambda terminates your function's execution, the log name, and the stream associated with your function and much more.

The `context` object also comes with its own methods that you can call to correctly terminate your function's executions such as, `context.succed()`, `context.fail()`, and `context.done()`. However, post April 2016, Lambda has transitioned the Node.js runtime from v0.10.42 to v4.3 which does support these methods. However, it encourages the use of `callback()` function for performing the same actions.

Here are some of the commonly used `context` object methods and properties described as follows:

- `getRemainingTimeInMillis()`: It returns the number of milliseconds left for execution before Lambda terminates your function. This comes in really handy when you want to perform some corrective actions before your function exits or times out.
- `callbackWaitsForEmptyEventLoop`: This property is used to override the default behavior of a `callback()` function, that is, to wait till the entire event loop is processed, and only then return back to the caller. If set to `false`, this property causes the `callback()` function to stop any further processing in the event loop even if there are any other tasks to be performed. The default value is set to `true`.
- `functionName`: It returns the name of the executing Lambda function.
- `functionVersion`: The current version of the executing Lambda function.
- `memoryLimitInMB`: The amount of resource in terms of memory that is set for your Lambda function.
- `logGroupName`: It returns the name of the CloudWatch Log group that stores the function's execution logs.
- `logStreamName`: It returns the name of the CloudWatch Log stream that stores the function's execution logs.
- `awsRequestID`: It returns the request ID associated with that particular function's execution.

 If you are using Lambda functions as mobile backend processing services, you can then extract additional information about your mobile application using the context of the `identity` and `clientContext` objects. These are invoked using the AWS Mobile SDK. To learn more, visit `http://docs.aws.amazon.com/lambda/latest/dg/nodejs-prog-model-context.html`.

Let us look at a simple example to understand the `context` object a bit better. In this example, we are using the `context` object `callbackWaitsForEmptyEventLoop` and demonstrating its working by setting the object's value to either `yes` or `no` on invocation:

1. Login to the AWS Management Console and select **AWS Lambda** from the dashboard.
2. Select the **Create a Lambda function** option as done in the earlier chapter.
3. From the **Select blueprint** page, select the **Blank Function** blueprint.
4. Since we are not configuring any triggers for now, simply click on **Next** at the **Configure triggers** page.
5. Provide a suitable **Name** and **Description** for your Lambda function and paste the following code in the inline code editor:

```
exports.myHandler = (event, context, callback) => {
  console.log("Hello, Starting Lambda Function");
  console.log("We are going to learn about context object
   and its usage");
  console.log('value1 =', event.key1);
  console.log('value2 =', event.key2);
  console.log('value3 =', event.key3);
  console.log('remaining time =',
   context.getRemainingTimeInMillis());
  console.log('functionName =', context.functionName);
  console.log('AWSrequestID =', context.awsRequestId);
  console.log('logGroupName =', context.logGroupName);
  console.log('logStreamName =', context.logStreamName);
  switch (event.contextCallbackOption) {
    case "no":
      setTimeout(function(){
        console.log("I am back from my timeout of 30
        seconds!!");
      },30000); // 30 seconds break
      break;
    case "yes":
      console.log("The callback won't wait for the setTimeout()
      n if the callbackWaitsForEmptyEventLoop is set to
      false");
      setTimeout(function(){
        console.log("I am back from my timeout of 30
        seconds!!");
      },30000); // 30 seconds break
      context.callbackWaitsForEmptyEventLoop = false;
      break;
    default:
      console.log("The Default code block");
  }
  callback(null, 'Hello from Lambda');
};
```

6. Next, in the **Lambda function handler and role** section on the same page, type in the correct name of your **Handler*** as shown. The handler name should match with the handler name in your function to work. Remember also to select the **basic-lambda-role** for your function's execution.

7. The final change that we will do is, to change the **Timeout** value of our function from the default 3 seconds to 1 minute specifically for this example. Click **Next** to continue:

8. In the **Review** page, select the **Create function** option.

9. With your function now created, select the **Test** option to pass the sample event to our function.

10. In the **Sample event** section, pass the following event and select the **Save and test** option:

```
{
    "contextCallbackOption": "yes"
}
```

You should see a similar output in the **Log output** window shown as follows:

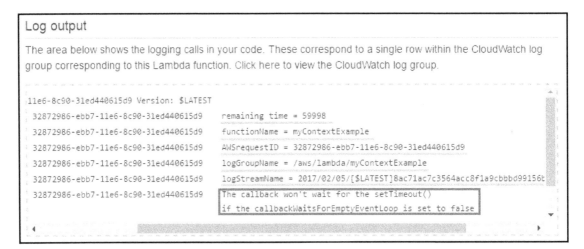

With the `contextCallbackOption` set to `yes`, the function does not wait for the 30 seconds `setTimeout()` function but it will exit, however, it prints the function's runtime information such as the remaining execution time, the function name, and so on. Now set the `contextCallbackOption` to `no`, and re-run the test and verify the output. This time, you can see the `setTimeout()` function, and verify the same by comparing the remaining time left for execution with the output of the earlier test run:

```
11e6-b491-6191bf96cdfb Version: $LATEST
32872986-ebb7-11e6-8c90-31ed440615d9    I am back from my timeout of 30 seconds!!
8c2e0785-ebba-11e6-b491-6191bf96cdfb    remaining time = 59992
8c2e0785-ebba-11e6-b491-6191bf96cdfb    functionName = myContextExample
8c2e0785-ebba-11e6-b491-6191bf96cdfb    AWSrequestID = 8c2e0785-ebba-11e6-b491-6191bf96cdfb
8c2e0785-ebba-11e6-b491-6191bf96cdfb    logGroupName = /aws/lambda/myContextExample
8c2e0785-ebba-11e6-b491-6191bf96cdfb    logStreamName = 2017/02/05/[$LATEST]8ac71ac7c3564acc8f1a9cbbbd99156b
8c2e0785-ebba-11e6-b491-6191bf96cdfb    I am back from my timeout of 30 seconds!!
```

Logging

You can always log your code's execution and activities using simple log statements. The following statements are supported for logging with Node.js runtime:

- `console.log()`
- `console.error()`
- `console.warn()`
- `console.info()`

The logs can be viewed using both the AWS Management Console as well as the CLI. Let us quickly explore both these options:

- **Using the AWS Management Console**: We have already been using Lambda's dashboard to view the function's execution logs, however, the logs are only for the current execution. To view your function's logs from the past, you need to view them using the CloudWatch Logs section.

  To do so, search, and select **CloudWatch** option from the AWS Management Console. Next, select the **Logs** option to display the function's logs as shown in the following screenshot:

You can use the **Filter** option to filter out your Lambda logs by typing in the `Log Group Name Prefix` as `/aws/lambda`.

Select any of the present **Log Groups** and its corresponding log stream name to view the complete and detailed execution logs of your function.

If you do not see any Lambda logs listed out here it is mostly due to your Lambda execution role. Make sure your role has the necessary access rights to create the log group and log stream along with the capability to put log events.

- **Using the CLI**: The CLI provides two ways using which you can view your function's execution logs. The first is using the Lambda function's `invoke` command itself. The `invoke` command when used with the `--log-type` parameter will print the latest 4 KB of log data that is written to CloudWatch Logs. To do so, first list out all the available functions in your current region using the following command:

  ```
  # aws lambda list-functions
  ```

  Next, pick a Lambda function that you wish to invoke and substitute that function's name and payload with the example snippet written as follows:

  ```
  # aws lambda invoke
  --invocation-type RequestResponse
  --function-name myFirstFunction
  --log-type Tail
  --payload '{"key1":"Lambda","key2":"is","key3":"awesome!"}'
  output.txt
  ```

  The second way, is by using a combination of the `context()` object and the CloudWatch CLI. You can obtain your function's `--log-group-name` and the `--log-stream-name` by using the `context.logGroupName` and the `context.logStreamName`. Next, substitute the data gathered from the output of these parameters in the following command:

  ```
  # aws logs get-log-events
  --log-group-name "/aws/lambda/myFirstFunction"
  --log-stream-name
    "2017/02/07/[$LATEST]1ae6ac9c77384794a3202802c683179a"
  ```

If you run into the following error `The specified log stream does not exist` in spite of providing the correct values for the log group name and stream name; then make sure to add the \ escape character in the [$LATEST] as shown.

Let us look at a few options that you can additionally pass with the `get-log-events` command:

- `--start-time`: The start of the log's time range. All times are in UTC.
- `--end-time`: The end of the log's time range. All times are in UTC.
- `--next-token`: The token for the next set of items to return. (You received this token from a previous call.)

- `--limit`: Used to set the maximum number of log events returned. By default the limit is set to 10,000 log events.

Alternatively, if you don't wish to use the `context()` objects in your code, you can still filter out the log group name and log stream name by using a combination of the following commands:

```
# aws logs describe-log-groups
--log-group-name-prefix "/aws/lambda/"
```

The `describe-log-groups` command will list all the log groups that are prefixed with `/aws/lambda`. Make a note of your function's log group name from this output. Next, execute the following command to list your log group name's associated log stream name:

```
# aws logs describe-log-streams --log-group-name
"/aws/lambda/myFirstFunction"
```

Make a note of the log stream name and substitute the same in the next, and the final command to view your log events for that particular log stream name:

```
# aws logs get-log-events --log-group-name
"/aws/lambda/myFirstFunction"
--log-stream-name "2017/02/07/[$LATEST]1ae6ac9c77384794a3202802c683179a"
```

Once again, make sure to add the backslash \ in the `[$LATEST]` to avoid the `The specified log stream does not exist` error. With the logging done, let's move on to the next piece of the programming model called **exceptions**.

Exceptions and error handling

Functions have the ability to notify AWS Lambda in case it failed to execute correctly. This is primarily done by the function passing the error object to Lambda which converts the same to a string and returns it to the user as an error message.

The error messages that are returned also depend on the invocation type of the function; for example, if your function performs a synchronous execution (the `RequestResponse` invocation type), then the error is returned back to the user and displayed on the AWS Management Console as well as in the CloudWatch Logs. For any asynchronous executions (the `event` invocation type), Lambda will not return anything. Instead it logs the error messages to CloudWatch Logs.

Let us examine a function's error and exception handling capabilities with a simple example of a calculator function that accepts two numbers, and an operand as the test event during invocation:

1. Login to the AWS Management Console and select **AWS Lambda** from the dashboard.
2. Select the **Create a Lambda function** option as done in the earlier chapter.
3. From the **Select blueprint** page, select the **Blank Function** blueprint.
4. Since we are not configuring any triggers for now, simple click on **Next** at the **Configure triggers** page.
5. Provide a suitable **Name** and **Description** for your Lambda function and paste the following code in the inline code editor:

```
exports.myHandler = (event, context, callback) => {
  console.log("Hello, Starting the "+ context.functionName
  +" Lambda Function");
  console.log("The event we pass will have two numbers and
  an operand value");
  // operand can be +, -, /, *, add, sub, mul, div
  console.log('Received event:',
  JSON.stringify(event, null, 2));
  var error, result;
  if (isNaN(event.num1) || isNaN(event.num2)) {
    console.error("Invalid Numbers");
    // different logging
    error = new Error("Invalid Numbers!");
    // Exception Handling
    callback(error);
  }
  switch(event.operand)
  {
    case "+":
    case "add":
      result = event.num1 + event.num2;
      break;
    case "-":
    case "sub":
      result = event.num1 - event.num2;
      break;
    case "*":
    case "mul":
      result = event.num1 * event.num2;
      break;
    case "/":
    case "div":
      if(event.num2 === 0){
```

```
        console.error("The divisor cannot be 0");
        error = new Error("The divisor cannot be 0");
        callback(error, null);
      }
      else{
        result = event.num1/event.num2;
      }
      break;
    default:
      callback("Invalid Operand");
      break;
  }
  console.log("The Result is: " + result);
  callback(null, result);
};
```

6. Next, in the **Lambda function handler and role** section on the same page, type in the correct name of your **Handler***. The handler name should match the handler name in your function to work. Remember also to select the **basic-lambda-role** for your function's execution.

7. Leave the rest of the values to their defaults and click **Next** to continue.

8. In the **Review** page, select the **Create function** option.

9. With your function now created, select the **Test** option to pass the sample event to our function.

10. In the **Sample event**, pass the following event and select the **Save and test** option. You should see a similar output in the **Log output** window shown as follows:

```
{
  "num1": 3,
  "num2": 0,
  "operand": "div"
}
```

The following screenshot shows the execution result for the preceding code:

```
❶ Execution result: failed (logs)

{
    "errorMessage": "The divisor cannot be 0",
    "errorType": "Error",
    "stackTrace": [
      "exports.myHandler (/var/task/index.js:32:25)"
    ]
}
```

So what just happened there? Well first, we can print simple user friendly error messages with the help of the `console.error()` statement. Additionally, we can also print the `stackTrace` of the error by passing the error in the `callback()` as shown in the following snippet:

```
error = new Error("The divisor cannot be 0");
callback(error, null);
```

You can also view the custom error message and the `stackTrace` JSON array both from the Lambda dashboard as well as from the CloudWatch Logs section. Next, give this code a couple of tries with some different permutations and combinations of events and check out the results. You can even write your own custom error messages and error handlers that can perform some additional task when an error is returned by the function.

With this we come towards the end of a function's generic programming model and its components. In the next section, we will be taking up few advanced topics such as function versioning and aliases along with a look at how to configure your functions with environment variables.

Versioning and aliases

In the real world, we often have different environments to work out of, for example development, QA, staging, pre-production, production, and so on. Having to manage a single Lambda function across all these environments can be a real pain, and also tricky especially, when each of your environments provide different configuration options, such as different connection strings for databases hosted for development and production, different roles and resource settings.

Lambda thus provides few add-on services that help you better categorize, and manage functions in the form of versions and aliases.

Versioning is a simple way to create one or more versions of your working Lambda code. Each version that you create is basically a snapshot of your origin function. Versions are also immutable which means, that each version you create from the origin or [$LATEST] branch cannot be edited or its configuration parameters change as well. Lambda assigns simple incremental version numbers *(1, 2, 3, ..., n)* to your versions each time they are created.

Following is a simple example depicting a function and its associated versions. Note however, that the version numbers are never reused, even if your function gets deleted or re-created:

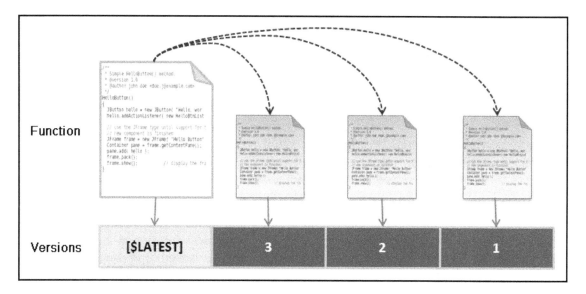

You can create and assign your function's versions using both, the AWS Management Console as well as the CLI.

In the following scenario, I'll be reusing the `calculator.js` code that we published and executed from our earlier steps however feel free to try these steps on any function of your own as well.

Let us look at the AWS Management Console first:

1. From the Lambda dashboard, select your function for which you wish to create the version.
2. Next, from the **Actions** tab, select the **Publish new version** option.
3. At this point, you will be publishing a new version of the code from the **$LATEST** version. Provide a suitable description for your new version in the **Version description** field and click **Publish** when done.
4. Note that the function is an exact copy of our $LATEST code with the same configurations as well, however we are not able to edit this code. To go back to the $LATEST version, simply select the **Version: 1** drop-down list and pick the **$LATEST** version as shown as follows:

You can similarly create versions using the CLI as well. With the CLI, you get two options: The first is to create the version when you first create the function itself. This can be done by using either the create-function or the update-function-code command and pass the parameter --publish along with it as shown in the following snippet:

```
# aws lambda create-function
--function-name myNewFunction
--zip-file fileb://myNewFunction.zip
--role arn:aws:iam::001234567890:role/basic-lambda-role
--handler index.myHandler
--runtime nodejs4.3
--memory-size 128
--publish
```

Alternatively, you can also publish a function's version explicitly using the `publish-version` command. But first, let us list out the current versions associated with our function using the `list-versions-by-function` command as shown:

```
# aws lambda list-versions-by-function
--function-name myCalculatorFunction
```

The preceding command's output can be seen in the following screenshot:

```
{
    "Version": "$LATEST",
    "CodeSha256": "uqPrE+DeUan8/QvsXstvlVOhbMTNxl31a875JwUua2c=",
    "FunctionName": "myCalculatorFunction",
    "FunctionArn": "arn:aws:lambda:us-east-1:8        7:function:myCalculatorFunction:$LATEST",
    "Handler": "index.myHandler",
    "Description": "Simple Calculator example"
},
{
    "Version": "1",
    "CodeSha256": "uqPrE+DeUan8/QvsXstvlVOhbMTNxl31a875JwUua2c=",
    "FunctionName": "myCalculatorFunction",
    "FunctionArn": "arn:aws:lambda:us-east-1:8        7:function:myCalculatorFunction:1",
    "Handler": "index.myHandler",
    "Description": "My First Version"
}
```

From the output, we can see that our calculator example has two versions associated with it. Each version also has its own unique ARN that you can use to invoke that particular function.

Now to publish a new version, we first need to make some change in our [$LATEST] version as Lambda will not create a newer version of your function unless, there is actually some change in it. So go ahead and either tweak some resource parameter or change some text around in your code; you can use the AWS Management Console to do the same. Make sure to save the changes performed in the [$LATEST] version and once done, type in the following command as shown:

```
# aws lambda publish-version
--function-name myCalculatorFunction
--description "A second version created by CLI"
```

Once executed successfully, you should now see a new version (in this case: *2*) of your code along with a new ARN of the following format:

```
arn:aws:lambda:[REGION]:[ACCOUNT_ID]:function:[FUNCTION_NAME]:[VERSION_NUMB
ER]
```

However as time goes by, you would end up with a lot of different versions of a particular function. This can be problematic, especially if you are working with environments like development or production where you need to frequently change a function's versions to match the environment. That's where aliases help out. Aliases are nothing but simple pointers that point to a particular Lambda function at a given point in time. They are basically simple name-like values that get invoked by a caller and thus abstract the version value that the alias was pointing to.

For example, consider a scenario where a developer pushes some function code from the base [$LATEST] version to a new version **1**. Let us assign this version **1** an alias called as **DEV**. When invoked, the alias **DEV** that points to version **1** gets invoked by the caller:

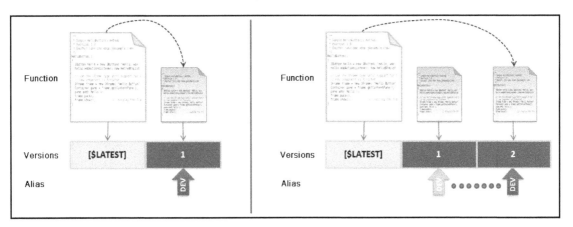

Now, the developer makes some modifications to the code from the base version again and pushes out a new version **2**. Rather than updating the invoker each time a new version is created, all the developer has to do now is, remap the alias **DEV** from version **1** to version **2**. In this way, the developer can map and unmap the alias to any current function version without changing the invoker.

 Each alias that you create gets its own individual ARN as well.

Aliases can also help in simplifying event source mappings where instead of using your Lambda function's ARN, you substitute it with an alias ARN. This makes it easier for developers to work with event source mappings as now, they don't have to worry about changing the function's ARN each time they update to a newer version.

Here is an example format of an alias's ARN:

```
arn:aws:lambda:[REGION]:[ACCOUNT_ID]:function:[FUNCTION_NAME]:[ALIAS]
```

You can create, associate, and disassociate an alias with a version anytime you want. This makes them mutable unlike versions which cannot be changed once created. Let us look at a few essential examples of working with aliases using both the AWS Management Console, as well as the AWS CLI with a simple example:

1. First up, from the Lambda dashboard, select a particular function for which you wish to create the alias. In my case, I'll be using the same calculator code example that we used to create the two versions. From the **Actions** tab, select the **Create alias** option.
2. In the **Create a new alias** dialog box, provide a suitable **Name**, **Description**, and finally, select the **Version** for which you wish to associate the alias. In this case, I've associated it with the **$LATEST** version as shown in the following screenshot:

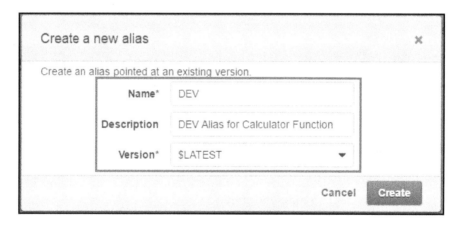

3. Click on **Create** to complete the process.

With this completed, your [$LATEST] version is now associated with the DEV alias. Let us quickly look at few commands from the CLI as well that can help us in creating and managing aliases.

First up, let us associate the version 1 of our calculator function with the alias PROD. To do so, we use the create-alias command as shown:

```
# aws lambda create-alias
--function-name myCalculatorFunction
--name PROD
--function-version 1
--description "PROD alias for my function"
```

With your new alias created, you can list out all associated aliases to your function using the list-aliases command as shown:

```
# aws lambda list-aliases
--function-name myCalculatorFunction
```

You should get a similar output as shown in the following screenshot. Note the individual alias ARNs, and the function versions to which they are mapped to:

```
"Aliases": [
    {
        "AliasArn": "arn:aws:lambda:us-east-1:8          7:function:myCalculatorFunction:DEV",
        "FunctionVersion": "$LATEST",
        "Name": "DEV",
        "Description": "DEV Alias for Calculator Function"
    },
    {
        "AliasArn": "arn:aws:lambda:us-east-1:8          7:function:myCalculatorFunction:PROD",
        "FunctionVersion": "1",
        "Name": "PROD",
        "Description": "PROD alias for my function"
    }
]
```

You can now substitute these ARNs for your event source mappings and go ahead with creating newer function versions as well. Let's assume you publish a new version of your code (in this case, version 2) and this new version has to be published to the PROD environment. All you need to do is update the alias PROD, and point it to the new version 2 using the update-alias command as shown:

```
# aws lambda update-alias
--function-name myCalculatorFunction
> --name PROD
> --function-version 2
```

Run the `list-aliases` command once again and verify the changes. Remember, all this time we have not touched the event source mapping for this function. We have only used aliases to point the new version of the function to the environment abstracting out. Simple isn't it!

With versioning and aliases done, let us quickly learn about environment variables and how you can use them with your Lambda functions.

Environment variables

Environment variables are special key value pairs that you can use to configure your function code or set some variable values dynamically. In simple terms, environment variables is an awesome mechanism to make your Lambda function reusable across different environments as now you don't have to make alterations to your application code each time a particular variable has to be changed.

For example, by declaring your database string as an environment variable, you can now use the exact same Lambda function for development, QA, or production environments by simply making the necessary connection string changes in the environment variable itself.

And to make things more interesting, environment variables can be leveraged with your Lambda function's versions and aliases as well. Once you have created a new copy of your function code in the [$LATEST] version along with the required resource settings, and the environment variables, you can create newer immutable snapshots or versions of the same and reuse them across your environments as needed. Let us look at how to work with environment variables using a simple code example:

```
exports.myHandler = (event, context, callback) => {
  console.log("Starting Version "+
   process.env.AWS_LAMBDA_FUNCTION_VERSION +" of "+
   context.functionName +" in "+process.env.AWS_REGION);
  // operand can be +, -, /, *, add, sub, mul, div
  console.log('Received event:', JSON.stringify(event, null, 2));
  var error;
  if (isNaN(process.env.NUM1) || isNaN(process.env.NUM2)) {
    console.error("Invalid Numbers");
    error = new Error("Invalid Numbers!");
    callback(error);
  }
  var res = {};
  res.a = Number(process.env.NUM1);
  res.b = Number(process.env.NUM2);
  var result;
  switch(process.env.OPERAND)
```

```
{
  case "+":
  case "add":
    result = res.a + res.b;
    break;
  case "-":
  case "sub":
    result = res.a - res.b;
    break;
  case "*":
  case "mul":
    result = res.a * res.b;
    break;
  case "/":
  case "div":
    if(res.b === 0){
      console.error("The divisor cannot be 0");
      error = new Error("The divisor cannot be 0");
      callback(error, null);
      //break;
    }
    else{
      result = res.a/res.b;
      //break;
    }
    break;
  default:
    callback("Invalid Operand");
    break;
}
console.log("The Result is: " + result);
callback(null, result);
};
```

There's a lot we are doing with this particular version of the calculator code example. First up, the code is going to print certain values in the form of `process.env.AWS_LAMBDA_FUNCTION_VERSION` and `process.env.AWS_REGION`. These are a certain form of environment variables that are internal to Lambda functions. For instance, `AWS_LAMBDA_FUNCTION_VERSION` prints the current executing function's version number while the `AWS_REGION` key prints the current AWS region executing the function. You can additionally obtain other useful information such as `LAMBDA_RUNTIME_DIR` that provides information on the runtime related artifacts and much more by reading the complete list provided here at `http://docs.aws.amazon.com/lambda/latest/dg/current-supported-versions.html#lambda-environment-variables`.

Next up, we can also see a few environment variables being read using the Node.js `process.env` property. This property returns an object containing the corresponding environment variable that was set. To set the environment variables, you can either use the AWS Management Console or the CLI as well. Let us look at the AWS Management Console first:

1. From the Lambda management dashboard, select the calculator function that we have been using throughout this chapter.
2. Copy and paste the preceding code into the inline code editor.
3. Next, in the **Environment variables** section, set the key and values for our function's execution:
   - NUM1: <NUMERIC_VALUE>
   - NUM2: <NUMERIC_VALUE>
   - OPERAND: <add>,<+>,<sub>,<->,<mul>,<*>,<div>,</>

4. You can optionally select the **Enable encryption helpers** checkbox to enable Lambda to encrypt your environment variables using the AWS **Key Management Service** (**KMS**). By default, AWS will create a default KMS key for encrypting and decrypting your environment variables however, you can always provide your own KMS keys here as well.
5. Next, from the **Actions** tab, select the **Publish new version** option. Provide a suitable **Description** for your new version and click **Publish** when done. Do remember that by doing so, your function version is now immutable, so you won't be able to change the environment variables as well. If you wish to change the values, you will need to create a new version out of it.

6. With the new version created (version 3 in this case), you can now simply select the **Test** option and validate the output as well:

```
⊘ Execution result: succeeded (logs)                          ☒ ▣ ▢

┌─────┐
│ 13  │
└─────┘

Log output

f14 Version: 3
-922c-65bb86e8ef14    Starting Version 3 of myCalculatorFunction in us-east-1
-922c-65bb86e8ef14    Received event: {}
-922c-65bb86e8ef14    The Result is: 13
4
ef14  Duration: 27.89 ms    Billed Duration: 100 ms    Memory Size: 128 MB    Max Memory Used: 13 MB

◄                                                                        ►
```

You can even use the CLI to pass environment variables during your function's creation using the `--environment` parameter in the `create-function` command as shown:

```
# aws lambda create-function
--function-name myCalculatorFunction
--zip-file fileb://myCalculator.zip
--role arn:aws:iam::001234567890:role/basic-lambda-role
--handler index.handler
--runtime nodejs4.3
--environment Variables="{NUM1=5,NUM2=6,OPERAND=add}"
--memory-size 128
```

With the core creation and writing concepts out of the way, let us move on to the final stage that covers how to package and deploy your functions to Lambda!

Packaging and deploying

As a developer we always want to make the deployment and management of our codes simpler and hassle free, especially when it comes to working with a lot of Lambda projects at the same time. These tools accelerate time to development and also help us reduce any errors that may occur when working with the AWS Management Console or the AWS CLI. In this section we will be exploring two such tools that are gaining a lot of momentum in the market today: APEX and Claudia.js.

APEX

APEX is by far the most versatile and easy deployment and management tool that I've come across. It is extremely simple to install, and get started with. To install the tool on most major Linux distributions, you simply need to copy and paste the following command on your Terminal:

```
# curl https://raw.githubusercontent.com/apex/apex/master/install.sh | sudo
sh
```

 You can get APEX working on Windows as well. Check out the latest APEX releases from `https://github.com/apex/apex/releases`.

Before we go any further, make sure you have the AWS access and secret keys set in the `~/.aws/credentials` directory of your Linux workstation or alternatively if you are planning to perform these steps from an EC2 instance, then make sure the EC2 instance has at least the basic Lambda full access role attached to it in order to work.

With APEX installed, all you need to do now is initialize and create your first working Lambda project. The project is a high-level folder that contains all your functions and other resources required by Lambda to work. To do so, simply type in the following command:

```
# mkdir workdir && cd workdir
# apex init -r us-east-1
//Assuming you want to deploy the function in the us-east-1 region
```

This will bring up a wizard that simply requires you to provide a suitable **Project name** and **Project description**. Yes! That's all there is to it! The rest of the work is all done by Apex itself and that includes creating an IAM role for Lambda to execute your function, creation of a CloudWatch policy that will enable to function to log its output to CloudWatch, and finally the creation of a `project.json` and a directory to house all your Lambda functions called as functions.

The `project.json` file contains metadata about your functions such as the function name, description, the resources that the function will use (by default it is set to 128 MB and timeout to 5 seconds), and the IAM role required by the function to run. You can edit the `project.json` file to make changes as required by your functions:

```
    Project name: apex-helloworld
Enter an optional description of your project.
    Project description: My first function deployed using Apex

[+] creating IAM apex-helloworld_lambda_function role
[+] creating IAM apex-helloworld_lambda_logs policy
[+] attaching policy to lambda_function role.
[+] creating ./project.json
[+] creating ./functions

Setup complete, deploy those functions!
```

The project directory will resemble something similar to the one shown as follows with all your functions falling under the master directory:

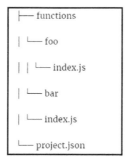

```
├── functions
│   └── foo
│   │   └── index.js
│   └── bar
│   └── index.js
└── project.json
```

Now by default, APEX will create a simple *hello world* node.js code and place it in the `index.js` file of your project. In this case we will use the same trusty example to demonstrate the ease of deploying your Lambda functions. To do so, simply type in the following command:

```
# apex deploy
```

Yes! That's it! With this command, APEX will automatically upload your function, assign it the IAM role for execution, and create a corresponding version for it as well! But that's not all, you can even invoke your function from the command line as well, and no prizes for guessing the command there:

```
# apex invoke hello
```

The name `hello` comes from the `functions/hello` folder name. This is created by default when we first initialized the directory using the `apex init` command:

```
[root@YoYoNUX workdir]#
[root@YoYoNUX workdir]# apex deploy
   • creating function       env= function=hello
   • created alias current   env= function=hello version=1
   • function created        env= function=hello name=apex-helloworld_hello version=1
[root@YoYoNUX workdir]#
[root@YoYoNUX workdir]# apex invoke hello
{"hello":"world"}
[root@YoYoNUX workdir]#
```

You can view your function's execution logs as well by using the following command:

```
# apex logs hello
```

Updating your functions is even more easier with APEX. Just make the required changes to your code and simply redeploy! APEX will automatically create a new version of your code and deploy it to Lambda. But the real power of APEX I guess, lies in its ability to even package and run functions that are written in other languages such as Java, Python, and even golang. This is made possible by a combination of a golang library and Node.js shim stdio interface. It also provides a variety of sub-tools using which you can perform rollbacks, view logs and metrics, and much more. To read more about APEX and its capabilities and features, read here at `http://apex.run/`.

Claudia.js

Unlike APEX, Claudia.js is designed to work only with Node.js. It simplifies the creation, deployment and management of your Node.js functions without having the need to make any alterations to your code. The prerequisites to get started with Claudia.js remain the same as APEX. Make sure your workstation has the AWS secret key and access key supplied in the ~/.aws/credentials file or alternatively provide the basic IAM roles if you are working out off an EC2 instance itself.

Next, install Claudia.js using the following command:

```
# npm install claudia -g
```

 You will need Node 4.x installed on your local development workstation. You can download the correct Node.js version for your Linux distro from here at https://nodejs.org/en/download/package-manager/.

Next, create a separate work directory and create a simple *hello world* index.js file as shown as follows:

```
# vi index.js
console.log('starting function')
exports.handle = function(e, ctx, cb) {
  console.log('processing event: %j', e)
  cb(null, { hello: 'world' })
}
```

To deploy the function using Claudia.js, type in the following command:

```
# claudia create --region us-east-1 --handler index.handle
```

Remember to name the --handler parameter correctly to match the module.method format. In this case, the module is index and the method is called handle.

At this point, Claudia.js will validate the code, upload the same to Lambda and create the associated IAM roles as well for execution. Once your code is uploaded successfully, you can invoke the same using just a single command as shown as follows:

```
# claudia test-lambda
```

```
[root@YoYoNUX claudia]#
[root@YoYoNUX claudia]# claudia test-lambda
{
    "StatusCode": 200,
    "Payload": "{\"hello\":\"world\"}"
}
```

With the deployment and invocation done, you can further make changes to your code and upload newer versions of the same with relative ease. To know more about the various command-line arguments, as well as the packaging options provided by Claudia.js, visit `https://claudiajs.com/documentation.html`. With this we come towards the end of this chapter.

16
Testing Lambda Functions

In the previous chapter, we explored the basics of writing simple Lambda functions as well as diving deep into Lambda's unique programming model that comprised of modules such as the context object, logging methods, and how to handle exceptions and errors. We also learned a bit about the concepts and benefits of versioning as well as how to create reusable functions with the help of environment variables.

The following chapter is a continuation of the previous chapter where we take a step further from writing the Lambda functions and look at the various ways and techniques used to test them. The following topics are covered in this chapter:

- Understanding the need for testing your Lambda functions
- Getting started with simple test cases using Mocha and Chai
- Exploring Lambda test harness
- Implementing third-party tools for testing your Lambda functions locally

The need for testing Lambda function

If you are new to the world of testing or don't write test cases, then you may be thinking "Hey, I am here to write and develop Lambda functions, why do I even need to read this chapter, right?" Well, not so right. Testing is a very crucial part of any code development and should be enforced at all times. The reason is that, tests are an effective way of documenting your codebase and they can also act as a safeguarding mechanism which ensures that only code that is working as expected, and nothing else, is pushed into a production environment.

There are a variety of different tests that you can run on your code, however, for simplicity we can always refer the following *test pyramid* as a reference:

To know more about the test pyramid, check out this link `https://martinfowler.com/bliki/TestPyramid.html`.

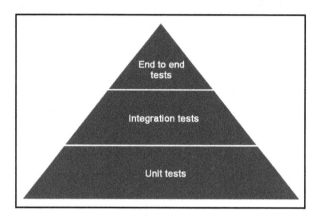

The following image depicts the three basic steps that you as a developer have to keep in mind when developing Lambda functions:

- **Unit Tests**: A unit test is a process in which you take the smallest piece of testable code from your application, isolate it from the remainder of the application, and subject it to a number of tests in order to verify it's proper operation. Each such piece of testable code is thus called as a **unit**.
- **Integration Tests**: As the name suggests, here many units effectively are combined and tested as a whole system. The main purpose of this testing is to expose any faults in the integration between multiple units.
- **End to End Tests**: These tests are conducted to ensure the flow of the application right from start to finish, check if they are behaving as expected and that data integrity is maintained between various systems and their components as well.

As a part of my experience, I have always gone ahead and created both unit tests as well as integration tests for my Lambda functions. The unit tests can be executed locally on the development system itself, as here we are simply testing the code's individual functionality and making sure each unit is working as expected. But, when it comes to integration testing, we generally have to deploy the function to AWS Lambda and then test its functionality as a whole.

Manually testing your functions with the AWS Management Console

We are definitely not new towards testing the functions manually using the AWS Management Console. Let us have a quick look at it once again before we go any further:

1. To test any of your functions manually, all you need to do is select the **Configure test event** option from the **Actions** drop-down list of your Lambda function. In this case, I'm using my trusty *Calculator* code example for this exercise (version: 2, alias: PROD).

2. In the **Input test event** dialog box, provide the test event as shown in the following screenshot. Remember, you can use either of these values as the operand variable: +, −, /, *, add, sub, mul, div.

3. Once you have provided the sample event, click on **Save and test**:

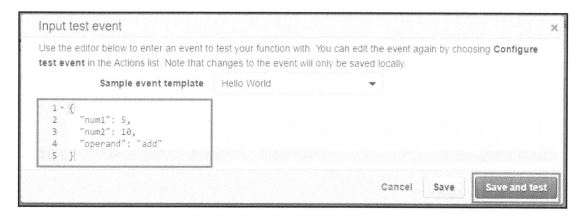

If all goes well, you should see the output of your function's execution in the **Execution result** area. Similarly, you can use the **Configure test event** option to simulate a variety of test events for your Lambda function ranging from simulated SNS messages to commits made to your repo in AWS CodeCommit and so on. This however, can become a very tedious and time consuming effort, especially when you have to develop various versions of the code, test it, run the code, and again repeat the entire cycle all over again. Fortunately for us, there are a few easier ways to test your functions even before you actually deploy them to Lambda. Let us take a look at how we can achieve this.

Testing functions with Mocha and Chai

The first step to creating a continuously deployable Lambda function is to write unit tests. One of the easiest and simplest ways to do so is by using a combination of two frameworks called **Mocha** and **Chai**.

First, a little bit about the two frameworks without going into too much information:

- **Mocha**: Mocha is a simple test framework for Node.js created to be easily extensible and fast for testing. It is used for unit and integration testing. You can read more about it at `https://mochajs.org/`.
  Mocha provides a unique ability to describe the features that we are implementing in our code by giving us a `describe` function that encapsulates our expectations:

  ```
  describe('myLambda',function(){
    //assertions about your code go here
  }
  ```

- **Chai**: Chai is a **Behaviour Driven Development (BDD)/ Test Driven Development (TDD)** assertion library for Node.js that works together with Mocha. You can read more about Chai here at `http://chaijs.com/guide/styles/`.
  Chai provides the following expressive assertion types that you can use to assert the behavior of the test result:

  - `assert`
  - `expect`
  - `should`
  - `difference`

For the purpose of this chapter, we will only concentrate on the `expect` interface. The `expect` interface uses simple chainable language to construct assertions, for example: `expect([1,2,3]).to.equal([1,2,3])`. Combining the `expect` assertion with the `describe` statement from Mocha looks something similar to the code snippet shown as follows:

```
describe('myLambda',function(){
  it('Check value returned from myLambda',function(){
  expect(retValue).to.equal('someValue');
}
```

Mocha has an assertion module of it's own, however I find Chai to be a little bit more flexible and extensible.

It is fairly simple and straightforward to setup Mocha and Chai on your development server. First up, create two folders; one to house the code that we are using and one to contain the test code:

```
# mkdir code
# mkdir test
```

Once this is done, install the Mocha framework and the Chai expectation library using the following commands:

```
# npm install mocha
# npm install chai
```

You can optionally add the --global parameter to save the npm modules globally over your dev system.

With the necessary packages downloaded, we move on to the code part. Copy and paste the calculator.js file in the recently created code directory. Next, copy and paste the following code into the test directory:

```
# vi test/calculatorTest.js
var expect = require('chai').expect;
var myLambda = require('../lib/calculator');
var retError, retValue ;

describe('myLambda',function(){
  context('Positive Test Case', function(){
    before('Calling myLambda function', function(done){
      var event = {
        num1: 3,
        num2: 2,
        operand: "+"
      };
      var context= {
        functionName: "calculator"
      };
      myLambda.handler(event, context, function (err, value) {
        retError = err ;
        retValue = value ;
```

```
        done();
      });
    });
    it('Check that error is not returned from myLambda',function(){
      expect(retError).to.be.a('null');
    });
    it('Check value returned from myLambda',function(){
      expect(retValue).to.equal(5);
    });
  });
  context('Negative Test Case - Invalid Numbers', function(){
    before('Calling myLambda function', function(done){
      var event = {
        num1: "num",
        num2: 2,
        operand: "div"
      };
      var context= {
        functionName: "calculator"
      };
      myLambda.handler(event, context, function (err, value) {
        retError = err ;
        retValue = value ;
        done();
      });
    });
    it('Check that error is returned from myLambda',function(){
      //var retErrorString = retError.toString();
      expect(retError).to.equal("Invalid Numbers!");
    });
    it('Check value returned from myLambda is undefined',function(){
      expect(retValue).to.be.an('undefined');
    });
  });
  context('Negative Test Case - Zero Divisor', function(){
    before('Calling myLambda function', function(done){
      var event = {
        num1: 2,
        num2: 0,
        operand: "div"
      };
      var context= {
        functionName: "calculator"
      };
      myLambda.handler(event, context, function (err, value) {
        retError = err ;
        retValue = value ;
        done();
```

```
        });
      });
      it('Check that error is returned from myLambda',function(){
        //var retErrorString = retError.toString();
        expect(retError).to.equal("The divisor cannot be 0");
      });
      it('Check value returned from myLambda is undefined',function(){
        expect(retValue).to.be.an('undefined');
      });
    });
    context('Negative Test Case - Invalid Operand', function(){
      before('Calling myLambda function', function(done){
        var event = {
          num1: 2,
          num2: 0,
          operand: "="
        };
        var context= {
          functionName: "calculator"
        };
        myLambda.handler(event, context, function (err, value) {
          retError = err ;
          retValue = value ;
          done();
        });
      });
      it('Check that error is returned from myLambda',function(){
        //var retErrorString = retError.toString();
        expect(retError).to.equal("Invalid Operand");
      });
      it('Check value returned from myLambda is undefined',function(){
        expect(retValue).to.be.an('undefined');
      });
    });
  });
});
```

Your final directory structure should resemble something like what is shown in the following screenshot:

```
ubuntu@ip-172-31-21-195:~/workdir$
ubuntu@ip-172-31-21-195:~/workdir$ tree -L 2
.
├── code
│   └── calculator.js
├── node_modules
│   ├── chai
│   └── mocha
└── test
    └── calculatorTest.js

5 directories, 2 files
ubuntu@ip-172-31-21-195:~/workdir$
```

With the setup all done, running your unit test on the calculator code is as easy as typing mocha!! Go ahead and execute the mocha command from your work directory. If all goes well, you should see a bunch of messages displayed on the screen, each taking about a particular test that was run against the calculator.js code. But where did all this come from? Let us look at it one step at a time.

First up, we wrote a bunch of unit test cases in the calculatorTest.js code using both Mocha and Chai.

The first couple of lines are to include the npm modules like Chai and the calculator.js code:

```
var expect = require('chai').expect;
var myLambda = require('../code/calculator');
var retError, retValue ;
```

Now, we will use the describe function of Mocha to describe the myLambda function. The describe function takes a simple string as its first argument and the second argument is a function while will represent the body of our expectations from the myLambda function:

```
describe('myLambda',function(){
```

Here we test the positive test case first. A *positive* test case is nothing more than providing the code with valid data to run.

Since myLambda is an asynchronous function and we need it to execute first before we can verify expect values, we use the done parameter with the before hook.

We define the `event` and `context` parameters and make a call to the `myLambda` function and calling done in its callback to let Mocha know that it can now move on to the expectations:

```
context('Positive Test Case', function(){
  before('Calling myLambda function', function(done){
    var event = {
      num1: 3,
      num2: 2,
      operand: "+"
    };
    var context= {
      functionName: "calculator"
    };
    myLambda.handler(event, context, function (err, value) {
      retError = err ;
      retValue = value ;
      done();
    });
  });
```

The output of this positive test block of unit test looks something like what is shown in the following screenshot:

```
 myHandler
    Positive Test Case
Hello, Starting the Version 1 of testLambda Lambda Function
The event we pass will have two numbers and an operand value
Received event: {
  "num1": 3,
  "num2": 2,
  "operand": "+"
}
The Result is: 5
    ✓ test success
```

Here, we use the `expect` interface from the `chai` module and check our error and result values respectively:

```
it('Check that error is not returned from myLambda',function(){
  expect(retError).to.be.a('null');
});
it('Check value returned from myLambda',function(){
  expect(retValue).to.equal(5);
});
});
```

Similarly, you can now add more assertions for positive and negative test cases as shown previously, changing the parameters with each test to ensure the `calculator.js` code works as expected.

Here is an example of a simple negative test case for our `calculator.js` code as well, we check how the code behaves if the values passed to it are non-numeric in nature (invalid data input):

```
context('Negative Test Case - Invalid Numbers', function(){
  before('Calling myLambda function', function(done){
    var event = {
      num1: "num",
      num2: 2,
      operand: "div"
    };
    var context= {
      functionName: "calculator"
    };
    myLambda.handler(event, context, function (err, value) {
      retError = err ;
      retValue = value ;
      done();
    });
  });
  it('Check that error is returned from myLambda',function(){
    //var retErrorString = retError.toString();
    expect(retError).to.equal("Invalid Numbers!");
  });
  it('Check value returned from myLambda is undefined',function(){
    expect(retValue).to.be.an('undefined');
  });
});
```

The following screenshot shows the output for the preceding code:

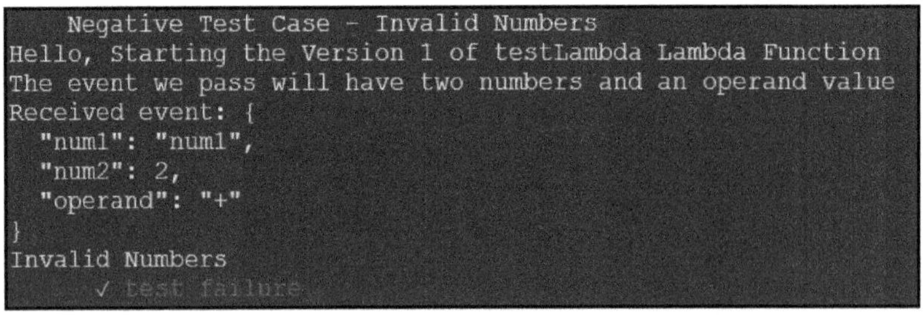

On similar lines, you can write and expand your own unit test cases to check and verify if the code is working as expected. Just do a few changes in the events and check the outcome!

Testing functions using the npm modules

There is a lot of testing that you can do with `mocha` and `chai`, however, with time, your test code becomes really long, complex, and difficult to manage. This can prove to be an issue, especially when it comes to adding newer functionality to your code and then requiring to retest it all over again.

That's one or more reasons why we now have a wide assortment of simpler, easier to use test frameworks that encapsulate a lot of the bulk validation code and help minimize the complexity of managing test cases. One such really interesting framework is provided as an npm module, so it makes it really easy to test Lambda functions that are written in Node.js and that module is called as `lambda-tester` created by Richard Hyatt.

The `lambda-tester` module is an open sourced, lightweight, and feature rich module that greatly simplifies writing and testing your Lambda functions. It is extremely easy to install and get started with.

I'll be comparing and demonstrating the `lambda-tester` module along with the `mocha` and `chai` example that we performed a while back so it's easier to see where `lambda-tester` brings it's uniqueness and flavor.

To install the `lambda-tester` npm module on your dev server, simply type the following command in your Terminal window:

```
# npm install lambda-tester
```

That's it! Simple, isn't it? Next, copy and paste the following code into a new file in your already existing `test` directory:

```
# vi test/calculatorLambdaTester.js

const LambdaTester = require( 'lambda-tester' );
var expect = require('chai').expect;
const myHandler = require( '../code/calculator' ).handler;

describe( 'myHandler', function() {
  context('Positive Test Case', function(){
    it( 'test success', function() {
      return LambdaTester( myHandler ).event( { num1: 3, num2: 2,
```

```
      operand: "+" } ).expectResult(function( result ) {
        expect( result ).to.equal( 5 );
      });
    });
  });
  context('Negative Test Case - Invalid Numbers', function(){
    it( 'test failure', function() {
      return LambdaTester( myHandler ).event( { num1: 'num1',
      num2: 2, operand: "+" } ).expectError(function( err ) {
        expect( err.message ).to.equal( 'Invalid Numbers!' );
      });
    });
  });
  context('Negative Test Case - Zero Divisor', function(){
    it( 'test failure', function() {
      return LambdaTester( myHandler ).event( { num1: 2, num2: 0,
      operand: "/" } ).expectError(function( err ) {
        expect( err.message ).to.equal( 'The divisor cannot be 0' );
      });
    });
  });
  context('Negative Test Case - Invalid Operand', function(){
    it( 'test failure', function() {
      return LambdaTester( myHandler ).event( { num1: 2, num2: 0,
      operand: "=" } ).expectError(function( err ) {
        expect( err.message ).to.equal( 'Invalid Operand' );
      });
    });
  });
});
});
```

If all goes well, your folder structure should look a bit like the following structure:

```
ubuntu@ip-172-31-21-195:~/workdir$ tree -L 2
.
├── code
│   └── calculator.js
├── node_modules
│   ├── chai
│   ├── lambda-tester
│   └── mocha
└── test
    ├── calculatorLambdaTester.js
    └── calculatorTest.js

6 directories, 3 files
```

To run the test, simply type in the following command as shown:

```
# mocha test
```

The output of this execution will be very similar to the one we got from our earlier `mocha` and `chai` test run, however, there's still a good amount of difference between the two approaches. Let us understand the code a bit better and compare it with the traditional approach of `mocha` and `chai`:

First up, is the declarative section which remains more or less same as the earlier test example:

```
const LambdaTester = require( 'lambda-tester' );
var expect = require('chai').expect;
const myHandler = require( '../code/calculator' ).handler;
```

Just like before, we describe `myHandler` function. Inside the `it` function we use `lambda-tester` module. This case simply verifies that the handler was called successfully that is, callback (null, result).

> I is important to return `lambda-tester` to the framework as `lambda-tester` is asynchronous in nature and it uses promises.

Notice that, while calling the `myHandler` function, we send the event we want to test it with and then use `expectResult` function where we use the expect from `chai`. The `expectResult` function is used when we are expecting a successful execution that is callback (null, result):

```
describe( 'myHandler', function() {
  context('Positive Test Case', function(){
    it( 'test success', function() {
      return LambdaTester( myHandler ).event( { num1: 3, num2: 2,
      operand: "+" } ).expectResult(function( result ) {
        expect( result ).to.equal( 5 );
      });
    });
  });
});
```

The following screenshot shows the output of the preceding code:

```
ubuntu@ip-172-31-21-195:~/workdir$ mocha test

  myHandler
    Positive Test Case
Hello, Starting the Version 1 of testLambda Lambda Function
The event we pass will have two numbers and an operand value
Received event: {
  "num1": 3,
  "num2": 2,
  "operand": "+"
}
The Result is: 5
      ✓ test success
```

Similarly, here is the case where we test our negative test case, where the handler calls the callback (err). In the event of a failure we use `expectError` in `lambda-tester`:

```
context('Negative Test Case - Invalid Numbers', function(){
  it( 'test failure', function() {
    return LambdaTester( myHandler ).event( { num1: 'num1', num2: 2,
    operand: "+" } ).expectError(function( err ) {
      expect( err.message ).to.equal( 'Invalid Numbers!' );
    });
  });
});
```

The following screenshot shows the output for the preceding code:

```
    Negative Test Case - Invalid Numbers
Hello, Starting the Version 1 of testLambda Lambda Function
The event we pass will have two numbers and an operand value
Received event: {
  "num1": "num1",
  "num2": 2,
  "operand": "+"
}
Invalid Numbers
      ✓ test failure
```

Similarly, we can go ahead and test the rest of the functionality as we did with `mocha` and `chai`. The main difference, however, is that the calculator test code with Mocha and Chai was 119 lines long whereas the same test cases code using `lambda-tester` is just 58 lines long! That's really impressive considering your code is now much cleaner and easier to test as well.

Testing with a simple serverless test harness

So far we have seen how simple and easy it becomes to test your Lambda functions out locally, right? But what happens once those Lambda functions are deployed on the cloud? How do you test those out? Don't worry, that's where Lambda can help out as well!

Our good folks at AWS have also provided us with a simple, customizable, and easy to use test harness function blueprint that in essence invokes unit test cases over other Lambda functions that are being tested, and stores the results of the tests in either DynamoDB, Kinesis or even S3 for that matter. The best part of this entire test harness is that you don't even bother about any of the underlying infrastructure, whether it's creating new resources for testing or shutting them down once the testing is over! It's all taken care by lambda itself!

Itching to give it a go? Let's get on with it then:

1. Login to the AWS Management Console and select **AWS Lambda** from the dashboard.
2. Select the **Create a Lambda function** option, as done in our earlier chapter.
3. From the **Select blueprint** page, select the `lambda-test-harness` blueprint. You can filter the blueprint using the **Filter** option as well.
4. The `lambda-test-harness` blueprint doesn't require any external triggers to be configured, so we will simply skip the **Configure triggers** page. Click **Next** to proceed.
5. Provide a suitable **Name** for your function.
6. Next, scroll down to the **Lambda function handler and role** section. Here, you will already have a predefined **Policy templates** already selected out for your function. Simply provide a suitable **Role name*** for the function as shown in the following screenshot:

7. Leave the rest of the values to their defaults and click on **Next** to proceed.
8. In the **Review** page, click the **Create function** once done.

With this step, the test harness is up and ready for use, but before we go ahead with the actual testing, we first need to create a really simple DynamoDB table that will store the results of the unit test cases.

The DynamoDB table will require just two attributes and a minimal of five read and write capacity for now:

- `testId` (string): Primary partition key
- `iteration` (number): Primary sort key

With the basics done, let us go ahead and test some functions with the test harness. The test harness comes in two execution modes, unit and load, which, as the names suggest, switch between unit testing and load testing of your Lambda functions. Let us examine the unit testing up first.

To unit test your Lambda function, you need to pass the following information to the test harness:

```
{
  "operation": "unit",
  "function": <Name/ ARN of the Lambda function under test>,
  "resultsTable": <DynamoDB table name that will store results>,
  "testId": <Some test identification>,
  "event": {<The event we want to pass to the function under test>}
}
```

Let us take a quick example to see how this works out. We had created our trusty `calculator.js` code and published it to Lambda back in Chapter 15, *Writing Lambda Functions* so I'm just going to reuse that itself and we will fire a few simple unit tests to make sure the code works as expected.

First up, from the test harness function's page, select the option **Configure test event** from the **Actions** drop-down list.

Next, in the **Input test event** section, provide the ARN of your calculator function as shown in the following code:

```
{
  "operation": "unit",
  "function": "arn:aws:lambda:us-east-1:01234567890:
    function:myCalculatorFunction:PROD",
  "resultsTable": "unit-test-results",
```

```
    "iteration": 1,
    "testId": "MyFirstRun1",
    "event": {
      "num1": 3,
      "num2": 7,
      "operand": "add"
    }
}
```

Once done, click on the **Save and test** option. The test harness function invokes the calculator function and passes the test events to it. The output is then recorded to the DynamoDB table that we had created earlier:

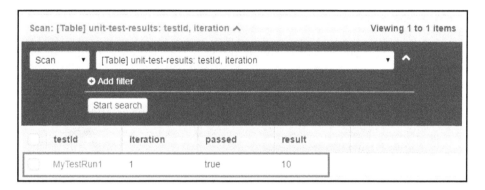

You can now play around with the test harness event and modify your test scenarios accordingly. For example, changing the iteration value to 5 or more to run the same test multiple number of times, or even changing the event values to make sure the calculator function is operating as expected, for example, passing the following event values will trigger the **Divisor cannot be zero** error, and so on.

```
    "event": {
      "num1": 8,
      "num2": 0,
      "operand": "div"
    }
```

You can alternatively run load tests as well using the same test harness function blueprint. The fundamentals stay the same once again with just a few minor exceptions. The first being the operation parameter now changes from unit to load; however, in the event section, we pass the same unit test case that we want to load test this time. What this will result in is a fleet of 10 functions executing the particular load test in parallel:

```
{
    "operation": "load",
```

```
"iterations": 10,
"function": "lambda_test_harness",
"event": {
  "operation": "unit",
  "function": "arn:aws:lambda:us-east-1:01234567890:
    function:myCalculatorFunction:PROD",
  "resultsTable": "unit-test-results",
  "testId": "MyTestRun2",
  "event": {
    "num1": 8,
    "num2": 12,
    "operand": "+"
  }
}
}
```

With the test completed, you can verify the load test output from the DynamoDB table as shown in the following screenshot:

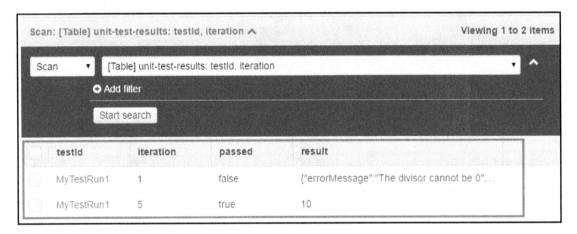

You can use this same functionality to load test your AWS API Gateways by simulating either POST or GET operations on the API Gateway endpoint. To learn more, visit `https://aws.amazon.com/blogs/compute/serverless-testing-with-aws-lambda/`.

 Remember to clean up the DynamoDB table once your tests are all done.

17
Event-Driven Model

So far, we have learned a thing or two about serverless and AWS Lambda. We started off by understanding the entire concept behind serverless architecture and, later, dived into the amazing world of serverless computing with AWS Lambda. We learned how to effectively write, develop, package, and test Lambda functions and also picked up on a few best practices and recommendations along the way.

From this chapter onwards, we will be taking a slightly different approach to understand how few core functionalities of Lambda actually work. For example, how do you trigger Lambda functions to execute based on a trigger? That's exactly what this chapter is going to be all about. In this chapter, we will be covering the following topics:

- What event-driven model is all about
- Understanding the event-driven model of Lambda along with a few simple event-driven architectures for better understanding
- Getting started with simple event-driven use cases of Lambda that range from basic data manipulations to automated infrastructure management and so on

So, without any more delay, let's get started!

Introducing event-driven architectures

Till now we have been working and understanding Lambda using our trusty calculator example code, that simply accepts few parameters and values as inputs, and, when run, provides you with some desired output. What you may not have noticed is that the inputs that we were providing for the code to run were actually part of an event, that would trigger the code into running. Similarly, you can write Lambda functions that get activated or triggered when a particular message or event is generated. This is perhaps one of the biggest reasons why I love Lambda so much and why Lambda is so much better than your traditional EC2 instances! But, before we begin exploring the various triggers and events that Lambda can respond to, let us understand what Event Driven architectures are all about and how are they so useful.

Event-driven architecture (EDA) is basically a software architecture pattern that deals with the generation, detection, consumption, and reaction to one or more events. Events can be anything; from simple messages, notification calls, to state changes. In our AWS Lambda case, events can be something such as an object getting uploaded to an S3 bucket or a row getting deleted from a DynamoDB table and so on.

An event-driven architecture in general comprises of three essential pieces: an event emitter, an event channel, and an event consumer. In simpler terms, the entire process flow looks a bit like the following image:

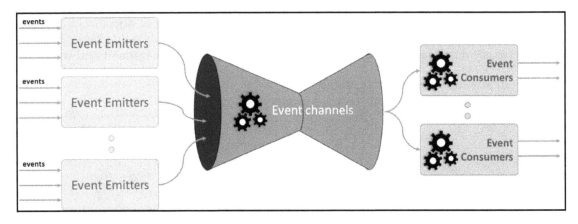

The event emitters are responsible for gathering state changes or events that occur within the event-driven system. They simply get the event and send it to the next step of the process which is the event channel. Here, the channels serve two purposes; one is to simply channel or funnel the event to a particular waiting consumer where the event will be processed and acted upon. Alternatively, the channel itself can react to the event, and perform some level of pre-processing on the event and then send it down to the consumers for the final processing as represented earlier.

Now, keeping these basics in mind, let us look at how AWS Lambda enables event-driven architecture along with a few easy to understand use cases as well.

Understanding events and AWS Lambda

Lambda works in a very similar way, as explained in the previous section. For instance, the emitters and channels act as the Lambda event source while the functions that we have been creating all this time act as the event consumers.

All in all, when an event is triggered by a particular AWS service, or even from an external source such as an application, that event gets mapped to a particular Lambda function which in turn, executes an action based on the code that you have written for it. This one-to-one mapping of events with their corresponding Lambda functions is what we call as **Event Source Mapping** and it is responsible for the automatic invocation of your Lambda functions whenever an event is fired.

There are two main categories of event sources supported by Lambda:

- **AWS services:** Lambda supports a few of AWS's services as preconfigured event sources that you can use to develop easy event-driven systems with. Few of the services namely S3, SNS, SES, Cognito, CloudFromation, CloudWatch fall under a branch relatively termed as regular AWS services; whereas DynamoDB and Kinesis fall under something called as stream based services as in both these cases, Lambda polls the streams for any updates and when it does find one, it triggers the corresponding function to run. In this chapter, we will be looking at few of the commonly used AWS services used as event mappings and how you can leverage them to perform simple tasks for your cloud environment.
- **Custom applications**: Custom applications are your own home grown applications or external world entities that can generate their own events. This can be anything from a simple web based application or even mobile device.

Before we actually begin with the event mapping examples and use cases, let us quickly glance through some of the architecture patterns and use cases where Lambda's event mapping system comes into play.

Lambda architecture patterns

In this section, we will be looking at some of the commonly used Lambda architecture patterns that you can use as blueprints for building your own serverless and event based applications.

- **Serverless microservices**: Microservices are designed and developed to be independent and self-sufficient, which is exactly why they are an amazing candidate for running with the help of Lambda. A Lambda function too, in its own is an independent code that can execute for a finite time when triggered by an external source. The only downside here is that, because of the deep granularity, the sheer number of microservices and the corresponding Lambda functions that you will end up with will be really high. Managing that many functions can be a challenge especially when you need to do changes, new deployments and so on.

In the following depiction, we can see a number of Lambda functions hosting microservices frontended by an API Gateway and having one or more databases as backends.

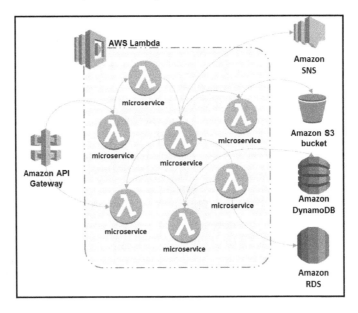

- **Serverless multi-tier applications**: Perhaps one of the most commonly used architecture patterns, Lambda is an ideal platform to host the business logic of your applications. With the presentation logic handled in S3 in the form of static website hosting, and the backend taken care of by a variety of database services ranging from DynamoDB, RDS to ElastiCache; Lambda is the perfect service to run the logic of your applications as shown in the image below:

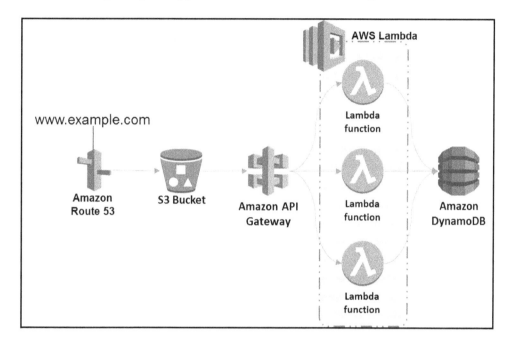

- **Real-time stream processing**: When we talk about streams and AWS, only one word comes to our mind and that is Kinesis. AWS Kinesis is a powerful and scalable solution that enables you to design and develop applications that can process as well as analyze large quantities of streaming data. Mix that with Lambda and you have yourselves a variety of use cases where this design becomes applicable such as transactions processing, log analysis, social media analytics, and much more!

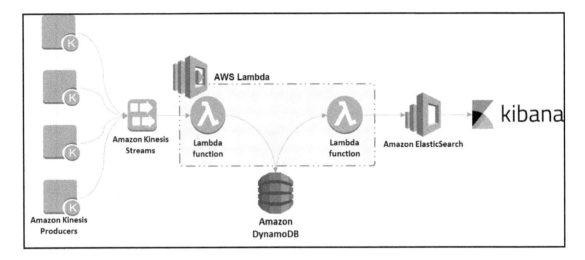

- **Backend services for mobile or IoT**: AWS Lambda can also be used to develop and support complete backend services for your IoT as well as mobile applications. You can use this pattern in conjunction with AWS API Gateway to create a REST API that invokes Lambda functions which in turn, performs some CRUD operations over data residing in DynamoDB or can even push notification messages to other users or systems using SNS as well.

With the architectural patterns done and dusted, let us move on to some seriously fun things by exploring some easy to use and practical event mapping examples!

Exploring Lambda and event mapping

We have already seen and learned a bit about how Lambda uses a notion called event mapping to map a particular AWS service to a corresponding Lambda function. In this section, we will be diving a bit further into event mapping with the help of some interesting real world use cases that most of you would find useful in your own AWS environments.

Mapping Lambda with S3

You can easily write and invoke Lambda functions for processing objects stored in an S3 bucket. The functions can be triggered using a set of notification configurations which trigger a corresponding Lambda function into action. The following is a list of few such notification configurations that can be used for triggering functions on S3 buckets:

- When an object is created in a bucket using either `put`, `post`, `copy` or a `completemultipartupload` operation
- When an object is deleted from a bucket using the `delete` operation
- When a bucket set with `ReducedRedundancy` storage option loses an object

How does it all work? Quite simple actually. When we first configure the event source mapping for a particular S3 bucket, we initially set the event source mapping of the bucket with it's corresponding Lambda function using the notification configuration we just talked about. Next, S3 begins to monitor the bucket for the particular event to be triggered. When the event is triggered, the corresponding notification configuration is activated which in turn invokes the assigned Lambda function.

Let us now look at a simple example of event source mapping between S3 and Lambda. In this scenario, we are going to simulate a simple image transformation example that gets triggered when a new object (image file) is uploaded or created in a particular S3 bucket (source bucket). This action, in turn, triggers a Lambda function that will first download the image from S3, transform it either to a grayscale, a negative image or a transparent image followed by uploading the new image into another S3 bucket (destination bucket).

This use case can be applied when you are hosting a simple website that runs some form of transformation techniques on images uploaded to it such as grayscale, creating thumbnail images and so on.

First up, let us explore the setup for this particular use case. We'll be using APEX to deploy the functions over to Lambda and I highly recommend you try out the same, although you could upload the following code snippets manually as well.

On my development server, I have already gone ahead and installed APEX.

 NOTE: You can read about installing and configuring APEX at `http://apex.run/`.

With APEX installed and set, you will now need to create a folder directory to work out of.

I have created a simple folder structure that makes it easy to work out APEX. You could follow a similar approach, or even try out something that suites your needs.

The folder structure I have for this use and other use cases to follow, looks something like this:

- `apex`: A primary working directory.
- `event_driven`: This is my project directory that will contain a `project.dev.json` (explained below) file.
- `functions`: This directory will contain all your Lambda functions that you are going to deploy for this chapter. The functions directory will have multiple sub folders, each one containing a master folder for our use cases. Since this is the first use case that we are performing, the only sub folder present in the functions directory is `myS3ToLambdaFunc`.
- Within the `myS3ToLambdaFunc` directory is where we will place the `index.js` (function code) and a `function.dev.json` file along with the `node_modules` directory as well:
  - `index.js`
  - `function.dev.json`
  - `node_modules/`

If the node modules directory is not present, simply copy and paste the `index.js` code and run the following command to install the necessary dependencies for the code to run:

```
# npm install async gm
```

The `index.js` file contains the actual Lambda function which will do the work of image transformation on the image that gets uploaded to a specified S3 bucket.

Here are a few key snippets of code for your understanding:

```
// dependencies
var async = require('async');
var AWS = require('aws-sdk');
var gm = require('gm')
            .subClass({ imageMagick: true });
```

The code starts off by declaring a few necessary variables, noticeably the `async Node.js` module and the `ImageMagick` module which is actually provided with the image transformation functions.

```
var transformFunc = process.env.TRANSFORM_FUNC;
```

In this example, we are setting the values of the image transformation function using Lambda's environment variables. You can select either `gray`, `negative`, or `transparent` based on your requirements.

```
exports.handler = function(event, context, callback) {
    // Read options from the event.
    console.log("Reading options from event:\n",
     util.inspect(event, {depth: 5}));
    var srcBucket = event.Records[0].s3.bucket.name;
    // Object key may have spaces or unicode non-ASCII characters.
    var srcKey = decodeURIComponent(event.Records[0].s3.object.key
     .replace(/\+/g, " "));
    var dstBucket = srcBucket + "-output";
    var dstKey    = "output-" + srcKey;
```

Here, we declare the handler function which Lambda invokes for execution. Our handler function will perform the following steps: download the image from S3 into a buffer, transform that image into the selected option (taken from the `env` variable), and then upload the image in the destination S3 bucket.

```
async.waterfall([
    function download(next) {
        // Download the image from S3 into a buffer.
        s3.getObject({
                Bucket: srcBucket,
                Key: srcKey
            },
            next);
        },
```

This is the transformation function which either generates a `gray`, `negative`, or `transparent` version of the uploaded image. A simple switch case will suffice.

```
function transform(response, next) {
            console.log("Here we have three option
             - negative, transparent and gray");
            console.log("Currently we have got the option of "
             + transformFunc+".");
            switch(transformFunc) {
                case "negative":
                    gm(response.Body).negative()
```

```
                          .toBuffer(imageType, function(err, buffer) {
                              if (err) {
                                  next(err);
                              } else {
                                  next(null, response.ContentType,
                                    buffer);
                              }
                          });
                      break;
```

You can find the complete code for this use case along with the other necessary files here:
`https://github.com/PacktPublishing/Mastering-AWS-Lambda`

Your final folder structure should resemble something as shown:

```
ubuntu@ip-172-31-21-195:~/workdir/apex$ tree -L 4
.
└── event_driven
    ├── functions
    │   └── myS3ToLambdaFunc
    │       ├── function.dev.json
    │       ├── index.js
    │       └── node_modules
    └── project.dev.json

4 directories, 3 files
ubuntu@ip-172-31-21-195:~/workdir/apex$
```

Let us examine a few of the important files related with APEX as well as the function deployment before moving on to the actual deployment process. First up is the `project.dev.json` file. The file basically is a descriptor for your `event_driven` project directory:

```
{
  "name": "eventDriven",
  "description": "event-driven use cases using pre-configured
    triggers",
  "profile": "example",
  "runtime": "nodejs4.3",
  "memory": 128,
  "timeout": 60,
  "role": "arn:aws:iam::<account-id>:role/myApexLambdaProjRole",
  "environment": {}
}
```

Here, you can set and modify default values that will be passed to your functions at runtime. For example, setting the default memory utilization, timeouts, as well as the role that Lambda functions will need to assume in order to get executed on your behalf. Here is a simple and minimalistic snippet of the `myApexLambdaProjRole` that we have used in this use case. Note that, in most cases, you will have to setup this role manually as APEX doesn't yet automate this for you. This proves yet another point: that there is a serious gap when it comes to Serverless Frameworks and tooling. For now, you could either do this manually or even use some automated deployment tool such as Terraform or Ansible to configure out this for you.

```
{
    "Version": "2012-10-17",
    "Statement": [
        {
            "Sid": "myLogsPermissions",
            "Effect": "Allow",
            "Action": [
                "logs:CreateLogGroup",
                "logs:CreateLogStream",
                "logs:PutLogEvents"
            ],
            "Resource": [
                "*"
            ]
        }
    ]
}
```

Now, the important point to note here is that, the `project.dev.json` file works at your project level, but what about my individual functions? That's where we have the `function.dev.json` file as described below. The `function.dev.json` file works very similarly to the `project.dev.json` file with the slight difference that here we pass the function's handler information along with the necessary information such as the environment variables that we need to pass to the function at runtime and the specific role required to run it.

```
{
    "description": "Node.js lambda function using S3 as a trigger to
transform the uploaded image and then upload the new image in S3",
    "role": "arn:aws:iam::<account-id>:role/myLambdaS3FuncRole",
    "handler": "index.handler",
    "environment": {
        "TRANSFORM_FUNC" : "negative"
    }
}
```

In the `function.dev.json` case, we also need to create and assign a role that is going to be required by S3 to get and put objects along with write logs to Amazon CloudWatch. This task too could be automated using the likes of Terraform or Ansible or you could even do it out manually. The following is a snippet of the `function.dev.role` that you can use and modify according to your own needs:

```
{
    "Version": "2012-10-17",
    "Statement": [
        {
            "Sid": "myLogsPermissions",
            "Effect": "Allow",
            "Action": [
                "logs:CreateLogGroup",
                "logs:CreateLogStream",
                "logs:PutLogEvents"
            ],
            "Resource": "arn:aws:logs:*:*:*"
        },
        {
            "Sid": "myS3Permissions",
            "Effect": "Allow",
            "Action": [
                "s3:GetObject",
                "s3:PutObject"
            ],
            "Resource": "arn:aws:s3:::*"
        }
    ]
}
```

Phew, that was a lot to digest, but I am sure with a few rounds of practice you will get to assigning and working with roles in no time. Now, for the fun part! We deploy the function as a package to Lambda using APEX. To do so, simply type in the following command as shown:

```
# apex --env dev deploy myS3ToLambdaFunc
```

 You will need to run this command from the `project` directory.

With the deployment underway, you should see an output similar to the one shown below. Do note however that, with each deployment, APEX will automatically create a new version of your function just as it has done in my case (*version 2*)

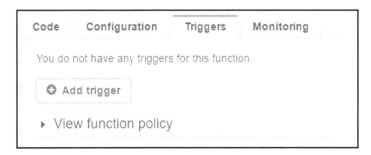

With the function deployed, the only thing left to do is configure the trigger mechanism out. To do this, you can login to the AWS Management Console or even use the AWS CLI or use Terraform to automate the process. We will use the simplest way to demonstrate the ease with which triggers can be created and set. First up, login to the AWS Management Console and Lambda service from the main landing page.

You should see your function already deployed out there. Select the function and click on the **Triggers** option as shown:

Code	Configuration	Triggers	Monitoring

You do not have any triggers for this function.

⊕ Add trigger

▸ View function policy

To create a new trigger, click on the **Add trigger** option. This will pop up an easy to use dialog box using which you can map a S3 bucket with your Lambda function.

Select the empty box adjacent to the Lambda function and from the drop down list provided and filter out **S3** as shown below. Select **S3** to view its corresponding event mapping properties:

- **Bucket name:** The bucket for which you wish to enable the trigger. In my case, I have already created a simple bucket with the name **image-processing-01**.
- **Event type:** From the dropdown, select the appropriate event for which you want to trigger the Lambda function. According to our use case, we want the function to run each time a new object/ image is uploaded to the S3 bucket. Hence, select the **Object Created (All)** option as shown as follows:

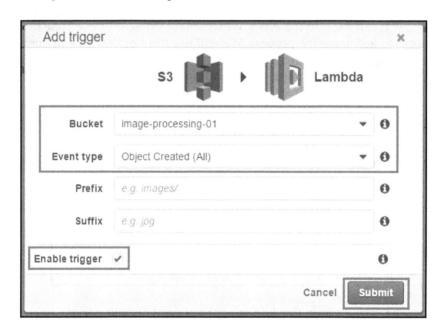

Leave the rest of the values to their defaults, but remember to check the **Enable trigger** option to yes before clicking on **Submit**. Your function is now mapped with the S3 bucket! It's that simple! With the trigger set, it's time to generate some events! In this case, simply upload an image (.jpg or .png) and watch the magic unfold. Depending on what was set in the function's environment variables during deployment (by default, its *negative*), the uploaded image will get transformed accordingly.

Go ahead and change the environment variable in the `function.dev.json` file from *negative* to *gray* to *transparent* and check the output in the S3 bucket that will be marked with the `*output*` keyword. Remember to deploy the updated functions using the same APEX command as done before. APEX will automatically handle the package uploads and the versioning for you! Here is a sample of an image I uploaded:

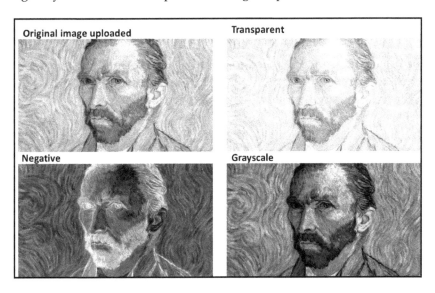

You can alternatively view the execution logs of your function using Amazon CloudWatch Logs.

Mapping Lambda with DynamoDB

Now that we've got a feel of mapping Lambda events with S3, let us give yet another service a go! This time its DynamoDB!

You can trigger Lambda functions in response to updates made to a particular DynamoDB table; for example, a new row that gets added in a table gets validated by a Lambda function, a row deletion operation resulting in Lambda sending a notification to a user, and so on. But, before you go ahead and implement triggers for DynamoDB, its important to note that, unlike S3, DynamoDB is a stream-based event source, which means that you first need to enable streams on your DynamoDB table before you create and map functions to it. Lambda actually polls the particular stream for events and when it finds one, it invokes the corresponding function mapped to it.

In the following use case, we shall see how to use a Lambda function to check a particular data column in the table for a pattern. If the pattern is invalid, the function should delete the entire data row, or else ignore it. Once again, I will be using APEX to deploy my functions, so first we need to get the folder directory all setup. Since we already have a work directory, and a project directory created, we will just go ahead and create a simple folder for this particular use case under the following folder structure:

```
# mkdir ~/workdir/apex/event_driven/functions/myDynamoToLambdaFunc
```

With the directory created, we only need to create a `function.dev.json` and `index.js` files here as well. Remember, the `function.dev.json` file is unique to each use case so in this case, the file will contain the following set of instructions:

```json
{
    "description": "Node.js lambda function using DynamoDB as a trigger to
validate the value of the inserted IP address and deletes it if it's
invalid.",
    "role": "arn:aws:iam::<account-id>:role/myLambdaDynamoFuncRole",
    "handler": "index.handler",
    "environment": {}
}
```

Once again, the code is self-explanatory. We once again have to create a corresponding IAM role to allow our Lambda function to interact and poll the DynamoDB table on our behalf. This includes providing Lambda with the necessary permissions to describe and list DynamoDB streams as well as get records from the table itself.

```json
{
  "Version": "2012-10-17",
  "Statement": [
    {
      "Sid": "myDynamodbPermissions",
      "Effect": "Allow",
      "Action": [
        "dynamodb:DescribeStream",
        "dynamodb:GetRecords",
        "dynamodb:GetShardIterator",
        "dynamodb:ListStreams",
        "dynamodb:DeleteItem"
      ],
      "Resource":
      [
        "arn:aws:dynamodb:us-east-1:<account-id>:table/LambdaTriggerDB*"
      ]
    },
    {
      "Sid": "myLogsPermissions",
```

```
      "Effect": "Allow",
      "Action": [
        "logs:CreateLogGroup",
        "logs:CreateLogStream",
        "logs:PutLogEvents"
      ],
      "Resource": "arn:aws:logs:*:*:*"
    }
    ]
  }
```

With the configurations of the function out of way, let us now have a quick look at the function code itself:

```
function isValidIPAddress(ipAddr, cb){
  if(/^(25[0-5]|2[0-4][0-9]|[01]?[0-9][0-9]?)\.(25[0-5]|2[0-4][0-9]|
    [01]?[0-9][0-9]?)\.(25[0-5]|2[0-4][0-9]|[01]?[0-9][0-9]?)\
    .(25[0-5]|2[0-4][0-9]|[01]?[0-9][0-9]?)$/.test(ipAddr)){
      cb(null, "Valid IPv4 Address");
  }
  else{
    cb("Invalid");
  }
}
```

The following code snippet simply checks and validates whether a supplied IP address is a valid or an invalid IP address. We have used a regex expression to do the check.

```
exports.handler = (event, context, callback) => {
  var ipAddr, eventName;
  var tableName = "LambdaTriggerDB";
  event.Records.forEach((record) => {
    eventName = record.eventName;
    console.log("Event: "+eventName);
    switch(eventName){
      case "MODIFY":
      case "INSERT":
      ipAddr = record.dynamodb.Keys.IP_ADDRESS.S;
```

Here, we check the `eventName` that is, MODIFY, INSERT, or REMOVE, to decide the different execution paths. For Modify and Insert events, we will check for the validity of the IP address and if it's invalid then delete that particular record from the DynamoDB table. In case of a remove event, we don't want to do anything.

We have used a simple switch case to achieve this task.

You can find the complete code along with all the necessary config files for your reference here: https://github.com/PacktPublishing/Mastering-AWS-Lambda.

We will once again use APEX to deploy our function to Lambda. To do so, we execute the APEX deploy command from the project level directory as shown below:

```
# apex --env dev deploy myDynamoToLambdaFunc
```

With your function successfully packaged and deployed, you can now create the DynamoDB table and the associated Lambda trigger as well. The table creation is a straight forward process. Select the **DynamoDB** option from the AWS Management Console. Click on **Create new table** and fill out the necessary information as shown in the image below. Make sure to provide the same table name as provided in your Lambda IAM role. For the **Primary key**, type in IP_ADDRESS and select the attribute as **String**. Click on **Create** once done.

 Make sure the DynamoDB table and the lambda function reside in the same region

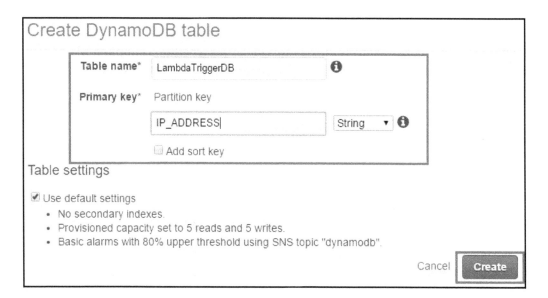

Once the table is copied, make sure to copy the table's stream ARN. The stream ARN will be required in the next steps when we map the table stream with our deployed Lambda function.

To configure the function's trigger, select the newly created function from Lambda's dashboard. Next, select the **Triggers** option to configure the event mapping. Click on the blank box adjacent to the Lambda function and choose the option **DynamoDB** as shown. Fill in the required details as described below:

- **DynamoDB table**: From the drop down list, select the stream enabled table that we just created a while back.
- **Batch size:** Provide a suitable value for the batch size operation. Here, I've opted for the default values.
- **Starting position:** Select the position from where the function must execute. In this case, we have gone with the **Latest** position marker.

Make sure the **Enable trigger** option is selected before you complete the configurations:

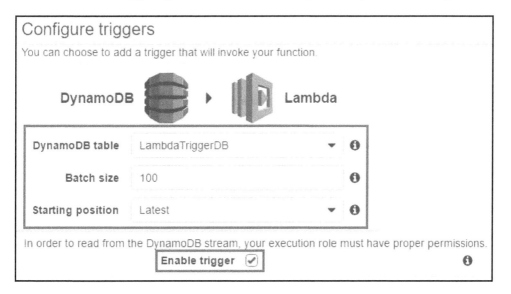

With this step completed, we are now ready to test our function. To do so, simply add a valid record in the DynamoDB table and check the function's logs using Amazon CloudWatch Logs. Once verified, try the same using an invalid IP address and see the results. You can use the same logic to verify data that is dumped into your DynamoDB table or even perform some level of processing over data in the table before it is either deleted or archived as a file to S3.

Mapping Lambda with SNS

Just as we have an event mapping for DynamoDB, AWS also provides event mapping for SNS and Lambda's integration. Lambda functions can get triggered each time a new message is published to an existing SNS topic. When triggered, a Lambda function can be used to perform tasks such as reading contents of the message payload, processing it or even forwarding it to other AWS services that can use the SNS notification to perform some action. An important thing to note here, while using SNS event mappings, is that, SNS will invoke Lambda functions in an asynchronous manner. If Lambda was successfully able to process the SNS event, it will send a successful delivery status. In the case of errors, SNS will try and invoke the particular function up to three times, post which, it will log an unsuccessful/failure message that can be viewed from Amazon CloudWatch.

Now, onward with the use case. This particular use case is a fairly simple representation of a simple user registration where a username is published via a SNS Topic which, in turn, triggers a Lambda function that reads the SNS Topic payload message, generates an MD5 checksum of the supplied username, and writes the first 10 characters of the MD5 checksum to a DynamoDB table.

To get started with the use case, we first create a corresponding directory structure. Type in the following command:

```
# mkdir ~/workdir/apex/event_driven/functions/mySnsToLambdaFunc
```

With the directory created, we only need to create a `function.dev.json` and our `index.js` files here as well. Remember, the `function.dev.json` file is unique to each use case so in this case, the file will contain the following set of instructions:

```
{
  "description": "Node.js lambda function using sns as a trigger to
    generate an md5 of the message received and store it in the
    database",
  "role": "arn:aws:iam::<account_id>:role/myLambdaSNSFuncRole",
  "handler": "index.handler",
  "environment": {}
}
```

Next, create the corresponding IAM role for providing permissions to the Lambda function to create and publish logs in CloudWatch as well as add items to a particular DynamoDB database:

```
{
  "Version": "2012-10-17",
  "Statement": [
    {
```

```
      "Sid": "myLogsPermissions",
      "Effect": "Allow",
      "Action": [
        "logs:CreateLogGroup",
        "logs:CreateLogStream",
        "logs:PutLogEvents"
      ],
      "Resource": [
        "*"
      ]
    },
    {
      "Sid": "myDynamodbPermissions",
      "Effect": "Allow",
      "Action": [
        "dynamodb:PutItem"
      ],
      "Resource": [
        "arn:aws:dynamodb:us-east-1:<account_id>:table/LambdaTriggerSNS"
      ]
    }
    ]
  }
```

Remember, the IAM role will not get pushed to AWS IAM by APEX. You will have to use some other means to achieve this action for now.

Finally, create the `index.js` file and paste the code as provided here: `https://github.com/PacktPublishing/Mastering-AWS-Lambda`.

The first section of the code is fairly understandable on its own. We check if the message string is not empty or undefined. If so, we simply return the `callback()` with a message. Else, we create an MD5 checksum of the supplied message and slice the first 10 characters off from it:

```
function getMessageHash(message, hashCB){
  if(message === ""){
    return hashCB("Message is empty");
  }
  else if((message === null) || (message === undefined)){
    return hashCB("Message is null or undefined");
  }
  else{
    var crypto = require('crypto');
    var messageHash =
      crypto.createHash('md5').update(message).digest("hex");
      return hashCB(null, messageHash.slice(0,10));
  }
```

```
    }
```

The second piece is where we define the `insert` function that will populate the DynamoDB table.

```
function insertItem(insertParams, insertCB){
  var AWS = require('aws-sdk');
  AWS.config.update({
    region: "us-east-1",
    endpoint: "http://dynamodb.us-east-1.amazonaws.com"
  });
  var dynamodb = new AWS.DynamoDB({apiVersion: '2012-08-10'});
  dynamodb.putItem(insertParams, function(err, data) {
  if(err){
    insertCB(err);
  }
  else{
    insertCB(null, data);
  }
});
}
```

And finally, we have the handler of our function defined.

```
exports.handler = (event, context, callback) => {
var tableName = "LambdaTriggerSNS";
var message, recordVal;
```

With the basic steps done, your work directory should resemble the following screenshot a bit:

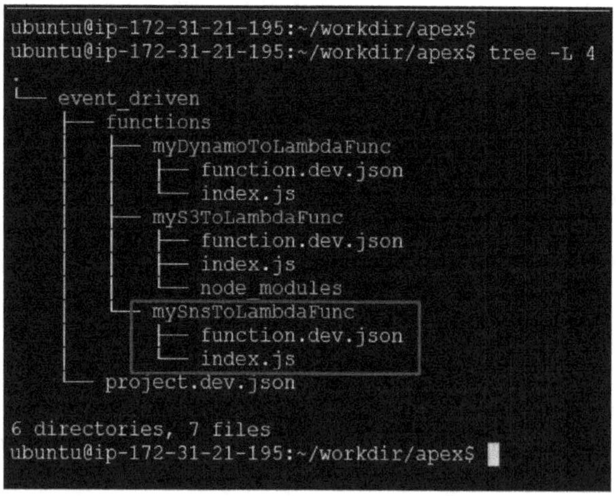

With this, we are ready to package and upload the function to Lambda. To do so, simply run the following command from your project directory:

```
# apex --env dev deploy mySnsToLambdaFunc
```

Next up, create a simple DynamoDB table and provide it with the same name as done in the function's role, that is, `LambdaTriggerSNS`. Make sure the **Primary key** of the table is set as `userName`. Accept the default settings for the table, and click on **Create** to complete the process.

Similarly, go ahead and create the corresponding SNS Topic. Login to the AWS Management Console and select the SNS service from the main landing page. Next, create a simple Topic by selecting the **Topics** option from the navigation pane to the left of the SNS Dashboard. Click on **Create topic** and fill out the **Topic name** and **Display name** for your **Topic** in the popup dialog box. Click **Create topic** once done.

With the topic created, the only thing left to do is subscribing the Lambda function to a particular topic. To do so, select the newly created Topic and from the **Actions** tab, select the option **Subscribe to topic**. This will bring up the **Create subscription** dialog, as shown as follows:

- **Topic ARN**: Provide the SNS Topic ARN here
- **Protocol**: Select AWS Lambda from the dropdown list
- **Endpoint**: From the drop down list, you will have to select the ARN of our deployed function
- **Version or alias**: You can leave this value to **default** as of now, however, you can always use the $LATEST flag to point to the latest version of your function code.

Verify that event mapping was indeed created successfully by viewing the **Triggers** tab of your function. You should see the SNS trigger configured there automatically as well. So, that should pretty much do it! You can now go ahead and test the event mapping. To do so, simply publish a username as a message in your Topic using the SNS dashboard itself. Back at Lambda, our deployed function will automatically get triggered once SNS publishes the message. It will read the contents of the message payload, create an MD5 checksum of the same, accept only the first 10 characters of the checksum and store that in the DynamoDB table we created a while back.

You can verify the output by viewing the logs of your functions' execution using Amazon CloudWatch as well:

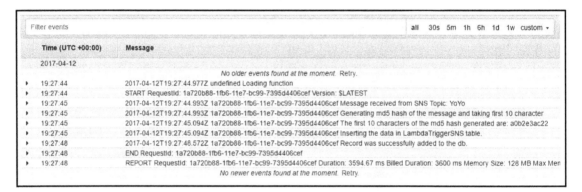

Mapping Lambda with CloudWatch events

CloudWatch offers easy event mapping integrations with Lambda using which you can execute Lambda functions either based on triggered events or even schedule their execution using CloudWatch events.

The following use case uses CloudWatch events to take periodic backups of data stored in a DynamoDB table over to S3. There are different ways to export data from your DynamoDB table and store it for later by using services such as data pipeline and EMR, but these approaches make sense when you have a really huge database consisting of millions of rows of data. What if you have a minimalistic DynamoDB table with a 100 or 200 rows of data only? In that case, it makes sense to write a simple function using Lambda that executes periodically, collecting the data from the table into a CSV file, and uploading the same to S3 for archival.

To get started with the use case, we once again create the necessary project directory folder for APEX:

```
# mkdir ~/workdir/apex/event_driven/functions/myCWScheduleToLambdaFunc
```

Next, we create the `function.dev.json` file that contains few descriptive elements with respect to the function code:

```
{
    "description": "Node.js lambda function using CloudWatch Scheduled
      events as a trigger to export a dynamodb table to s3",
    "role": "arn:aws:iam::<account_id>:role/myLambdaCWScheduleFuncRole",
    "handler": "index.handler",
    "environment": {}
}
```

Once created, go ahead and create the required IMA role as well. Remember to name the IAM role `myLambdaCWScheduleFuncRole` as done in the earlier step.

```
{
    "Version": "2012-10-17",
    "Statement": [
        {
            "Sid": "myLogsPermissions",
            "Effect": "Allow",
            "Action": [
                "logs:CreateLogGroup",
                "logs:CreateLogStream",
                "logs:PutLogEvents"
            ],
            "Resource": [
                "*"
            ]
        },
        {
            "Sid": "myS3Permissions",
            "Effect": "Allow",
            "Action": [
                "s3:PutObject"
            ],
            "Resource": [
                "arn:aws:s3:::dynamodb-backup-s3*"
            ]
        },
        {
            "Sid": "myDynamodbPermissions",
            "Effect": "Allow",
            "Action": [
```

```
                    "dynamodb:Scan"
            ],
            "Resource": [
                "arn:aws:dynamodb:us-east-1:
                <account_id>:table/LambdaExportToS3*"
            ]
        }
    ]
}
```

Finally, we create the `index.js` file that will house the actual function's code. You can download the entire code and it's associated support files at `https://github.com/PacktPublishing/Mastering-AWS-Lambda`:

```
console.log('Loading function');
exports.handler = function(event, context, callback) {
  var csvExport = require('dynamodbexportcsv');
  var exporter = new csvExport(null, null, 'us-east-1');

  exporter.exportTable('LambdaExportToS3', ['userName'], 1,
  true, 250, 'dynamodb-backup-s3', '04-17-2017', function(err) {
    if(err){
      console.log("An error occurred while exporting the
        table to s3. The error is: "+err);
      return callback(err);
    }
    console.log("Succesfully exported the table to S3!");
    callback(null, "success");
  });
};
```

The function code is extremely streamlined and simple to use. Internally, we make use of a third-party npm module called `dynamodbexportcsv` that exports a DynamoDB table's records to a CSV and then writes that to local a file system or streams it to S3 as we are performing in this case. The module calls the `exportTable` function that takes the following parameters to execution:

- **table**: The name of DynamoDB table from which we need to export the contents.
- **columns**: The column name or names from where the data has to be extracted.
- **totalSegments**: The number of parallel scans to run on the table.
- **compressed**: The compresses the CSV file using GZIP compression.

- **filesize**: The maximum size of each file in megabytes. Once a file hits this size it is closed and a new file is created.
- **s3Bucket**: This is the name of the S3 bucket where you wish to stream the CSV file. If no value is provided, the file is streamed to a local directory instead.
- **s3Path**: Used as a prefix for the files created.
- **callback (err)**: A callback which is executed when finished and includes any errors that occurred.

Before we go ahead with the deployments, ensure that you compile the necessary npm modules into the project directory using the following command:

```
# node index.js
```

 To read more about the npm module and how to use it, check out its man page here: `https://www.npmjs.com/package/dynamodbexportcsv`.

With all the preparations completed, you can now go ahead and deploy your function to Lambda using the following command:

```
# apex --env dev deploy myLambdaCWScheduleFuncRole
```

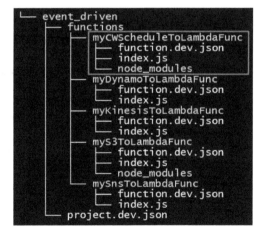

With the function deployed, let us move on the creation of the CloudWatch events that will schedule and execute the functions on our behalf. To do this, log on to the AWS Management Console and select the CloudWatch option from the main page.

In the CloudWatch dashboard, select **CloudWatch Events** to get started. Click on **Create rule** to bring up the scheduler wizard. Here, you can configure a particular event source based on which you would want your function to get triggered. In this case, I've opted to configure a **Schedule** with a **Fixed rate** of execution set as **1** day. You can, optionally, even configure an equivalent cron expression for the same:

With the **Event Source** configured, we move on towards configuring the **Targets** that is, the Lambda functions. From the dropdown list, select **Lambda function** as the **Target**. Next, furnish the necessary details such as the name of the **Function** to trigger, the particular version/ alias of the function that you wish to invoke. Once completed, select **Next** to proceed. In the final step of the wizard, provide a suitable **Name** for the CloudWatch event and make sure to check the **State** option as **Enabled** before creating the rule.

You can now go ahead and run a few tests to make sure the code works as expected. First up, create a DynamoDB Simple Table named **LambdaExportToS3** containing a column called as **username**. Fill out few rows of the column and based on the scheduled time that you have specified during the CloudWatch event rule configuration, the associated Lambda function would then get triggered and export the contents of the table to a CSV in S3.

You can always verify the results by using the Function's CloudWatch Logs as shown as follows:

```
No older events found at the moment. Retry.
2017-04-22T20:56:53.373Z undefined Loading function
START RequestId: 366f4f9f-279e-11e7-8bca-a7dc5830a5a4 Version: $LATEST
2017-04-22T20:57:04.191Z 366f4f9f-279e-11e7-8bca-a7dc5830a5a4 Succesfully exported the table to S3!
END RequestId: 366f4f9f-279e-11e7-8bca-a7dc5830a5a4
REPORT RequestId: 366f4f9f-279e-11e7-8bca-a7dc5830a5a4 Duration: 10817.46 ms Billed Duration: 10900
```

The important point to note here again is that this technique is only going to be useful if you have a few set of records or at least the number of records that a function can consume within its maximum runtime limit of five minutes.

Mapping Lambda with Kinesis

The final use case in this chapter, but an equally interesting one, Kinesis is just one of another AWS services that provides stream based event sources just as we say with DynamoDB.

Kinesis and Lambda have by far the most exhaustive set of real world use cases; from log processing of streams of log data, to transactional processing, social media analytics and much more!

To get started with Kinesis and Lambda, we follow the same pattern as performed for DynamoDB. We start by creating a Kinesis Stream and mapping it to a particular Lambda function. Lambda then polls the stream for any new records and when it gets a new record (either a single record or in the form of a batch) it invokes the mapped function to execute its code. In the following example we will be using Kinesis to Stream Apache web server logs from a dummy EC2 instance. This log data is then processed by our trusty Lambda function that will send email notifications to a particular set of administrators each time an error is found in the Apache logs.

For simplicity, let's break this use case into two parts: the first is where we set up our dummy EC2 instance with Apache, a Kinesis Stream, and a Kinesis Agent, and the second part will contain the Lambda function code and how to deploy and package it using Apex.

Creating the Kinesis Stream

1. From the AWS Management Console or from the AWS CLI create a simple Kinesis Stream with the name `myKinesisStream`. Keep the **Number of shards** to the default value of **1** and create the steam. Make a note of the stream ARN as that will be required in subsequent steps.

2. Next, create a new **SNS Topic** as we performed in the earlier use case, however this time, in the **Create subscription** popup dialog, select the **Protocol** as **Email** as shown in the image below. This will enable our Lambda function to send out email based alerts whenever it gets an error log from our Kinesis Stream:

With this basic setup completed, move on to configuring our EC2 instance to send logs to this stream.

Setting up the log streaming

For this use case, I'll be using a simple EC2 instance with Apache web server installed in it. You could alternatively use any other software so long as it has the ability to produce logs.

1. Install `httpd` package:

   ```
   # sudo yum install httpd
   ```

2. Once the package is installed, edit the `httpd.conf` file to change the `error_log` file location to the `/tmp/` directory:

   ```
   # sudo vi /etc/httpd/conf/httpd.conf
   ```

3. Search for `ErrorLog` and change the path to the `/tmp` directory as shown as follows:

```
ErrorLog /tmp/logs/error_log
```

4. With the changes done, restart the `httpd` service:

```
# sudo service httpd restart
```

5. The next step is to install the Kinesis agent on our instance. You can follow this straight forward link for the same: `https://docs.aws.amazon.com/streams/latest/dev/writing-with-agents.html`.

6. With the agent installed, the only thing left to do is edit the agent's config file so that you can set the file pattern as well as the Kinesis Stream name where the logs will get streamed to:

```
{
  "CloudWatch.emitMetrics": true,
  "kinesis.endpoint": "kinesis.us-east-1.amazonaws.com",
  "flows": [
  {
    "filePattern": "/tmp/logs/error_log",
    "kinesisStream": "myKinesisStream"
  }
  ]
}
```

 Make sure the `kinesis.endpoint` points to the same region where your Lambda functions are going to get created.

7. With all the configurations out of the way, go ahead and start the agent:

```
# sudo kinesis-agent start
```

 Remember, with each change you make in the Kinesis config file, you will need to restart the service once again for the changes to take effect.

8. You can tail the logs of the Kinesis agent:

```
# sudo tail -f /var/log/aws-kinesis-agent/aws-kinesis-agent.log
```

Packaging and uploading the function

With the log server set up along with the Kinesis Stream and the SNS based email notification, we can now move on to packaging and deploying the function using APEX.

Like always, we first start off by creating a directory for our code:

```
# mkdir ~/workdir/apex/event_driven/functions/mykinesisToLambdaFunc
```

Next, we create the `function.dev.json` file that contains few descriptive elements with respect to the function code:

```
{
  "description": "Node.js lambda function using Kinesis streams as
   a trigger to send an sns for error messages received from the
   stream",
  "role": "arn:aws:iam::<account_id>:role/myLambdaKinesisFuncRole",
  "handler": "index.handler",
  "environment": {}
}
```

Don't forget to create the associated `myLambdaKinesisFuncRole` IAM role as well. You can use either the AWS IAM Management Console or the AWS CLI to create this. The role will basically provide our Lambda function with the necessary access rights to describe and get records from the Kinesis Stream, as well as to create and add logs to Amazon CloudWatch and publish email notifications to an SNS topic.

```
{
  "Version": "2012-10-17",
  "Statement": [
  {
    "Sid": "myKinesisPermissions",
    "Effect": "Allow",
    "Action": [
      "kinesis:DescribeStream",
      "kinesis:GetRecords",
      "kinesis:GetShardIterator",
      "kinesis:ListStreams"
    ],
    "Resource": [
      "arn:aws:kinesis:us-east-1:<account_id>:stream/myKinesisStream"
    ]
  },
  {
    "Sid": "myLogsPermissions",
    "Effect": "Allow",
    "Action": [
```

```
        "logs:CreateLogGroup",
        "logs:CreateLogStream",
        "logs:PutLogEvents"
      ],
      "Resource": [
        "*"
      ]
    },
    {
      "Sid": "mySnsPermissions",
      "Effect": "Allow",
      "Action": [
        "sns:Publish"
      ],
      "Resource": [
        "arn:aws:sns:us-east-1:<account_id>:myHTTPSns"
      ]
    }
  ]
}
```

Finally, we create the index.js file that will house the actual function's code. You can download the entire code and its associated support files at https://github.com/PacktPublishing/Mastering-AWS-Lambda.

The only place where you will be required to modify the code is in the handler section where you will have to provide your SNS topic's ARN as shown as follows:

```
exports.handler = function(event, context, callback) {
  event.Records.forEach(function(record) {
    var snsTopicArn = "arn:aws:sns:us-east-1:<account_id>:myHTTPSns";
    // Kinesis data is base64 encoded so decode here
    var payload = new Buffer(record.kinesis.data,
      'base64').toString('ascii');
    console.log("Decoded error log is: ", payload);
    console.log("Sending SNS topic - Alert to xyz@email.com");
    var snsParams = {
      Message: payload, /* required */
      Subject: 'HTTP Error',
      TopicArn: snsTopicArn
    };
```

With all the preparations completed, you can now go ahead and deploy your function to Lambda using the following command:

```
# apex --env dev deploy myKinesisToLambdaFunc
```

Remember to run this command from your project directory, as follows:

```
ubuntu@ip-172-31-21-195:~/workdir/apex/event_driven$ ll
total 16
drwxrwxr-x 3 ubuntu ubuntu 4096 Apr 10 12:12 ./
drwxrwxr-x 3 ubuntu ubuntu 4096 Apr  9 19:51 ../
drwxr-xr-x 6 ubuntu ubuntu 4096 Apr 10 12:12 functions/
-rw-rw-r-- 1 ubuntu ubuntu  285 Apr 10 12:12 project.dev.json
ubuntu@ip-172-31-21-195:~/workdir/apex/event_driven$
ubuntu@ip-172-31-21-195:~/workdir/apex/event_driven$ apex --env dev deploy myKinesisToLambdaFunc
   • creating function         env=dev function=myKinesisToLambdaFunc
   • created alias current     env=dev function=myKinesisToLambdaFunc version=1
   • function created          env=dev function=myKinesisToLambdaFunc name=eventDriven_myKinesisToLambdaFunc version=1
ubuntu@ip-172-31-21-195:~/workdir/apex/event_driven$
```

With the function now deployed, the final step involves setting up the event mapping of your function with the Kinesis Stream. To do so, from the AWS Lambda dashboard, select your newly deployed function and click on the **Triggers** tab. Next, select the **Add trigger** option. This will pop up the **Add trigger** configuration page where just as before, we select the appropriate service we wish to map to this particular Lambda function. Next, provide the details as shown below:

- **Kinesis Stream**: Provide the name of the Kinesis Stream that we created. Remember the stream has to be in the same region as your Lambda function to work.
- **Batchsize**: Keep it to it's default value of 100 for now.
- **Startingposition**: Select **latest** as the starting position.

Remember to select the option **Enable trigger** before completing the trigger configuration.

That's it! We are all ready to test now! Open up a browser window and type in the URL of your Apache web server. You should see the default welcome page. Now, go ahead and type in some additional parameters in the URL that will force the Apache server to send out an error in the logs as shown as follows:

```
                              No older events found at the moment.  Retry.
▶   17:17:14          2017-04-10T11:47:14.652Z undefined Loading function
▶   17:17:14          START RequestId: 16e4849d-4109-405b-9e37-17b5e2cfc20b Version: $LATEST
▼   17:17:14          2017-04-10T11:47:14.664Z 16e4849d-4109-405b-9e37-17b5e2cfc20b Decoded error log is: [Mon Apr 10 11:46:12 2017] [error] [client 52.76.2(

2017-04-10T11:47:14.664Z 16e4849d-4109-405b-9e37-17b5e2cfc20b │Decoded error log is: [Mon Apr 10 11:46:12 2017] [error] [client 52.76.202.190] File does not exist:│
/var/www/html/index4.html


▼   17:17:14          2017-04-10T11:47:14.665Z 16e4849d-4109-405b-9e37-17b5e2cfc20b Sending SNS topic - Alert to xyz@email.com

2017-04-10T11:47:14.665Z 16e4849d-4109-405b-9e37-17b5e2cfc20b │Sending SNS topic - Alert to xyz@email.com│

▼   17:17:18          2017-04-10T11:47:18.385Z 16e4849d-4109-405b-9e37-17b5e2cfc20b SNS sent successfully

2017-04-10T11:47:18.385Z 16e4849d-4109-405b-9e37-17b5e2cfc20b │SNS sent successfully│

▶   17:17:18          END RequestId: 16e4849d-4109-405b-9e37-17b5e2cfc20b
▶   17:17:18          REPORT RequestId: 16e4849d-4109-405b-9e37-17b5e2cfc20b Duration: 3733.35 ms Billed Duration: 3800 ms Memory Size: 128 MB Max Me
                              No newer events found at the moment.  Retry.
```

Each error message that gets streamed triggers the Lambda function to send an email notification to the people who have subscribed to the Topic. In this way, you can leverage Kinesis and Lambda to perform similar tasks on your transactional data, as well as social data for real time analytics.With this we come towards the end of this chapter.

Extending AWS Lambda with External Services

18

In the previous chapter, we learned how to leverage and execute few Lambda functions based on triggers. However, one key aspect of that chapter was that the events were generated by sources or services residing within AWS. But, what if the triggers are generated by an external service provider or a third-party tool? Is Lambda even capable of handling such external services and events? Well, that's exactly what we are going to discuss and talk about in this chapter!

In this chapter, we will be covering the following topics:

- Understanding the concept of Webhooks and how they can be used to trigger Lambda functions remotely
- Triggering Lambda functions with the help of a few commonly used third-party tools and services, such as Git, Teamwork, and Slack
- Triggering Lambda functions from an external application

Introducing Webhooks

Webhooks are simple callbacks that are rapidly growing in popularity with a lot of developers. Webhooks work in a very similar way to Lambda functions; they are invoked when a particular event is fired by an application on the web. This makes them highly applicable to a variety of web development use cases where, rather than having a traditional API that polls for data on a frequent basis, you use a Webhook to get data at real time.

With most APIs there's a request followed by a response, whereas in the case of Webhooks, they simply send the data whenever it's available.

The way a Webhook works is quite simple! To use a Webhook, you register a URL with the Webhook provider, for example IFTTT or Zapier. The URL is a place within your application that will accept the data and do something with it. In some cases, you can tell the provider the situations when you'd like to receive data. Whenever there's something new, the Webhook will send it to your URL.

Here's a common example of a Webhook--open up any of your GitHub pages from your browser. There, in your repository's **Setting** page, you will see a **Webhooks** section as shown in the following image. You can always add a new Webhook to your repository by selecting the **Add webhook** option. There, you can provide a URL that will receive an event each time you either push or commit code into your repository and so on. On the event getting triggered, GitHub sends a POST request to the URL with details of the subscribed events. You can also specify which data format you would like to receive the request in, for example, JSON or `x-www-form-urlencoded`. In this way, you can easily create open ended integrations with other arbitrary web services without having to spin up any new infrastructure or manage any complex code integrations as well.

This is the exact same case that we are going to explore and learn about in this chapter. We will learn how to effectively use Webhooks to hook into third-party services and sites, and trigger some Lambda action on it's behalf. Since we have already taken up the topic of GitHub, let us look at how Lambda, Webhooks and a GitHub repository can be tied together functionally with minimal efforts.

Integrating GitHub with AWS Lambda

Before we begin with the actual integration, let us take some time to understand the purpose of this particular use case. For starters, we will be using two third-party tools, namely GitHub and Teamwork. For those of you who don't know or haven't used Teamwork before; it is basically a productivity and communication tool that helps with project management activities. You can read up more about Teamwork here at `https://www.teamwork.com/`.

The end goal of this exercise is to simulate the automated creation tasks in Teamwork each time a new issue is created in GitHub with the help of AWS Lambda. So, each issue created will in turn create a corresponding task in our Teamwork project for the team to work on:

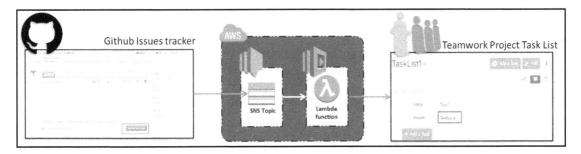

To begin with ,you will require a GitHub account along with a Teamwork account. You can sign up for a Teamwork account for 30 days absolutely free of charge. So, without further ado, let's get started!

The first step that we are going to start off with is the creation of an SNS topic. Why SNS? Well, it's simple. Lambda functions do not have an endpoint or unique URL on which we can send event payloads, and hence we need an AWS service that provides some form of notification services that other third-party services like GitHub can subscribe to, but also can be used as a trigger in combination with Lambda--enter SNS!

Following are steps to create a topic:

1. Log in to the AWS Management Console and select the **SNS** service from the main landing page.
2. Next, create a simple topic by selecting the **Topics** option from the navigation pane to the left of the SNS dashboard.

3. Click on **Create topic** and fill out the **Topic name** and **Display name** for your topic in the popup dialog box. Click **Create topic** once done.

4. Select the newly created topic and make a note of its **Topic ARN**:

With the SNS created, we move ahead with the next step of creating a separate user which will be used to publish messages from GitHub to our SNS topic:

1. From the IAM console, select the **Users** option from the panel. Click on the **Add user** option.

2. Provide the user's name and make sure to check the **Programmatic access** checkbox before you proceed any further with the wizard.

3. Once done, click on **Next** and it will ask you for permissions to be given to this user. Click on the **Create Policy** option. Provide the policy with a suitable **Name** and **Description**.

4. Paste the following code in the policy window. Make sure to edit the **Resource** field with the correct SNS ARN:

```
{
  "Version": "2012-10-17",
  "Statement": [
  {
    "Sid": "mySnsPermissions",
    "Effect": "Allow",
    "Action": [
      "sns:Publish"
    ],
    "Resource": [
      "arn:aws:sns:us-east-1:<account-id>:myGitSNS"
    ]
  }
  ]
}
```

5. With the policy created, go back to **IAM User Permissions** and choose the **Attach existing policies** option and select the policy we just created. Complete the user creation process by reviewing the user settings and selecting the **Create user** option.

With the basics configured, let us now focus our attention to configuring the GitHub repository.

Login into your GitHub account and select your repository for which you wish to enable the integration:

1. Go to the **Settings** tab in your repository and, from the left-hand side panel, select the **Integration and services** option.
2. Click on **Add service** and select **Amazon SNS** option as shown in the following screenshot:

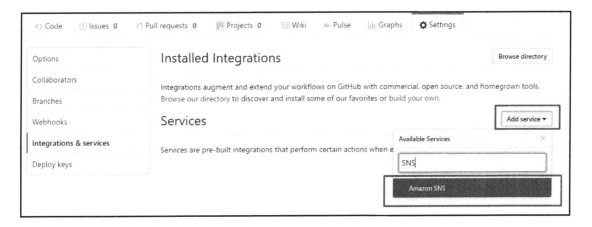

3. In the **Add service** dialog box, provide the AWS GitHub user's **Aws key**, **SNS topic** ARN, and **Sns region** details. Once done, click on **Add service**. Make sure the **Active** checkbox is selected before you add the service. This will enable the service to run when a corresponding trigger is invoked.

An important point to note here is that the service integration responds only to push events, however, we need responses for any **Issues** and **Pull request** events as well. For that, we will have to create a hook using *GitHub API*. Here is a simple Node.js script which will create the hook for us in our repository, but before we do that we will need a GitHub **Personal access tokens** to be able to authenticate and create the hook. For this, follow these simple steps from your GitHub account:

1. Go to your GitHub **Settings**. On the left hand-side panel, you will see **Personal access tokens**. Click on **Generate new token** as shown in the following screenshot:

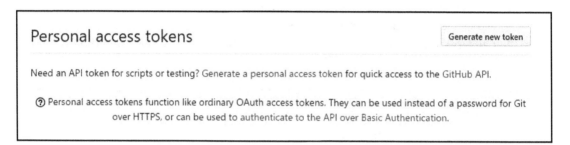

2. In the next dialog box, provide a suitable description for the token and select **repo** and **gist** options from the list of scopes. Once completed, you will receive the token from GitHub. Make sure you save it safely somewhere!

Creating the hook Node.js code:

```
var GitHubApi = require("github") // npm i github
var github = new GitHubApi({version: "3.0.0"})
var gitToken = process.env.gitToken;
github.authenticate({type:"oauth", token: gitToken})
github.repos.createHook({
  owner : process.env.owner,
  user: process.env.user,
  repo: process.env.repoName,
  name: "amazonsns",
  config: {
    "aws_key": process.env.awsAccessKey,
    "aws_secret": process.env.awsSecretKey,
    "sns_topic": process.env.snsTopicARN,
    "sns_region": process.env.AWS_SNS_REGION || "us-east-1"
  },
  events: ["pull_request", "issues"]
}, function(err, result) {
console.log(arguments)
});
```

The code is pretty self-explanatory. All we have done is added all the variable details like `aws_key`, `gitToken`, and so on as environment variables for our function. We have also used the `createHook` call and in the events, we have passed the `pull request` and `issues` objects to the same.

With this step completed, we now move on to creating the all-important lambda function. Start by creating a role for our function:

```
{
  "Version": "2012-10-17",
  "Statement": [
  {
    "Sid": "myLogsPermissions",
    "Effect": "Allow",
    "Action": [
      "logs:CreateLogGroup",
      "logs:CreateLogStream",
      "logs:PutLogEvents"
    ],
    "Resource": [
      "*"
    ]
  },
  {
    "Sid": "myKMSPermissions",
    "Effect": "Allow",
    "Action": [
      "kms:Decrypt"
    ],
    "Resource": [
      "*"
    ]
  }
  ]
}
```

The role is basically required for two things--adding the function's logs to CloudWatch and decrypting the API key that we will be using to create tasks in Teamwork.

Why encrypt the keys in the first place? Since API keys are sensitive data, we will be encrypting those using KMS keys and then decrypt the same key in our code before using it. This is more or less a best practice when it comes to handling keys in Lambda functions. Once the role is created, make a note of it's ARN value.

As we have been using APEX till now to create our Lambda functions, we will use APEX once again to create this Lambda function too.

To get started, create the necessary project directory folder for APEX:

```
# mkdir ~/workdir/apex/event_driven/functions/myGitAWSIntegration
```

Next, we create the necessary `function.dev.json` file that contains few descriptive elements with respect to the function code:

```
{
  "description": "Node.js lambda function to show integration
    between Git and lambda via SNS service",
  "role": "arn:aws:iam::<accountid>:role/myGitRole",
  "handler": "index.handler",
  "environment": {
    "kmsEncryptedAPIKey" : "<your API key>",
    "taskListID" : "<Task List ID>",
    "teamworkCompany" : "<Teamwork company name>"
  }
}
```

You can obtain the `taskListID` by searching the in the URL of our Teamwork webpage

Next, we create the `index.js` file that will house the actual function's code. You can download the entire code and it's associated support files from `https://github.com/PacktPublishing/Mastering-AWS-Lambda`.

The code has two parts--a `handler` function and a `createTask` function.

The `handler` function first checks whether the trigger was for an *issue* or something else. If it was for an *issue* then it checks whether the KMS encrypted API key is present or not. If yes, then it decrypts it and sends the event and the API key to the `createTask` function:

```
'use strict';
const request = require('request');
const AWS = require('aws-sdk');
const company = process.env.teamworkCompany;
const kmsEncryptedAPIKey = process.env.kmsEncryptedAPIKey;
const taskListID = process.env.taskListID;
let teamworkAPIKey;
exports.handler = function(event, context, callback) {
  var githubEvent = JSON.parse(event.Records[0].Sns.Message);
```

```
console.log('Received GitHub event:', githubEvent);
if (!githubEvent.hasOwnProperty('issue') || githubEvent.action
 !== 'opened') {
  // Not an event for opening an issue
  console.log("Event isn't for issue opening!");
  callback(null, "Event isn't for issue opening!");
}
else{
  // Event for opening an issue
  console.log("Issue was opened!");
  if(teamworkAPIKey){
    // Container re-use
    createTask(githubEvent, callback);
  }
  else if (kmsEncryptedAPIKey && kmsEncryptedAPIKey !==
   '<kmsEncryptedAPIKey>') {
    const encryptedBuf = new Buffer(kmsEncryptedAPIKey, 'base64');
    const cipherText = { CiphertextBlob: encryptedBuf };
    const kms = new AWS.KMS();
    kms.decrypt(cipherText, (err, data) => {
      if (err) {
        console.log('Decrypt error:', err);
        return callback(err);
      }
      teamworkAPIKey = data.Plaintext.toString('ascii');
      createTask(githubEvent, callback);
    });
  }
  else{
    console.error("API Key has not been set.");
    callback("API Key has not been set.");
  }
 }
};
```

Now, the `createTask` function takes the event and the API key, forms the request URL to be hit, and sends a POST request to the Teamwork API. Using this, it creates the corresponding task in Teamwork which our project team can work on:

```
function createTask(githubEvent, callback){
  let taskName = githubEvent.issue.title;
  let path = "/tasklists/" + taskListID + "/tasks.json";
  let date = new Date();
  let month = date.getMonth();
  let day = date.getDate();
  let endDate = date.getFullYear() + ((month+2) < 10 ? '0' : '')
   + (month+2) + (day < 10 ? '0' : '') + day;
  let startDate = date.getFullYear() + ((month+1) < 10 ? '0' : '')
```

```
    + (month+1) + (day < 10 ? '0' : '') + day;
let base64 = new Buffer(teamworkAPIKey + ":xxx").toString("base64");
let json = {"todo-item": {"content": taskName,
 "startdate": startDate, "enddate": endDate }};
let options = {
  uri: "https://"+ company + ".teamwork.com" + path,
  hostname: company + ".teamwork.com",
  method: "POST",
  encoding: "utf8",
  followRedirect: true,
  headers: {
    "Authorization": "BASIC " + base64,
    "Content-Type": "application/json"
  },
  json: json
};
request(options, function (error, res, body) {
  if(error){
    console.error("Request Error: " + error);
    callback(error);
  }
  else{
    console.log("STATUS: " + res.statusCode);
    res.setEncoding("utf8");
    console.log("body: " + body);
    callback(null, "Task Created!");
  }
});
}
```

As you can see, our code has used some of the environment variables, so don't forget to add those to the `function.dev.json` file's `environment` section as shown in the following snippet:

```
"environment": {
  "kmsEncryptedAPIKey" : "<your API key>",
  "taskListID" : "<you Task List ID>",
  "teamworkCompany" : "<your company>"
}
```

Next, deploy the function to Lambda using the `apex deploy` command:

```
# apex deploy --env dev myGitAWSIntegration
```

With the function deployed, log in to the AWS Lambda web console and verify whether the environment variables were added successfully or not. Click on the **Enable encryption helpers** checkbox and encrypt the `kmsEncryptedAPIKey` key value as shown in the following screenshot:

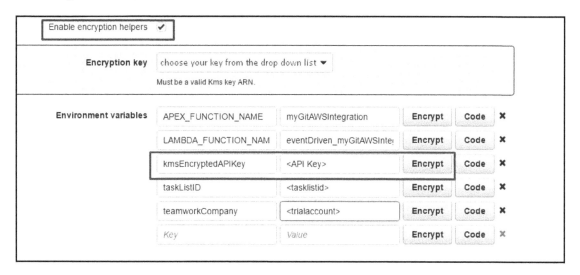

TO create your own KMS key, visit `http://docs.aws.amazon.com/lambda/latest/dg/tutorial-env_console.html`.

With the function deployed, go ahead and configure the SNS trigger for the function. Select the **Trigger** tab from the AWS Lambda console, select the **SNS** service from the trigger and populate the **SNS topic** field with the SNS we created in our earlier steps. Remember to check the **Enable trigger** option before you click on **Submit**:

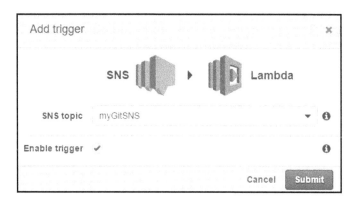

If you made it this far, then the only thing left is to test the setup! Go ahead and create an issue in your GitHub repository. If all settings were done correctly, you should have a new task created within Teamwork, as shown in the following screenshot:

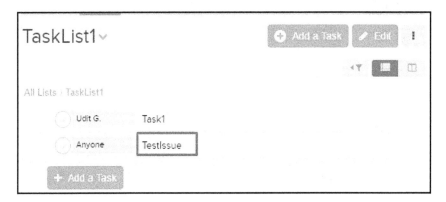

You can use a similar setup to trigger actions from GitHub to other services, such as Jenkins, for triggering automated code builds and deploys as well.

In the next use case, we are going to explore yet another very commonly used team collaboration and communication tool that uses interactive notifications to inform us of the health of our EC2 instances.

Integrating Slack with AWS Lambda

I'm a big fan of Slack and have been using it for quite some time now. It's perhaps one of the trendiest collaboration tools, just because of it's intuitiveness and ability to program things around it! Perhaps that's why this particular use case is also one of my favorites. In this scenario, we will be using Slack as our custom EC2 alerting dashboard by integrating it with AWS Lambda and a few other services. The alerts will be sent out to a custom made Slack channel that the IT team will use to track alerts and other important notifications.

In a broader sense, here are the list of things that we plan to do for this activity:

- Create SNS topic which will act as the Lambda trigger.
- Create a CloudWatch alarm for one of our EC2 machines. Say if CPU utilization goes higher than 80% then, trigger the alarm.
- The CloudWatch alarm will post the notification to an SNS topic.

- The SNS topic will act as a trigger to our Lambda function.
- As soon as the Lambda function gets a trigger, it will post the notification to our Slack channel.

Sounds simple? Let's get down to implementing it then.

We will once again begin by creating an SNS topic which will act as a trigger for the Lambda function. A CloudWatch alarm would hit this SNS topic which will in turn set in motion the Lambda function that publishes the CloudWatch alert on Slack.

Go ahead and create another simple SNS topic as we did in our earlier use case. Once completed, make a note of the SNS topic's ARN as well. In this case, our SNS is configured to send a simple notification to an IT admin email alias.

Next up, we create our CloudWatch alarm. To do so, select the **CloudWatch** service from the AWS Management Console and click on **Alarms** in the left-hand side panel. Select the option **Create alarm** to get started.

Since we will be monitoring the EC2 instances in our environment, I've gone ahead and selected the **EC2 Metrics** option. Alternatively, you can select any other metric, as per your requirements.

In our case, we have gone ahead and configured a simple **CPUUtilization** alarm as shown in the following screenshot:

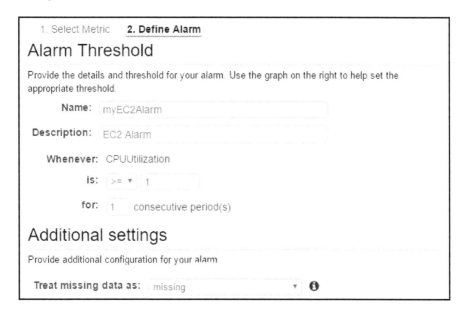

Make sure to set up a notification for the alerts and point it to the newly created SNS topic as shown in the following screenshot:

Once the alarm is created, it will show up as it's in **OK** state in CloudWatch's dashboard.

Next, we need to configure a Slack channel where the notifications will be posted. For that we will need an incoming Webhook to be set and a hook URL that will be used to post the notifications. To do so, go to your Slack team's settings page and select the **Apps & integrations** option as shown in the following screenshot:

Once you click on **Apps & integrations**, it will take you to a new page of apps. Search for `Incoming` and select the **Incoming WebHooks** from the options that show up.

Next, click on **Add Configuration**. It will ask you to select the channel to post to along with a few other necessary parameters. Make sure to copy and save the *Webhook URL* before you proceed any further with the next steps.

Now that we have our Slack hook URL ready, we can finally get started with deploying our Lambda function. Since the hook URL is sensitive data, we will be encrypting it the same way we did in the earlier use case and then decrypt it in our code before using it. For this exercise, we will be using an existing AWS Lambda function blueprint designed for Slack integration using Node.js 4.3 version.

Since we already have the AWS template, here is a quick explanation of what it does.

The code has three functions: `handler`, `processEvent`, and `postMessage`.

The `handler` function is where the execution will start. It checks whether the KMS encrypted key is present or not. If yes, it decrypts it and forms the hook URL.

After that, it calls the `processEvent` function:

```
const AWS = require('aws-sdk');
const url = require('url');
const https = require('https');
// The base-64 encoded, encrypted key (CiphertextBlob) stored in the
  kmsEncryptedHookUrl environment variable
const kmsEncryptedHookUrl = process.env.kmsEncryptedHookUrl;
// The Slack channel to send a message to stored in the slackChannel
  environment variable
const slackChannel = process.env.slackChannel;
let hookUrl;
exports.handler = (event, context, callback) => {
  console.log("EVENT: ", JSON.stringify(event));
    if (hookUrl) {
      // Container reuse, simply process the event with the key
      in memory
      processEvent(event, callback);
    }
    else if (kmsEncryptedHookUrl && kmsEncryptedHookUrl !==
    '<kmsEncryptedHookUrl>') {
      const encryptedBuf = new Buffer(kmsEncryptedHookUrl, 'base64');
      const cipherText = { CiphertextBlob: encryptedBuf };
      const kms = new AWS.KMS();
      kms.decrypt(cipherText, (err, data) => {
        if (err) {
          console.log('Decrypt error:', err);
          return callback(err);
        }
        hookUrl = `https://${data.Plaintext.toString('ascii')}`;
```

```
      processEvent(event, callback);
    });
  }
  else {
    callback('Hook URL has not been set.');
  }
};
```

Now, the `processEvent` function extracts the required information from the event and forms the Slack message that's going to be posted on the Slack channel. Once the message is formed, it calls the `postMessage` function:

```
function processEvent(event, callback) {
  const message = JSON.parse(event.Records[0].Sns.Message);
  const alarmName = message.AlarmName;
  const newState = message.NewStateValue;
  const reason = message.NewStateReason;
  const slackMessage = {
    channel: slackChannel,
    text: `${alarmName} state is now ${newState}: ${reason}`,
  };
  console.log("slack msg: ", slackMessage);
  postMessage(slackMessage, (response) => {
    if (response.statusCode < 400) {
      console.info('Message posted successfully');
      callback(null);
    }
    else if (response.statusCode < 500) {
      console.error(`Error posting message to Slack API:
        ${response.statusCode} - ${response.statusMessage}`);
      callback(null);
      // Don't retry because the error is due to a problem with
      the request
    }
    else {
      // Let Lambda retry
      callback(`Server error when processing message:
       ${response.statusCode} - ${response.statusMessage}`);
    }
  });
}
```

The `postMessage` function uses the `https` and `url` npm modules to form the `options` to hit the Slack URL. We are doing a `POST` request in this case. The syntax of these modules is very simple and can be obtained from the documentation itself:

```
function postMessage(message, callback) {
  const body = JSON.stringify(message);
  const options = url.parse(hookUrl);
  options.method = 'POST';
  options.headers = {
    'Content-Type': 'application/json',
    'Content-Length': Buffer.byteLength(body),
  };
  //console.log("options: ", options);
  const postReq = https.request(options, (res) => {
    const chunks = [];
    res.setEncoding('utf8');
    res.on('data', (chunk) => chunks.push(chunk));
    res.on('end', () => {
      if (callback) {
        callback({
          body: chunks.join(''),
          statusCode: res.statusCode,
          statusMessage: res.statusMessage,
        });
      }
    });
    return res;
  });
  postReq.write(body);
  postReq.end();
}
```

The function takes two environment variables: `hookUrl` and the slack channel name. Add those to the `function.dev.json` file. Also, make sure the hook's URL environment variables in `function.dev.json` file doesn't contain the `https` protocol appended to it:

```
{
  "description": "Node.js lambda function to show integration
    between lambda and Slack via SNS service",
  "role": "arn:aws:iam::<account_id>:role/mySlackBotRole",
  "handler": "index.handler",
  "environment": {
    "slackChannel" : "<channel name>",
    "kmsEncryptedHookUrl" : "<slack_hook_url_without_protocol>"
  }
}
```

As we have been following APEX to deploy Lambda functions, we will be doing the same this time too. First, let's create a role for the Lambda function to assume when it executes:

```
{
  "Version": "2012-10-17",
  "Statement": [
    {
      "Sid": "myLogsPermissions",
      "Effect": "Allow",
      "Action": [
        "logs:CreateLogGroup",
        "logs:CreateLogStream",
        "logs:PutLogEvents"
      ],
      "Resource": [
        "*"
      ]
    },
    {
      "Sid": "myKMSPermissions",
      "Effect": "Allow",
      "Action": [
        "kms:Decrypt"
      ],
      "Resource": [
        "*"
      ]
    }
  ]
}
```

With the role created, we are now ready to deploy the Lambda function using APEX.

Run the following command to get the deployment started:

```
# apex deploy --env dev mySlackLambdaIntegration
```

Once the function is deployed, using the **Lambda Management Console**, encrypt the hookURL environment variable just as we performed in the earlier use case. Review the configurations and remember to **Save** your changes:

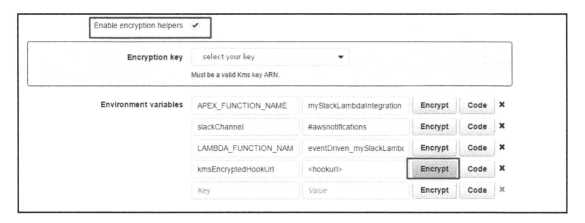

With the function ready to deploy, you can now go ahead and configure the function's trigger using the **Trigger** tab from the **Lambda Management Console**. Select the **SNS** service and make sure you populate the correct **SNS topic** for this exercise as created earlier. Don't forget the check the **Enable trigger** checkbox before selecting **Submit**.

Now our function and Slack integration is ready and primed! All that is required is increasing the CPU load on our EC2 instance and we should start getting custom alert notifications on our Slack channel. In our case, we used an open source CPU load testing tool called as **stress** to generate a synthetic load on our instance. When the CloudWatch alarm thresholds were crossed, the alert was triggered from CloudWatch and the corresponding SNS event was generated. The SNS triggered Lambda to publish the alert to our Slack channel as depicted in the following screenshot:

You can use a similar set of notifications and alert mechanisms to provide your IT admins with a more intuitive and customizable response rather than the traditional alerting via email approach.

Invoking Lambda using an external application

So far, we have seen how to integrate third-party services such as GitHub and Slack with Lambda functions. In this section, we will be looking into yet another simple example where an application is used to invoke a particular Lambda function.

The use case is pretty straightforward--we have a simple Node.js application that accepts any city's name as a parameter and as a response, provides you with the detailed weather conditions of that city. The city name is passed to the Lambda function in the form of an event using SNS. Once the event is provided to the function, it makes a call to an open sourced API called as `openweather` by passing the city name as a parameter. The API in turn returns the current temperature as well as other miscellaneous weather details of that city. If the current temperature of the city is greater than say 25 degrees, the function automatically sends a customized SNS email to the specific user. Sounds simple? Then let's see how it all fits together.

> To learn more about the `openweather` API and how to use it, check out it's main documentation at `https://openweathermap.org/api`.

Once again, like all our examples, we will begin by creating a simple SNS topic for our Lambda functions to send the email notifications out. Make sure you copy the ARN of the SNS topic as we will be requiring that in the later steps.

With the SNS topic created, let us go ahead and create the Lambda function. First up, creating the IAM role for our function to execute.

Here is the role:

```
{
  "Version": "2012-10-17",
  "Statement": [
  {
    "Sid": "myLogsPermissions",
    "Effect": "Allow",
    "Action": [
      "logs:CreateLogGroup",
      "logs:CreateLogStream",
      "logs:PutLogEvents"
    ],
    "Resource": [
      "*"
```

```
      ]
    },
    {
      "Sid": "myKMSPermissions",
      "Effect": "Allow",
      "Action": [
        "kms:Decrypt"
      ],
      "Resource": [
        "*"
      ]
    },
    {
      "Sid": "mySNSPermissions",
      "Effect": "Allow",
      "Action": [
        "sns:Publish"
      ],
      "Resource": [
        "arn:aws:sns:us-east-1:<account-id>:myWeatherSNS"
      ]
    }
    ]
}
```

As you can see we have logs permissions, as usual, but we also have KMS decrypt along with SNS publish permissions. Since the code uses the `openweather` API, we will be requiring an API key for the same. So just as we did in our previous use cases, we are encrypting the API key and then decrypting it by our code before using it.

> The SNS publish permission is present because we will be publishing an SNS to the email address if the temperature is greater than 25 degrees Celsius.

Next, create a new folder structure for our new Lambda function and copy the following contents into the `function.dev.json` file:

```
{
  "description": "Node.js lambda function to show lambda invocation
    from a custom application",
  "role": "arn:aws:iam::<account-id>:role/myWeatherLambdaRole",
  "handler": "index.handler",
  "environment": {
    "snsTopicARN": "arn:aws:sns:us-east-1:<account-id>:myWeatherSNS",
    "kmsEncryptedAPIKey": "<API key>",
    "language" : "en",
```

```
    "units" : "metric"
  }
}
```

Finally, go ahead and create the `index.js` file that will house the code that will pass the `city` parameter to the `openweather` API. The code is divided into two functions--one is the `handler` function and the other is the `processEvent` function.

The `handler` function first checks whether the encrypted API key is present or not. If it is, then it decrypts the key and sends the event for further processing to the `processEvent` function. The `processEvent` function then takes the event which has the city name mentioned and gets the required info using the `openweather` API. It also checks whether the temperature of that particular city is greater than 25 degrees Celsius or not. If it is, then it will send an SNS alert to the subscribed SNS topic.

```
'use strict';
const weather = require('openweather-apis');
const AWS = require('aws-sdk');
const sns = new AWS.SNS({apiVersion: '2010-03-31'});
const kmsEncryptedAPIKey = process.env.kmsEncryptedAPIKey;
const snsTopicARN = process.env.snsTopicARN;
let language = process.env.language;
let units = process.env.units;
let apiKey;

function processEvent(event, callback) {
  let city = event.city;
  weather.setAPPID(apiKey);
  weather.setLang(language);
  weather.setUnits(units);
  weather.setCity(city);
  weather.getSmartJSON(function(err, smart){
    if(err){
      console.log("An error occurred: ", err);
      callback(err);
    }
    else{
      if(Number(smart.temp) > 25){
        console.log("Temperature is greater than 25 degree celsius!!");
        let snsParams = {
          Message: "Its Hot outside!! Avoid wearing too many layers!
          WEATHER UPDATE: "+ JSON.stringify(smart),
          Subject: 'WEATHER UPDATE',
          TopicArn: snsTopicARN
        };
        sns.publish(snsParams, function(snsErr, data) {
          if (snsErr){
```

```
          console.log("An error occurred while sending SNS Alert:
            "+snsErr, snsErr.stack); // an error occurred
          callback(snsErr);
        }
        else{
          console.log("SNS Alert sent successfully:
            ", snsParams.Message); // successful response
          callback(null, "Done");
        }
      });
    }
    else{
      console.log("WEATHER UPDATE: ", smart);
      callback(null, "Done");
    }
  }
  });
}

exports.handler = function(event, context, callback) {
  //var weatherEvent = JSON.parse(event);
  console.log('Received custom event:', event);
  if (apiKey) {
   // Container reuse, simply process the event with the key in memory
    processEvent(event, callback);
  }
  else if (kmsEncryptedAPIKey && kmsEncryptedAPIKey
   !== '<kmsEncryptedAPIKey>') {
    const encryptedBuf = new Buffer(kmsEncryptedAPIKey, 'base64');
    const cipherText = { CiphertextBlob: encryptedBuf };
    const kms = new AWS.KMS();
    kms.decrypt(cipherText, (err, data) => {
      if (err) {
        console.log('Decrypt error:', err);
        return callback(err);
      }
      apiKey = data.Plaintext.toString('ascii');
      processEvent(event, callback);
    });
  }
  else {
    callback('API Key has not been set.');
  }
};
```

Make sure to run the following command before you deploy the function to Lambda. Since the code uses the `openweather-apis` npm module, you will also need to install the same locally:

```
# npm install -save openweather-apis
```

With the function and it's necessary dependencies sorted out, go ahead and upload the package using the following command:

```
# apex deploy --env dev myCustomAppToLambda
```

The following screenshot shows the output for the preceding command:

```
ubuntu@ip-172-31-21-195:~/workdir/apex/event_driven$
ubuntu@ip-172-31-21-195:~/workdir/apex/event_driven$ apex deploy --env dev myCustomAppToLambda
  • creating function          env=dev function=myCustomAppToLambda
  • created alias current      env=dev function=myCustomAppToLambda version=1
  • function created           env=dev function=myCustomAppToLambda name=eventDriven_myCustomAppToLambd
a version=1
ubuntu@ip-172-31-21-195:~/workdir/apex/event_driven$
```

With the function deployed, you will need to enable the encryption enablers for encrypting the API key using the Lambda Management Console. Select the checkbox **Enable encryption helpers** and encrypt the API key as shown in the following screenshot:

Remember to save the changes before proceeding further with the configurations.

Now that our function is in place, we need to create our custom application and invoke the Lambda function from it. The application will simply accept a parameter (city) from the user and invoke the function with the following event in JSON format:

```
{
  "city":"<city_entered_by_user>"
}
```

The code is really simple to understand. We are will be using an npm module named prompt which will help us prompt our users to enter a city name and then we send it to our Lambda function using the invoke function from the AWS SDK itself.

 The only required parameter is the function name; the rest all are optional. You can read more about this from the AWS SDK documentation.

```
const AWS = require('aws-sdk');
AWS.config.update({
  region: 'us-east-1',
  maxRetries: 20
});
const lambda = new AWS.Lambda({apiVersion: '2015-03-31'});
const prompt = require('prompt');
console.log("Greetings!!");
console.log("Please enter the city name for weather updates.");
// Start the prompt
prompt.start();
// Get city
prompt.get(['city'], function (err, result) {
  // Log the results
  console.log('Command-line input received:');
  console.log('city: ' + result.city);
  // Create lambda event
  var event = "{\"city\":\""+ result.city + "\"}";
  // Form lambda params
  var params = {
    FunctionName: "<lambda_function_name>", /* required */
    InvocationType: "Event",
    Payload: event
  };
  // invoke lambda function
  lambda.invoke(params, function(err, data) {
    if (err) console.log(err, err.stack); // an error occurred
    else console.log(data);               // successful response
```

```
        });
});
```

With the application created, simply run it using the following command:

```
# node weatherApp.js
```

When prompted, type in the city name for which you would like to check the weather. In our case, we have given the city as `Mumbai` as it's really nice and hot during the summers.

You can verify the output of the application's output by viewing the CloudWatch Logs for the same:

2017-05-21	
	No older events found at the moment. Retry.
▶ 23:43:09	START RequestId: 24ad0060-3e51-11e7-a704-cb4965690426 Version: $LATEST
▶ 23:43:09	2017-05-21T18:13:09.576Z 24ad0060-3e51-11e7-a704-cb4965690426 Received custom event: { city: 'mumbai' }
▶ 23:43:10	2017-05-21T18:13:10.613Z 24ad0060-3e51-11e7-a704-cb4965690426 Temperature is greater than 25 degree celsius!!
▼ 23:43:10	2017-05-21T18:13:10.978Z 24ad0060-3e51-11e7-a704-cb4965690426 SNS Alert sent successfully: Its Hot outside!! Avoid wearing too many

```
2017-05-21T18:13:10.978Z 24ad0060-3e51-11e7-a704-cb4965690426 SNS Alert sent successfully: Its Hot outside!! Avoid wearing too many layers! WEATHER UPDATE:
{
    "temp": 28.84,
    "humidity": 97,
    "pressure": 1020.22,
    "description": "clear sky",
    "weathercode": 800,
    "rain": 0
}
```

▶ 23:43:11	END RequestId: 24ad0060-3e51-11e7-a704-cb4965690426
▶ 23:43:11	REPORT RequestId: 24ad0060-3e51-11e7-a704-cb4965690426 Duration: 1430.97 ms Billed Duration: 1500 ms Memory Size: 128 MB Max
	No newer events found at the moment. Retry.

Also, since you can see that the temperature is greater than 25 in Mumbai, we received an email stating the same! The following screenshot depicts this:

In this way, you can also create custom applications and integrate them with SNS and Lambda functions to perform some backend processing. With this use case, we come towards the end of this chapter.

19
Build and Deploy Serverless Applications with AWS Lambda

In the previous chapter, we saw how easy it is to build and integrate your applications and third party services with AWS Lambda functions. In this chapter, we will be taking things up a notch by learning how to design and build simple serverless applications with Lambda and a few other AWS services in the form of **Serverless Application Model** (**SAM**) and a newly launched service called as Step Functions.

In this chapter we will be learning:

- What the SAM template is and how to build serverless applications with it
- Using SAM to build and deploy serverless applications using simple examples
- Introducing AWS step functions
- Building coordinated Lambda services using step function's visual workflows

So without any further delays, let's get started!

Introducing SAM

The story of SAM starts back with few of the caveats faced by AWS CloudFormations. Although immensely powerful in it's automated infrastructure deployment capabilities, CloudFormations is still a tool that's not that easy to work with and maintain. A simple infrastructure deployment template can range anywhere from a 100 lines to even a 1,000 lines depending on the way the template is authored. More so, CloudFormation lacked the specialized resource types optimized for defining serverless applications which is why project Flourish was established which later on became known as SAM.

SAM is an extension of CloudFormation and basically provides developers with a really simplified way of writing CloudFormation-like templates for serverless services such as API Gateway, DynamoDB and even Lambda.

 NOTE: SAM is released under the Apache 2.0 License

The main goal of SAM is to define a standard application model for serverless applications which in turn helps developers design, deploy, and manage these applications using CloudFormation templates.

SAM is structured similarly to CloudFormation and just like it's counterpart, provides template support using both JSON and YAML. You can easily define and create S3 buckets to store the individual Lambda function deployment packages, create an API Gateway with the necessary configurations, create Simple DBs, configure SNS notifications, and much more using simple **commandlets** that make it far easier to read and manage your templates.

Writing SAM templates

Before we get going with writing our own SAM templates, it is important to understand a few SAM terms and terminologies. For starters; SAM is built on top of the standard CloudFormation service itself, so most of the SAM templates are nothing more than simplified CloudFormation templates that you can deploy just as you would deploy a standard CloudFormation stack! Even the concepts of resources, parameters, properties, and so on are all reused in SAM as well. The main difference however, is that simplified support for serverless AWS services namely API Gateway, Lambda functions, and DynamoDB makes these templates far easier to write and maintain than traditional CloudFormation ones.

Writing a SAM template starts off just as any other CloudFormation template does, with an `AWSTemplateFormatVersion` followed by a transform section that is specific to SAM. The transform section takes a value of `AWS::Serverless-2016-10-31` as shown in the snippet below:

```
AWSTemplateFormatVersion: '2010-09-09'
Transform: 'AWS::Serverless-2016-10-31'
```

After the transform section, you can have the resources section where you can define one or more serverless resource types. While writing this book, SAM supports three resource types namely:

- AWS::Serverless::Function
- AWS::Serverless::Api
- AWS::Serverless::SimpleTable

AWS::Serverless::Function

The AWS::Serverless::Function resource type is used to define and create Lambda functions and it's associated event source mappings which trigger the function.

Consider the flowing example snippet for creating a simple Lambda function using SAM:

```
Handler: index.js
Runtime: nodejs4.3
CodeUri: 's3://myS3Bucket/function.zip'
Description: A simple function for demonstrating SAM
MemorySize: 128
Timeout: 15
Policies:
  - LambdaFunctionExecutePolicy
  - Version: '2012-10-17'
    Statement:
      - Effect: Allow
        Action:
          - s3:GetObject
          - s3:GetObjectACL
        Resource: 'arn:aws:s3:::myS3Bucket/*'
Environment:
  Variables:
    key1: Hello
    key2: World
```

From the following snippet, most of the properties should be well known by now, including the Handler, Runtime, MemorySize, Timeout, and so on. The CodeUri refers to the S3 URI or any other valid location from where SAM will obtain the Lambda function for deployment. It's important to note, however, that this has to be a packaged Lambda function (.zip) even if it contains just a single index.js file.

The Policies section contains the names of either the AWS managed IAM policies or IAM policy documents that this function will require for execution; and finally we have the Environment section that can be used to set the function's environment variables as well.

AWS::Serverless::Api

You can use the `AWS::Serverless::API` resource type to define one or more Amazon API Gateway resources and methods that can be invoked through HTTPS endpoints. SAM supports two ways of creating API Gateways; both are explained as follows:

- **Implicitly**: In this case, the API is created implicitly by combining one or more API events defined using the `AWS::Serverless::Function` resource. For example, consider this simple example where we create an API Gateway using the `Events` parameter of the `AWS::Serverless::Function` resource. In this case, SAM will auto-generate that API for you. The API that is going to be generated from the three API events above looks like the following:

  ```
  Resources:
    GetFunction:
      Type: AWS::Serverless::Function
      Properties:
        Handler: index.js
        Runtime: nodejs4.3
        Policies: myAWSLambdaReadOnlyPolicy
        Environment:
          Variables:
            Key: Hello
        Events:
          GetSomeResource:
            Type: Api
            Properties:
              Path: /resource/{resourceId}
              Method: get
  ```

- **Explicitly**: You can additionally create and configure API Gateway resources by using the `AWS::Serverless::Api` resource type followed by a valid Swagger file and a Stage name as shown in the example below:

  ```
  Resources:
    ApiGatewayApi:
      Type: AWS::Serverless::Api
      Properties:
        DefinitionUri: s3://myS3Bucket/swagger.yaml
        StageName: Dev
  ```

The `StageName` parameter is used by the API Gateway as the first path segment for the invocation of the URI.

AWS::Serverless::SimpleTable

You can use the AWS::Serverless::SimpleTable resource to create a DynamoDB table with a single attribute primary key (hence the name SimpleTable). You can additionally provide the name and type of your primary key along with the table's provisioned throughput as parameters, as shown in the following example:

```
MySimpleTable:
    Type: AWS::Serverless::SimpleTable
    Properties:
        PrimaryKey:
            Name: userId
            Type: String
        ProvisionedThroughput:
            ReadCapacityUnits: 5
            WriteCapacityUnits: 5
```

You can optionally even use the AWS::DynamoDB::Table resource instead of the SimpleTable if, you require more advanced functionalities for your tables.

Putting it all together, you will end up with a ready to use template that can deploy a simple serverless application based on API Gateway, Lambda functions, and a simple backend in the form of DynamoDB as described in the next section.

Building serverless applications with SAM

Now that we have the basics covered, let us stitch together and deploy a simple application using SAM. To do so, we are going to use a readymade template provided by Lambda itself. Go to the AWS Lambda dashboard and select the option **Create a Lambda function**. Next, from the **Select blueprint** page, type in the filter **microservice** as shown below. Select the download icon adjoining to the blueprint and download the associated microservice-http-endpoint.zip on your workstation.

The following blueprint will provide a simple backend service using API Gateway that is able to read and write data to a particular DynamoDB table using a simple Lambda function!

Once the zip is downloaded, extract it's contents to a folder. You will now have two files present namely `index.js` and `template.yaml`. The SAM template is declaring a Lambda resource and we are using the same to create an API (implicit) as well. The `index.js` file contains the necessary code that queries any DynamoDB table based on the parameters (`PUT`, `GET`, `DELETE`, `POST` and so on) that are passed to it via the API Gateway.

Have a look at the `template.yaml` file. You will notice that the `CodeUri` parameter under the `AWS::Serverless::Function` resource simply has a dot provided in it. Leave this as it is for now, we will be explaining that in a short while. The rest of the template should be pretty self-explanatory.

Now there are two ways in which we could have deployed this entire template. First up is by using the Lambda dashboard itself. You can simply select the `microservice-http-endpoint` blueprint and continue to setup the Lambda function just as you would have done during the initial deployment chapters. The second way is by uploading the template file to CloudFormation and executing it from there. We will give the second way a try by using AWS CLI.

For this setup, you will need AWS CLI installed and configured on your workstation. Make sure the CLI is the latest by either upgrading it by using python pip, or manually by installing a latest version of the CLI from here: `https://aws.amazon.com/cli/`.

 NOTE: You can refer to the following site for configuring the AWS CLI:
`http://docs.aws.amazon.com/cli/latest/userguide/cli-chap-getting-started.html`

Next, cd into the `microservice-http-endpoint` directory and run the following command:

```
# aws cloudformation package \
--template-file template.yaml \
--output-template-file output.yaml
--s3-bucket sam-codebase
```

The following code simply takes the existing `template.yaml` file and packages it for the CloudFormation stack by replacing the `CodeUri` with the one that will be used for the deployment. You can clearly see the difference in the `template.yaml` and the `output.yaml` file as shown below:

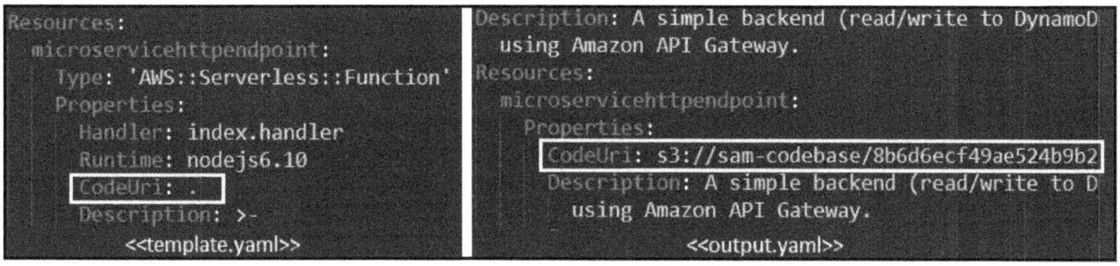

This comes in really handy when we want to implement a CICD pipeline for our Lambda functions. The CloudFormation `package` command does all the work for us by zipping the files, uploading them to the required S3 bucket, and even updating the `CodeUri` parameter with the correct URI. In this way, you can package your code and create multiple versions of the deployment packages without having to manually go and change the `CodeUri` each time. Simple, isn't it?

With the code uploaded, the next step is to deploy the code using the newly generated `output.yaml` as a CloudFormation stack. Type in the following command:

```
# aws cloudformation deploy \
--template-file output.yaml \
--stack-name MyFirstSAMDeployment \
--capabilities CAPABILITY_IAM
```

The `--capabilities CAPABILITY_IAM` parameter enables CloudFormation to create roles on our behalf for executing the Lambda function. If all goes well, your new application should be deployed over to CloudFormation as a Stack. Verify this by viewing the newly created Stack from the CloudFormation dashboard as shown below:

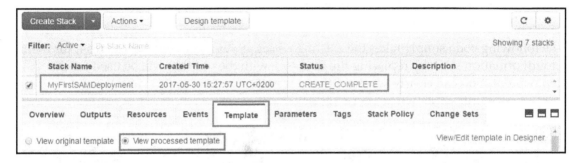

Select the newly deployed Stack and click on the **Template** tab as shown. You will see two checkboxes here: **View original template** and **View processed template**. Selecting the second option shows you just how few of the necessary permissions, as well as event parameters, were auto-filled by CloudFormations to ensure that Lambda Function executes properly.

With the stack deployed, you will now need the API Gateway URL to send POST or GET requests. You can obtain that by going over to the Lambda Dashboard, selecting the newly deployed Lambda function (`MyFirstSAMDeployment-microservicehttpendpoint-15L1RPRD4QGZ` in my case) and then selecting the **Triggers** tab, as shown:

Make a note of the API Gateway URL that is displayed there. You can now use a tool such as Postman (`https://www.getpostman.com/`) to fire queries at the URL. You can pass the **TableName** of your DynamoDB table as a key-value pair and **Send** the request.

Corresponding to your table, you will be provided with a list of the table's items as shown below:

```
{
    "Items": [
        {
            "IP_ADDRESS": "10.0.0.0"
        },
        {
            "IP_ADDRESS": "192.168.76.90"
        }
    ],
    "Count": 2,
    "ScannedCount": 2
}
```

You can use the same steps to build and deploy your own serverless applications using SAM. Let us look at yet another example where we take our trusty calculator code and modify it to accept the operator and operands using an API Gateway. When a user posts these values using the gateway, it triggers the Lambda function that calculates the answer and stores the relevant data in a simple DynamoDB table.

First up, let us have a look at the calculator function code. The code is modified a bit to accept parameters from the API Gateway and write the output to a DynamoDB table:

```
'use strict';
console.log('Loading the Calc function');
let doc = require('dynamodb-doc');
let dynamo = new doc.DynamoDB();
const tableName = process.env.TABLE_NAME;
const createResponse = (statusCode, body) => {
    return {
        "statusCode": statusCode,
        "body": body || ""
```

```
    }
};
let response;

exports.handler = function(event, context, callback) {
    console.log('Received event:', JSON.stringify(event, null, 2));
    let operand1 = event.pathParameters.operand1;
    let operand2 = event.pathParameters.operand2;
    let operator = event.pathParameters.operator;

    if (operand1 === undefined || operand2 === undefined
    || operator === undefined) {
        console.log("400 Invalid Input");
        response = createResponse(400, "400 Invalid Input");
        return callback(null, response);
    }
    let res = {};
    res.a = Number(operand1);
    res.b = Number(operand2);
    res.op = operator;
    if (isNaN(operand1) || isNaN(operand2)) {
        console.log("400 Invalid Operand");
        response = createResponse(400, "400 Invalid Operand");
        return callback(null, response);
    }

    switch(operator)
    {
        case "add":
            res.c = res.a + res.b;
            break;
        case "sub":
            res.c = res.a - res.b;
            break;
        case "mul":
            res.c = res.a * res.b;
            break;
        case "div":
            if(res.b === 0){
                console.log("The divisor cannot be 0");
                response = createResponse(400, "400 The
                 divisor cannot be 0");
                return callback(null, response);
            }
            else{
                res.c = res.a/res.b;
            }
            break;
```

```
        default:
            console.log("400 Invalid Operator");
            response = createResponse(400, "400 Invalid Operator");
            return callback(null, response);
            break;
    }
    console.log("result: "+res.c);
    console.log("Writing to DynamoDB");

    let item = {
        "calcAnswer": res.c,
        "operand1": res.a,
        "operand2": res.b,
        "operator": res.op
    };

    let params = {
        "TableName": tableName,
        "Item": item
    };

    dynamo.putItem(params, (err, data) => {
        if (err){
            console.log("An error occured while writing to Db: ",err);
            response = createResponse(500, err);
        }
        else{
            console.log("Successfully wrote result to DB");
            response = createResponse(200, JSON.stringify(res));
        }
        callback(null, response);
    });
};
```

Copy and save the code in an `index.js` file. Next up, we will create the all-important SAM file (`template.yaml`) for our calculator application.

```
AWSTemplateFormatVersion: '2010-09-09'
Transform: AWS::Serverless-2016-10-31
Description: Simple Calc web service. State is stored in a DynamoDB table.
Resources:
  CalcGetFunction:
    Type: AWS::Serverless::Function
    Properties:
      Handler: index.handler
      Policies: AmazonDynamoDBFullAccess
      Runtime: nodejs4.3
      Role: <role arn>
```

```
        Environment:
          Variables:
            TABLE_NAME: !Ref: Table
        Events:
          GetResource:
            Type: Api
            Properties:
              Method: get
              Path: /calc/{operand1}/{operand2}/{operator}
    Table:
      Type: AWS::Serverless::SimpleTable
      Properties:
        PrimaryKey:
          Name: calcAnswer
          Type: Number
        ProvisionedThroughput:
          ReadCapacityUnits: 5
          WriteCapacityUnits: 5
```

With the SAM all set up, let us run a few commands to generate the all-important output.yaml file and later deploy our application using CloudFormation as well. First up, we package the template.yaml with the command as shown below:

Change into the calculator application directory where the index.js file and the template.yaml file are saved and run the following command:

```
# aws cloudformation package \
--template-file template.yaml \
--output-template-file output.yaml
--s3-bucket sam-codebase
```

The output of this packaging command will be an output.yaml file. The output file will have the CodeUri parameter autofilled with a unique S3 URI.

With the code uploaded, the next step is to deploy the code using the newly generated output.yaml as a CloudFormation stack. Type in the following command as shown:

```
# aws cloudformation deploy \
--template-file output.yaml \
--stack-name MyCalcSAMDeployment \
--capabilities CAPABILITY_IAM
```

Remember to add the `--capabilities CAPABILITY_IAM` parameter that enables CloudFormation to create roles on our behalf for executing the Lambda function. A few minutes later, you should have your application stack created. You can verify the same using the CloudFormation dashboard as shown below:

Now, over to the fun part! Testing and making sure the entire application setup works as expected or not. To do so, we will first require the API Gateway URL for posting the requests. You can obtain the same using either the API Gateway dashboard or even by using the Lambda dashboard as explained in the steps below.

First up, open up the Lambda management dashboard and select the newly created functions from the **Functions** page. The function name will be prefixed by the CloudFormation Stack name followed by some random string of characters; for example: `MyCalcSAMDeployment-CalcGetFunction-18T7IJLS4F53L`

Next, select the **Triggers** option and copy the API Gateway URL as shown in the image below:

You can use a tool such as Postman to send the requests to the API Gateway URL. To download the latest version of Postman, click here: `https://www.getpostman.com/`

Paste the API Gateway URL and substitute the {Operator1}, {Operator2}, and the {Operand} with your own values as shown in the image below. Once done, click on **Send** to send the request. If the application is setup correctly, you should see the output displayed in the **Body** section as shown. You can even verify the output by checking against the application's table from DynamoDB. The **Table** will have a similar naming convention as used for the Lambda function; prefixed by the name of the CloudFormation Stack and ending with some randomly added set of characters, for example: MyCalcSAMDeployment-Table-9G02RMWZ9O4M.

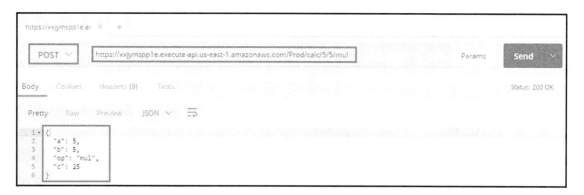

In similar ways, you can easily build out and deploy complete serverless applications such as this, using a standardized SAM template. But, as your applications gains in complexity with the introduction of more and more Lambda functions, it becomes even more difficult to write and coordinate the interactions among all these components. But fret not! You will be really happy to know that there's yet another AWS service that makes building and orchestrating serverless apps a breeze! Here's introducing AWS step functions!

Introducing AWS step functions

Working with Lambda functions so far has been really great for us and I hope it's been a similar experience for you as well! But there's a slight hitch that the Lambda service alone cannot help solve: how do you effectively coordinate and orchestrate Lambda functions so that they form a backbone for some really distributed applications that rely on complex workflows for execution? For most of you, working with AWS for a long time, the obvious answer would be to use something like AWS **Simple Workflow Service** (**SWF**) or maybe even create a single Lambda function that acts as an orchestrator for some other worker functions, but both these techniques have their own sets of pros and cons. To solve this, AWS unfolded the Step Functions web service during the *AWS re:Invent* 2016 event!

AWS Step Functions is basically an orchestration service for Lambda functions, using which you can orchestrate and control multiple Lambda function executions. Using Step Functions, you build individual functions that perform a particular "task", with each task being capable of scaling independently of each other. The scaling, retries in case of failure, and the coordination among other components is all taken care of, by Step Functions itself, leaving you to design the workflows as you see fit.

Under the hood

Under the hood, AWS step functions mainly relies on two things apart from few other essential components: tasks and state machines. Let us take a quick peek into what each of these component performs:

- **State machine**: State machine is basically a JSON-based structured language used to define one or more "states". States can be used to perform some specific set of tasks, for example, the "task states" can be used to perform some activity, the "choice states" determine which states to transition to next, the "Fail states" are designed to stop an execution with an error, and so on. States can run in a sequence or even in parallel with each copy of the state machine called as an "execution." Multiple executions can run independently at any given point in time.

    Here is a simple representational example of a state machine:

    ```
    {
      "Comment": "A Hello World example of the Amazon
        States Language using a Pass state",
      "StartAt": "HelloWorld",
      "States": {
        "HelloWorld": {
           "Type": "Pass",
           "Result": "Hello World!",
           "End": true
        }
      }
    }
    ```

- **States**: States are individual elements or helper functions that together combine to form the state machine. They can be used to perform a variety of functions in your state machine such as:
- **Task state**: Used to perform activities in your state machine.

- **Choice state:** Used to make decisions between multiple executions.
- **Pass state:** Simply used to pass some data from one point to another.
- **Wait state:** Used to provide a timed delay between executions.
- **Parallel state:** Starts a parallel execution of tasks.
- **Succeed/ fail state:** Used to stop an execution based on it's success or failure.
- **Tasks and activities:** Each work performed by your state machine is termed as a Task. Tasks can be further subdivided into two categories: A Lambda function that performs some task based on the code that's written and a second category called as activities which is basically any and all code that's either hosted on EC2, ECS containers, physical infrastructure, or even mobile devices!
- **Transitions**: Transitions are points in your state machine's execution that define the next state that step functions have to advance to. In some states, you can provide only a single transition rule however, this does not hold true if you are using the choice state which can require more than one transition rules.

Besides these concepts, step functions also provide a really simple and easy to use visual workflow editor of sorts that provides you with a color coded representation of your workflow during it's execution. This comes in real handy during debugging of your workflows as well as helps to view the various input and output values passed by the State Machine.

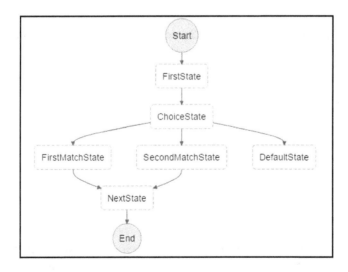

Let us now look at a couple of examples on how we can leverage Step Functions to co-ordinate and organize our Lambda functions.

Getting started with step functions

In this section, we are going to walk you through a fairly simple example of how to set up and get started with your very first step function state machine.

The scenario is fairly straight forward: I have two Lambda functions that are used to either switch on or switch off the light bulbs in my house! Don't worry, we are not going to set up any AWS IoT out here! The functions simply simulate the actions of switching on and off the light bulbs; the real idea here is to understand how to create a minimalistic state machine that will help you do so.

Before we go ahead and create the state machine, the first order of business is to create our Lambda functions. In this case, the functions are really just place holders, so you can actually use the same function with a slight modification for simulating both the switch on and off of the light bulbs.

```
'use strict';
console.log('Loading function');
exports.handler = (event, context, callback) => {
    console.log('Some magical code to turn on my lightbulb goes
     here!', event.onoff);
    callback(null, "Light Bulb is switched on");
};
```

The function simply takes an event parameter and returns a message in it's `callback()`. Go ahead and deploy this function to Lambda by providing it a meaningful name (in my case, I named it `switchOn`). The event for triggering the `switchOn` function is supplied in the following format:

```
{
    "onoff": "on"
}
```

With the code deployed, make a note of it's ARN as well, this will be required during the state machine creation phase. Similarly, go ahead and create the `switchOff` function as well. With our functions created, it's time to move on to the second part of this exercise which is basically creating the state machine itself.

To do so, from the AWS Management Console, filter and select the service **Step Functions**. Select the **Get started** option on the dashboard. This will bring you to the **Create State Machine** page as shown below. Here, we provide a suitable name for your **State Machine**:

Next, scroll down towards the **Code** section and paste the following machine state code there:

```
{
    "Comment": "Change Power State of my light bulbs",
    "StartAt": "SwitchState",
    "States": {
        "SwitchState": {
            "Choices": [
                {
                    "Next": "OnSwitch",
                    "StringEquals": "on",
                    "Variable": "$.onoff"
                },
                {
                    "Next": "OffSwitch",
                    "StringEquals": "off",
                    "Variable": "$.onoff"
                }
            ],
            "Default": "DefaultState",
            "Type": "Choice"
        },
        "DefaultState": {
            "Cause": "No Matches!",
            "Type": "Fail"
        },
        "OffSwitch": {
            "End": true,
            "Resource": "arn:aws:lambda:us-east-1:12345678910:
              function:switchOff",
            "Type": "Task"
        },
        "OnSwitch": {
            "End": true,
```

```
            "Resource": "arn:aws:lambda:us-east-1:12345678910:
              function:switchOn",
            "Type": "Task"
        }
    }
}
```

Lets us understand what we pasted into the **Code** section a bit. First up, is the all-important **StartAt** parameter that defines the start of our state machine code. This is followed up by the **Choices** parameter that provides us with one or more choices to follow; in this case, what choice do I need to take if the function receives an *on* or an *off* event. Within each **Choice** we also pass a **Next** parameter that defines the name of the next logical step that the state machine has to follow in case that particular choice is met. We can also see a **Default** state being created which basically handles the actions that are required to be performed if neither of the choices are met. In this case the default state will simply fail with an error message if no match is found during the choices state.

Towards the end of the State Machine is where we have actually defined the actionable states (**OffSwitch** and **OnSwitch**) that call the necessary Lambda functions when invoked. Replace the ARN of your Lambda functions with the ones shown in the above state machine and click on the **Preview** button to visually view the state machine. You will end up with a similar flowchart as shown as follows:

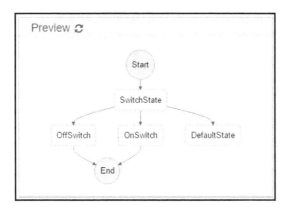

Click on **Create State Machine** option to complete the creation process. At this point, you will be prompted to select an IAM role for your task. To do so, you will need to create an IAM Role with the following policy:

```
{
    "Version": "2012-10-17",
    "Statement": [{
        "Effect": "Allow",
```

```
            "Action": [
                "lambda:InvokeFunction"
            ],
            "Resource": ["*"]
        }]
    }
}
CODE:
```

Once the Role is created, you will also need to establish a trust relationship of that role with Step Functions. To do so, copy the following policy in the "Trusted entities" section of your Role:

```
{
    "Version": "2012-10-17",
    "Statement": [
        {
            "Sid": "",
            "Effect": "Allow",
            "Principal": {
                "Service": "states.us-east-1.amazonaws.com"
            },
            "Action": "sts:AssumeRole"
        }
    ]
}
```

Once completed, you should be able to select your newly created role and complete the creation of your first state machine, as shown below:

To test and execute the state machine, select the **New execution** option, as shown. This will provide you with a JSON editor where you can type in the required event you want to pass to the state machine. In this case, the event should look something like this:

```
{
    "onoff": "on"
}
```

Once done, click on **Start Execution** to begin your state machine. If all goes according to plan, you should see a successful execution of your state machine as shown in the image below. You can select the **SwitchState** and the **OnSwitch** states to view more details about them. For example, selecting the **Output** tab from the **OnSwitch** state will display the message **Light bulb is switched on** and so on.

You can additionally drill down into your state machine's execution by selecting other tasks and checking the input and output parameters supplied. Remember, however, that each time you wish to run the state machine; you will have to create new executions of the same.

With this, we come towards the end of this section. In the next section, we will take what we have learned so far with step functions and apply it to our calculator example.

Building distributed applications with step functions

The whole idea behind step functions is to make it easier for developers to write and orchestrate multiple Lambda functions with ease. This comes in really handy when you have a really large number of Lambda functions, each performing a very specific task, and you wish to coordinate the actions among them. In this scenario, we will be taking our monolithic calculator example code from the earlier deployed SAM template and re-engineer it to work with Step Functions. To begin with, let us examine the Lambda functions that we have created for this scenario. First up, are the basic addition, subtraction, and multiplication functions that all follow the same code as shown below:

```
'use strict';
console.log('Loading the Addition function');

exports.handler = function(event, context, callback) {
    console.log('Received event:', JSON.stringify(event, null, 2));
    let operand1 = event.a;
    let operand2 = event.b;
    let operator = event.op;

    let res = {};
    res.a = Number(operand1);
    res.b = Number(operand2);
    res.op = operator;

    res.c = res.a + res.b;
    console.log("result: "+res.c);
    callback(null, res);
};
```

The function is very simple to understand and implement. It takes three parameters (operand1, operand2 and operator) as events, calculates the results, and simply passes all the details to an object as a callback().

The function code for dividing is a bit different, in the sense that it does a few checks before actually running a divide operation on the two operands as shown in the snippet below:

```
function ZeroDivisorError(message) {
    this.name = "ZeroDivisorError";
    this.message = message;
}

    if(res.b === 0){
        console.log("The divisor cannot be 0");
```

```
        const zeroDivisortError =
          new ZeroDivisorError("The divisor cannot be 0!");
        callback(zeroDivisortError);
    }
    else{
        res.c = res.a/res.b;
        console.log("result: "+res.c);
        callback(null, res);
    }
```

Apart from these two functions, we have also gone ahead and created a function that basically checks whether all the required values are entered or not, as well as, whether the operands are numbers or not. If the operands clear the checks, they are then passed to the respective Lambda function for further calculation.

```
'use strict';
console.log('Loading the Calc function');

function InvalidInputError(message) {
    this.name = "InvalidInputError";
    this.message = message;
}

function InvalidOperandError(message) {
    this.name = "InvalidOperandError";
    this.message = message;
}

exports.handler = function(event, context, callback) {
    console.log('Received event:', JSON.stringify(event, null, 2));
    let operand1 = event.operand1;
    let operand2 = event.operand2;
    let operator = event.operator;

    InvalidInputError.prototype = new Error();
    if (operand1 === undefined || operand2 === undefined
     || operator === undefined) {
        console.log("Invalid Input");
        const invalidInputError =
          new InvalidInputError("Invalid Input!");
        return callback(invalidInputError);
    }
    let res = {};
    res.a = Number(operand1);
    res.b = Number(operand2);
    res.op = operator;
    InvalidOperandError.prototype = new Error();
```

```
    if (isNaN(operand1) || isNaN(operand2)) {
        console.log("Invalid Operand");
        const invalidOperandError =
          new InvalidOperandError("Invalid Operand!");
        return callback(invalidOperandError);
    }

    callback(null, res);
};
```

Once the calculations are all completed, the final results are stored in a predefined DynamoDB table using the final function code snippet as shown below:

```
let item = {
        "calcAnswer": event.c,
        "operand1": event.a,
        "operand2": event.b,
        "operator": event.op
    };

    let params = {
        "TableName": tableName,
        "Item": item
    };

    dynamo.putItem(params, (err, data) => {
        if (err){
            console.log("An error occured while writing to Db: ",err);
            callback(err);
        }
        else{
            console.log("Successfully wrote result to DB");
            callback(null, "success!");
        }
```

So, all in all, we have taken our standard calculator code and split it's functionality into six different Lambda functions! Once all the functions are deployed to Lambda, the last thing left is to go ahead and create the associated state machine for step functions! Let us have a look at the state machine one section at a time:

The first section is where we are defining the starting state FetchAndCheck that will basically accept the operands and operator as events and pass them through a series of validation checks. If an error is found, the FailState is invoked with the appropriate error message else the execution continues with the invocation of the ChoiceStateX.

```
    {
        "Comment": "An example of the Amazon States Language using
```

```
        an AWS Lambda Functions",
  "StartAt": "FetchAndCheck",
  "States": {
    "FetchAndCheck": {
      "Type": "Task",
      "Resource": "arn:aws:lambda:us-east-1:12345678910:
          function:fetchandCheckLambda",
      "Next": "ChoiceStateX",
      "Catch": [
            {
                "ErrorEquals": ["InvalidInputError",
                    "InvalidOperandError"],
                "Next": "FailState"
            }
        ]
    },
```

The `ChoiceStateX` state decides the task to invoke, based on the operator parameter passed during the state machine's execution

```
    "ChoiceStateX": {
      "Type": "Choice",
      "Choices": [
        {
          "Variable": "$.op",
          "StringEquals": "add",
          "Next": "Addition"
        },
        {
          "Variable": "$.op",
          "StringEquals": "sub",
          "Next": "Subtraction"
        },
        {
          "Variable": "$.op",
          "StringEquals": "mul",
          "Next": "Multiplication"
        },
        {
          "Variable": "$.op",
          "StringEquals": "div",
          "Next": "Division"
        }
      ],
      "Default": "DefaultState"
    },
```

With the choice state defined, the next step in the state machine's definition is the individual task itself. Here, we will provide the individual Lambda function ARN's that we created earlier:

```
"Addition": {
  "Type" : "Task",
  "Resource": "arn:aws:lambda:us-east-1:12345678910:
    function:additionLambda",
  "Next": "InsertInDB"
},

"Subtraction": {
  "Type" : "Task",
  "Resource": "arn:aws:lambda:us-east-1:12345678910:
    function:subtractionLambda",
  "Next": "InsertInDB"
},

"Multiplication": {
  "Type" : "Task",
  "Resource": "arn:aws:lambda:us-east-1:12345678910:
    function:multiplication",
  "Next": "InsertInDB"
},

"Division": {
  "Type" : "Task",
  "Resource": "arn:aws:lambda:us-east-1:12345678910:
    function:divisionLambda",
  "Next": "InsertInDB",
  "Catch": [
      {
          "ErrorEquals": ["ZeroDivisorError"],
          "Next": "FailState"
      }
    ]
},

"DefaultState": {
  "Type": "Pass",
  "Next": "FailState"
},
```

The `InsertInDB` state is the final state in the state machine's execution where the operands, the operator, and the calculated value are stored in a pre-defined DynamoDB table:

```
"InsertInDB": {
  "Type": "Task",
  "Resource": "arn:aws:lambda:us-east-1:12345678910:
    function:insertInDBLambda",
  "Next": "SuccessState",
  "Catch": [
        {
            "ErrorEquals": ["States.ALL"],
            "Next": "FailState"
        }
     ]
},

"FailState": {
  "Type": "Fail"
},

"SuccessState": {
  "Type": "Succeed"
  }
 }
}
```

With the code pasted, click on the **Preview** option to visually see the state machine. You should see a flowchart similar to the one shown as follows:

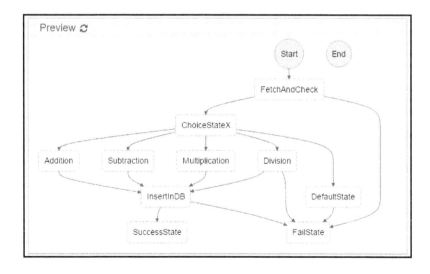

Once completed, click on **Create State Machine** option to select the IAM role for our state machine. Unlike the previous IAM role for our example, we need to add few specific policies for logging the events to CloudWatch, as well as inserting items to a specific DynamoDB table. Note that, in my case, I'm reusing one of my table's for this exercise.

```
{
    "Version": "2012-10-17",
    "Statement": [
        {
            "Sid": "Stmt1497293444000",
            "Effect": "Allow",
            "Action": [
                "logs:CreateLogGroup",
                "logs:CreateLogStream",
                "logs:PutLogEvents"
            ],
            "Resource": [
                "*"
            ]
        },
        {
            "Sid": "Stmt1497293498000",
            "Effect": "Allow",
            "Action": [
                "dynamodb:PutItem"
            ],
            "Resource": [
                "arn:aws:dynamodb:us-east-1:12345678910:
                table/myCalcResults"
            ]
        }
    ]
}
```

With the IAM role created and assigned to the state machine, you can now go ahead and create an execution for the same.

Click on the **New execution** option and pass the following event in the events pane as shown:

```
{
    "operand1": "3",
    "operand2": "5",
    "operator": "mul"
}
```

With the event parameters passed, you should see a flowchart along with the **Input** and **Output** values as shown in the following flowchart:

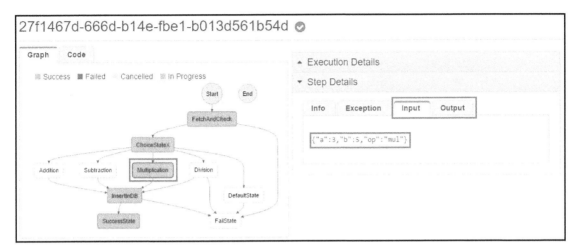

You can run similar permutations and combinations of executions on the following state machine as per your requirements. Make sure to check the DynamoDB table whether the records are inserted or not, as well as the CloudWatch logs of your individual Lambda functions for troubleshooting and error checking.

Monitoring and Troubleshooting AWS Lambda

20

So far, we have been learning about how to write, test, and build serverless applications using the AWS Lambda service. This chapter is going to cover few different aspects with regards to Lambda functions, namely: how to effectively monitor and troubleshoot your functions and applications using a combination of both AWS CloudWatch, as well as a few third-party tools in the form Datadog and Loggly.

In this chapter we will be learning:

- How to monitor Lambda functions using CloudWatch
- How to leverage AWS X-Ray for monitoring your serverless applications
- How to get started on monitoring your Lambda functions using Datadog
- How to log and analyze your application as well as your functions logs to Loggly
- Some basic steps and tricks to troubleshoot your Lambda functions

So, without any further delays, let's get started!

Monitoring Lambda functions using CloudWatch

Throughout the book we have been talking about checking and monitoring your Lambda functions using CloudWatch. It's really not that difficult to set it up and once you have the base ready, you can reuse the same setup for monitoring almost all of your functions. So, let us quickly recap on how to monitor Lambda functions using CloudWatch!

To start off, we first need to prepare the base that we talked about. The base here is nothing more that the correct set of policies that allow your function to send its logs to CloudWatch. In most cases, your functions will require rights to create log groups and streams in CloudWatch, as well as to put log events into that particular stream. The log group creation, as well as the stream creation, is all taken care of by CloudWatch itself. Here is a simple IAM policy that will basically allow your functions to dump their logs into CloudWatch. Remember, this is just a template so you should always follow the practice of creating specific IAM policies and roles for your functions, especially if they are going to be running on a live production environment:

```
{
  "Version": "2012-10-17",
  "Statement": [
  {
    "Effect": "Allow",
    "Action": [
      "logs:CreateLogGroup",
      "logs:CreateLogStream",
      "logs:PutLogEvents"
    ],
    "Resource": "*"
  }
  ]
}
```

Once the base is ready, you can write, package, and upload your functions to Lambda and when your functions get triggered, they will ideally start pumping logs to CloudWatch. You can view your function's logs by selecting CloudWatch Logs option from the CloudWatch dashboard and typing the name of your function in the filter text as shown as follows:

```
/aws/lambda/<Name_Of_Your_Function>
```

Select your function and you should see a log stream created already for you. If you don't see a log stream, it is probably because you haven't configured the IAM role to grant the necessary permissions to write the logs to CloudWatch.

You can then use the CloudWatch Logs dashboard to scroll and filter your application logs as you see fit. Here's a sample CloudWatch Logs dashboard view for one of our calculator functions that we created in the previous chapter:

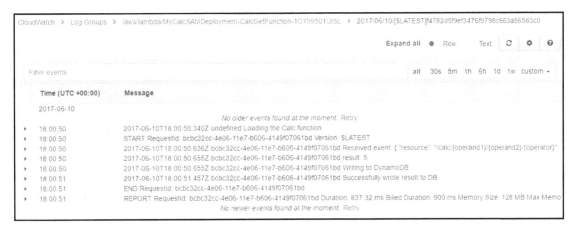

Apart from the standard logs, you can also use CloudWatch metrics to view and analyze a few of your function's runtime parameters, such as **Errors**, **Invocations**, **Duration**, and **Throttles**; each is explained briefly as follows:

- **Invocations**: This metric measures the number of times a particular function was invoked either by an API call or an event response.
- **Errors**: The errors metric only counts the number of invocations that failed due to errors present in the function. It does not take into account internal service errors or errors caused by other AWS services connected to Lambda functions.
- **Duration**: This metric measures the elapsed time from when a function is invoked to run till the time it stops execution.
- **Throttles**: This metric counts the number of invocations that are throttled in case the invocation rates exceed the set concurrent execution limit.

To view your function's metrics, simply select the **Metrics** option from the CloudWatch dashboard. Next, search for the **Lambda** metrics group from the **All metrics** tab. You can now drill further down to your individual functions by selecting either the **By Resource** or **By Function Name** options. You can alternatively view the collective metrics for all your functions using the **Across All Functions** option as well.

In this case, I have opted for the **By Function Name** option and selected the **Error,**
Throttles, Invocations, and **Duration** metrics for the calculator function that we deployed
from our earlier chapter. You can select any of the function metrics as you see fit. Once the
metrics are selected, you will automatically be shown a simple **Line** graph that depicts the
overall duration of the function's execution, as well as whether there were any error or
throttle events. You can switch between **Line** graphs or **Stacked area** graphs by selecting
the **Graph options** tab provided beneath your graph area:

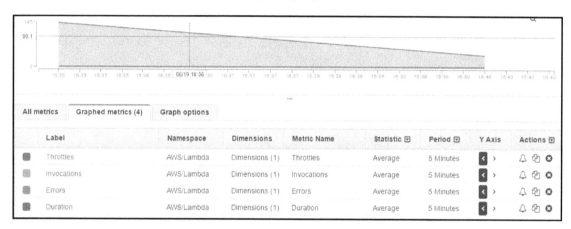

Alternatively, you can even configure CloudWatch alarms by selecting the individual
metric from the **Graphed metrics** tab and clicking on the adjoining alarm icon as depicted
in the previous image.

Although CloudWatch provides a good assortment of services for monitoring your Lambda
functions, it still had some clinks in its armor. First up, as we know, Lambda functions are
more or less designed around the principles of microservices, where each service gets its
own functional container for hosting. However, unlike the traditional EC2 instances that
hosted monolithic apps, thousands of containers can be spun up within fractions of seconds
using Lambda. This, along with the large number of other moving parts in the form of AWS
services such as DynamoDB and API Gateway, can prove too much for even CloudWatch
to handle. A specialized tool was required that could effectively trace each request made by
functions against other services and also that could be used to analyze performance
bottlenecks and remediate against them. Enter the newest kid on the block! AWS X-Ray!

Introducing AWS X-Ray

AWS X-Ray was first introduced during *AWS re:Invent 2016* as a tool that would enable developers to debug their distributed applications by analyzing and tracing the calls that occur between the application and its various components. By analyzing this performance, you can easily isolate and remediate issues caused either due to bottlenecks or errors. The best part of X-Ray is its ability to work with a wide variety of applications and services; for example, your application maybe running on a single EC2 instance or it might even be a highly distributed application containing thousands of Lambda functions! X-Ray can easily get integrated with your code; whether it is written in Node.js, .NET, or Java, and start providing performance metrics for the same. This, along with the support for tracing requests from services such as EC2, ECS, Beanstalk, DynamoDB, SNS, SQS, and Lambda makes, X-Ray a really important tool from an application performance management perspective.

How does it all work? X-Ray provides an SDK that you will be required to incorporate in your applications for performance monitoring. You can even leverage an X-Ray agent provided by X-Ray that can be installed on applications hosted on EC2 instances. If your application is hosted on an Elastic Beanstalk environment, the agent comes pre-installed so the only activity that you need to do is plug in the SDK with your app and you can get started with the traces immediately. The traces are used to track each request made to your application. The data that passes through each of the services or application component is recorded as a trace and displayed using a visual map format using the X-Ray dashboard:

Before we begin with the actual monitoring of your application, we need to have a quick understanding of some of the concepts and terminologies that are commonly used in X-Ray:

- **Segments**: Segments are small work units that contains data about your running application. Segments with common requests are grouped into what we call traces. A segment provides the resource's name, details about the request, the response, and details about the work done.
- **Subsegments**: Subsegments are smaller groups of more granular data present within one segment. They provide more information about a particular response that your application might make against a request.
- **Service graph**: Service graphs are generated by X-Ray using the metrics that are passed by your application. Each AWS resource that sends data to X-Ray appears as a service in the graph.
- **Trace**: A trace, as the name suggests, tracks the path of a request made through your application. A single trace can be a collection of requests (GET/ POST) that propagate all the way from the time your application was invoked either by a Load Balancer, all the way to the code itself, and finally to some other AWS service or an external API.

With the basics out of the way, let us look at how to enable your serverless applications for monitoring using X-Ray.

To demonstrate X-Ray's usage for tracing purposes, we are going to re-use the same calculator code that leveraged an API Gateway, a single Lambda function and a DynamoDB as a backend. You can refer to Chapter 6, *Build and Deploy Serverless Applications with AWS Lambda* for this code's explanation and details. That being said, we are going to look into using X-Ray for our Lambda functions. The good thing here is, it's as easy as checking a box to activate X-Ray tracing for your Lambda function! No, I am not kidding! It's literally a checkbox on your Lambda console. To enable X-Ray monitoring for your functions, select the **Configuration** tab and under **Advanced settings**, you should be able to see a checkbox that reads **Enable active tracing**. Go ahead and select that and remember to **Save** the configuration settings before running your function code.

Additionally, you will also need to provide your Lambda function with an IAM role that enables Lambda to create traces in X-Ray for you.

This is a predefined policy provided by AWS under the name
`AWSXrayWriteOnlyAccess` as shown as follows:

```
{
    "Version": "2012-10-17",
    "Statement": [
    {
        "Effect": "Allow",
        "Action": [
            "xray:PutTraceSegments",
            "xray:PutTelemetryRecords"
        ],
        "Resource": [
            "*"
        ]
    }
    ]
}
```

So, remember to add this to your Lambda execution role before you start using X-Ray's
tracing.

Now, if you go through the extensive X-Ray documentation, you will see that X-Ray has
three types of nodes on the service map for requests served by Lambda:

- Lambda service (`AWS::Lambda`)
- Lambda function (`AWS::Lambda::Function`)
- Downstream service calls

The trace will display the in-depth info regarding the Lambda function in the form of
segments and subsegments. Now there are various kinds of segments and subsegments
depending on the event type--synchronous or asynchronous, and so on. By default, once
you activate X-Ray on your function, the basic segments and subsegments are visible in the
trace view but if you want to see custom segments, annotations, or subsegments for
downstream calls, you might need to include additional libraries and annotate your code.

In our example, we do have a downstream call made to DynamoDB and hence we will be including the additional libraries. To do so, you first need to include the AWS X-Ray SDK for Node.js in your deployment package. In addition, you will also need to wrap your AWS SDK's `require` statement as depicted in the snippet below:

```
'use strict';
console.log('Loading the Calc function');
var AWSXRay = require('aws-xray-sdk-core');
var AWS = AWSXRay.captureAWS(require('aws-sdk'));
```

Then, use the AWS variable defined in the preceding example to initialize any service client that you want to trace with X-Ray, for example:

```
s3Client = AWS.S3();
```

 These additional capabilities of custom segments, annotations and subsegments for downstream calls are only present for Java and Node.js runtimes.

The rest of the code remains practically unchanged. Here too, we are going to use the SAM template to deploy our entire calculator code.

```
AWSTemplateFormatVersion: '2010-09-09'
Transform: AWS::Serverless-2016-10-31
Description: Simple Calc web service. State is stored in a DynamoDB table.
Resources:
  CalcGetFunction:
    Type: AWS::Serverless::Function
    Properties:
      Handler: index.handler
      Runtime: nodejs4.3
      Policies: AmazonDynamoDBReadOnlyAccess
      Role:
        arn:aws:iam::012345678910:
        role/MyCalcSAMDeployment-CalcGetFunctionRole-1JSUDGR70YYON
      Environment:
        Variables:
          TABLE_NAME: !Ref Table
      Events:
        GetResource:
          Type: Api
          Properties:
            Path: /calc/{operand1}/{operand2}/{operator}
            Method: post
  Table:
    Type: AWS::Serverless::SimpleTable
```

```
Properties:
  PrimaryKey:
    Name: calcAnswer
    Type: Number
  ProvisionedThroughput:
    ReadCapacityUnits: 5
    WriteCapacityUnits: 5
```

Here are the CLI commands to deploy the SAM template. Replace the content in the brackets < > with your values:

```
# aws cloudformation package --template-file <templateName.yaml> --s3-
bucket <bucketName> --output-template-file <packaged-templateName.yaml>
# aws cloudformation deploy --template-file <packaged-templateName.yaml> --
stack-name <stackName>
```

Once the stack gets deployed, go to the Lambda function and activate the X-Ray tracing as shown in the following screenshot:

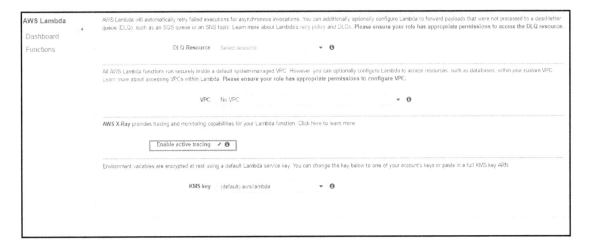

Go ahead and pass a few values to the deployed application using the API Gateway. Next, jump on to the X-Ray console and select the **Service map** tab on the left-hand side panel. You should see a graph populated as shown in the following screenshot:

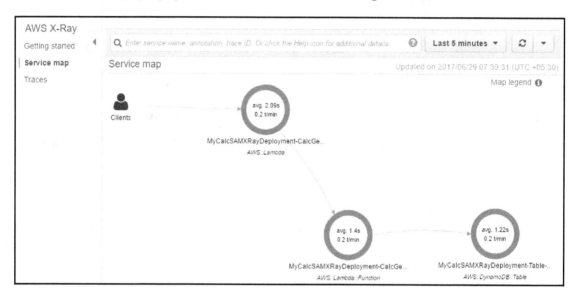

Select the **Traces** tab to view the trace list for this particular application. Select the trace **ID** to view an in-depth analysis of your application's performance and traces as shown in the following screenshot:

This is just one of the ways using which you can effectively analyze and monitor the performance of your serverless applications using one or more combinations of AWS services such as CloudWatch and X-Ray. In the next section, we will be exploring some really awesome third-party tools that are real handy when it comes to monitoring and analyzing performances of your serverless applications.

Monitoring Lambda functions using Datadog

Although CloudWatch and X-Ray are really awesome tools, there are times when these tools are simply not enough to work with at an *enterprise* level. This can hold true for a variety of reasons; take for example maturity--now, although X-Ray provides you with some real time trace statistics, it's still a very young service and will take time to evolve, into say, something provided by an enterprise transaction monitoring tool such as Dynatrace. Dynatrace actually leverages artificial intelligence to detect performance and availability issues and pinpoints their root causes; something that X-Ray doesn't support today. The same can be said for CloudWatch as well. Although you can monitor your AWS infrastructure using CloudWatch, sometimes you may require some extra tools such as Datadog, New Relic, Splunk, and so on to do some customized monitoring for you. Mind you, this doesn't mean there's something wrong in using AWS services for monitoring or performance tuning. It's simply a matter of perspective and your requirements.

So, that's what this section will cover mostly! We will understand how to leverage third-party tools for monitoring your serverless applications and infrastructure. We begin with a small walkthrough of Datadog!

Datadog is cloud infrastructure and an application monitoring service that comes packaged with an intuitive dashboard for viewing performance metrics along with notifications and alert capabilities. In this section, we will walk through few simple scenarios using which you can integrate Datadog with your own AWS environment and start monitoring your Lambda and rest of the serverless services with ease.

To start off with Datadog, you will first need to sign up for it's services. Datadog offers a 14-day trial period in which you can get complete access to all of its services for free. You can read about the entire integration process by visiting the site `http://docs.datadoghq.com/integrations/aws/`. With the integration completed, all you need to do is filter and select the **AWS Lambda** dashboard from the **List Dashboard** section. This is a prebuilt dashboard that you can start using immediately out of the box for your Lambda function monitoring. You can, alternatively, copy or **Clone Dashboard** into a new custom dashboard and add more metrics for monitoring, or change the overall setup of the dashboard as well:

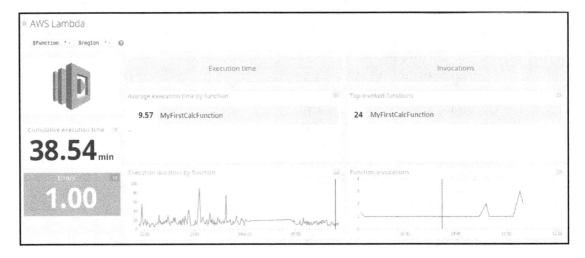

Simple enough, isn't it? There's still a lot more you can do and achieve with the dashboard, so feel free to give it a few tries.

With the basics out of the way, let us try something a bit different with Lambda as well. In this use case, we will be using a Lambda function to report our custom metrics obtained from monitoring a sample website running on an EC2 instance. These metrics will then be sent to Datadog for visualizations.

You can start of by installing a simple Apache web server on an EC2 instance with it's default `index.html` page being able to load when invoked by the instance's URL. The function's code will check whether it's getting a successful `200` response code from the website that you just created. If yes, then the function will send a `gauge` metric called `websiteCheck = 1` back to Datadog for visualization, else it will send a `gauge` metric called `websiteCheck = 0`.

Before we begin with the actual setup, here are a few pointers to keep in mind when working with Lambda and Datadog integration:

- At time of writing, Datadog supports only `gauge` and `count` metrics for Lambda
- Datadog Agent monitors our AWS account and sends metrics every 10 minutes
- Most of the service integrations with dashboards are already provided out of the box in Datadog, so you don't have to go around creating dashboards for your custom metrics as well

To get started, we first need to integrate our AWS account with Datadog. For this, we will be installing a Datadog Agent on an EC2 instance in our AWS account. This agent will monitor the AWS resources and periodically send metric data back to Datadog. The Agent requires certain permissions to be provided to it so that it is able to collect the metrics and send it back to Datadog. You will be required to create AWS role using the steps provided in this link: `http://docs.datadoghq.com/integrations/aws/`.

The role can be modified as per your requirements, but make sure the role in this case has at least permissions to describe and get EC2 instance details as well as logs.

We can create a role with the following snippet:

```
{
  "Version": "2012-10-17",
  "Statement": [
  {
    "Action": [
      "ec2:Describe*",
      "ec2:Get*",
      "logs:Get*",
      "logs:Describe*",
      "logs:FilterLogEvents",
      "logs:TestMetricFilter"
    ],
    "Effect": "Allow",
    "Resource": "*"
  }
  ]
}
```

With the role created, you now need to install the Datadog Agent in your AWS environment. If you already have an account in Datadog, then simply go to **Integrations** and select the **Agent** option from there. Here, you can select the option **Amazon Linux**, and click on **Next** to continue.

This will bring up a few extremely easy to follow and straightforward steps using which you can install and configure your Datadog Agent on the Amazon Linux EC2 instance.

For installing the Datadog Agent on the Amazon Linux instance, login to your Datadog account and follow the steps mentioned at `https://app.datadoghq.com/account/settings#agent/aws`.

With the Datadog Agent installed, the final steps required are simply to configure your service and Agent integration. This can be achieved by selecting the **Integrations** option from the Datadog dashboard and selecting the **Amazon Web Services** integration tile. Next, filter and select **Lambda** from the services list as shown in the following screenshot. You will also need to select the **Collect custom metrics** option for this case. Finally, fill in the required AWS account information along with the Datadog Agent role that we created at the beginning of this use case. With all settings completed, select the **Update Configuration** option to complete the Agent's configuration:

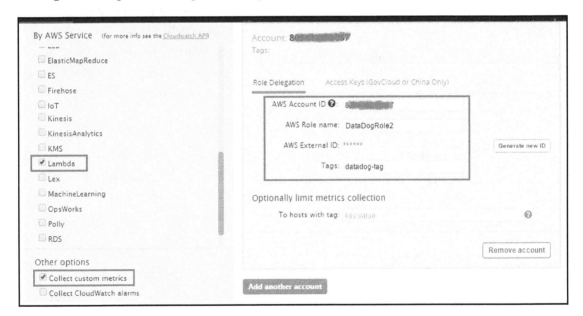

Now that you are done with AWS and Datadog integration, the next steps are all going to be Lambda specific configurations. First up, we need to understand how the metric data is going to be sent to Datadog by our Lambda function.

To send custom metrics to Datadog, you must print a log line from your Lambda, using the following format:

```
MONITORING|unix_epoch_timestamp|value|metric_type|my.metric.name|#tag1:valu
e,tag2
```

In the preceding code:

- `unix_epoch_timestamp`: It is a timestamp value calculated in seconds.
- `value`: It is the actual value of the metric.
- `metric_type`: It defines the type of metric. While writing, only `gauge` and `count` metrics are supported.
- `metric.name`: It is your custom name. In our case it is `websiteCheckMetric`.
- `tag`: is the tag name you wish to give to your custom metric so that you can filter out from the Datadog dashboard.

Here's a quick look at the metrics provided by Datadog for monitoring Lambda functions:

`aws.lambda.duration` (gauge)	Measures the average elapsed wall clock time from when the function code starts executing as a result of an invocation to when it stops executing. It is shown in millisecond.
`aws.lambda.duration.maximum` (gauge)	Measures the maximum elapsed wall clock time from when the function code starts executing as a result of an invocation to when it stops executing. It is shown in millisecond.
`aws.lambda.duration.minimum` (gauge)	Measures the minimum elapsed wall clock time from when the function code starts executing as a result of an invocation to when it stops executing. It is shown as millisecond.
`aws.lambda.duration.sum` (gauge)	Measures the total execution time of the lambda function executing. It is shown in millisecond.
`aws.lambda.errors` (count every 60 seconds)	Measures the number of invocations that failed due to errors in the function (response code 4XX).
`aws.lambda.invocations` (count every 60 seconds)	Measures the number of times a function is invoked in response to an event or invocation API call.

	Measures the number of Lambda function invocation attempts that were throttled due to invocation rates exceeding the customer's concurrent limits (error code 429). Failed invocations may trigger a retry attempt that succeeds.
`aws.lambda.throttles` (count every 60 seconds)	

Table source: Datadog Lambda integration (http://docs.datadoghq.com/integrations/awslambda/)

 Make sure that your IAM role contains the following permissions in order for the function to collect and send metric data to Datadog: `logs:describeloggroups`, `logs:describelogstreams`, and `logs:filterlogevents`.

Next, we prepare our Lambda function code that will be monitoring our simple website whether it is up and running, or down. Make sure to replace the `<Your_URL>` field with the URL of your website that you wish to monitor:

```
'use strict';
const request = require('request');
let target = "<Your_URL>";
let metric_value, tags;
exports.handler = (event, context, callback) => {
  // TODO implement
  let unix_epoch_timeshtamp = Math.floor(new Date() / 1000);
  // Parameters required for DataDog custom Metrics
  let metric_type = "gauge";
  // Only gauge or count are supported as of now.
  let my_metric_name = "websiteCheckMetric";
  // custom name given by us.
  request(target, function (error, response, body) {
    // successful response
    if(!error && response.statusCode === 200) {
      metric_value = 1;
      tags = ['websiteCheck:'+metric_value,'websiteCheck'];
      console.log("MONITORING|" +unix_epoch_timeshtamp+ "|" +metric_value+
        "|"+ metric_type +"|"+ my_metric_name+ "|"+ tags.join());
      callback(null, "UP!");
    }
    // erroneous response
    else{
      console.log("Error: ",error);
      if(response){
        console.log(response.statusCode);
      }
      metric_value = 0;
      tags = ['websiteCheck:'+metric_value,'websiteCheck'];
```

```
        console.log("MONITORING|" +unix_epoch_timeshtamp+ "|" +metric_value+
         "|"+ metric_type +"|"+ my_metric_name+ "|"+ tags.join());
        callback(null, "DOWN!");
      }
    });
};
```

With the code in place, package, and upload the same to Lambda. Make sure you build the code at least once so that the necessary npm modules are downloaded as well. With this step completed, we can now test our custom metrics by simply accessing the web URL of our Apache web server instance. If the page loads successfully, it will send a 200 response code that is interpreted by our Lambda function as a custom metric of value 1 to Datadog. You can even verify the output by viewing the functions' logs either from the Lambda dashboard or from CloudWatch as shown as follows:

Coming back to Datadog, to view your custom metrics, Datadog provides out-of-the-box dashboards that are able to display the custom metrics as well. You could alternatively even use the existing pre-created Lambda monitoring dashboard and add a new widget specifically for these custom metrics as well.

To view the custom metrics, select the **Custom Metrics** (no namespace) dashboard from Datadog's **List Dashboard**. Here, you can edit the graph's properties and provide customized values as per your requirements. To do so, click on the **Edit this graph** option:

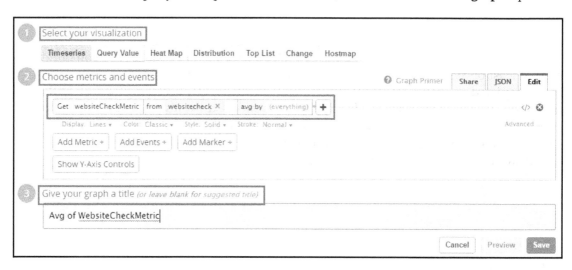

Here, you can edit the graph's visualization type from **Timeseries** to **Heat Map** as well as configuring the graph to display the outcome of our custom metric using the **Choose metrics and events** section. In our case, the query string is pretty straightforward: where we simply get the metric value by providing the metric name that we configured a while back in our Lambda function. Once you are done with your changes, remember to click on **Save** and exit the graph properties window. You should automatically see your custom metric get populated here after a short while. Remember, it can take time to display the metric as the Datadog Agent sends metrics in 10 minute intervals, so be patient! By default, the graph will show the average value of the metric. However you can always clone the dashboard and then make changes to the graph as you see fit. Here are a few examples of what the graph looks like once it is configured correctly:

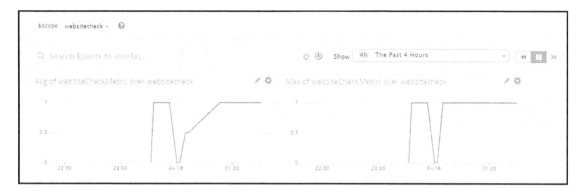

In this case, we are displaying the *average* as well as the *maximum* occurrence of the `websiteCheckMetric` over a period of 4 hours. In similar ways, you can configure custom metrics using more than one Lambda functions and visualize the same using Datadog's custom dashboards. Once the dashboards are all setup, you can even configure advanced alerts and notification mechanisms that trigger out in case an error or threshold value is detected.

In the next and final section of this chapter, we take a look at yet another popular tool that can prove to be a real life saver when it comes to churning through your functions logs and making some sense of your applications as well. Welcome to the world of Loggly!

Logging your functions with Loggly

You might have already used CloudWatch log streams since the time we have started working with Lambda functions in this book. Although a pretty neat tool; CloudWatch still lacks a good interface for performing log filtering and analysis. That's where Loggly steps in! Loggly is a centralized logging solution that offers powerful filtering capabilities along with the ability to analyze historical data to help detect anomalies within log data.

In this section, we will be exploring two simple use cases where Lambda functions and Loggly can be used together--the first is where we use Lambda to pump logs from CloudWatch all the way to Loggly and the second is by leveraging a few npm modules supported by Loggly for sending your application's logs to Loggly. So, without further ado; let get started!

First up, register for a Loggly account. You can sign up for one free of charge for a period of one month. You can sign up by visiting `https://www.loggly.com/signup/`.

Once you have signed up, you will need to generate a unique token called as **Customer Token** that will basically authenticate and send your CloudWatch logs from your AWS account over to your newly created Loggly account. To do so, select the **Source Setup** tab on the navigation bar and select **Customer Tokens** option from under it as shown:

With the token created, move over to your Lambda dashboard and filter out a blueprint with the name of `cloudwatch-logs-to-loggly`. This is perhaps the best part of working with Lambda! You have readymade starter templates for connecting to almost any service you can think of! Let us go ahead and deploy a function from this template.

In the **Configure triggers** page, select a log group whose logs you wish to send to Loggly for analysis. You can optionally provide a suitable **Filter Name** and **Filter Pattern** as well for your logs here. Once completed, click on **Next** to proceed with the next steps. Remember to select the **Enable trigger** option as well before you continue further.

In the **Configure function** page, provide a suitable **Name** for your function. Next, scroll down to the **Environment variables** section and provide the following information as shown in the following screenshot:

- `kmsEncryptedCustomerToken`: Provide the customer token that you created using Loggly dashboard here. Remember to encrypt the same using the KMS **Encryption key**.
- `logglyTags`: These are simple tags to identify your logs using Loggly.
- `logglyHostName`: Provide a suitable hostname for your Loggly function here. The name can be any meaningful identifier.

Finally, create, and assign your function an execution role. The role only needs to have full access to the logs as shown in the following snippet:

```
{
  "Version": "2012-10-17",
  "Statement": [
  {
    "Action": [
      "logs:*"
    ],
    "Effect": "Allow",
    "Resource": "*"
  }
  ]
}
```

Review the function's configurations and finally go ahead and create the function. You can simulate tests on your new function by simply selecting the **Test** option and passing the sample **CloudWatch Logs** as shown in the following screenshot:

Use the editor below to enter an event to test your function with. You can edit the event again by choosing **Configure test event** in the Actions list. Note that changes to the event will only be saved locally.

Sample event template   CloudWatch Logs

```
1 ▼ {
2 ▼   "awslogs": {
3       "data": "H4sIAAAAAAAAAHWPwQqCQBCGX0Xm7EFtK+smZBEUgXoLCdMhFtKV3akI8d0bLYmibvPPN3wz00CJxmQnT
4     }
5 }
```

To verify whether the events were passed to Loggly or not, log in to your Loggly account and select the **Search** tab and pass the `tag` name that you provided during the lambda function's creation as shown as follows:

```
tag:CloudWatch2Loggly
```

You should see the sample events passed during the tests as shown in the following screenshot:

Simple, isn't it? With this part over, let us move on to the second part of this section where we use a Loggly provided npm module and send our application logs over to Loggly for analysis.

For this scenario, we will be looking at a few communities provided npm modules that actually, make logging your application's logs to Loggly a breeze. To start with, here are four of the most commonly used npm modules that comply with Loggly's API:

- **Node-Loggly**: Node-Loggly can be used to send log data, search within log data, and retrieve relevant information as well. The Node-Loggly module is also capable of logging data with tags and supports sending log messages either as simple or as complex JSON objects.
- **Winston**: Winston is the most preferred out of the lot when it comes to logging and is also a recommended module by Loggly themselves. It is capable of accomplishing much more than the Node-Loggly module. It has the ability to perform profiling, handle logging exceptions, create custom error levels, and much more.
- **Bunyan**: Bunyan is also a very similar tool, in terms of functionality, to Winston. For this scenario we will be using Bunyan's logging module.
- **Morgan**: Unlike it's counterparts, Morgan is not very powerful or flexible. However it is specifically designed to work best with Express.js applications.

To know more about Bunyan, check out its documentation here: `https://github.com/trentm/node-bunyan`.

First up, we will need to create an IAM role for our application to be able to create and put logs into CloudWatch as well as permissions to decrypt the KMS keys. Here's a small snippet of the same:

```
{
  "Version": "2012-10-17",
  "Statement": [
    {
      "Sid": "myLogsPermissions",
      "Effect": "Allow",
      "Action": [
        "logs:CreateLogGroup",
        "logs:CreateLogStream",
        "logs:PutLogEvents"
      ],
      "Resource": [
        "*"
      ]
    },
    {
      "Sid": "myKMSPermissions",
      "Effect": "Allow",
      "Action": [
        "kms:Decrypt"
      ],
      "Resource": [
        "*"
      ]
    }
  ]
}
```

With the IAM role created, we can now move on to our application and injecting the Bunyan code within it as well. Copy the code to an `index.js` file and install the `bunyan` and `bunyan-loggly` npm modules using the `npm install` command. Once the code is up and ready, create a zip and upload the same to Lambda either manually, or by using APEX as performed in our earlier chapters.

The code relies on two environment variables; one for customer token and another for the Loggly subdomain. During execution, the code simply creates a new logger stream named `myloggylog`. We specify our customer token (which is first decrypted) and our Loggly subdomain during configuring the environment variables for the function:

```
'use strict';
const bunyan = require('bunyan');
const Bunyan2Loggly = require('bunyan-loggly');
const AWS = require('aws-sdk');
const kms = new AWS.KMS({ apiVersion: '2014-11-01' });
const decryptParams = {
  CiphertextBlob: new Buffer(process.env.kmsEncryptedCustomerToken,
  'base64'),
};
let customerToken;
let log;
exports.handler = (event, context, callback) => {
  kms.decrypt(decryptParams, (error, data) => {
    if (error) {
      console.log(error);
      return callback(error);
    }
    else {
      customerToken = data.Plaintext.toString('ascii');
      log = bunyan.createLogger({
        name: 'myloggylog',
        streams: [
        {
          type: 'raw',
          stream: new Bunyan2Loggly({
            token: customerToken,
            subdomain: process.env.logglySubDomain,
            json: true
          })
        }
        ]
      });
      log.info("My first log in loggly!!!");
      return callback(null, "all events sent to loggly!");
    }
  });
```

With the code uploaded, make sure you check **Enable encryption helpers** and fill out the **Environment variables**, namely the customer token and the Loggly subdomain as shown in the following screenshot:

With this step completed, you can now test the application. The code doesn't require any specific events to be passed during execution. You should see the output in your function's logs, as shown in the following screenshot:

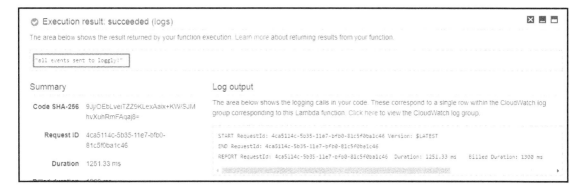

Bunyan in it's output to Loggly includes the **process id (pid)**, hostname, and timestamp, along with the log message as shown in the following screenshot:

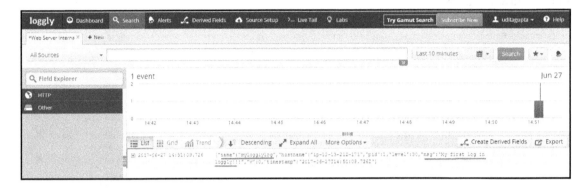

Using such npm modules or other third-party libraries written in languages such as C#, Java, and so on, you can easily create and send logs to Loggly for analysis.

AWS Lambda - Use Cases
21

In this chapter, we will be looking at some of the most commonly used Lambda use cases and how you can leverage them to manage your AWS environments. The use cases are broadly classified into the following categories:

- Infrastructure management--this section will demonstrate how to leverage Lambda functions
- Managing the costs of your AWS account by shutting down large instance types during off hours
- Tagging untagged instances for better governance and cost control
- Taking scheduled snapshots of your volumes for data backups
- Data transformation--how to use Lambda functions to transform either streaming or static data before it gets uploaded to a database

Sounds interesting, right? Then what are you waiting for! Let's get started right away!

Infrastructure management

One of the core and most frequently used use cases for Lambda has been effective management of the AWS infrastructure, mainly around EC2 instances, as this is where a majority of the costs are incurred unnecessarily. Before the advent of Lambda functions, a lot of organizations had to rely on third-party automation tools and services to run simple and straightforward tasks on their instances, such as taking periodic backups of an EBS volume, checking whether an instance is tagged or not, or shutting down large instances if they are not required to run 24/7, just to name a few. The worst issue in this case was also the management of the automation tool itself! In most cases, you would have to run it off an EC2 instance, and this just created an unnecessary overhead for administrators. But not anymore! With Lambda, administrators can now create simple functions that are capable of performing a lot of these tasks without the need for complex third-party tools that were required to perform earlier. Let's take a look at each of these use cases in a bit more depth and see how you can use them for your environments as well.

Scheduled startup and shutdown of instances

First up, we have a simple function that shuts down your instances and powers them back on, based on CloudWatch scheduled events.

To begin, we first create a simple function that will start up a particular instance or set of instances using the following code. You will need to replace the <YOUR_INSTANCE_ID_GOES_HERE> field with the actual IDs of your instances; the rest of the code remains the same:

```
'use strict';
console.log('Loading function');
exports.handler = (event, context, callback) => {
  var AWS = require('aws-sdk');
  AWS.config.region = 'ap-southeast-1';
  var ec2 = new AWS.EC2();
  var params = {
    InstanceIds: [ /* required */
      '<YOUR_INSTANCE_ID_GOES_HERE>'
      /* more items */
    ]
    //AdditionalInfo: 'STRING_VALUE',
    //DryRun: true || false
  };
  ec2.startInstances(params, function(err, data) {
    if (err) console.log(err, err.stack); // an error occurred
    else     console.log(JSON.stringify(data));
```

```
    });
  }
```

For the functions to start and stop instances on our behalf, we will also need to provide a custom IAM role for them. Remember to provide your function's ARN in the IAM role's resource section, as shown in this example:

```
{
  "Version": "2012-10-17",
  "Statement": [
    {
      "Sid": "Stmt1483458245000",
      "Effect": "Allow",
      "Action": [
        "ec2:StartInstances",
        "ec2:StopInstances"
      ],
      "Resource": [
        "*"
      ]
    },
    {
      "Sid": "Stmt1483458787000",
      "Effect": "Allow",
      "Action": [
        "logs:CreateLogGroup",
        "logs:CreateLogStream",
        "logs:PutLogEvents"
      ],
      "Resource": [
        "*"
      ]
    },
    {
      "Sid": "Stmt148345878700",
      "Effect": "Allow",
      "Action": [
        "lambda:InvokeFunction"
      ],
      "Resource": [
        "arn:aws:lambda:ap-southeast-1:01234567890:function:Instance_Stop",
        "arn:aws:lambda:ap-southeast-1:01234567890:function:Instance_Start"
      ]
    }
  ]
}
```

So far, so good; we have just one small bit to take care of for the last--the trigger for our function that will be created using CloudWatch Event Rule. Now, you can create and configure the Event Rule using the CloudWatch dashboard as well as by leveraging the **Configure triggers** configuration page on the function's dashboard, which is what we are going to be using for this use case. The triggers' configuration page on the function's dashboard, is what we are going to be using for this use case.

Select the **CloudWatch Events** option from the **Add trigger** page, as shown here. This will pop up some simple fields that you will need to fill out for your *instance start* rule. Provide a suitable **Rule name** and **Rule description**, as shown in the following screenshot:

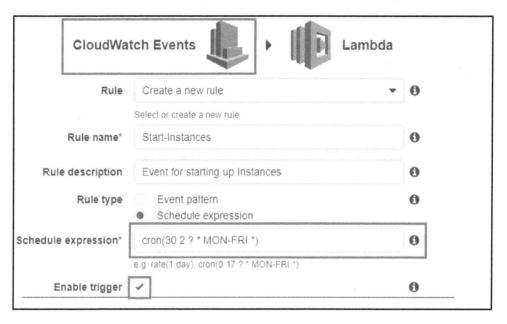

Next, select **Schedule expression** from the **Rule type** choice and provide a valid Cron expression based on your requirements. In my case, the Cron expression looks a bit like this: `cron(30 2 ? * MON-FRI *)`.

 You can get more examples of the Cron expression at
`https://docs.aws.amazon.com/AmazonCloudWatch/latest/events/ScheduledEvents.html`.

Remember to select the **Enable trigger** option before saving the trigger. With this, we have created a simple event-driven function that will start up a set of EC2 instances at a particular time. Similarly, you can create a second function that will stop the EC2 instances based on another CloudWatch Event. You can actually reuse the previous code and simply change the `ec2.startInstances` method to `ec2.startInstances`, as shown in the following snippet, and that's it! You are good to go!

```
ec2.stopInstances(params, function(err, data) {
  if (err) console.log(err, err.stack); // an error occurred
  else     console.log(JSON.stringify(data));
});
```

You can additionally modify these functions to accept the instance IDs as environment variables or even pass them as event parameters at runtime, but that is something I leave completely up to you.

Let's look at a similar use case, where we leverage a Lambda function to take periodic snapshots of your EBS volumes.

Periodic snapshots of EBS volumes using Lambda

This use case follows along the same lines as the earlier one, where we take backup of our instances in the form of an AMI as well as conduct a snapshot of that instance's EBS volume if the instances have a tag named `backup`.

To get started, your Lambda function needs to have permissions to be able to create snapshots, create an AMI, as well as change some snapshot attributes, and so on. Here is a snippet of the function's IAM role that we have created for this exercise:

```
{
  "Version": "2012-10-17",
  "Statement": [
  {
    "Sid": "myEC2Permissions",
    "Effect": "Allow",
    "Action": [
      "ec2:Describe*"
    ],
    "Resource": [
      "*"
    ]
  },
```

```
    {
      "Sid": "myEC2AMIPermissions",
      "Effect": "Allow",
      "Action": [
        "ec2:CreateImage",
        "ec2:Describe*",
        "ec2:ModifyImageAttribute",
        "ec2:ResetImageAttribute"
      ],
      "Resource": [
        "*"
      ]
    },
    {
      "Sid": "myEC2SnapshotPermissions",
      "Effect": "Allow",
      "Action": [
        "ec2:CreateSnapshot",
        "ec2:ModifySnapshotAttribute",
        "ec2:ResetSnapshotAttribute"
      ],
      "Resource": [
        "*"
      ]
    },
    {
      "Sid": "myLogsPermissions",
      "Effect": "Allow",
      "Action": [
        "logs:CreateLogGroup",
        "logs:CreateLogStream",
        "logs:PutLogEvents"
      ],
      "Resource": [
        "*"
      ]
    }
  ]
}
```

With the IAM role setup, let's quickly understand how the function code actually works out. The code maintains two arrays--one for instance IDs and the other comprising their corresponding EBS volume IDs:

- The code first filters instances with the `backup` tag and adds all the instance IDs returned in the response to the `instanceIDs` array.
- It then uses the `describeVolume` call to get all the EBS volumes IDs of those particular instances and adds them to the corresponding `volumeIDs` array.
- Once done, the code will call the `createImage` function and provide each instance ID in the `instanceIDs` array to create an AMI out of them.
- It will also invoke `createSnapshot` along with the `createImage` function and provide each volume ID in the `volumesIDs` array to create snapshots out of it-- simple, isn't it?

Let's take a look at the function code itself now:

```
'use strict';
console.log('Loading function');
const aws = require('aws-sdk');
const async = require('async');
const ec2 = new aws.EC2({apiVersion: '2016-11-15'});
let instanceIDs =[];
let volumeIDs = [];
function createImage(instanceID, createImageCB){
  let date =
   new Date().toISOString().replace(/:/g, '-').replace(/\..+/, '');
  //console.log("AMI name: "+instanceID+'-'+date);
  let createImageParams = {
    InstanceId: instanceID, /* required */
    Name: 'AMI-'+instanceID+'-'+date /* required */
  };
  ec2.createImage(createImageParams,
  function(createImageErr, createImageData) {
    if (createImageErr){
      console.log(createImageErr, createImageErr.stack);
      // an error occurred
      createImageCB(createImageErr);
    }
    else{
      console.log("createImageData: ",createImageData);
      // successful response
      createImageCB(null, "AMI created!!");
    }
  });
}
```

```
function createSnapShot(volumeID, createSnapShotCB){
  let createSnapShotParams = {
    VolumeId: volumeID, /* required */
    Description: 'Snapshot of volume: '+volumeID
  };
  ec2.createSnapshot(createSnapShotParams,
  function(createSnapShotErr, createSnapShotData) {
    if (createSnapShotErr){
      console.log(createSnapShotErr, createSnapShotErr.stack);
      // an error occurred
      createSnapShotCB(createSnapShotErr);
    }
    else{
      console.log("createSnapShotData: ", createSnapShotData);
      // successful response
      createSnapShotCB(null , "SnapShot created!!");
    }
  });
}
exports.handler = (event, context, callback) => {
  instanceIDs = [];
  volumeIDs =[];
  let describeTagParams = {
    Filters: [
    {
      Name: "key",
      Values: [
        "backup"
      ]
    }
    ]
  };
  let describeVolParams = {
    Filters: [
    {
      Name: "attachment.instance-id",
      Values: []
    }
    ]
  };
  ec2.describeTags(describeTagParams,
  function(describeTagsErr, describeTagsData)
  {
    if (describeTagsErr){
      console.log(describeTagsErr, describeTagsErr.stack);
      // an error occurred
      callback(describeTagsErr);
    }
```

```
else{
  console.log("describe tags data: ",
  JSON.stringify(describeTagsData));
  // successful response
  for(let i in describeTagsData.Tags){
    instanceIDs.push(describeTagsData.Tags[i].ResourceId);
    describeVolParams.Filters[0].Values.push(
      describeTagsData.Tags[i].ResourceId);
  }
  console.log("final instanceIDs array: "+instanceIDs);
  console.log("final describeVolParams: ",describeVolParams);
  ec2.describeVolumes(describeVolParams,
  function(describeVolErr, describeVolData) {
    if (describeVolErr){
      console.log(describeVolErr, describeVolErr.stack);
      // an error occurred
      callback(describeVolErr);
    }
    else{
      console.log("describeVolData:",describeVolData);
      // successful response
      for(let j in describeVolData.Volumes){
        volumeIDs.push(describeVolData.Volumes[j].VolumeId);
      }
      console.log("final volumeIDs array: "+volumeIDs);
      async.parallel({
        one: function(oneCB) {
          async.forEachOf(instanceIDs,function (instanceID,
          key, imageCB)
          {
            createImage(instanceID, function(createImageErr,
            createImageResult){
              if(createImageErr){
                imageCB(createImageErr);
              }
              else{
                imageCB(null, createImageResult);
              }
            });
          }, function (imageErr) {
              if (imageErr){
              return oneCB(imageErr);
              }
              oneCB(null, "Done with creating AMIs!");
          });
        },
        two: function(twoCB) {
          async.forEachOf(volumeIDs,
```

```
                        function (volumeID, key, volumeCB)
                        {
                          //console.log("volumeID in volumeIDs: "+volumeID);
                          createSnapShot(volumeID, function(createSnapShotErr,
                          createSnapShotResult){
                            if(createSnapShotErr){
                              volumeCB(createSnapShotErr);
                            }
                            else{
                              volumeCB(null, createSnapShotResult);
                            }
                          });
                        }, function (volumeErr) {
                            if (volumeErr){
                               return twoCB(volumeErr);
                            }
                            twoCB(null, "Done with creating Snapshots!");
                        });
                    }
                }, function(finalErr, finalResults) {
                    if(finalErr){
                       callback(finalErr);
                    }
                    callback(null, "Done!!");
                });
            }
        });
    }
  });
};
```

With the code and IAM roles created, you can now go ahead to create the trigger. We are going to trigger this function using a CloudWatch scheduled event. You can alternatively even use a cron job or rate expression, as per your requirements. For this exercise, we have gone ahead and created rate expression for simplicity, as shown here:

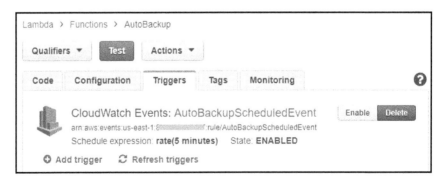

Make sure your trigger is set to **ENABLED** before testing the function out. To test the function, simply create a new instance with a tag of `backup` or create a new tag with the same `backup` name to an existing set of instances as well.

Once the function is triggered based on the rate expression or cron job execution, you should see new AMIs and EBS volume snapshots created, as shown in the following screenshot:

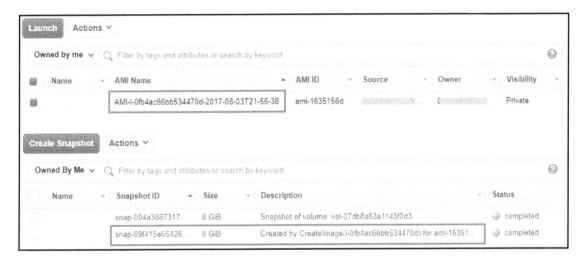

Here's a handy tip! Although we have created a really useful instance backup utility here, it's equally important to have an automatic backup deletion system in place as well; otherwise, your account will be soon flooded with too many copies of AMIs and EBS volumes, which will pile up on your overall costs.

With this use case completed, let's look at yet another simple yet useful infrastructure management use case that can potentially enable you to govern your AWS accounts much better, as well as cut some costs in the process.

Enabling governance using EC2 tags and Lambda

Governance has always been of one of the key issues faced by cloud administrators, especially when it comes to tracking EC2 instances for cost and compliance purposes. In this use case, we are going to automate the tagging of EC2 instances and its corresponding resources using a simple Lambda function used in conjuncture with AWS CloudTrail and CloudWatch. The function will ensure that users can work only on those resources that they have created based on resource tags.

How it all works is as follows. We start off by creating a *trail* in CloudTrail to track all the API calls and events taking place within the AWS account. Next, we create a dummy user in IAM, which will not only have permissions of creating tags, but also the permission to create and use their own resource. This is essential as if the user has the permission to create tags; then, they can manipulate the tags themselves, which is something we don't want. After this, we create a function that will tag the resources automatically with the following tag key values:

- `Owner`: The current user's name value or the resource creator's name value
- `PrincipalId`: The current user's `aws:userid` value

The code will also get triggered for the following events:

- EBS volume creation
- Snapshot creation
- AMI creation
- Run instances

Let's get started by creating a simple trail in CloudTrail. You can refer to the steps mentioned in this guide to get started with CloudTrail: `http://docs.aws.amazon.com/awscloudtrail/latest/userguide/cloudtrail-create-and-update-a-trail-by-using-the-console.html`.

In our case, we have provided the following values for the trail's parameters:

- **Trail name**: Provide a suitable name for your trail. In this case, we have provided it with the name `taggerTrail`.
- **Apply trail to all regions**: You can select **Yes** for this option.

- **Read/Write events**: These events are correspondents to operations that occur in your AWS account. For this use case, we have selected **All** as the option.
- **Storage location**: Here, you can either select an S3 bucket to store your trial logs or, alternatively, go ahead and create one:

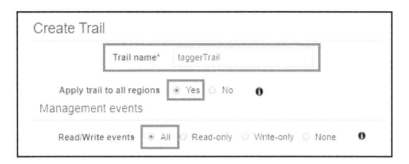

With the trail created, we now move on toward creating a policy for our IAM users. The policy basically states that if you are the owner of that particular EC2 resource, then you can stop, start, reboot, and terminate your machine; otherwise, you won't be permitted to perform it. Running and describing instance operations is, however, allowed to all users.

Create a new policy using IAM and attach this policy to your users or user groups:

```
{
  "Version": "2012-10-17",
  "Statement": [
  {
    "Sid": "LaunchEC2InstancesPermissions",
    "Effect": "Allow",
    "Action": [
      "ec2:Describe*",
      "ec2:RunInstances"
    ],
    "Resource": [
      "*"
    ]
  },
  {
    "Sid": "AllowActionsIfYouAreTheOwnerPermissions",
    "Effect": "Allow",
    "Action": [
      "ec2:StopInstances",
      "ec2:StartInstances",
      "ec2:RebootInstances",
      "ec2:TerminateInstances"
    ],
```

```
        "Condition": {
          "StringEquals": {
            "ec2:ResourceTag/PrincipalId": "${aws:userid}"
          }
        },
        "Resource": [
          "*"
        ]
      }
    ]
  }
```

With the IAM policy created and the trail enabled, let's us go ahead and set up the Lambda function and its triggers. To start with, you will first need to create the function's IAM role, as described in the following snippet:

```
{
    "Version": "2012-10-17",
    "Statement": [
    {
      "Sid": "Stmt1501655705000",
      "Effect": "Allow",
      "Action": [
        "cloudtrail:LookupEvents"
      ],
      "Resource": [
        "*"
      ]
    },
    {
      "Sid": "Stmt1501655728000",
      "Effect": "Allow",
      "Action": [
        "ec2:CreateTags",
        "ec2:Describe*"
      ],
      "Resource": [
        "*"
      ]
    },
    {
      "Sid": "Stmt1501655809000",
      "Effect": "Allow",
      "Action": [
        "logs:CreateLogGroup",
        "logs:CreateLogStream",
        "logs:PutLogEvents"
      ],
```

```
    "Resource": [
      "*"
    ]
  }
 ]
}
```

Next, we move on to creating the Lambda function for this use case. The function's code has been broken down here for simplicity and ease of understanding. You can always get the complete code using this link as well: `https://github.com/masteringAWSLambda/Mastering-AWS-Lambda`.

Here's a look at what the code does snippet by snippet.

First up, the code uses an ID array to store all the resource IDs it needs to create tags for. The code will get all parameters, such as `region`, `eventname` (the API call the user makes: for example, `RunInstances`), `PrincipalId`, and so on from the event it receives:

```
Id = [];
region = event.region;
detail = event.detail;
eventname = detail.eventName;
arn = detail.userIdentity.arn;
principal = detail.userIdentity.principalId;
userType = detail.userIdentity.type;
if(userType === 'IAMUser'){
  user = detail.userIdentity.userName;
}
else{
  user = principal.split(':')[1];
}
```

After this, the code looks for the resource IDs in the CloudWatch Event. For each API call (for example, `RunInstances`, `CreateVolume`, and so on) the resource IDs can be found in different sections of the received event response:

```
To process this, we have implemented a switch case that checks for the
event name and then appropriately gathers all the resource IDs and adds
them to the id array.
switch(eventname){
  case "CreateVolume":
    id.push(detail.responseElements.volumeId);
    console.log("id array: "+id);
    createTag(function(err, result){
      if(err){
        callback(err);
      }
```

```
          else{
            callback(null, "Done tagging!!");
          }
      });
      break;
    case "RunInstances":
      runInstances(function(err, result){
        if(err){
          callback(err);
        }
        else{
          createTag(function(createTagErr, createTagResult){
            if(createTagErr){
              callback(err);
            }
            else{
              callback(null, "Done tagging!!");
            }
          });
        }
      });
      break;
    case "CreateImage":
      id.push(detail.responseElements.imageId);
      console.log("id array: "+id);
      createTag(function(err, result){
        if(err){
          callback(err);
        }
        else{
          callback(null, "Done tagging!!");
        }
      });
      break;
    case "CreateSnapshot":
      id.push(detail.responseElements.snapshotId);
      console.log("id array: "+id);
      createTag(function(err, result){
        if(err){
          callback(err);
        }
        else{
          callback(null, "Done tagging!!");
        }
      });
      break;
    default:
      console.log("None of the options matched!!!");
```

```
        callback(null, "None of the options matched!!!");
    }
```

Since the `runInstances` and `createTag` functions were a little more complicated, we decided to take them out, create them as functions, and call them from our handler.

Here are the functions:

```
function createTag(tagCB){
  async.forEachOf(id, function (resourceID, key, cb) {
    var tagParams = {
      Resources: [
        resourceID
      ],
      Tags: [
        {
          Key: "Owner",
          Value: user
        },
        {
          Key: "PrincipalId",
          Value: principal
        }
      ]
    };
    ec2.createTags(tagParams, function(tagErr, tagData) {
      if (tagErr){
        console.log("Couldn't tag the resource "+tagParams.Resources+"
         due to: "+tagErr); // an error occurred
        cb(tagErr);
      }
      else{
        console.log("Tagged successfully");
        // successful response
        cb(null, "tagged!");
      }
    });
  }, function (err) {
      if (err){
        console.log(err);
        tagCB(err);
      }
      else{
        console.log("Done tagging!");
        tagCB(null, "Done!!");
      }
  });
}
```

```
function runInstances(runCB){
  let items = detail.responseElements.instancesSet.items;
  async.series({
    one: function(oneCB) {
      async.forEachOf(items, function (item, key, cb) {
        id.push(item.instanceId);
        cb(null, "added");
      }, function (err) {
          if (err){
            console.log(err);
            oneCB(err);
          }
          else{
            console.log("id array: "+id);
            oneCB(null, "Done!!");
          }
      });
    },
    two: function(twoCB){
      describeParams = {
        InstanceIds: [
        ]
      };
      async.forEachOf(id, function (instanceID, key, cb) {
        describeParams.InstanceIds.push(instanceID);
        cb(null, "added");
      }, function (err) {
          if (err){
            console.log(err);
            twoCB(err);
          }
          else{
            //console.log("describeParams: ", describeParams);
            twoCB(null, "Done!!");
          }
      });
    },
    three: function(threeCB){
      ec2.describeInstances(describeParams, function(err, data) {
        if (err){
          console.log(err, err.stack); // an error occurred
          threeCB(err);
        }
        else{
          console.log("data: ",JSON.stringify(data));
          // successful response
          let reservations = data.Reservations;
          async.forEachOf(reservations, function (reservation,
```

```
key, resrvCB)
{
  console.log("******** inside reservations foreachof
  async loop! ************");
  let instances = reservation.Instances[0];
  //console.log("Instances: ",instances);
  // get all volume ids
  let blockdevicemappings = instances.BlockDeviceMappings;
  //console.log("blockdevicemappings: ",blockdevicemappings);
  // get all ENI ids
  let networkinterfaces = instances.NetworkInterfaces;
  console.log("networkinterfaces: ",networkinterfaces);

  async.each(blockdevicemappings,
  function (blockdevicemapping, blockCB) {
    console.log("************** inside blockdevicemappings
    asyn each loop! ***********");
    id.push(blockdevicemapping.Ebs.VolumeId);
    console.log("id array from blockdevicemapping: "+id);
    blockCB(null, "added");
  }, function (err) {
      if (err){
        console.log(err);
        resrvCB(err);
      }
      else{
        async.each(networkinterfaces,
        function (networkinterface, netCB) {
         console.log("******** inside networkinterfaces each
          async loop! *******");
         id.push(networkinterface.NetworkInterfaceId);
         console.log("id array from networkinterface: "+id);
         netCB(null, "added");
        }, function (err) {
            if (err){
              console.log(err);
              resrvCB(err);
            }
            else{
              resrvCB(null, "Done!!");
            }
        });
      }
  });
  }, function (err) {
      if (err){
        console.log(err);
        threeCB(err);
```

```
                        }
                        else{
                         threeCB(null, "Done!!");
                        }
                   });
               }
           });
       }
   }, function(runErr, results) {
       if(runErr){
          console.log(runErr);
          runCB(runErr);
       }
       else{
          //console.log("id array from final runInstances: "+id);
          runCB(null, "got all ids");
       }
   });
}
```

Phew! That's some code! But, if you have gotten this far, then we are just a few more steps away from testing our setup. But before that, we need to create and configure a CloudWatch Event rule that will trigger the Lambda function each time it receives a log from the CloudTrail trail we created earlier.

To do that, simply select the **Create rule** option from the **Rules** section in your CloudWatch dashboard. This brings up the **Create rule** wizard, using which we will configure our trigger.

First up, from the **Event Source** section, ensure that the **Event pattern** option is selected, as shown in the following screenshot. Select **EC2** from the **Service Name** drop-down list and **AWS API Call via CloudTrail** as its corresponding **Event Type**.

Next, specify the operations for which you wish to trigger the function. In this case, we have opted for the EC2 instance's **CreateImage**, **CreateSnapshot**, **CreateVolume**, and **RunInstances**, as shown in the following screenshot:

You can even copy and paste the following in the **Event Pattern Preview** dialog box:

```
{
  "source": [
    "aws.ec2"
  ],
  "detail-type": [
    "AWS API Call via CloudTrail"
  ],
  "detail": {
    "eventSource": [
      "ec2.amazonaws.com"
    ],
    "eventName": [
      "CreateImage",
      "CreateSnapshot",
      "CreateVolume",
      "RunInstances"
    ]
  }
}
```

Next, select your newly created **Function** from the **Targets** section, as shown here:

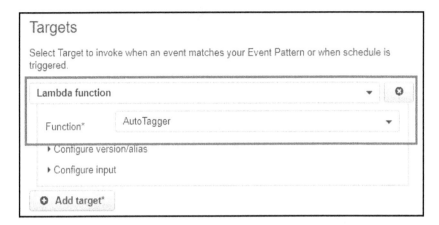

Now let's look at this in action--to test the setup, simply launch a new EC2 instance in your account. Once the instance is up and running, it will obtain two tags--Owner and PrincipalId values. The associated EBS volume of the instance as well as the **Elastic Network Interface** (**ENI**), *if attached* should also get tagged with these two tags!

Here is a screen grab of the instance showing the two tags, as described earlier:

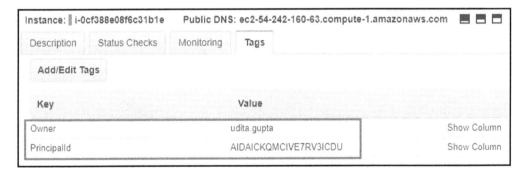

With this, we come toward the end of the infrastructure management use cases for Lambda. In the next section, we will be looking at a simple example of leveraging Lambda functions for conduction data transformation.

Data transformation

Yet another key use case for Lambda has been its ability to transform data on the fly. Say you have a stream of data coming into an S3 bucket in the form of one or more CSV files, each CSV file being different in size. For your application to process this data, it first needs to be transformed into a JSON file and then uploaded to a DynamoDB table. So, how do you get this done effectively? One way is to leverage an EC2 instance that will periodically poll or pull the CSV files from S3, transform it, and upload it to DynamoDB. However, this can have potential issues, for example: what happens when there are no files coming into S3 for a long time? Do you keep the EC2 instance up and running all this time? Also, polling or pulling the files from S3 will require its own set of logic that you will have to maintain, which can be an additional burden. So, what's the easy way out? You guessed it: Lambda functions!

For this particular use case, we will be creating a simple S3 bucket that will host our CSV files. A corresponding Lambda function will be used to convert the CSVs into JSON files and push the transformed data to a DynamoDB table.

For this to work, we will additionally need to configure a trigger on our S3 bucket so that it triggers the Lambda function whenever a new CSV file is uploaded to it. This will be achieved by leveraging the *S3 object created event* as the trigger for our Lambda function, which we will explain in the upcoming steps.

Go ahead and create a new bucket in S3. For this use case, you can name the bucket anything you want; however, the CSV files are all going to be placed within a folder in the bucket with the name csv. With the bucket created, configure a simple DynamoDB table in the same region with the following structure:

ID	Name	Age
1	John	23
2	Sarah	45

Next, create a Lambda function in the same region as the bucket. Copy and paste the following code in an index.js file:

```
'use strict';
console.log('Loading function');
const aws = require('aws-sdk');
const async = require('async');
const s3 = new aws.S3({ apiVersion: '2006-03-01' });
const csv = require("csvtojson");
const jsonfile = require('jsonfile');
const fs = require('fs');
```

```
const docClient = new aws.DynamoDB.DocumentClient();
exports.handler = (event, context, callback) => {
  async.auto({
    download: function(callback) {
      console.log('Received event:', JSON.stringify(event, null, 2));
      const bucket = event.Records[0].s3.bucket.name;
      let key =
       decodeURIComponent(event.Records[0].s3.object.key
       .replace(/\+/g, ' '));
      const downloadParams = {
        Bucket: bucket,
        Key: key
      };
      // removing the csv/ from the actual key-name
      key = key.replace('csv/', '');
      // files can be downloaded in the /tmp directory in lambda
      let csvFile = "/tmp/"+key;
      let file = fs.createWriteStream(csvFile);
      s3.getObject(downloadParams).createReadStream().on('error',
      function(err){
        console.log("Error while downloading the file from S3: ",err);
        callback(err);
      }).pipe(file);
      file.on('finish', function() {
        file.close();  // close() is async, call cb after close completes.
        console.log("Download complete! "+csvFile);
        callback(null, {'csvFile':csvFile, 'bucketName':bucket,
         'key':key});
      });
      file.on('error', function(err){
        console.log("Error while downloading the Id3 file from S3:
         ",err);
        callback(err);
      });
    },
    csvtojson: ['download', function(results, callback){
      console.log("Inside csvtojson function");
      let csvFile = results.download.csvFile;
      csv()
      .fromFile(csvFile)
      .on("end_parsed",function(jsonArrayObj){
        //when parse finished, result will be emitted here.
        console.log(jsonArrayObj);
        // Final file will have a .json extention
        let keyJson = results.download.key.replace(/.csv/i, ".json");
        console.log("Final file: "+keyJson);
        // we are writing the final json file in the /tmp directory itself
         in lambda
```

```
      let jsonFile = "/tmp/"+keyJson;
      jsonfile.writeFile(jsonFile, jsonArrayObj, function (err) {
        if(err){
          console.error(err);
          callback(err);
        }
      });
      callback(null, {'keyJson':keyJson, 'jsonFile':jsonFile});
    });
  }],
  sendToDynamo: ['download', 'csvtojson', function(results, callback)
{
    console.log("Inside sendToDynamo function");
    console.log("Importing data into DynamoDB. Please wait.");
    fs.readFile(results.csvtojson.jsonFile, function (err, data) {
      if (err){
        console.log(err);
        return callback(err);
      }
      let obj = JSON.parse(data);
      async.forEachOf(obj, function (obj, key, cb) {
        let params = {
          TableName: process.env.TABLE_NAME,
          Item: {
            "ID":  obj.ID,
            "Name": obj.Name,
            "Age":  obj.Age
          }
        };
        docClient.put(params, function(err, data) {
          if (err) {
            console.error("Unable to add ", data.Name,
             ". Error JSON:", JSON.stringify(err, null, 2));
            cb(err);
          } else {
              console.log("PutItem succeeded");
              cb(null, "PutItem succeeded");
          }
        });
      }, function (err) {
          if (err){
            console.log(err);
            callback(err);
          }
          else{
            callback(null, "Done!!");
          }
      });
```

```
        });
      }]
    },
    function(err, results) {
      if(err){
        console.log("Finished with error!");
      }
      else{
        console.log(results);
      }
    });
  };
```

The code is pretty self-explanatory. We first download the `.csv` file from the `/csv` folder present in your S3 bucket locally into Lambda. The file gets downloaded into the function's `/tmp` directory as this is the only available local filesystem you can write to in a function. Once the function downloads the file to `/tmp`, it is converted into a new JSON file. The JSON file is written into the `/tmp` directory as well. Now that the file is converted, the `sendToDynamo` function gets invoked, which reads the JSON file and writes its contents to our previously created DynamoDB table.

Make sure you have provided the function the necessary permissions before saving the function. In this case, the function will require permissions to retrieve the CSV file from the S3 bucket, write logs to CloudWatch, as well as write the data into your DynamoDB table. You can use the following snippet to configure your IAM role; just remember to substitute the `<YOUR_BUCKET_NAME>` and `<YOUR_TABLE_NAME>` fields with the values from your setup:

```
{
  "Version": "2012-10-17",
  "Statement": [
  {
    "Sid": "myS3Permissions",
    "Effect": "Allow",
    "Action": [
      "s3:GetObject"
    ],
    "Resource": [
      "arn:aws:s3:::<YOUR_BUCKET_NAME>/*"
    ]
  },
  {
    "Sid": "myLogsPermissions",
    "Effect": "Allow",
    "Action": [
      "logs:CreateLogGroup",
```

```
      "logs:CreateLogStream",
      "logs:PutLogEvents"
    ],
    "Resource": [
      "*"
    ]
  },
  {
    "Sid": "myDynamodbPermissions",
    "Effect": "Allow",
    "Action": [
      "dynamodb:PutItem"
    ],
    "Resource": [
      "arn:aws:dynamodb:us-east-1:01234567890:table/<YOUR_TABLE_NAME>"
    ]
  }
  ]
}
```

With the function created and all set, the final step is to configure the trigger for the function. Make sure you provide the **Prefix** in the trigger's configuration, as shown here:

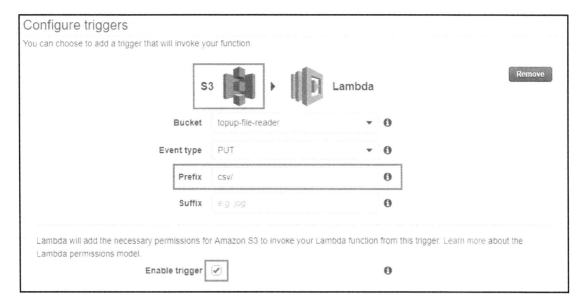

With this step completed, test the entire setup by uploading a sample CSV file to the /csv directory. Remember the CSV file will have to be of the same tabular format as we discussed earlier at the beginning of this use case. Once the file is uploaded, check whether the contents are populated successfully in the DynamoDB table or not. You can even verify this by looking at the function's logs in CloudWatch, as shown in the following screenshot:

With this, we come toward the end of our use cases.

22
Next Steps with AWS Lambda

It's been quite a long journey so far, and yet here we are--the last chapter of this book! If you made it until here, then you definitely need to take a moment and give yourself a well-deserved pat on the back!

So far in this book, we have seen how to write, test, deploy, monitor, and manage your serverless applications using AWS Lambda and a bunch of other interesting tools and services. In this last and final chapter, I wanted to provide you with just a small glimpse into what you can expect from Lambda over the next few years and how is it going to change the way we view and do computing in the cloud!

In this chapter, we will be glancing through some new and recent product releases that are based on or work with AWS Lambda, namely the following:

- **Lambda@Edge**: Trigger Lambda to run functions in CloudFront edge locations based on CloudFront events
- **AWS Snowball Edge**: Store terabytes of data in a Snowball device and leverage Lambda to analyze and process data streams locally
- **Lambda bot and Amazon Lex**: Use Lambda functions to fulfill requests generated by the Lex chatbot framework
- **AWS Greengrass**: Execute Lambda functions locally on your IoT devices for near real-time responses and processing

Sounds interesting! Then what are you waiting for? Let's get started right away!

Processing content at the edge with Lambda@Edge

Lambda@Edge was launched by AWS during the 2016 *AWS re:Invent* summit; however, it had been in the preview mode until right now. The service basically allows you to execute Lambda functions in edge locations in response to CloudFront events. With this service, you now don't need to install, configure, or scale servers globally in order to customize your content. With Lambda@Edge, all this work is handled by the Lambda service itself. All you need to do is write the function and deploy it, and that's it!

At the time of writing, Lambda@Edge supports writing functions for the following CloudFront events:

- **Viewer request**: When CloudFront receives a request from a viewer
- **Viewer response**: Before CloudFront returns the response to the viewer
- **Origin request**: Before CloudFront forwards a request to the origin
- **Origin response**: When CloudFront receives a response from the origin

Where can I use Lambda@Edge? Well, the service has a few very specific use cases, some of which are explained here:

- You can use a Lambda function to generate custom HTTP responses when a CloudFront viewer request or origin request event occurs. A Lambda function can additionally be used to inspect headers or authorization tokens and insert the applicable header to control access to your content before CloudFront forwards a request back to the origin.
- A Lambda function can be used to add, drop, or modify headers, and can rewrite URL paths so that CloudFront returns different objects.
- You can even write Lambda functions that inspect cookies and rewrite URLs so that users see different versions of a site for A/B testing.
- CloudFront can return different objects to viewers based on the User-Agent header, which includes information about the devices that users are using in order to view your content. For example, CloudFront can return different images based on the screen size of devices. Similarly, the Lambda function could consider the value of the Referer header and cause CloudFront to return the images that have the lowest available resolution to bots.

How does it all work together? Well, it is a very simple and straightforward process! You first author a function using either the AWS Lambda management dashboard or the set of tools that we discussed earlier in this book, such as APEX, serverless, and so on. Once the function is created, you can configure its trigger by selecting a CloudFront distribution that you want to propagate the function over, along with a cache behavior in the distribution. Once these values are filled in, you can configure the trigger that will essentially execute your function over the edge location. These triggers can be any one of the four (viewer request/response, origin request/response) that we discussed a while back. With the trigger created, Lambda replicates the function to all the AWS regions and CloudFront edge locations around the globe.

 Note that once the replica functions are created and distributed across the globe, you will not be permitted to perform any changes on them, not even deleting them.

Let's examine Lambda@Edge with a simple use case walkthrough. For this section, we will be looking at how to leverage Lambda@Edge to generate a custom **404 Not Found** HTTP redirect for one of our static hosted websites on S3.

First up is creating the function. For this, log in to your AWS Management Console and select the **AWS Lambda** service from the main dashboard.

Next, from the Lambda management dashboard, select the **Create a Lambda function** option to get things started.

On the **Select blueprint** page, you can choose to use an existing Lambda@Edge boiler template for this use case as well. Simply type **Edge** in the filter and select the **cloudfront-response-generation** template, as shown in the following screenshot:

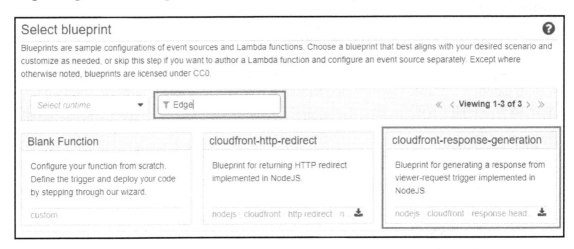

Alternatively, you can also select the **Blank Function** template and copy and paste the following code snippet:

```
'use strict';
let content = `
<\!DOCTYPE html>
<html lang="en">
  <head>
    <meta charset="utf-8">
    <title>404 - Not Found</title>
  </head>
  <body>
    <p>Looks like the page you are looking for is not available for
      the moment... try again after a while.</p>
  </body>
</html>
`;
exports.handler = (event, context, callback) => {
  const response = {
    status: '404',
      statusDescription: 'Not Found',
        headers: {
          'cache-control': [{
            key: 'Cache-Control',
            value: 'max-age=100'
          }],
          'content-type': [{
```

```
          key: 'Content-Type',
          value: 'text/html'
        }],
        'content-encoding': [{
          key: 'Content-Encoding',
          value: 'UTF-8'
        }],
      },
      body: content,
    };
    callback(null, response);
};
```

Next, from the **Configure triggers** section, select the particular CloudFront **Distribution ID** for which you need to enable Lambda@Edge. Note that the static website in my case is hosted on S3, and its content is distributed globally using a specific CloudFront **Distribution ID**.

Next, from the **CloudFront Event** drop-down list, select the appropriate event for which you wish to enable this function. In my case, I've selected the **Viewer Request** option, as shown in the following screenshot:

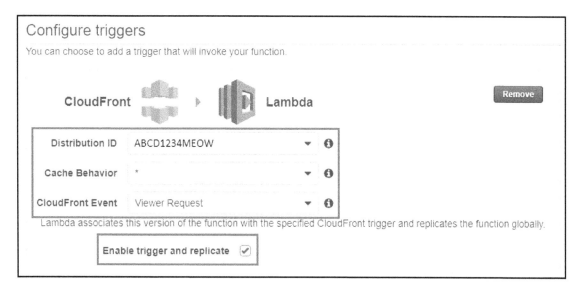

Remember to check the **Enable trigger and replicate** option as well before you select the **Next** option.

On the **Configure function** page, start off by providing a suitable **Name** for your function. Before you go ahead and paste the function code, you will be provided with a list of restrictions that currently apply to Lambda@Edge functions:

- **Memory (MB)** is limited to 128 MB.
- The uncompressed size of the code and associated libraries that upload for a function is limited to 1 MB. Deployment packages must be compressed in the `.zip` or `.jar` format.
- The **Timeout** for CloudFront origin request and origin response events is three seconds. For these events, the function can make network calls.
- The **Timeout** for the CloudFront viewer request and viewer response events is one second. For these events, the function cannot make network calls.
- The `/tmp` space is not available.
- Environment variables, the **Dead Letter Queues** (**DLQ**), and Amazon VPCs cannot be used.

Next, paste the preceding code in the code editor window. Provide a suitable name for your Lambda@Edge IAM role and select the **Basic Edge Lambda permissions** option from the list of existing **Policy templates**, as shown here:

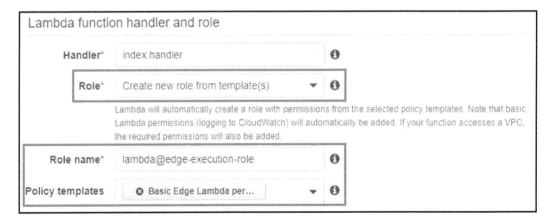

Leave the rest of the fields at their default values and go ahead and complete the function's creation process. Once your function is deployed, it will take a good few minutes for the function to replicate and propagate to the CloudFront edge locations. You can verify the state of the propagation from the CloudFront dashboard as your **Distribution Status** would now be in a **InProgress** state. Once the state changes to **Deployed**, open your favorite web browser and type in your static website's URL. Pass an incorrect page at the URL, and you should get the customized error response page that we had configured earlier! You can use similar techniques to generate custom HTTP responses when a CloudFront viewer request or origin request events occurs. There's still a lot more that you can do and achieve using Lambda@Edge, such as optimizing latencies, compressions, added security, and so on. To learn more about how to leverage Lambda@Edge for your use cases, visit `http://docs.aws.amazon.com/AmazonCloudFront/latest/DeveloperGuide/lambda-at-the-edge.html`.

Building next generation chatbots with Lambda and Lex

Chatbots are all the craze right now, with practically each cloud provider dishing out its chatbot framework for end users and developers to build conversational interfaces with voice- and text-based applications, which brings us to the introduction of Amazon Lex--a powerful and scalable chatbot framework built using Amazon's intelligent personal assistant named *Alexa*.

Lex essentially provides you with a readymade framework complete with all the necessary integration capabilities to kick start your bot creation process without having to learn or have expertise in with Lex! All you need to do is specify the basic conversational flow using the Lex management console and let Lex take care of the rest by provisioning the required infrastructure and services as well as adjusting responses to your conversations. This enables you to build, test, and publish chatbots at lighting pace on various mobile, web applications, and even other chat platforms.

Amazon Lex also provides prebuilt integrations with AWS Lambda, using which you can trigger off custom actions based on your chat conversations! This proves extremely effective as both Lex and Lambda are completely serverless, which means you don't have to bother about the underlying infrastructure at all! Just create the framework, integrate it with the right set of Lambda functions, and you have a complete chatbot all ready for use!

To summarize, here are some of the key features provided by Lex:

- **Fully managed service**: Lex is backed by the AWS infrastructure, which makes it that much easier to scale with no operational overheads whatsoever.
- **Simpler to learn and use**: Amazon Lex provides **automatic speech recognition (ASR)** and **natural language understanding (NLU)** technologies to create a **Speech Language Understanding (SLU)** system. Through SLU, Amazon Lex takes natural language speech and text input, understands the intent behind the input, and fulfills the user intent by invoking the appropriate business function.
- **Backed by Lambda**: The brains behind the chatbot's logic execution, Lambda essentially enables you to write code to fulfill the user's intent without having to worry about the scale or underlying infrastructure requirements.
- **Built-in integrations**: Lex also provides out-of-the-box integration capabilities with other messaging frameworks, such as Facebook Messenger, Twilio, and Slack.

With this in mind, let's understand some Lex concepts and terminologies:

- **Bots**: At a high-level, bots in Lex are the entities that perform some tasks. These tasks can be anything, from booking a restaurant table to ordering food, and so on. The bot is powered by ASR and NLU capabilities, the same technology that internally powers Amazon Alexa.
- **Intents**: As the name suggests, intents are actions that the user wishes the bot to perform. For example, a bot that books a restaurant table for you can have these three intents--check the availability of a table, book a table for two, and notify the chef's specials for that day. Each intent requires some special phrases or *utterances* that convey what sort of action you wish the bot to take. For example, "Can you book a table for me?" or "Can you let me know what's the chef's special tonight?" and so on. Once the utterances are created, you can choose one or more Lambda functions to fulfil your intent.
- **Slots**: Slots are nothing more than simple parameters that your intents can use as a part of the intent's configuration. For example, for the intent "Can you book a table for me at (restaurant)", Lex will prompt the user to provide the value for (restaurant) at the bot's runtime. Without this value, the bot will not be able to fulfil its intent. Lex also provides a few built-in slot types; for example, AMAZON.NUMBER is a built-in slot type that you can use for the number of pizzas ordered, and so on.

With these points in mind, let's quickly look at a simple example to get started with Lex and Lambda.

First up, log in to the AWS Management Console and select the **Lex** service from the main dashboard.

At the time of writing this, Lex is currently only provided out of the N. Virginia region. This means that your associated Lambda function will also need to be hosted out of the N. Virginia region.

On the main **Bots** page, choose **Create**.

Once selected, you will be provided with the following screen. Here, you can select any one of the three sample Lex examples to get started or alternatively select **Custom bot** to create your own chatbot. For this case, we will build a simple coffee ordering chatbot, so go ahead and select the **Custom bot** option:

Next, provide a suitable name for your bot in the **Bot name** field. You can select your bot to provide an optional **Output voice** for your conversations; however, for this exercise, I've chosen to keep this bot a strictly text-based application.

Next up, provide a value for the bot's **Session timeout**, as shown in the preceding screenshot. This field is used to configure the time for which your bot should retain context before dropping it. Fill out the rest of the details and select **Create** to get started.

With the bot created, we now need to create its subsequent **Slot types** and **Intents**. To do that, first, select the add sign + next to the **Slot types** option. This will pop up the **Add slot type** dialog, as shown here:

For this exercise, we have created three slot types, namely:

- beverageType: latte, coffee, mocha, chai
- beverageSize: small, medium, large, extra large
- beverageStrength: single, double, triple, quad, quadruple

Create the rest of the **Slot types** and click on **Save slot type** for each of the slots that you create. With the slots created, we now move on to the creation of the intent!

To create the intent, select the add sign + adjoining the **Intent types** option. This will pop up the **Add intent** dialog. Here, select the **Create new intent** option and provide a suitable name for it. Click on **Add** once done! Your intent should be created and displayed as shown here. Now you can go ahead and create a few utterances that will help the user order their coffee. In this case, I have created three utterances with different values in each case:

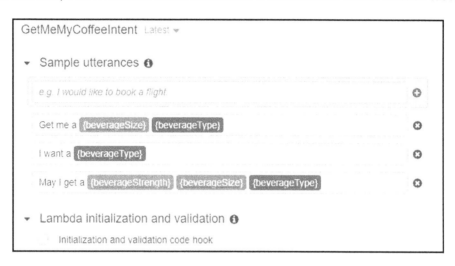

With the utterances populated, move on to the **Slots** section, where we can actually map the **Slot types** we created earlier with some meaningful **Name** and a user **Prompt**.

Remember, the **Slot types** were created during the earlier steps, whereas the names were simple placeholders for the slots:

Required	Name	Slot type	Prompt
Yes	beverageType	beverageType	What kind of beverage would you like? For example, mocha, chai, and so on.
Yes	beverageSize	beverageSize	What size? Small, medium, or large?
Yes	beverageStrength	beverageStrength	What kind of milk or creamer?

You can optionally even check the **Confirmation prompt** option and provide a suitable message for the user to confirm their order and even a custom message when the user cancels the order as shown in the following screenshot:

Finally, in the **Fulfilment** section, select **Return parameters to client** for now and test the chatbot first by saving the intent and selecting the **Build** option toward the top-right corner of the Lex dashboard. The build takes a few minutes to complete, and if no errors are present, it will pop up the **Test Bot**, using which you can test your intent by typing the **Sample utterances** you created a while back.

You should get an all success response similar to the one shown here:

ReadyForFulfillment beverageSize:small beverageStrength:single beverageType:coffee

This is a simple response generated by the Lex framework itself, and it indicates that our chatbot is now ready to be integrated with the Lambda function. So now let's create a simple Lambda function in the same N. Virginia region.

Create a new Lambda function with the following code in it:

```
'use strict';
function close(sessionAttributes, fulfillmentState, message) {
  return {
    sessionAttributes,
    dialogAction: {
      type: 'Close',
      fulfillmentState,
      message,
    },
  };
}
function dispatch(intentRequest, callback) {
  console.log('request received for userId=${intentRequest.userId},
  intentName=${intentRequest.currentIntent.intentName}');
  const sessionAttributes = intentRequest.sessionAttributes;
  const slots = intentRequest.currentIntent.slots;
  const type = slots.beverageType;
  const size = slots.beverageSize;
  const strenght = slots.beverageStrength;
  callback(close(sessionAttributes, 'Fulfilled',
```

```
    {'contentType': 'PlainText', 'content': `Okay, I have placed your ${size}
    ${type} order!`}));
  }
  exports.handler = (event, context, callback) => {
    try {
      dispatch(event, (response) => { callback(null, response); });
    } catch (err) {
        callback(err);
    }
  };
```

The code is very straightforward. It essentially comprises three sections: first up is the close() function that reports the state of the fulfillmentState object--whether it has failed or succeeded. The second is the dispatch() function that receives the data from the slots, processes it, and provides a callback() with the success message toward the end, and finally, the handler that routes the incoming request based on the specified intent.

Once you have pasted the function in the inline code editor, in the **Lambda function handler and role** section, select the **Choose a new role from template(s)** option and just provide a name for the role; that's it. The role will be created and assigned by Lex automatically when we attach this Lambda function to the chatbot. Go ahead and complete the creation of the function, and once it is all done, test it by selecting the **Configure test event** option from the **Actions** drop-down list and providing the following test sample data to it:

```
{
  "messageVersion": "1.0",
  "invocationSource": "FulfillmentCodeHook",
  "userId": "user-1",
  "sessionAttributes": {},
  "bot": {
    "name": "GetMyCoffeeChatBot",
    "alias": "$LATEST",
    "version": "$LATEST"
  },
  "outputDialogMode": "Text",
  "currentIntent": {
    "name": "GetMyCoffee",
    "slots": {
      "type": "Chai",
      "size": "small",
      "strength": "single"
    },
    "confirmationStatus": "None"
  }
}
```

You can modify the `type`, `size`, and `strength` parameters as per your requirements. Once done, click on the **Save and test** option and verify the results. You should see an output similar to the one shown here:

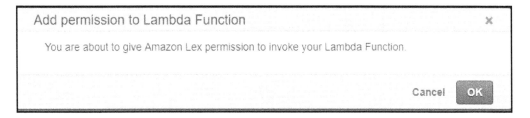

With this, you can now integrate your function to your chatbot. To do that, simply go back to your Lex dashboard and change the **Fulfilment** from **Return parameters to client** to **AWS Lambda function**. Next, select your newly created Lambda function from the drop-down list provided. On selecting your function, you will be provided with the following dialog, which will essentially provide your function with the necessary permissions to get invoked by Lex. Click on **OK**:

Finally, select the **Build** option to complete the chatbot's build. Test the chatbot once again using **Test Bot**. This time on your order's successful completion, you should see the success message that was passed using your Lambda function! This means that the function was able to obtain the parameters passed by the slots and successfully return an order fulfillment summary as well. You can create similar chatbots using Lex and Lambda and integrate them with other AWS services, such as AWS Mobile Hub, Cognito, and so on or even with other messaging platforms such as Twilio, Slack, and Facebook Messenger. To read more about how to leverage Lex with such messaging platforms, visit `http://docs.` `aws.amazon.com/lex/latest/dg/example1.html`.

Processing data at the edge with Greengrass and Lambda

Greengrass is yet another recent offering in the space of IoT provided by AWS. In simpler terms, Greengrass is an extension of AWS's own IoT service, and it is specifically designed to extend AWS cloud capabilities to local IoT devices, thus making it possible for them to collect and analyze data closer to the source of information. This is made possible by enabling developers to write and execute serverless code. More specifically, developers who use AWS Greengrass can author serverless code using AWS Lambda either on the cloud or on the device itself and conveniently deploy it for the local execution of applications. Here is a representational architecture of Greengrass depicting the Greengrass Core SDK interconnecting various devices with the AWS Cloud:

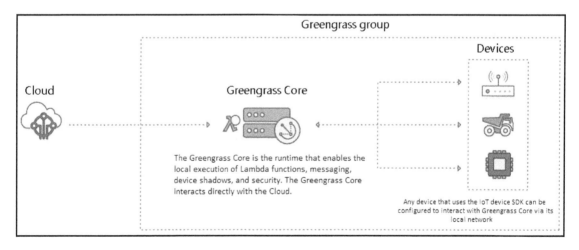

The AWS **Greengrass Core** software primarily consists of:

- A message manager that routes messages between devices, Lambda functions, and AWS IoT. The pub/sub message manager can intelligently buffer and resend messages if the connectivity to the cloud is disrupted or lost.
- A Lambda runtime that runs user-defined Lambda functions.
- An implementation of the *thing shadows* service that provides a local copy of thing shadows that represent your **Devices**. Thing shadows can be configured to sync with the **Cloud**.
- A deployment agent that is notified about new or updated AWS **Greengrass group** configuration. When a new or updated configuration is detected, the deployment agent downloads the configuration data and restarts the AWS **Greengrass Core**.

Besides the message manager and the local Lambda runtime, Greengrass also provides features such as Group management and Discovery services for your local IoT devices. Here's a quick look at a simple example of how you can connect your local devices (in this case, *a Raspberry Pi*) with Greengrass and run simple Lambda functions using it.

First up, we'll look at configuring and making the device ready for Greengrass! AWS has a really simple and straightforward tutorial for this, so I'll not be going too deep into this one. You can refer to the steps mentioned in this link to configure and prepare your device for AWS Greengrass: `http://docs.aws.amazon.com/greengrass/latest/developerguide/prepare-raspi.html`.

With the device prepped and ready, the next step involves the download of the Greengrass Core software from the AWS IoT dashboard and transferring it over to your device. To do that, log in to your AWS account and filter and select **AWS IoT** from the **Services**. You should have the IoT dashboard in front of you. Select the **Get started** option to view the various options for your IoT device management. Here, select **Software** from the options pane on the left-hand side to view a different version of the Greengrass Core software.

Follow the wizard and download the correct version of the Greengrass Core software, as shown here:

With the software downloaded, transfer it to your IoT device, in my case, the Raspberry Pi device. Extract the contents of your software using the following command:

```
# sudo tar -zxvf greengrass-<platform_version>.tar.gz -C /
```

With the extraction completed, we need to use the IoT dashboard and create something called a *Greengrass group*. A Greengrass group is a container that lists and describes your local device environment. The group contains an AWS Greengrass Core device with which all other devices in the group communicate, a list of devices that belong to the group, a list of Lambda functions, and a subscription table that defines how messages are passed between devices, the AWS Greengrass Core, and Lambda functions.

To create the group, from the AWS IoT dashboard, select **Greengrass** from the options pane. On the **Define a Greengrass group** tile, select the **Use easy creation** option and follow the wizard to create a certificate and key pair that your AWS Greengrass Core will use to authenticate with AWS IoT and AWS Greengrass:

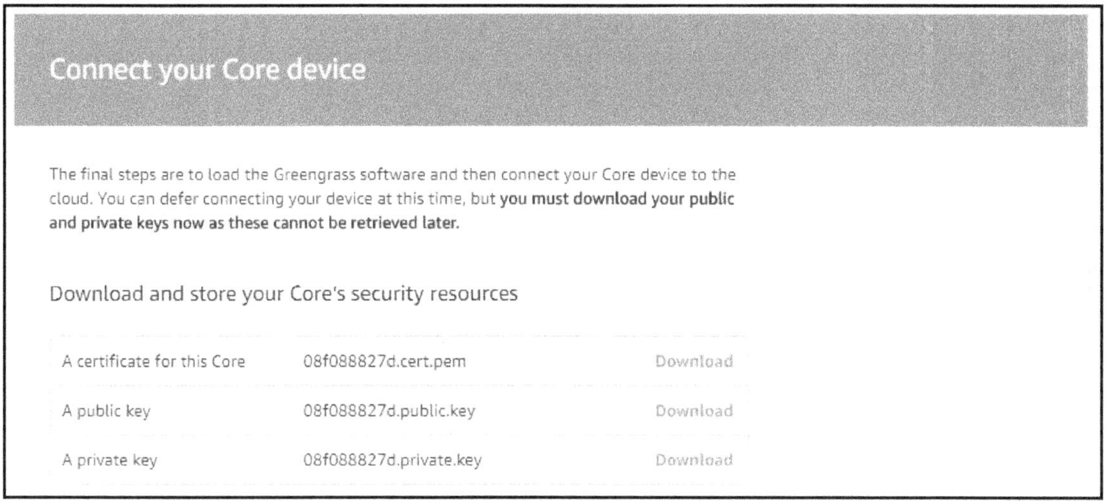

Download and transfer the certificate and the private key over to your IoT device. Next, open the Greengrass code `config.json` file and substitute the filenames, as depicted here:

```
# sudo nano /greengrass/configuration/config.json
```

The preceding command opens the following code:

```
{
  "coreThing": {
    "caPath": "rootca.pem",
    "certPath": "<your_CRT_Filename>",
    "keyPath": "<your_Private_Key_Filename>",
    "thingArn": "<your_Device_ARN>",
    "iotHost": "<IoT_Host_Prefix>.iot.[AWS_REGION_HERE].amazonaws.com",
    "ggHost": "greengrass.iot.[AWS_REGION_HERE].amazonaws.com",
    "keepAlive": 600
  },
  "runtime": {
    "cgroup": {
      "useSystemd": "yes"
    }
  }
}
```

For a list of complete steps and how to obtain the root CA certificate, check out the complete link at `http://docs.aws.amazon.com/greengrass/latest/developerguide/gg-setup.html`.

With the certificates in place and all configs done, we are now ready to start the Greengrass Core daemon service. Use the following command to start the service. You should see output similar to what's shown here:

```
# sudo ./greengrassd start
```

```
pi@raspberrypi:/greengrass $
pi@raspberrypi:/greengrass $ sudo ./greengrassd start
Setting up greengrass daemon
Validating execution environment
Found cgroup subsystem: cpu
Found cgroup subsystem: cpuacct
Found cgroup subsystem: blkio
Found cgroup subsystem: memory
Found cgroup subsystem: devices
Found cgroup subsystem: freezer
Found cgroup subsystem: net_cls

Starting greengrass daemon.....
Greengrass daemon started with PID: 1815
pi@raspberrypi:/greengrass $
```

If you got this far, congratulations! You are that much closer to setting up the device with Greengrass. Next, we need to add our IoT device to the Greengrass group. To do that, from the Greengrass group, select the **Device** option, and from the **Add a device** dialog, select the **Use an existing IoT Thing as a Device** option. You can select your newly added device on the next page and click on **Finish** once done. The device takes a few minutes to sync with Greengrass. You can verify the status by viewing `/greengrass/var/log/system/runtime.log` from the device's Terminal. With this process completed, we will now create a Lambda function in the same region as the region for our Greengrass deployment.

From the Lambda dashboard, select **Create a Lambda function** and filter `greengrass` from the filter box, as shown here. You should see a `greengrass-hello-world` example template; select it to proceed with the function's configuration:

Now this example function doesn't require any triggers as such, so we will skip through the **Configure triggers** section. On the next page, provide a suitable **Name** for your function and select the `lambda_basic_execution` role for your function's execution. At the time of writing this, Greengrass supports only Python as the programming language, with more languages possibly getting added as the service matures.

Back to the IoT dashboard, select the **Lambda** option from **Greengrass groups**. Here, you will need to select the newly created function from our earlier step. If your function is not visible here, make sure the function and Greengrass are both present in the same region.

To test your Lambda function, you first need to deploy it. To do that, simply select the **Actions** button from the Greengrass group and opt for the **Deploy** option. Wait until the state of the deployment turns successful and then select the **Test** option from the IoT dashboard. Under **Subscription**, type `hello/world` and then choose **Publish to topic** to subscribe to the `hello/world` topic.

If your `hello-world` Lambda function is running on your AWS Greengrass Core device, it publishes messages to the `hello/world` topic and is displayed in the AWS IoT console, as shown here:

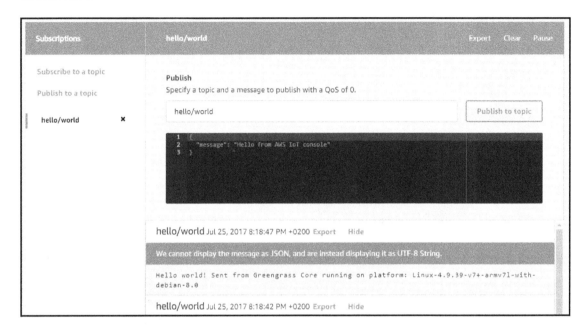

This was just a high-level view of what you can achieve with Greengrass and Lambda. You can leverage Lambda to perform all kinds of preprocessing on data at your IoT device itself. To know more about Greengrass service and how you can leverage it for your devices, visit `http://docs.aws.amazon.com/greengrass/latest/developerguide/gg-storyline.html`.

Other Books You May Enjoy

If you enjoyed this book, you may be interested in these other books by Packt:

Learning AWS - Second Edition
Aurobindo Sarkar, Amit Shah

ISBN: 9781787281066

- Set up your AWS account and get started with the basic concepts of AWS
- Learn about AWS terminology and identity access management
- Acquaint yourself with important elements of the cloud with features such as computing, ELB, and VPC
- Backup your database and ensure high availability by having an understanding of database-related services in the AWS cloud
- Integrate AWS services with your application to meet and exceed non-functional requirements
- Create and automate infrastructure to design cost-effective, highly available applications

AWS Certified Developer - Associate Guide
Vipul Tankariya, Bhavin Parmar

ISBN: 9781787125629

- Create and manage users, groups, and permissions using AWS Identity and Access Management services
- Create a secured Virtual Private Cloud (VPC) with Public and Private Subnets, Network Access Control, and Security groups
- Get started with Elastic Compute Cloud (EC2), launching your first EC2 instance, and working with it
- Handle application traffic with Elastic Load Balancing (ELB) and monitor AWS resources with CloudWatch
- Work with AWS storage services such as Simple Storage Service (S3), Glacier, and CloudFront
- Get acquainted with AWS DynamoDB – a NoSQL database service
- Coordinate work across distributed application components using Simple Workflow Service (SWF)

Leave a review - let other readers know what you think

Please share your thoughts on this book with others by leaving a review on the site that you bought it from. If you purchased the book from Amazon, please leave us an honest review on this book's Amazon page. This is vital so that other potential readers can see and use your unbiased opinion to make purchasing decisions, we can understand what our customers think about our products, and our authors can see your feedback on the title that they have worked with Packt to create. It will only take a few minutes of your time, but is valuable to other potential customers, our authors, and Packt. Thank you!

Index

www.ingramcontent.com/pod-product-compliance
Lightning Source LLC
Chambersburg PA
CBHW060110090326
40690CB00064B/4389

9 781788 835770